I0823015

GREEN

English language edition published by Princeton University Press,
41 William Street, Princeton, New Jersey 08540
In the United Kingdom: Princeton University Press, 6 Oxford Street,
Woodstock, Oxfordshire OX20 1TW

press.princeton.edu

Library of Congress Cataloging-in-Publication Data
Pastoureau, Michel, 1947–
[Vert. English]
Green : the history of a color / Michel Pastoureau.
pages cm
Includes bibliographical references.
ISBN 978-0-691-15936-2 (hardcover : alk. paper)
1. Green. 2. Color—Psychological aspects—History. 3. Color—Social aspects—History.
4. Symbolism of colors—History. I. Title.
BF789.C7P39513 2014
155.9'1145—dc23
2013043893

British Library Cataloging-in-Publication Data is available

Printed on acid-free paper.

Photogravure: Quadrilaser, Ormes, France

Printed by Toppan Leefung, China

3 5 7 9 10 8 6 4 2

Michel
PASTOUREAU

GREEN

THE HISTORY OF A COLOR

Translated by Jody Gladding

PRINCETON UNIVERSITY PRESS

Princeton and Oxford

Contents

God said, "Let the earth grow green with vegetation, plants yielding seed and trees bearing fruit, each according to its kind." And it was so. The earth turned green with vegetation, plants yielded seed and trees bore fruit, each according to its kind. And God saw that it was good. There was evening and there was morning; it was the third day.

Genesis 1:11–13

Introduction

Do you like green? To this simple question, responses today are divided. In Europe, one out of six people names green as their favorite color, but almost ten percent do not like it or think that it does not become them. Green seems to be an ambivalent, if not an ambiguous, color: a symbol of life, luck, and hope on the one hand, an attribute of disorder, poison, the devil and all his creatures on the other.

In the following chapters I have attempted to recount the long social, cultural, and symbolic history of green in European societies, from Greek antiquity to the present. Long difficult to produce and even more difficult to fix, green is not only the color of vegetation, it is also and most importantly the color of destiny. Chemically unstable, as much in painting as in dyeing, through the centuries it has been associated with all that was changing, changeable, and fleeting: childhood, love, hope, luck, play, chance, money. It was only in the Romantic period that it definitively became the color of nature and thus of freedom, health, hygiene, sports, and ecology. Its history in the West is, in part, one of a reversal of values. Long unnoticed, disliked, or rejected, now it is entrusted with the impossible mission of saving the planet.

The present book is not unique but the third in an ongoing series. Two works preceded it: *Blue: The History of a Color* (2001) and *Black: The History of a Color* (2009), published by the same press. Two other volumes are to follow, one devoted to red and one to yellow. As with the preceding volumes, the framework of this one is deliberately chronological; it is very much a history of green, not an encyclopedia of the color, and even less a study of its place only in the contemporary world. It is a history book that examines green over the long term and from all angles. Too often histories of color—what few there are—are limited to the most recent periods and to artistic matters, which is very reductive. The history of painting is one thing, the history of colors is another—and altogether more vast.

As with the two preceding works, this one only appears to be a monograph. A color does not occur alone; from a social, artistic, and symbolic perspective it only takes its meaning, it only fully "functions" insofar as it is combined with or opposed to one or many other colors. By the same token, it is impossible to view it in isolation. To speak of green is necessarily to speak of blue, yellow, red, and even black and white.

These first three works—and the two forthcoming—constitute the building blocks of an edifice I have been constructing for almost half a century: the history of colors in European societies from classical antiquity to the nineteenth century. Even if it is necessary for me to look beyond and before those two periods, as you will read in the following pages, the essence of my research is located within that slice of time. Similarly, my research is limited to European societies because, for me, the issues of color are first of all issues of society. As a historian I am not competent to speak of the entire planet and not interested in compiling third- or fourth-hand research conducted by others on non-European cultures. In order to avoid making foolish claims or plagiarizing or recopying others' books, I am limiting myself to what I know and what was the subject of my seminars for over thirty years at the École Pratique des Hautes Études and the École des Hautes Études en Sciences Sociales.

Attempting to construct a history of colors, even limited to Europe, is not an easy exercise. In fact, it is a particularly arduous task that historians, archeologists, and art historians (including those who study painting!) have refused to tackle until recently. It is true that the difficulties were—and remain—numerous. Reviewing them in the introduction to this present book is worthwhile because they are fully part of its subject and help us to understand the reasons for the gaps in our knowledge. Here more than elsewhere there is no real boundary between history and historiography.

These difficulties can be grouped into three categories. The first are documentary in nature. We see the objects, images, artworks, and monuments that past centuries have left to us not in their original colors but as time has made them. The disparity between their original state and their present state is sometimes immense. What should be done? Recapture and restore the original colors at any cost? Or should we acknowledge that the work of time is a document of history? Furthermore, we see these colors in lighting conditions very different from those of the societies preceding ours. The torch, oil lamp, candle, and gaslight produce different illumination than electricity provides. That is obvious. But who among us remembers it when visiting a museum or exhibition? And how many historians take it into account in their work? And finally, for decade upon decade, researchers were in the habit of studying objects, artworks, and monuments through the means of black-and-white reproductions—first engravings, then photographs—to the point that over time their ways of thinking and perceiving seemed to have become "black and white" as well. Accustomed to working from documents, from books and collections of images largely dominated by black and white, they considered and studied the past as a world from which color was absent.

The difficulties in the second category are methodological. Historians are often stymied when they try to understand the status or the function of a color in an image or artwork. All the problems—material, technical, chemical, iconographical, ideological, symbolic—present themselves at the same time. How to organize them? How to conduct an analysis? What questions should be asked and in what order? To this day, no researcher, no research team has yet proposed relevant methods for helping the entire scholarly community better study the issues of color. That is why, facing the proliferation of inquiries and the multitude of vested interests, all researchers—and me first among them, no doubt—tend to retain only what suits them in relation to whatever they are in the process of demonstrating and, inversely, overlooking whatever does not suit them. That is clearly a bad way of working.

The difficulties in the third category are epistemological in nature: we cannot thoughtlessly project our present-day definitions, classifications, and conceptions of color, just as they are, onto the past. They are not those of the societies preceding ours (and will not be those of the societies following ours). All the more so because what is true of knowledge is also true of perception: the antique or medieval eye, for example, did not perceive colors or contrasts as the twenty-first-century eye does. Whatever the historical period, perception is always cultural. By the same token, for the historian, the danger of anachronism seems to lurk behind every document's corner, especially when it is a matter of the spectrum (unknown before the late seventeenth century), the theory of primary and complementary colors, the distinction between warm and cool colors, the law of simultaneous contrast, or the alleged physiological or psychological effects of colors. Our knowledge, our sensibility, our present-day "truths" were not those of yesterday and will not be those of tomorrow.

All these difficulties together underscore the strictly cultural nature of the questions concerning color. For the historian—as for the sociologist or the anthropologist—color is defined first as a social phenomenon, not as matter or fragment of light, still less as sensation. It is the society that "makes" the color, that gives it its definitions and meaning, that constructs its codes and values, that organizes its uses and determines its stakes. That is why any history of color must first be a social history. Unless we acknowledge that, we could lapse into reductive pseudo-neurobiology or dangerous scientism.

In attempting to construct such a history, the researcher's work is twofold. The first task is trying to define what the universe of colors could have been for societies of the past, taking into account all the components of that universe: the lexicon and phenomena of language, the chemistry of pigments, techniques of dyeing, dress systems and their accompanying codes, color's place in everyday life, rules handed down by authorities, moral standards of the church, scientific speculations and artistic creations. The areas of inquiry and reflection are multifold and present the historian with multiform questions. After defining a given cultural area, the second task in a diachronic study is to examine the changes, losses, innovations, and mergers that affect all historically observable aspects of the color in question.

In that dual process all documents must be examined. Color is essentially an interdocumentary and interdisciplinary area. But certain areas have proven to be more fruitful than others. The lexicon is an example; the history of words provides much information relevant to our knowledge of the past. With regard to colors, it underscores how their primary function in all societies is to classify, mark, associate, and oppose. Another example is the area of dyeing, fabrics, and clothing. That is probably where the issues of chemistry and technique merge most closely with the issues of ideology and symbolism.

Lexicons, fabrics, dyes: in matters of color, the poets and dyers have at least as much to teach us as the painters, chemists, and physicists. The history of the color green in European societies is a case in point.

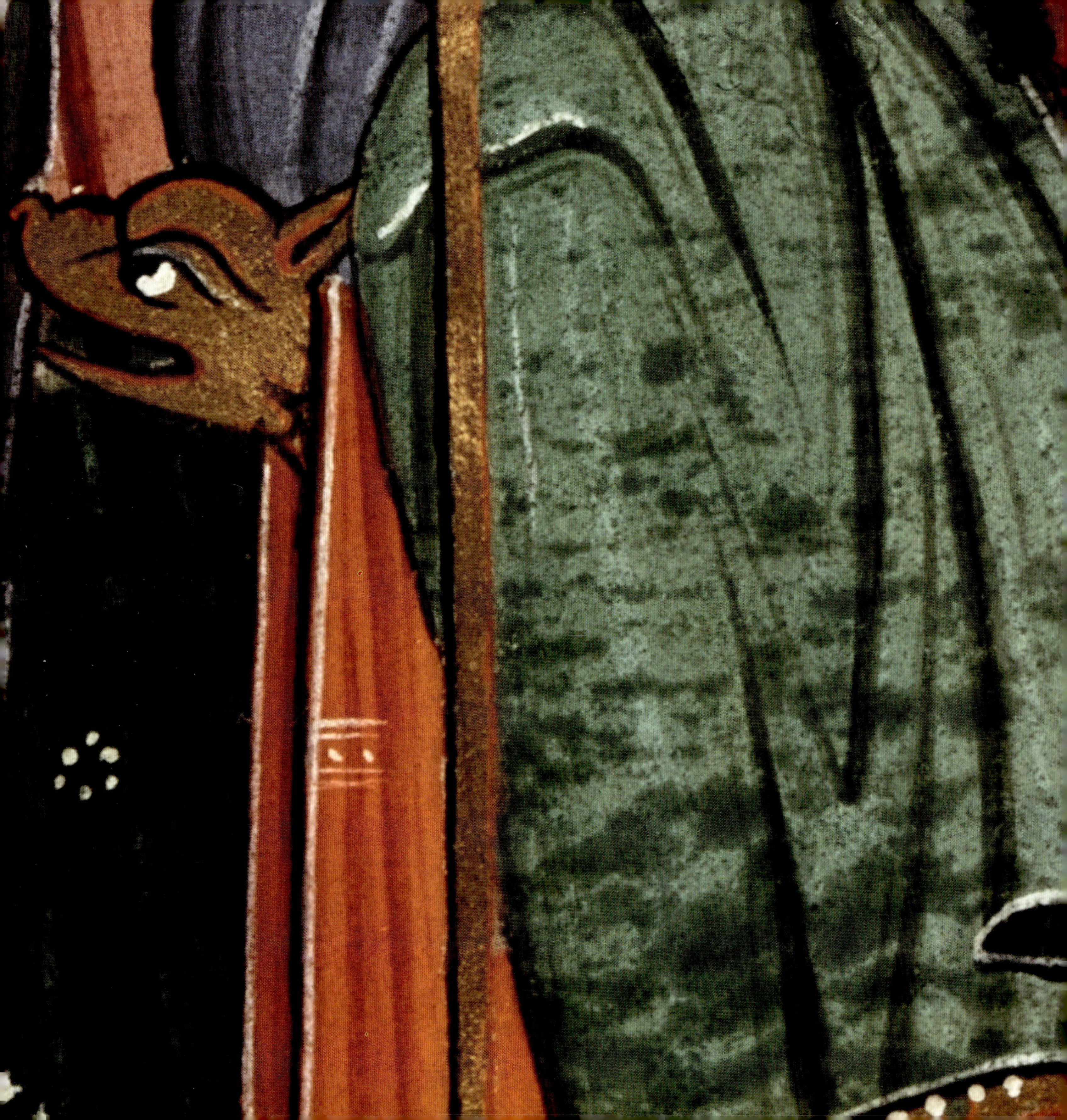

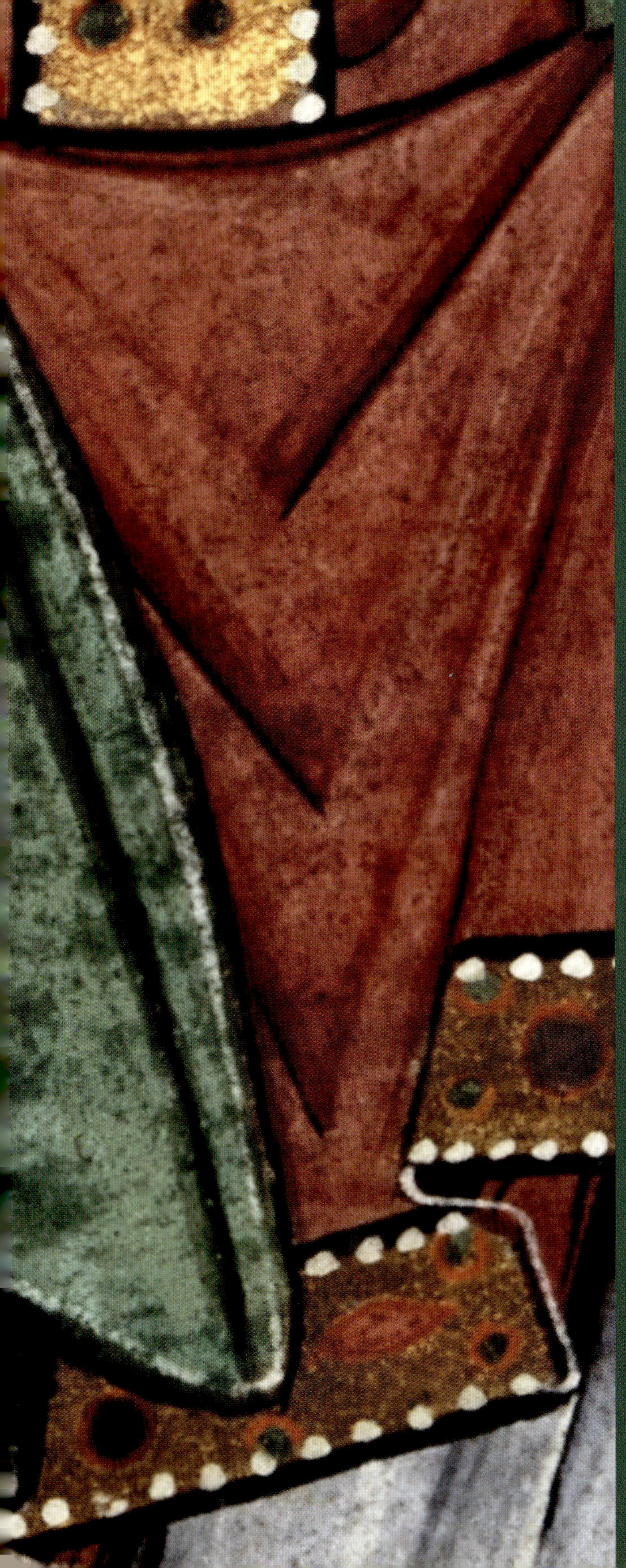

An **uncertain** color

FROM THE BEGINNING TO THE YEAR 1000

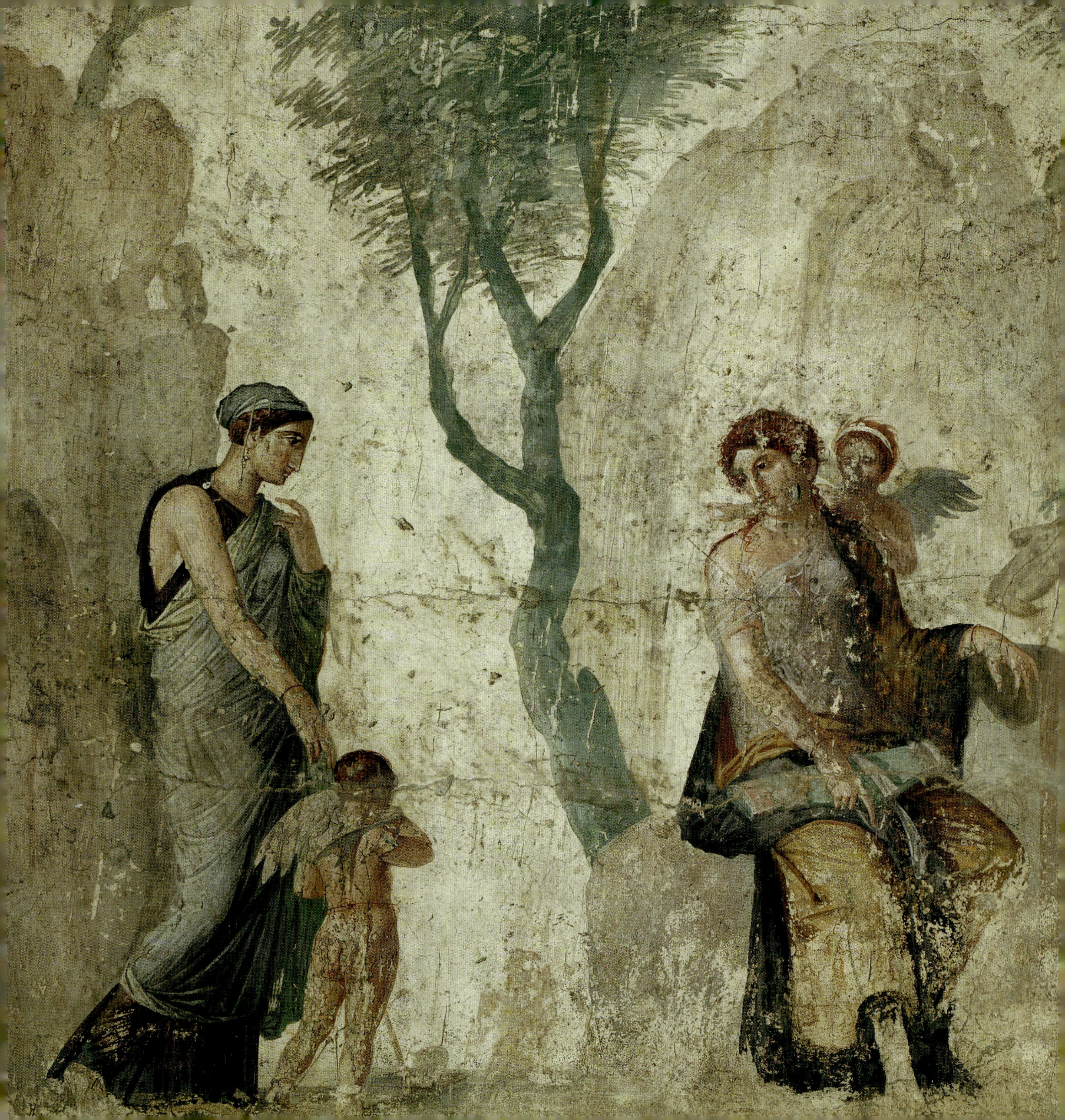

Long before painting or dyeing, humans observed colors in nature. They first admired them, then distinguished them, and finally identified them. Later, when they were still nomadic but had lived for a long time in societies, they named, thought about, and classified them. In a good many places the green of vegetation was dominant among those colors. Is that why this color is absent from the first palettes that humans conceived and produced? When they began to make their own colors, did humans deliberately avoid reproducing the one that proliferated in the universe surrounding them? Or was green absent for other reasons, material, technical, biological, even ideological or symbolic in nature?

It is difficult to answer these questions. But we must note that not a single color belonging to the range of greens is present in Paleolithic paintings. On cave walls we find tones of red, black, brown, and ochers in different shades but no green or blue and scarcely any white. And that is more or less the case a few thousand years later in the Neolithic period, when the first dyeing practices appeared. Having become sedentary, humans dyed in red and yellow tones long before dyeing in greens or blues. Ubiquitous in the plant world, green is a color that humans reproduced, made, and mastered late and with difficulty. Perhaps that explains why in the West it long remained a minor color, playing practically no role in social life, religious rituals, or artistic creation, not totally absent as in the Paleolithic period, but inconspicuous. Compared to red, white, and black—the three "basic" colors in most ancient European societies—the symbolic power of green was undoubtedly too limited to prompt emotions, transmit ideas, or structure classifications or systems; classifying is the first social function of color, even in communicating with the beyond.

The inconspicuous place of green in human activities and the difficulty of naming that color in many ancient languages led many late nineteenth-century scholars to wonder if the men and women of classical antiquity were blind to green or if at least they saw it differently from how it was later seen. Those questions are no longer pertinent today. But the minor material and ideological role that green played in most European societies for many thousands of years, from the Neolithic period to the beginning of the Middle Ages, remains an undeniable historical fact worth examining.

Did the Greeks see green?

PAGE 12: **MURAL PAINTING FROM POMPEII**

Green shades appear abundantly in Roman painting from the time of the Roman empire. Artists liked to paint trompe l'oeil gardens and landscapes and feature a variety of flora. Even though they were city dwellers, the Romans remained country people and retained a strong attraction for nature and the vegetable kingdom. Green pigments are in general well conserved, often better than blues, which fall victim to the effects of time.

From the Pompeii villa "of Fatal Love," ***Nemesis Bringing Love before Venus*****, first half of the 1st century. Naples, Museo Nazionale Archeologica.**

The phenomena of language and lexicon are the first areas into which the historian must venture. Often words have more to teach us than pigments or dyes, or at least they allow us to establish our first inquiries and derive a few solid ideas upon which to base our subsequent research. Ancient Greece is a case in point. It offers us a fascinating historiographical record to consider, thus letting us better discern the relationship between perception and nomenclature.

Ancient Greek possesses a relatively poor, imprecise chromatic lexicon. Only two terms seem stable and correspond to a very limited field: *leukos* (white) and *melanos* (black). A third term, *erythros*, covers an indeterminate field in the range of reds. All the other words are unstable, uncertain, or polysemous, especially in the archaic period. Often they convey qualities of light or material more than true coloring. Sometimes they do not concern the color so much as the sensations or emotions it prompts. It is not easy to translate these words into a modern language. In many of their usages, the terms for color provide more of a "feeling of the color" than precise information on this or that coloration.[1] The difficulties of translating—and even of understanding—color terms are not unique to Greek; we encounter them in most ancient languages beginning with those of the Bible, and even in Latin and the

THE LASCAUX PALETTE

Like blues, greens are absent from the palette of the Paleolithic painters, where reds, blacks, browns, and ochers predominate.

Second "Chinese" horse, c. –17,000. Lascaux cave.

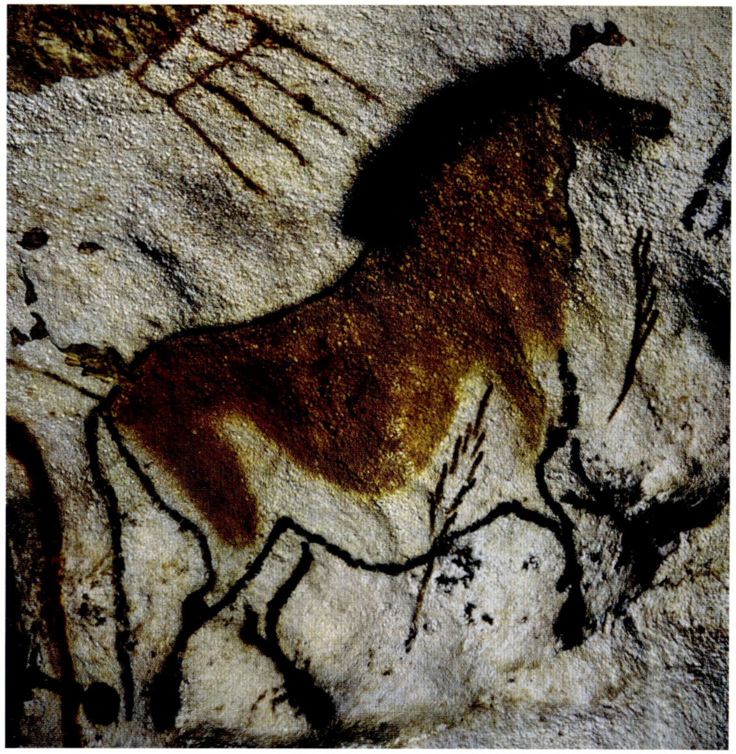

Germanic languages, although to a lesser degree. Too often we want to read color information where it is only a matter of light or dark, vivid or dull, glossy or matte, or even smooth or rough, clean or dirty, sumptuous or crude. The precise coloring of the object counts less than those other characteristics.

In addition to these difficulties, the chromatic boundaries of each color term are uncertain. Greek vocabulary is notable in this regard; aside from the three words mentioned above, all the other commonly used terms seem to vacillate among several colors. They waver particularly among the ranges of blue and green. Thus *kyaneos*—from which is derived the modern and scholarly French *cyan*—almost always designates a dark color, but it might as easily be dark blue as purple, black, or brown. Thus again *glaukos*, which the archaic poets use extensively, can sometimes express green, sometimes gray or blue, sometimes even yellow or brown. It conveys the idea of a color's paleness or weak concentration rather than a precisely defined shade. That is why it is used in Homer to name the color of water as well as the color of eyes, leaves, or honey. As for *chloros*, it moves constantly between green and yellow, and like *glaukos* it almost always conveys a weak, washed-out, desaturated color, rendered effectively in modern French with the suffix *-âtre*: *verdâtre*, *jaunâtre*, *grisâtre*, greenish, yellowish, grayish.

Thus naming green in ancient Greek is not easy. Not only are there fluid boundaries between green and other colors (blue, gray, yellow, brown), but green appears to be without density, pale, dull, almost colorless. Not until the Hellenistic period does it acquire more strength, and a term of little consequence until then begins to play an increasingly greater lexical role, to the point of competing with *glaukos* and *chloros*: *prasinos*. Etymologically, this adjective means "the color of leeks," but as it was commonly used beginning in the third to second centuries BCE, *prasinos* designates all the pronounced shades of green, especially the dark greens.[2] These gradual changes may be due to the influence of Latin, which experiences no difficulty

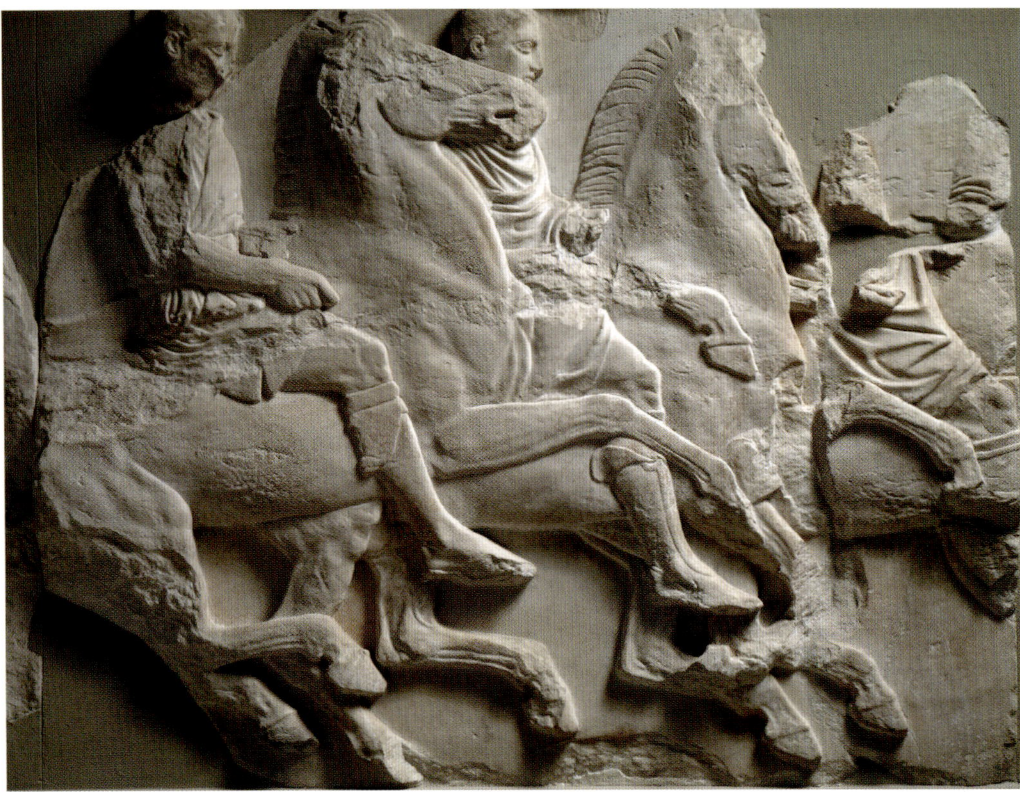

naming the color green. In any case they attest to a more manifest interest in colors in general, especially colors appearing in nature, and to a greater ease, no doubt, in producing and varying them, both in painting and dyeing. Until that time, it is more or less the historian's impression that the colors of nature were not really colors for the Greeks, and taking the trouble to name them hardly made sense, which explains the apparent imprecision in Homer and among most of the poets when they speak of the sky, the sea, water, earth, plants, and even animals.[3] A "true" color was above all a manufactured color, not a color present by itself in the natural world. Fabric and clothing were the principal mediums of color. Some philosophers—Plato, for example—go even further and speak of colors only when they are seen or perceived by human beings. Others, even when they are discussing the rainbow, seem uncomfortable clearly stating the colors of which it is comprised.[4]

All the difficulties in naming colors in ancient Greek, especially blue and green, were already noted by a few scholars in the Ancien Régime. Goethe echoes them in the appendixes to his famous treatise on colors (*Farbenlehre*) published in 1810. In doing so, he opened the way to a debate and controversies that would last several decades and constitute an important stage in research and reflection on the relationship between vision and nomenclature.

With this vacillating, imprecise lexicon for greens and blues as their evidence, many historians, philolo-

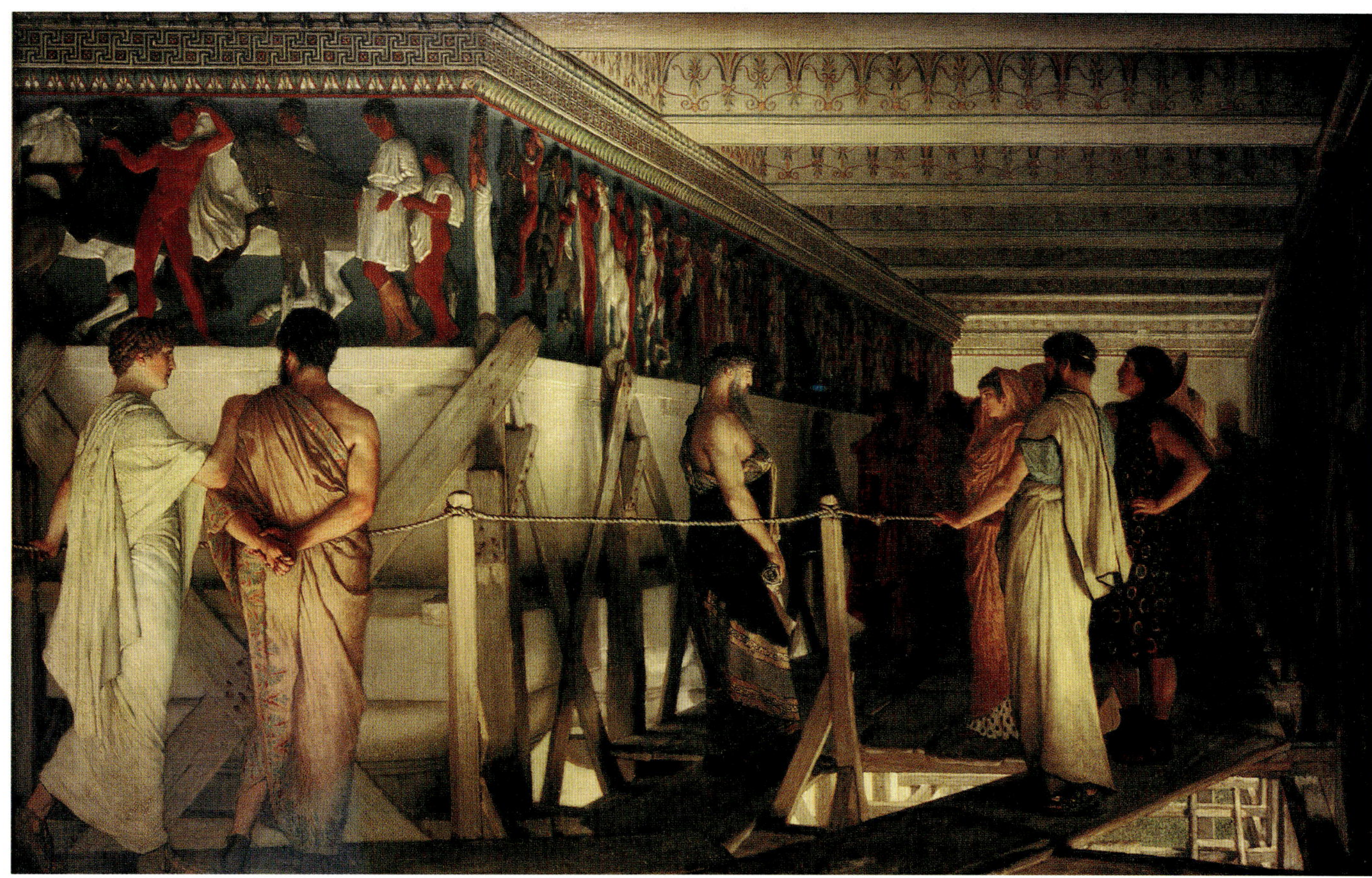

gists, doctors, and ophthalmologists in the second half of the nineteenth century really did wonder whether the Greeks were blind to those two colors and even more generally whether they had difficulty perceiving most color shades.[5] William Gladstone opened the debate. In a long study published in 1858, he underscored how rare color terms are in Homer: out of sixty adjectives describing natural elements and landscape in the *Iliad* and the *Odyssey*, only three are true color terms. On the other hand, words referring to light are extremely numerous. As for the sky, there may be different shades but never blue, and the same is true for the sea: "color of bronze," "crimson color," or "wine colored" but never green or gray. Expanding his inquiry to other more recent poets, Gladstone empha-

POLYCHROMATIC SCULPTURE IN CLASSICAL GREECE

For a long time, historians and archeologists refused to acknowledge that Greek temples were painted, both the architecture and the sculpture. That the marbles by the great Phidias (at left) could have been covered in bright colors was unthinkable. Gradually however, they had to yield to the evidence: everything was polychromatic and dramatically contrasting, even the celebrated friezes of the Parthenon (at right).

Opposite page: Group of horses from the south frieze of the Parthenon, attributed to the workshop of Phidias, 5th century BCE. Acropolis Museum, Athens.

Above: Sir Lawrence Alma-Tadema, *Phidias Showing the Frieze of the Parthenon to his Friends*, 1868. Birmingham, City Museum and Art Gallery.

sized the total absence of blue and the rarity of green. He thus concluded that the Greeks probably had difficulty perceiving those two colors.

Absorbed by his tasks as Prime Minister for Queen Victoria, Gladstone, though an excellent philologist, did not have the time to continue his work any further. But soon other scholars followed his lead, notably in Germany and Austria. Some recalled that Homer was blind and thus insensible to colors. Others surmised that the Greeks suffered from a form of color blindness or abnormal color vision that involved green and blue tones in particular. Still others, fascinated with the evolutionist theories of Darwin and his followers, claimed that until the Hellenistic period the Greeks were still "biologically in their childhood" and their sense of colors was hardly developed.[6] An Austrian ophthalmologist, Hugo Magnus, in two pamphlets published in 1871 and 1877, reopened the case, went even further, and claimed that the structure of the eye had evolved over the course of the centuries. The Greek eye had not yet fully developed its ability to distinguish colors clearly.[7] The Romans were supposedly more advanced in this area, but apparently they still had difficulties isolating and characterizing blue, as the Latin lexicon proves. It is not easy to say blue in Latin; different words exist for it but they are all imprecise, polysemous, and inconsistently used.[8] For example the most common one, *caeruleus*—which etymologically may stem from the color of wax, *cera* (between white, brown, and yellow)—first designated certain shades of green or black before it became specific to the range of blues.[9]

Magnus's works caused quite a stir and fueled debates until World War I and even beyond. Some authors took up and developed his hypotheses, others criticized them.[10] A few adopted intermediary positions, rejecting the evolutionist theories but accepting the idea of abnormal perception of green and blue among the Greeks.[11] For their part, the philologists extended Gladstone's investigations and endlessly disputed the meaning of certain Homeric adjectives.[12] Even the neurologists and philosophers joined in the general debate and made their voices heard in one camp or the other. Thus in 1881, in the preface to *Aurora*, his first book against moral prejudices, Nietzsche wrote:

> The Greeks saw nature in a different fashion than we do. Their eyes, we must admit, were blind to blue and green; instead of blue they saw a dark brown and instead of green a pale yellow. Moreover, they used the same term to designate the color of the greenest plants, honey and human skin. How different their natural world must have seemed to them than ours does to us! . . . That is probably why the first great Greek painters only used black, white, red and yellow to paint it.[13]

Nevertheless, the closer we get to World War I, the more the opponents of Gladstone's and Magnus's ideas make themselves heard.[14] Many philologists noted that our knowledge of ancient Greek is limited to the written language; what about the spoken language? Others emphasized that Gladstone and his followers only studied poetic texts; if texts of a technical or encyclopedic nature were examined, the lexicon of colors would be richer and more precise. On the part of doctors and ophthalmologists, there were many who objected to the idea of the structure of the eye differing between Greek and Roman, and even between ancient and modern times. Most importantly, some researchers noted that color vision and nomenclature constitute two different issues; not naming a color does not infer not seeing it. Jacques Geoffrey, a specialist in the French lexicon, notes for example that the word "blue" is completely absent from Corneille's tragedies and La Fontaine's *Fables.* Does that mean that those two authors were blind to blue? Of course not.[15]

Beginning in the years 1920–1930, the debate subsided a bit. But the partisans of evolutionist theories still piped up, especially in Nazi Germany. A few specialists in ancient Germanic languages observed that they presented no difficulties when it came to naming green and blue. They thus concluded that the Germans were more "evolved" than the Greeks and Romans; more "evolved" and therefore superior. Other researchers considered the visual capacities of Paleolithic painters: did the absence of blue and green from their palette mean that they did not see those two colors and thus that their perception of the world was still "in its childhood"?

Oddly enough, those very debatable hypotheses still have their advocates today. In *Basic Color Terms*, their 1969 book that created much controversy and relaunched inquiries into the perception and naming of colors, two American researchers, Brent Berlin and Paul Kay, maintained and attempted to demonstrate that the more technically advanced a society was, the richer and more solid its color lexicon.[16] This claim was immediately contested—even ridiculed—by many linguists and anthropologists.[17] But it is a somewhat disturbing claim that still has its supporters. I myself tend to think that if a color is never or rarely named in a given society, it is not because it is not seen but because it plays a minor role in the human occupations, social relationships, religious life, the world of symbols, and the imagination of that society. The issues of color are not only biological or neurobiological; they are also and above all social and cultural. For the historian it is first of all the society that "makes" the color, not nature, not the eye-brain relationship.[18] The ancient Greeks surely saw green quite well, but their opportunities for naming this color in writing were probably limited or not particularly noteworthy. Green may have been mentioned daily in speaking but more rarely in writing. On the other hand, like blue, it appeared in painting. Pictorial methods attest to its use in Greece from ancient times and to a very wide array of pigments (malachite, earth greens, and even artificial copper greens).

Today, studies on the Greeks' relationship with color have shifted. Vocabulary studies have given way to studies on architectural and sculpted polychromy. These are at the heart of the most recent and most relevant work, and they confirm that the Greeks not only saw colors perfectly but also had a very pronounced taste for vivid, contrasting hues.[19]

NEW WOMEN'S FASHIONS IN ROME

Green is not a common color for Roman clothing, at least under the Republic. Later, toward the end of the first century CE, it made its entry into the wardrobes of aristocratic women, first by way of Eastern fashions, and then in the third century by way of barbarian styles. This scandalized the moralists and upholders of traditional customs, who denounced the growing invasion of new colors, considered to be "dishonest" (*inhonesti*) and too "florid" (*floridi*).

Sir Lawrence Alma-Tadema, *A Coign of Vantage*, 1895. Private collection.

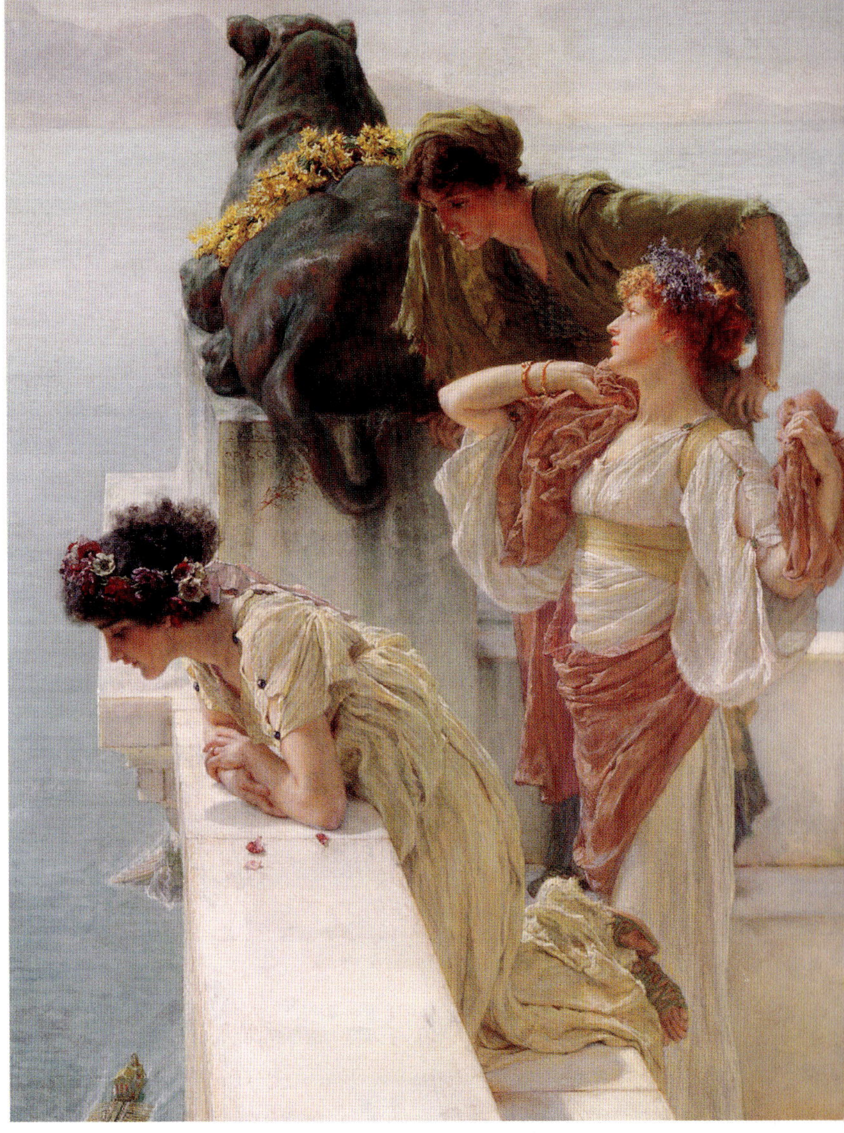

Green among the Romans

Unlike Greek, Latin experiences no difficulty in naming the color green. It possesses a basic term with an extensive semantic and chromatic range: *viridis*, from which are derived all the words designating the color green in the Romance languages, beginning with the French *vert*, the Italian *verde*, and the Castilian *verde*. Etymologically, *viridis* is related to a large family of words that evoke vigor, growth, and life: *virere* (to be green, to be vigorous), *vis* (strength), *vir* (man, masculine singular), *ver* (spring), *virga* (stem, rod), perhaps even *virtus* (courage, virtue).[20] In the first century BCE, the encyclopedist Varro, "the most learned of Romans," according to his friend Cicero, proposed in his history of the Latin language an etymology that will surface again in the modern era: *viride est id quod habet vires*, "green is that which has vigor" (word for word, "what which possesses strength").

The use of *viridis* is so extensive that it has almost no rivals for characterizing one or another shade of green. To do so, Latin adds prefixes to it: *perviridis*, dense green, dark green; *subviridis*, pale green, greenish. The adjective *virens*, the present participle of the verb *virere*, is only a doublet of *viridis*, especially used metaphorically to characterize youth, ardor, and courage. The other words for green are more rare: *herbeus*, green like grass; *vitreus*, light or bright green; *prasinus*, green like leeks, loud green, sometimes deep green; *glaucus*, gray-green, greenish, bluish green; *galbinus*, between yellow and green. Medieval Latin added only a single term to this list: *smaragdinus*, emerald green. But, as in classical Latin, *viridis* occupies nearly the whole semantic and chromatic field for the color.

We may wonder why the Romans did not experience the same difficulties as the Greeks did in naming green. Is it because, like the Germans, they were largely rural? Did country life and daily contact with vegetation make them pay more attention to green and name it more frequently? Or on the contrary, is it strictly a matter of lexicon? In fact, the Latin vocabulary seems better distributed and more precise than the Greek vocabulary (and even in some cases than the vocabulary of modern vernacular languages). Alternatively, is it a matter of technical skill? Were the Romans more skillful than the Greeks in dyeing and painting greens? Did their increasingly close relations with the Celts and the Germans make them

GALLO-ROMAN GLASSWARE

As experts in the art of glass, Romans and Gallo-Romans produced objects and receptacles of all shapes and sizes in splendid shades of greens and blues that have come down through the ages and exert great seductive power on our modern eye.

Gallo-Roman glass vases, 3rd–4th century BCE. Strasbourg, Musée d'archéologie du Palais Rohan.

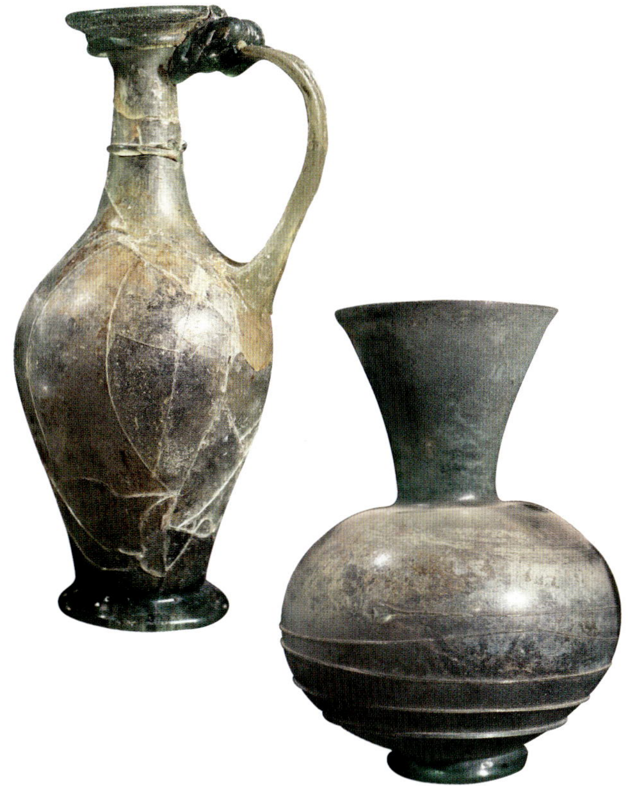

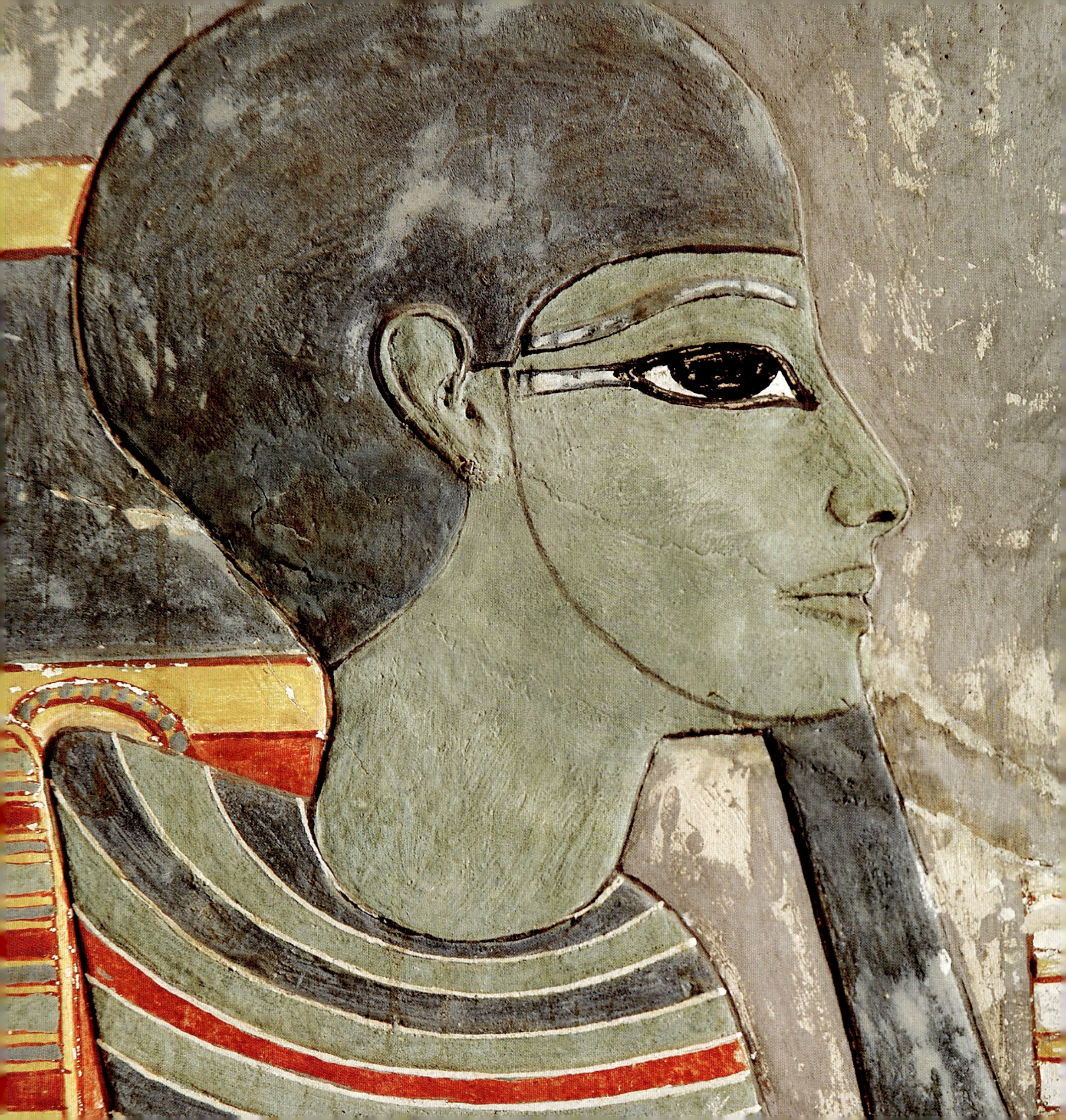

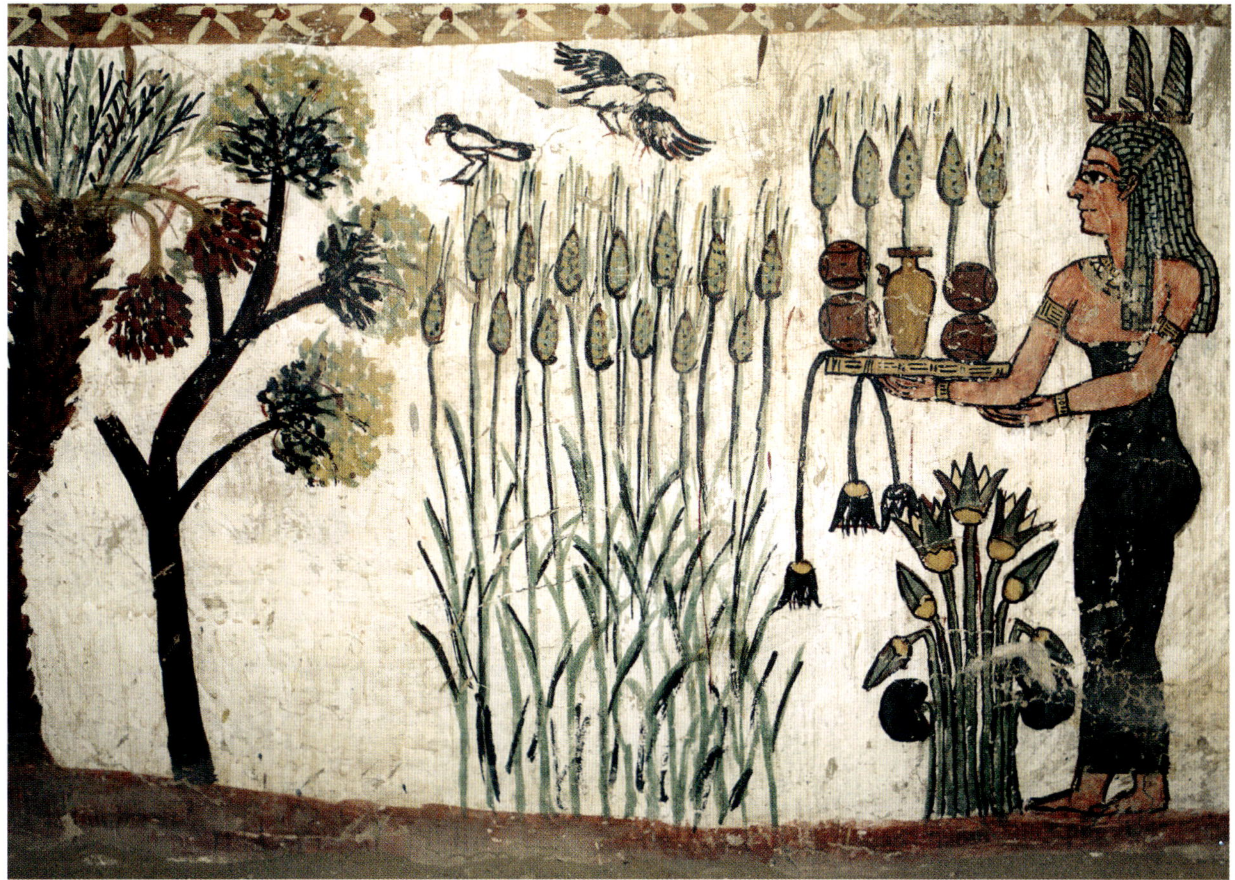

OPPOSITE PAGE: **THE GOD PTAH**

Like Osiris, to whom he is sometimes compared, the god Ptah, venerated in the region of Memphis, is represented with a face of green, a fertile and beneficial color.

Tomb of the Pharaoh Horemheb, KV 57, end of the 18th dynasty. Egypt, Valley of the Kings.

ABOVE: **FERTILE GREEN IN EGYPT**

In Egyptian painting, the color green is always seen as good and takes on various meanings: fertility, fecundity, youth, growth, regeneration, victory over disease and evil spirits. It is a beneficial color that wards off the forces of evil. Here, in a late necropolis with decor influenced by Roman painting, it is a fertile green that is presented: a goddess of the fields and harvests makes an offering.

Petosiris necropolis, turn of the 1st–2nd centuries. Egypt, Qaret el Mouzawak, Dakla oasis.

more familiar with dyestuffs and recipes unknown to the Greeks? That seems doubtful, especially because in daily life, green did not occupy an important place in Rome, unlike white, yellow, red, and all the brown, ocher, and brick tones.

Until the imperial era, green seems to have been absent from clothing except perhaps among the poorest classes. Dressing in green was not only demeaning, it was also technically difficult. Although more advanced than Greek dyeing, Roman dyeing was only truly impressive for the ranges of reds and yellows. To dye in green—a solid, dense, radiant green, that is—was a difficult enterprise since methods for mixing yellow and blue were still unknown and plant dyes (numerous in the range of greens) produced only grayish or faded shades. These appeared on the clothes of the poorest peasants. In town even slaves rejected them, preferring brown or dark-blue tones.

The same was true of everyday objects; they were rarely green in color. Even so, the Romans tended to color everything: wood, bone, metal, even leather and ivory, especially in the imperial era. But green was practically absent from that abundant and diverse palette, except with regard to glazed pottery and especially glassware. Under the Republic pottery and glass were already being produced in magnificent tones of green and blue. They became increasingly light and translucent over the centuries, attaining a certain perfection in the Gallo-Roman period. But that is almost an exception. Green played no major role in everyday life, in civic or religious rituals, or in the most festive or solemn occasions.

In that way, Rome differed greatly from the barbarian world where greens were plentiful on fabric and clothing, and even from Egypt where it was often considered beneficial and thus much sought after, even protected. Green animals like crocodiles were sacred. Artisans knew how to make artificial green pigments using copper filings as a base, mixed with sand and potash. By heating them to a very high temperature, they obtained splendid blue-green tones for use on small funerary furnishings (statuettes, figurines, pearls), often coated with a glaze that gave them a vitreous or precious look.[21] For the Egyptians, as for many other Near or Middle Eastern peoples, green and blue were beneficial colors that kept away evil powers. Associated with funeral rites, they were supposed to protect the dead in the world beyond.[22] Green itself is the color of Osiris, the funeral god but also the god of earth and vegetation; his face is often represented in this color, symbolic of fertility, growth, and resurrection. The hieroglyph that represents the color green is generally in the form of a papyrus stalk, always positive in its symbolism.

That was not at all the case in Rome, at least under the Republic. But the situation changed slightly under the Empire. As early as the first century CE, green, considered eccentric and even improper by the "old Romans," was making its appearance in women's clothing. In two or three generations, the dyers, who had until then experienced great difficulty with green dyes, made quick progress to respond to the demand. Had they discovered a new dyestuff? Did they have new mordants for the products that they had long used (ferns, black plum, plum leaves, leek juice)? Were they practicing mixing blue and yellow for the first time—as it seems the Celts and Germans did? We do not know. But we can observe that beginning with the reign of Tiberius green made its entry into women's wardrobes, and its presence would grow, scandalizing the defenders of good and ancient moral standards.

For the Romans green—and blue to perhaps an even greater extent—was indeed a "barbarian" color. The theater provides various examples of this in the figure of the strange and more or less ridiculous German: fat, flabby, pale or ruddy face, curly red hair, blue or green eyes, tall and thickset, dressed in stripes or checks in mostly green tones.[23] Over the course of decades and centuries, this extravagant character, for so long such a far cry from Roman standards of propriety, came to influence fashions, first women's fashions and later men's fashions. Beginning in the late first century, and even more in the second and third centuries, the women's *stola* (a long pleated dress, gathered at the waist) and *palla* (a kind of large rectangular shawl loosely draped), formerly white, red, or yellow (this last color was expensive and reserved for the most privileged classes) featured an increasingly varied palette. Historians of clothing have usually attributed these changes to the influence of Eastern fashions, which were then making themselves felt in Rome in various domains. That is not false, but with regard solely to dress, the influence of Germanic fashions was at least as great. Consider, for example, the yellow tones that formerly always tended toward orange (*luteus*, *aureus*): henceforth they were more green, more acid (*galbinus*), shades unknown in the East. As for green itself, it was gradually becoming a fashionable color, not so much for everyday life as for more ephemeral occasions in which eccentricity had a place. Indeed, green fabric did not stay green very long. Even in the first centuries CE, in this color range, Roman dyeing techniques remained inferior to German ones. Without an effective mordant dyestuffs penetrated textile fibers poorly and the color faded very quickly. That may explain why its use was limited to women's wardrobes, more extensive and unstable than men's. A pretty woman had to change clothes often, to match her complexion, her hair (well groomed and often colored), her makeup, and accessories. Moreover, her tunics and dresses were not only made of wool or linen but also of cotton and silk, two fabrics that better accepted green dyes. None of this was true for men. Green would not make its appearance on masculine togas until the third and fourth centuries, and even then it remained the exception.

The emerald and the leek

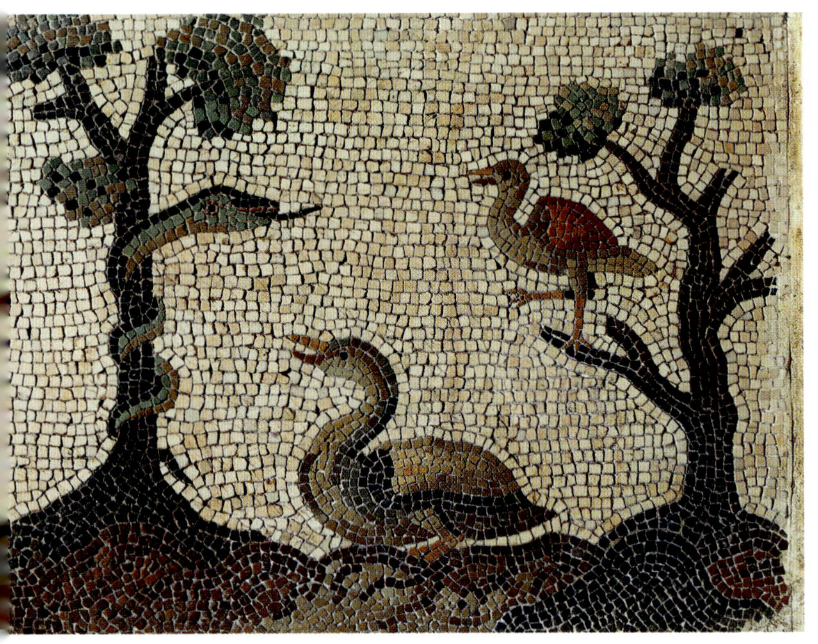

THE SERPENT AND THE BIRDS

Animals are abundantly represented in Roman mosaics, notably birds. Some scenes are drawn from fables and proverbs, others represent symbols or allegories. That is probably the case here.

Polychromatic mosaic of unknown origin, 2nd century. Rome, Museo Nazionale Romano.

As with clothing, green became more of a presence in artistic creations and the framework of everyday life under the Empire, at least among the wealthiest Romans. Here, the fashions were not so much barbarian as oriental. Beginning in the first century CE, the decor of a few grand Roman villas—the *Domus aurea* for example—as well as various Pompeian mansions featured green in a significant way. On the walls trompe-l'oeil paintings sought to imitate gardens and orchards as closely as possible; vegetation was prolific in them and employed a broad range of green tones. Painters had various pigments at their disposal—from light to dark, from bluish to yellowish—for conveying this greenery in all its shades—shades that Latin language would have had a very hard time naming. Moreover, unlike dyers, painters practiced mixing and superimposing colors, which provided them with a more extensive palette. On floors tiled mosaics took over and featured a great diversity in tones in the ranges of greens and blues. Even though these artists were more interested in the effects of light than in realistic color, they frequently represented hunting or fishing scenes with water, plants, and trees that led them to make abundant use of the color green.

In addition to its uses in decor, the color green was used in polychromatic architecture and sculpture. Here we must forget once and for all the neoclassical image of a Rome in which the temples and public buildings were supposedly entirely white and immaculate. That image is false. Everything, or nearly everything, was painted, including statues and all sculpture. Moreover the same was true in Greece, as much in the archaic period as in the classical and Hellenistic periods. Strangely, this long established fact is sometimes still found difficult to accept today. In this regard, the historiographical record is particularly instructive. In the

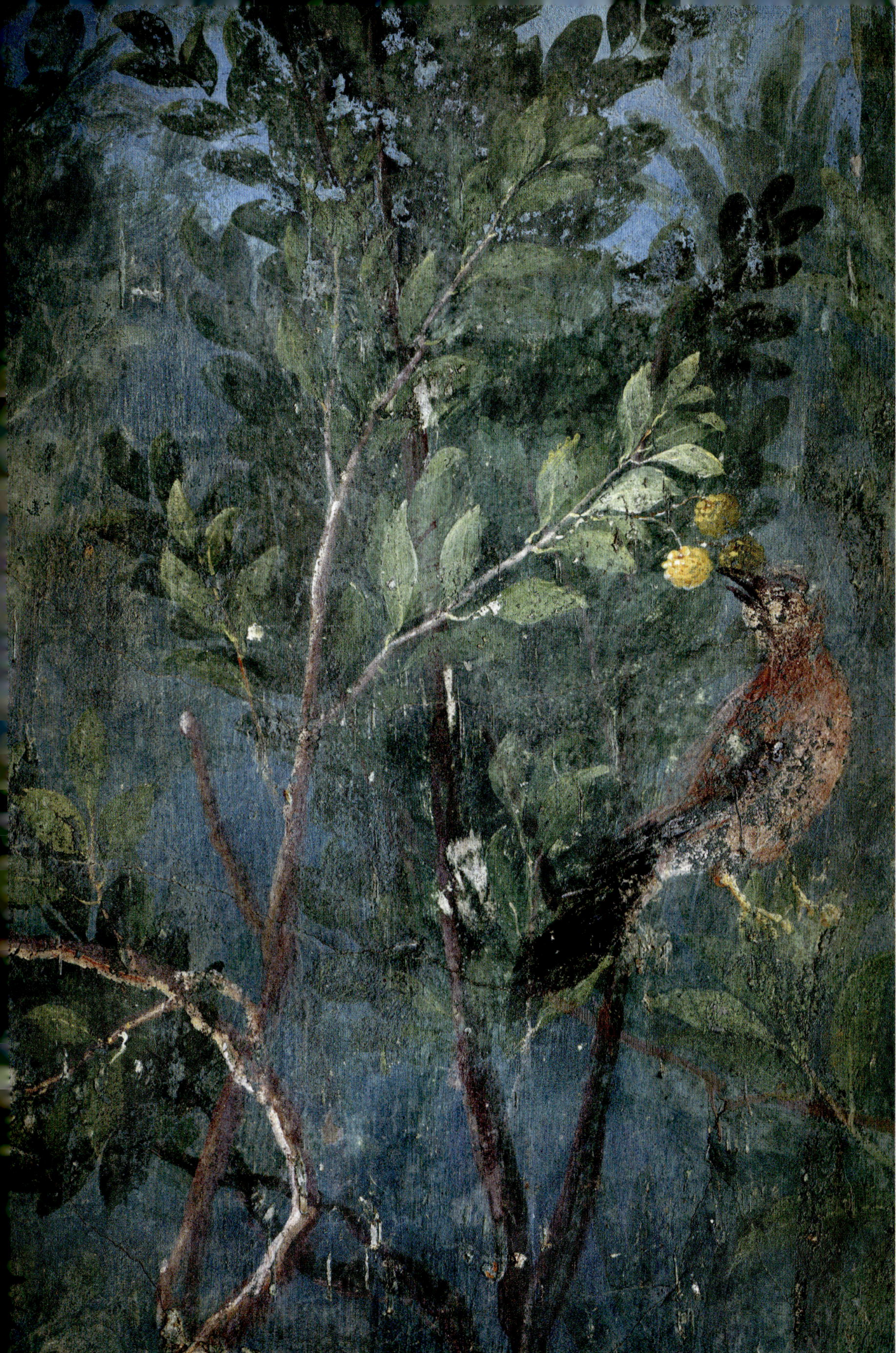

TROMPE L'OEIL GARDEN

Roman mural painters liked to represent gardens in trompe l'oeil. A variety of trees and bushes, plants and grasses, fruits and flowers can be found there, as well as many birds. All are represented in a realistic manner. Greens dominate and appear in a wide variety of shades thanks to the use of natural (earth greens, malachite) and artificial (copper greens) mineral pigments. We have retained many of the formulas for obtaining those artificial greens, which are very luminous and slightly bluish.

Mural painting from the Villa Livia, 20 BCE. Rome, Museo Nazionale Romano.

late eighteenth and early nineteenth centuries, when young archeologists and architects first travelled to the eastern Mediterranean, to Sicily and Greece and then beyond, they discovered many traces of polychromy on the walls of ruined temples and statues more or less defaced. They mentioned this in the reports they sent to the great scholars of the academies in London, Paris, and Berlin. But the scholars, who had never gone out into the field, did not believe them. It was inconceivable to them that the temples and sculptures of the Greco-Roman world could have been painted. Later, in the mid-nineteenth century, in the face of abundant evidence, some scholars finally acknowledged the existence of a "moderate polychromy," but it was not until many generations, countless voyages, and multiple reports later that the academic world yielded to the evidence: in Greece as in ancient Rome, polychromy was excessive and covered almost everything.[24] Today, not a single researcher contests it, and several exhibitions and excellent publications have recently underscored it again.[25] But to no avail; the general public still retains the image of Athens and Rome as entirely white, even brand new, as they are seen in films or comic strips.

In general, everyday life in Rome became more colorful under the Empire than it had been under the Republic. Among the new colors, green now played a role, as did purple, pink, orange, and even blue. These newcomers were not appreciated by everyone. Moralists and defenders of the tradition denounced the arrival of the *colores floridi* as frivolous, false, vulgar, too vivid, or too decorative, rarely used alone but in combination to produce strong contrasts and loud, flashy palettes. They opposed them to the *colores austeri* (white, red, yellow, black), restrained, dignified, and monochromatic, whose ancient use was responsible for the grandeur of Rome. Among the defenders of the tradition and good chromatic practices was Pliny, who proved to be one of the most extreme, not so much with regard to clothing as to painting and the decorative arts. In his immense *Natural History* he repeatedly rails against the new pigments arriving from the East, against mixing methods that distorted colors, and in a broader fashion against what we would call today "contemporary art."[26] Moreover, Pliny was not the only one to denounce the new fashions and the colors that accompanied them. Cato and Cicero preceded him; his contemporaries Seneca, Quintilian, and even Vitruvius joined him. Seneca ridiculed the new decor of the thermal baths and bathhouses where the men are naked but "the walls are dressed up like peacocks."[27] Later Tacitus, Juvenal, Tertullian, and others indulged in similar diatribes. In matters of color, whether for painting or for dyeing, any novelty was condemnable. Sometimes such coloring was seen as too artificial or too aggressive; sometimes a certain combination of discordant colors was considered crude or indecent. A medley of colors (*varietas colorum*) was considered especially repulsive, even when it was simply a matter of striped fabric or checkered decor. It was all indecent and barbarian.[28]

By denouncing these new fashions, condemning certain colors, and extolling others (white, red), Roman authors proved to be pioneers in a particularly fertile area: morality and color. Over the centuries they would have many followers who would distinguish between honest and "dishonest" colors in their speeches, sermons, creations, and rulings: Saint Bernard in the twelfth century; Franciscan adherents to voluntary poverty in the thirteenth century; legislators promulgating sumptuary laws in the late Middle Ages; the great Protestant reformers of the sixteenth century; bourgeois moralists in the nineteenth century; puritans of all types in the twentieth century. In this moral ranking of colors, which changed many times over the course of European history, green was always ranked with the bad colors, the false, unstable group unworthy of good citizens, virtuous Christians, and even simple honest men, as we will come to see.

For the moment, let us remain in Rome, where not all authors shared the opinion of Pliny and Seneca. On the contrary, some of them celebrated the new fashions and echoed the avid sponsors or patrons of change and originality, even eccentricity. They seemed to have been numerous under Nero's reign (54–68), beginning with the emperor himself, who loved the arts and considered himself a true artist, practicing poetry and music, acting in the theater, and not hesitating to descend into the amphitheater or the hippodrome.

Ancient history and historiography were harsh with Nero, a megalomaniac and unstable character, a despotic, incompetent emperor, surrounded by buffoons and drunken revelers. He was charged with many crimes (notably the burning of Rome in 64), the deaths of all his enemies, and horror of horrors, the assassination of his own mother, Agrippina. Recent historiography is more nuanced and has emphasized how Nero was the victim of Suetonius, who detested him and who painted a horrifying portrait of him in his *Lives of the Twelve Caesars*, written about 115–120. In fact, the early years of his reign were relatively peaceful, and Nero seemed to be a skilled politician in many instances. It was the end of his reign that was especially dramatic; it ended with the emperor's suicide and led to a crisis of succession and civil unrest unknown in the Empire since the death of Caesar. But that is not our concern here. Nero interests us because he seems to have been a remarkable champion of the color green.

NERO

Roman historians spoke at length about Nero. Thanks to them, we know some of his preferences in matters of color: his favorite color was green. He liked to dress in green, collected emeralds, supported the green stable in the chariot races, and when it came to cooking, relished leeks. The green patina on this coin, due to the oxidation of the bronze, seems to echo the emperor's tastes.

Imperial bronze coin, 60 BCE. Private collection.

Unlike for most of the Roman emperors, for Nero we actually know something about his taste in matters of color and clothing. Nero liked vivid colors, Greek-style clothing, Eastern fashions. Most importantly, in many areas he showed an undeniable penchant for green. First in his dress, especially when he made an appearance at the theater or the races. Secondly, in the decor of his palaces, where silk occupied an unprecedented place. But above all, in his collections of gems and stones, where emeralds held the most prominent position. A passage from Suetonius on this subject is still famous: at the amphitheater Nero supposedly watched the gladiator fights through a large emerald so as not to be bothered by the rays of the sun.[29] This passage has often been translated badly or misinterpreted. Of course Nero loved to watch such fights, but he did not observe the gladiators through an emerald, or even through less colorful, skillfully cut beryl. He would have seen nothing, or very little. The text must be understood differently. Nero delighted in the spectacle of gladiators, watched them for hours on end, and to rest his eyes he occasionally directed his gaze toward a large emerald because among its other virtues this stone was supposed to soothe the eyes.[30] Later, like Nero, medieval scribes and illuminators who spent a good part of their day bent over books and parchment, would similarly rest their eyes by gazing at an emerald from time to time.[31]

There is another area, odd and unexpected, that connects the emperor to the color green: cooking. Nero was a "porrophage:" he ate great quantities of leeks, entirely unusual for a man of his rank and his time. This trait struck many of his contemporaries, perhaps even more than his depraved behavior or ignominious crimes. Nero devoured leeks, a two-tone vegetable no doubt but in classical antiquity so frequently associated with the color green that one adjective was constructed from its name in Greek (*prasinos*), and two in Latin (*prasinus* and *porraceus*). All of them express the idea of a loud, garish green, corresponding more or less to the modern French expression *vert épinard*, spinach green.[32]

A few authors claim that it was to improve and protect his voice that Nero, who prided himself on his perfect singing, consumed so many leeks. Alternatively, many modern scholars have thought that this diet was prescribed to him by a doctor: leeks, like garlic and onion, have beneficial effects on the heart. But did Roman medicine know that? It considered the leek, which Romans used abundantly, first to be a powerful diuretic (confirmed by contemporary medicine), an aphrodisiac (among many others), and supposedly an effective remedy for snake bites (which is more debatable).[33] But in the end it hardly matters. What does matter is that Nero loved green, emeralds, greenery, and leeks—so much so that when he went to the hippodrome to participate in the chariot races, he donned the green stable tabard, the famous *factio prasina* that Petronius makes fun of in the *Satyricon*.[34]

Hippodrome green

For the historian of colors, sports provide particularly fertile fields for observation. Whether it is a matter of the Olympic Games, ancient or modern, medieval tournaments or jousts, or today's grand championships, they offer a fruitful harvest. Not only do colors abound in the stadium and the stands, not only do they help identify the participants, distinguish the two sides, and mark the supporters, but most importantly they obey codes and combinatory systems that function fully without either the participants or spectators being truly aware of them. On the sports fields colors are "at home" and play primary roles.

In Rome the chariot races were no exception to this rule. Arriving from Greece, where they had been part of the Olympic Games since 620 BCE, they became an important presence early in the Roman Republic and then rose to triumph in the Roman Empire, where they constituted the sport par excellence, in an almost modern sense of the word. The races took place in the hippodrome, that is, at the amphitheater. The greatest of them was the Circus Maximus, located between Palatine and Aventine. Rebuilt many times, under Augustus it measured 600 meters long by 180 meters wide, but it had to be expanded in the third century: it could then hold 385,000 spectators, nearly two-thirds of whom were seated. Men and women, young and old, free and slave mingled in an unusually free way there in rowdy crowds. The spectators were all the more excited since many of them wagered on this or that chariot, this or that stable. There were frequent quarrels, disputes, mob scenes and riots.

In the shape of a large oblong oval, the hippodrome was divided into two parts by a low central wall, the *spina*, more than 200 meters long. At both ends there were sharp curves that caused many accidents as each chariot attempted to get on the inside. Collisions, dirty

A CHARIOT RACE AT THE HIPPODROME

Chariot races were the Romans' favorite "sports" event. Every town, no matter how small, had to have a hippodrome, sometimes several. The largest was located in Rome: the Circus Maximus, which grew to its maximum size in the third century, when it could hold 385,000 spectators. In that period only two great stables remained: the Blues and the Greens. These stables also represented powerful, restless political factions. In general, the Senate and the patricians supported the Blues; the people supported the Greens.

Tiled mosaic, c. 300–310. Barcelona, Museu Nacional Arqueològic de Tarragona.

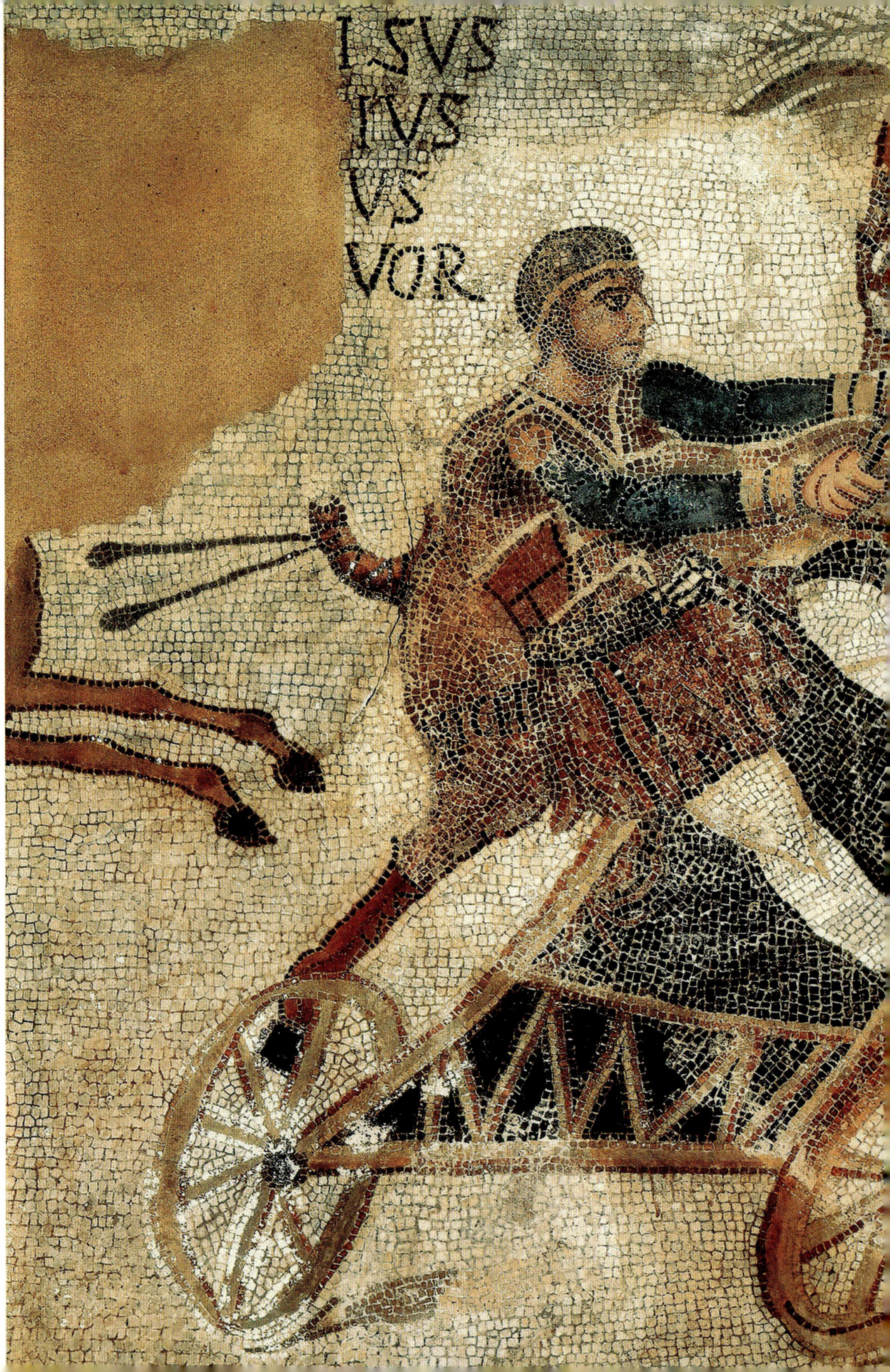

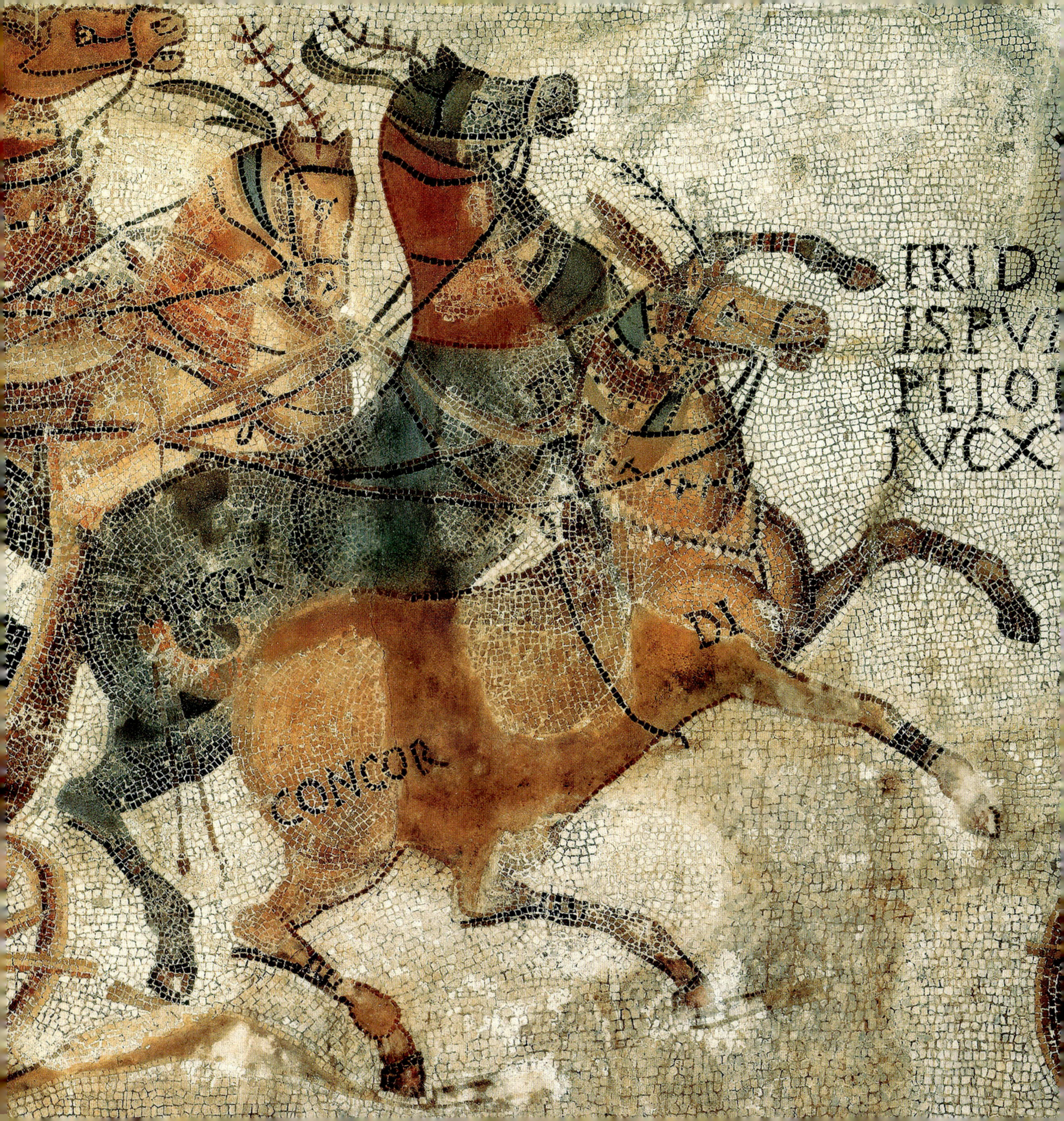
CONCOR
DI

tricks, cheating, falls, and broken wheels were not uncommon. At one end, the slightly larger one, were the starting stalls, twelve in number; closed by one door, they opened suddenly at a signal given by the magistrate presiding over the races. In the provinces many amphitheaters were constructed in the image of the great amphitheater in Rome; they were smaller, but the race tracks were organized in the same way.

Chariots could be drawn by one, two, three, or four horses. This last combination, with the four horses harnessed to the front, was the most spectacular. In Rome this was the star race. It lasted seven laps, the last one being the fastest, most violent, and the most dangerous. As time went on competitions became increasingly numerous: sixty-seven days per year and twelve races per day in Caesar's era; 175 days per year and up to thirty-four races per day three centuries later. The charioteers were then the "stars" as in today's great sports events. Former slaves, their successes freed and enriched them; sometimes statues were erected of them, and they were transformed into demigods. Thanks to funerary inscriptions, the names of a few champions have come down to us, such as that of Gaius Appuleius Diocles, originally from Lusitania; he raced for twenty-four years, participated in 4,237 races, scored 1,462 victories, and earned about thirty-six million sesterces. That, it seems, is the world's record.[35]

Charioteers usually did not race alone but in teams of two, three, or four chariots in a single race. They belonged to a stable (*factio*), and they wore its colors. Their monochrome tabards, a kind of sleeveless jerkin, helped to identify them. Under Augustus four stables participated in the races: the Whites, the Blues, the Greens, and the Reds. Later, others joined them (the Yellows and the Purples), but in the late Empire, only two great stables remained: the Blues (*factio venata*) and the Greens (*factio prasina*). They employed a large staff, were powerfully organized, and represented much more than sports teams or fan clubs. They were actual political factions, with their clientele, networks, and lobbies, whose influence extended beyond the hippodrome. In general, the Blues (*venetiani*) represented the Senate and the

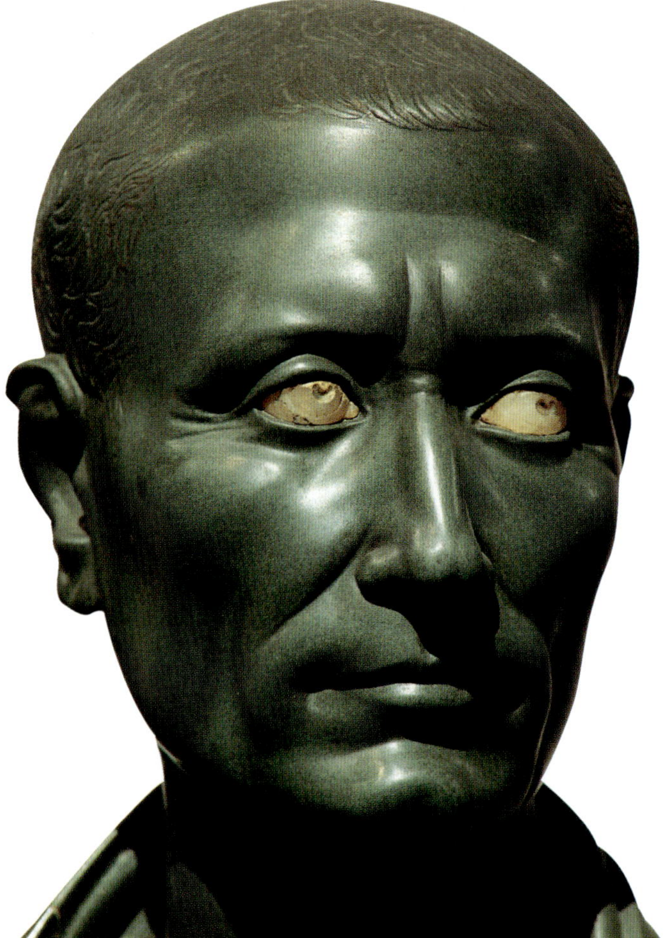

JULIUS CAESAR

This splendid bust in green schist from Egypt (the eyes are in marble) was commissioned by Cleopatra, probably in Caesar's lifetime.

Berlin, Pergamonmuseum.

patrician class, the Greens (*prasiniani*) the people. Many emperors supported the Blues, but over the decades a few particularly demagogic princes aligned themselves with the Greens. Nero, Domitian, and Commodus are primary examples.[36]

Let us pause at these two colors that gradually eliminated all the others. These were not ordinary colors; not only did blue and green play relatively minor roles in daily life, but they were expressed here by two terms and two shades that were rarely encountered outside the hippodrome. These were circus colors, loud, garish, and vulgar. The green of the *factio prasina* compared, as we have said, to that of leeks, relatively dark and more or less bluish. But above all, it was conspicuous. As for the blue of the *factio venata*, it is almost indefinable as the adjective *venetus* was practically only used for chariot races and circus games. Its etymology is much debated.[37] Was it linked to the Venetians? But, if so, which Venetians? Three people very distant from one another bore that name: the first in Armorica, the second in Venetia, the third in Cappadocia. Moreover, was it a matter of pale blue, bright blue or dark blue? Without anything to compare it to, an answer is impossible. I myself tend to see *venetus* as a very vivid turquoise blue, in opposition to the equally vivid emerald green of the other side.

Barring exceptions, the results of these chariot races are unknown to us. But it certainly seems that the green stable won more victories than the blue. Take, for instance, a passage from one of Juvenal's satires, written in the early second century. As was his habit, the author denounces the morals of his contemporaries, the behavior of women, the excesses of food and riches, the triumph of money and vices, and the circus and amphitheater games. Over the course of some lines recounting a chariot race, he ironically informs us of the Green stable's victory, making it clear to us that this is a welcome outcome because if the Blues had won, all the people of Rome would have been upset:

> All of Rome today is at the Circus. A clamor arises and pierces my ears: I thus conclude that the Greens have won. If they had not won, the city would have been overcome with an even greater sadness and despondency than the day when Hannibal vanquished the consuls in the dust of Cannes. Let youth attend these games; they are for the young. It suits that age to let out tumultuous cries, to make reckless bets, and to enjoy being seated beside elegant young women.[38]

The fall of Rome did not mark the end of the chariot races. In the West, Christianity was hostile to circus games and finally abolished them; the hippodrome was far too much "the refuge of Satan" (Tertullian). But in Byzantium, races continued for a long time. Even more so than in Rome, the "demes," or the factions, played the role of political parties, taking part in public affairs and on many occasions causing considerable unrest. That was the case in 532, early in Justinian's reign, when the Blues, who were supported by the empress Theodora, won a victory that provoked many riots, which then degenerated into deadly confrontations. They were followed by a huge fire, badly handled reprisals, and renewed violence. In the end more than thirty thousand people lost their lives.

In Byzantium, as in Rome, for public order the victory of the Greens was a safer bet.[39]

The silences of the Bible and the church fathers

THE THRONE OF THE LAMB SURROUNDED BY THE TETRAMORPH

Unlike blue, green appears abundantly in the illuminated manuscripts of the early Middle Ages. It is often paired with red, a color not at all its opposite but rather its neighbor on the axis of color classification: white, yellow, red, green, blue, black. The illuminators used natural pigments (earth greens, malachite, plant greens) as well as artificial ones (copper greens, brilliant but dangerous and corrosive).

Miniature from an *Apocalypse* from the Saint-Amand Abbey, 9th century. Valenciennes, Bibliothèque municipale, ms. 99, fol. 12.

For color historians the Bible poses complex and sometimes insoluble problems. Not only are terms and expressions for color rare in it, but the scant offerings that can be found there are more a matter of comparisons and metaphors than actual color notations. Furthermore, there is frequent confusion between the vocabularies for colors and for materials; words like "purple," "gold," "silver," "ebony," and "ivory" might refer to the material or the color, or even both at the same time. The context does not always provide clarification. Added to these difficulties is the delicate question of translations. The Bible is made up of a disparate assembly of heterogeneous books, compiled in different eras and in different places, each one having been revised, interpolated, altered, or transformed many times; the translations that have been done over the centuries belong to very distinct sociocultural environments.[40]

Thus the lexicon sometimes changed dramatically, especially with regard to colors.[41] Scant and vague in the Hebrew text and the Aramaic and Greek translations, it became richer—and above all more precise—in the first Latin translations and the Vulgate, then even more abundant in the translations into modern vernacular languages. A revelatory example in this regard: the Hebrew text never uses the generic word "color"; it is used only once in the Aramaic (*tseva'*) and Greek (*khrôma*) texts; the Vulgate on the other hand uses it about thirty times, usually accompanied by an adjective that specifies a hue or shade. The Latin text of the Bible is more colorful than the Hebrew or the Greek text. Where the Hebrew says "a rich cloth," the Latin says *pannus purpureus*, which the vernacular languages subsequently translated into "a

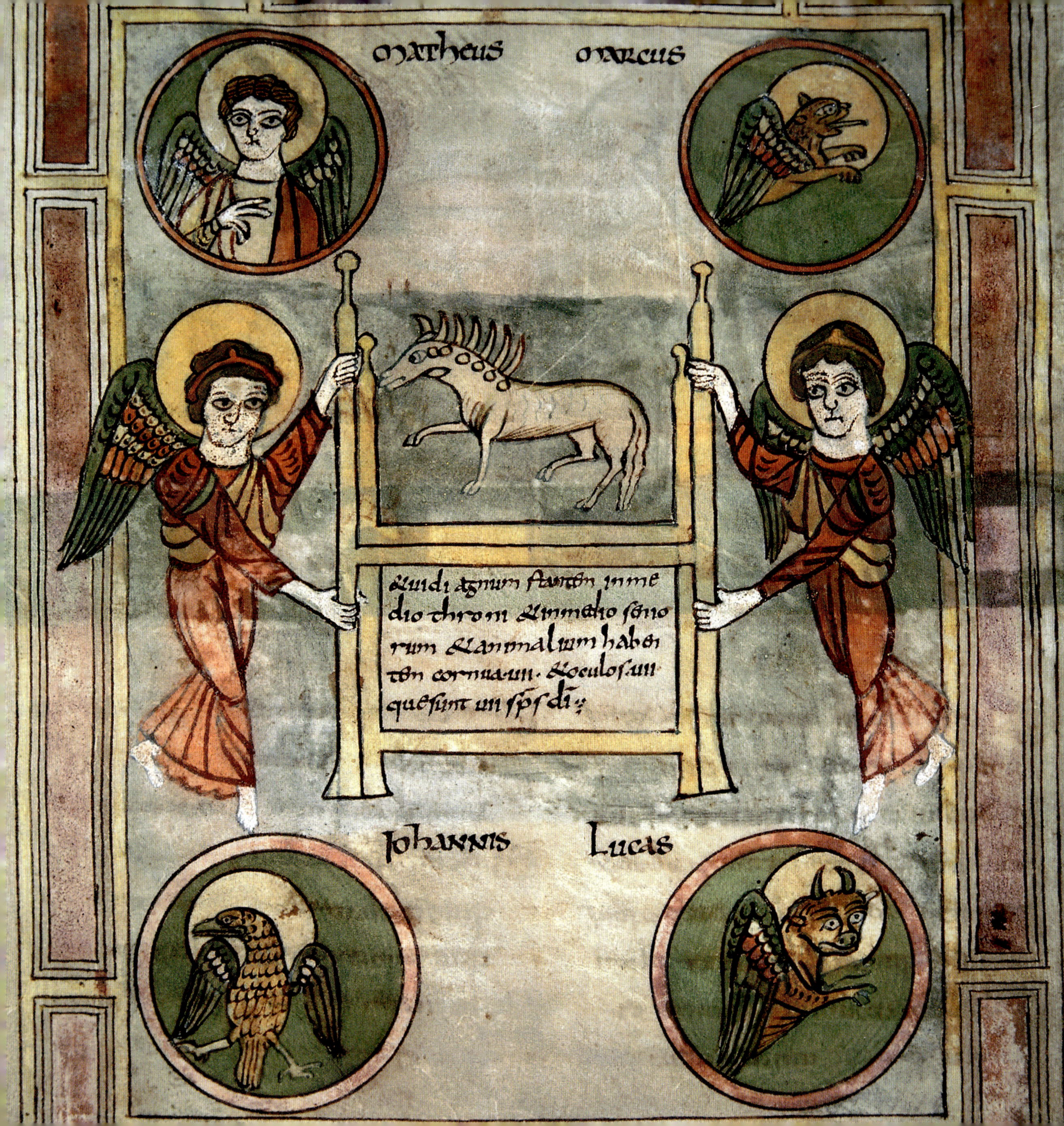
MATHEUS
MARCUS
&uidi agnum stantem in me
dio throni & in medio senio
rum & animalium haben
tem cornua .vii. & oculos .vii
que sunt vii sps di
IOHANNIS
LUCAS

splendid purple cloth" or even "a crimson red fabric." Where the Greek says "a column of dark marble," the Latin tends to translate *columna nigra marmorea*, introducing a black shade (*nigra*), which then appears in the vernacular languages as "a column in black marble." That is why the color historian must always know the state of the text in question when studying the colors in the Bible. What language, what period, what version, what translation? Beginning with modern Bibles recently translated into one Western language or another serves absolutely no purpose, no matter what worthy efforts were made to stay as close as possible to the ancient texts. The translation of color terms is always treason, more so than for any other area of the lexicon.

That said, in ancient versions and modern translations alike, the Bible is lacking in colors. Actual mention of colors is rare. Even in a book as narrative and descriptive as Esther, which offers sumptuous decor, a feast, rich fabrics, and luxurious clothing, the pickings are slim.[42] The biblical text is more interested in the light and the nature and quality of the materials than in the colors themselves. Very often it would rather convey the luster, brilliance, and rich (or poor) quality of a substance than its color. Nevertheless, if one does a quantitative study on the frequency with which each color occurs, white and red dominate. Their symbolism is twofold: white is pure and virginal on the one hand, bland, dirty, or diseased (leprosy) on the other; as for red and its many shades, they sometimes embody love, beauty, wealth and power, sometimes anger, pride, violence, and murder. In order of frequency, next comes black and the various tones of purple (which can, in certain cases, belong to the family of reds), then brown and russet (another red of a specific kind). Yellow and green are much rarer (and sometimes merge), and blue is totally absent.[43]

Such a count is deceptive however. It relies on modern concepts and categories. Red, blue, green, and yellow are clearly distinguished, individualized colors in our modern knowledge and sensibilities, but that was not the case in ancient societies. What we said regarding ancient Greece applies here to the peoples of the Bible; not only were the boundaries between the colors fluid, but the parameters of light, matter, brilliance, and density counted much more than the coloring. Hence the difficulty in translating terms and expressions, in assessing frequency and rarity, and what is more, in establishing true statistics. We can only discern a few broader tendencies: the primacy of white and red, and to a lesser degree black, the rarity of yellow and green, the absence of blue.

Actually, green as a color is practically absent in the Bible as well. When it is mentioned (*yereq* in Hebrew; *viridis* in Latin), it is nearly always a matter of grass or vegetation, never an object, fabric, or article of clothing. Only the emerald does credit to the color green; it is mentioned twice in a list of twelve precious gems, those that adorn the breast of the high priest (Exodus 28:17–20) and those that serve as foundation for the walls of the heavenly Jerusalem (Apocalypse 21:19–21). But those are the exceptions. True green is limited to greenery, the green of the fields, woods, and pastures, places of peace and rest; when it declines into "greenish," it is associated with corpses and death.

The rarity of green in the Scriptures seems to have disconcerted the church fathers, long-winded as they were regarding colors and their symbolism.[44] What is there to say about a color that the Bible does not mention, or only rarely? Nothing, or almost nothing. A quantitative survey done by François Jacquesson on patristic texts predating the mid-ninth century is very revealing in this regard. Compiling all the color terms present in the first 120 volumes of the *Patrologia latina* (an edition of all the Christian authors before the thirteenth century, published between 1844 and 1855 by the priest Jacques-Paul Migne and his collaborators), he was able to make very instructive calculations.[45] Words signifying white represent 32 percent of the total; red, 28 percent; black, 14 percent; gold (and yellow), 10 percent; purple, 6 percent; green, 5 percent; blue, less than 1 percent.[46] Of course the texts in question are specific and essentially a matter of exegesis, hagiography, and moral doctrine. But would more technical or encyclopedic treatises or more narrative or literary works change the results for the period in question? That is not clear.

Whatever the case, to define the symbolism of green for the church fathers proved to be a difficult task. At best we can note that they did not attribute to this color most of the virtues or the vices that were later associated with it: youth, vigor, hope on one side; disorder, greed, madness on the other. For them green is above all the color of vegetation. A few of them made it the color of the wood of the Cross and gave it a positive symbolism tied to the Resurrection. But that remained a minor association and was only really noted by the liturgists.

Before the birth of heraldry and the great chromatic changes of the twelfth and thirteenth centuries, it is, in fact, within the liturgical domain that historians can find the most information regarding the symbolism of colors, envisioned for the first time as concepts, that is to say abstract categories, and not as light, material, or simple coloring.

It is worthwhile to pause here.

A middle color

Unfortunately the question of the appearance and diffusion of liturgical colors has hardly attracted the interest of scholars. There are numerous histories of the liturgy, but they rarely address color. On many fronts our knowledge remains rudimentary.[47] Nevertheless let us summarize the major trends in the development of liturgical colors up to the thirteenth century.[48]

In earliest Christian times priests did not wear any particular clothing; to celebrate the mass they wore their ordinary clothes. Later a specific vestiary made its appearance (amice, alb, stole, chasuble, and maniple), but fabrics and clothing were not dyed as color was considered to be impure. However, undyed fabric shifted gradually to white, reserved for Easter and the most important holidays, then to black for times of affliction and penitence. The patristic texts are in agreement in considering white the most dignified color and black the color of sin and death. Later, in the Carolingian period, when luxury made its entry into the churches, gold and vivid colors began to appear on liturgical fabrics and clothing. Customs varied widely according to the diocese. After the year 1000 a certain unity developed for the first time, at least for the high holidays: white was chosen for Christmas and Easter; black for Good Friday and days of mourning; red for Pentecost and the holidays of the Cross. For the rest, notably the saints' days, and for ordinary times, local customs varied and persisted.

All that changed with Pope Innocent III (1198–1216)—the greatest pope of the Middle Ages—who succeeded in gradually imposing the idea that the customs of the Roman diocese must be adopted by all of Christendom. He himself had described those customs in an early work compiled in 1195, even though he was only Cardinal Lothar of Segni at the time and at some

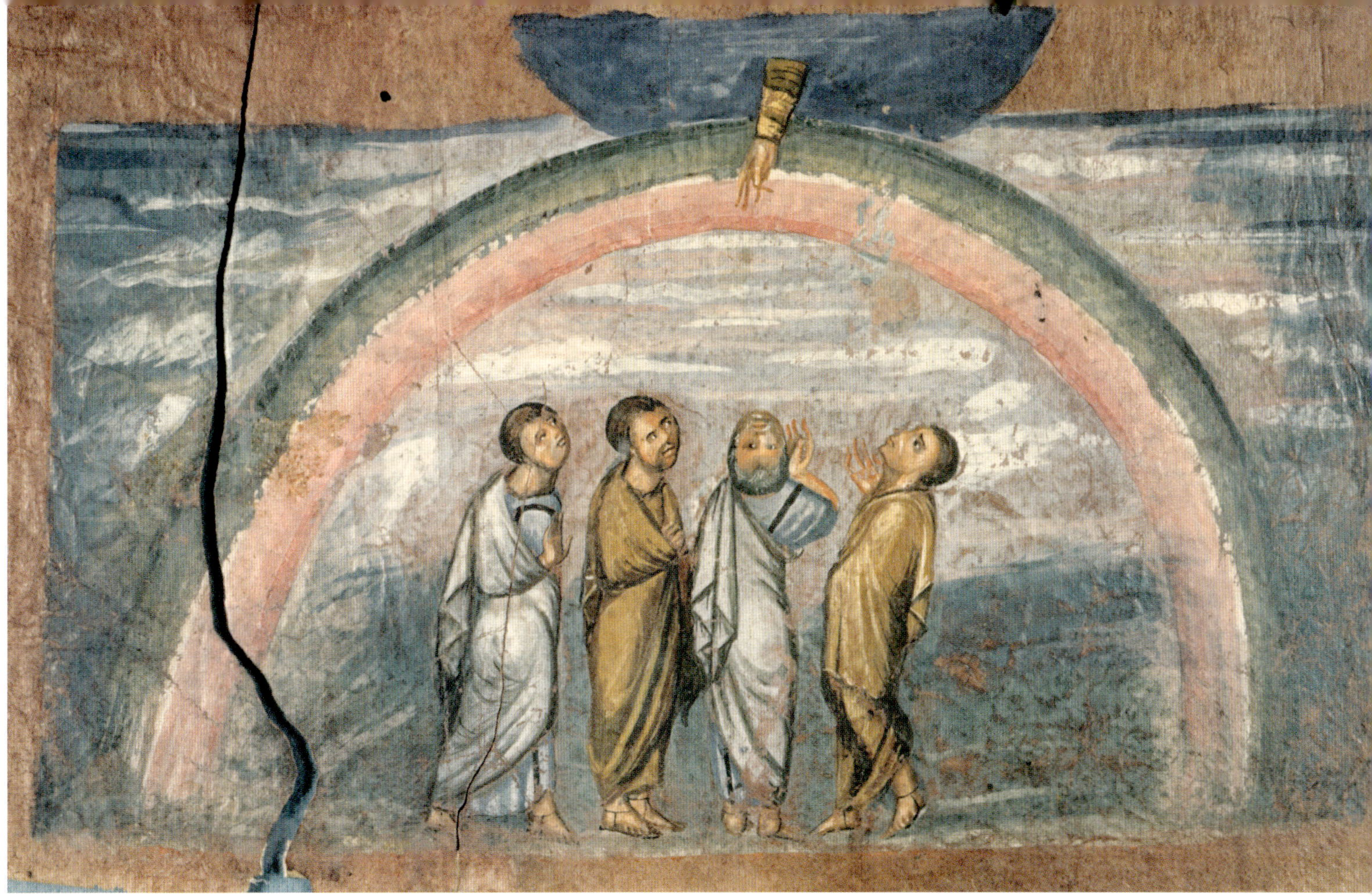

remove from the affairs of the Curia. It was a treatise on the mass, the *De sacro sancti altari mysterio*, in which the author compiled and cited many sources, according to the customs of the time.[49] Nonetheless, for us this treatise has the merits of going on for longer than earlier ones did about the symbolism of colors and of describing and commenting upon their liturgical role in the Roman diocese in the late twelfth century.

Regarding white, red, and black, Cardinal Lothar hardly broke new ground in relation to the liturgists who preceded him (Honorius, Rupert of Deutz, Jean Beleth), but he extended the list of the holidays in question. White, the symbol of purity, joy, and glory, was used for all the holidays for Christ, as well as for angels,

THE BIBLICAL RAINBOW

In Biblical exegeses the rainbow is considered an arc of alliance between God and man. The one shown here appears after the Flood; it is protective and pacifying. In medieval images the rainbow never resembles the one we are familiar with; not only does it lack seven colors, possessing only two (as is the case here), three or four, but those colors do not form a sequence ordered like the spectrum. In early medieval rainbows green is often present, blue never.

Miniature from the *Genesis of Vienna*, Syria, first half of the 6th century. Vienna, Österreichische Nationalbibliotheck, Theol. Gr. 31, fol. 3.

virgins, and confessors.[50] Red, which evokes both the fire of the Holy Spirit and the blood spilled by and for Christ, was used for the Pentecost, as well as for the feasts of the apostles and martyrs and for those of the Cross. Black, associated with mourning and penitence, served for Good Friday, as well as funeral masses and throughout Advent and Lent. But it was with regard to green that our author proved himself to be the most original. He made it the color of hope in life eternal—that was a new thing—and made this pronouncement, important for our purposes:

> Green must be chosen for the holidays and the days when neither white nor red nor black are suitable, because it is a middle color between white, red and black.[51]

Green is a middle color! This claim was not insignificant. Not only was green presented as the fourth color of Christian culture—from which yellow and blue were absent, let us note—but it was placed in the middle of a system (a triangle) for which white, red, and black served as the three poles.[52] On the one hand, Cardinal Lothar, the future Pope Innocent III, made himself heir to ancient traditions that, in many societies, beginning with those of the Bible and the Greco-Roman world, granted primacy to those three colors. But on the other hand, he granted green, formerly a very inconspicuous color, a very conspicuous place henceforth, essential for the whole to function properly. In his treatise, a "middle" color did not mean an unimportant one. Associated with holidays and ordinary days, green became de facto the color most often called upon throughout the liturgical year. That is not insignificant, especially given the general tendency in the thirteenth century toward liturgical unification. Most of the dioceses that had retained local customs gradually adopted those of Rome; green became a liturgical color in a large portion of Roman Christendom and thus acquired a certain prestige.[53] It was certainly less solemn that white, red, or black, but on the theological plane, it came before yellow, blue, purple, and all the other colors.

What accounts for this promotion? Scholars' speculations on the colors? At the turn of the twelfth to thirteenth centuries, they were numerous, especially with regard to the rainbow. Aristotle was gradually being rediscovered. Although he certainly never wrote a treatise devoted specifically to color, on many occasions in his works on natural philosophy he placed green at the center of an axis formed by all the other colors.[54] For Aristotle, green was very much a "middle" color. This idea was taken up again in a small late treatise (second or third century) that was not by him but was attributed to him, *De coloribus*. This text circulated among scholars in the early Middle Ages and gradually

EMPEROR OTTO III IN MAJESTY

The Carolingian emperors had made red an imperial color, evoking the crimson of Rome and Byzantium. The Ottonian emperors continued this custom but sometimes combined green and red, at least in images. Later the Salian and especially the Staufen dynasties would do the same. Red thus represented the imperial majesty and green the reigning dynasty. This practice disappeared in the early fourteenth century with the accession of the house of Luxembourg.

Miniature from the Gospels of Otto III, Reichenau, c. 998–1000. Munich, Bayerische Staatsbibliothek, Clm 4453, fol. 23.

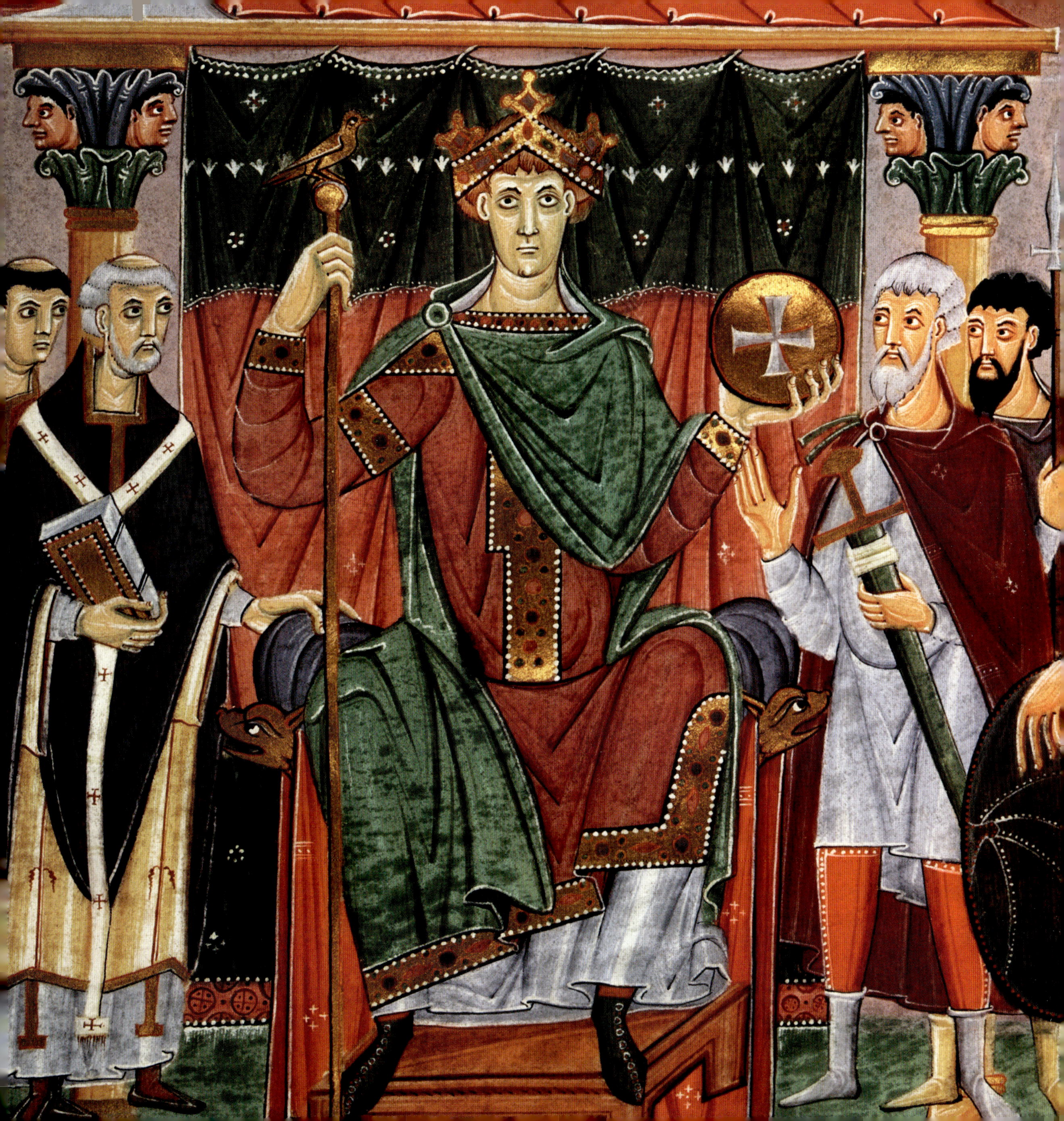

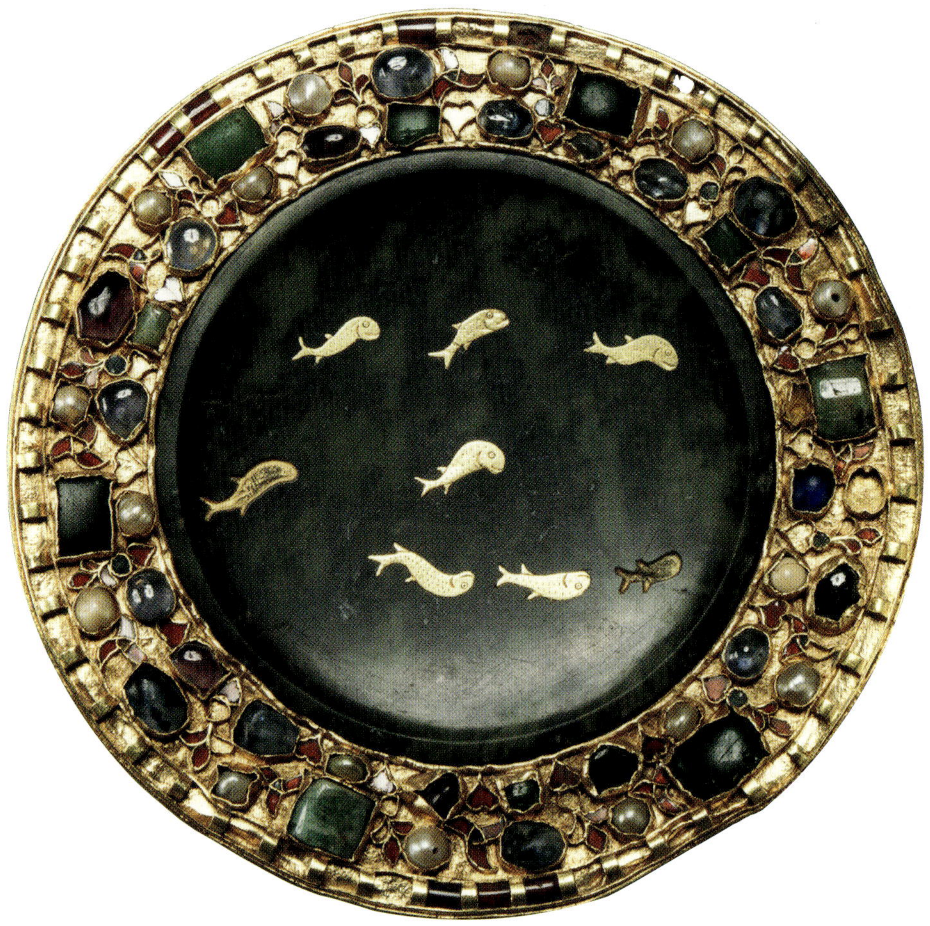

established a supposedly "Aristotelian" classification for colors: white, yellow, red, green, blue, purple, black. This would become the basic scientific classification system until the seventeenth century. Was the Roman Curia already aware of it in the late twelfth century?

That is a difficult question to answer, and perhaps the explanation must be sought elsewhere, for example in the material culture. We have seen that green played a minor role in the everyday life of the Romans. The "barbarian" fashions of the late Empire were not sufficient to expand that role. Only aristocratic women, capricious and versatile in matters of dress, resorted to it in various periods. After the great Germanic invasions of the fifth century, things changed. The Germans brought with them dyeing methods and clothing customs that were not those of the long-Romanized populations. In matters of color, the palettes differed widely: white, red, yellow, monochrome on one side; blue, green, yellow, combinations of vivid, distinct colors on the other. Even the yellows contrasted: tending toward orange for the Romans, more or less greenish for the Germans. A Latin term was even created to characterize this yellow, so disagreeable to the Mediterranean eye: *galbinus*.[55]

How long did it take for Roman and Germanic customs to merge? It is not easy to say given the silence of the sources on this question. Clothing fashions in the Merovingian period remain terra incognita for the historian, even with regard to princely circles. Moreover, here as elsewhere romantic imagery replaced historic reality and dressed the kings and princes of the sixth and seventh centuries in costumes they might never have worn: short tunics and mantles, legs bare or wrapped with strips of cloth, vivid colors, stripes, checks, abundant furs and animal skins. Later, representational documents are more numerous, at least for the aristocracy. They tend to show a mixture of Gallo-Roman and "barbarian" fashions: the forms remained Roman, the colors became Germanic. The Germans' superior dyeing techniques in part explain this change, especially in the range of greens and to a lesser degree for blues, even though blue had not yet experienced its great promotion. That would not take place until the central Middle Ages.

Thus Charlemagne and his successors wore more green than the emperors of the late Empire, not green in isolation but green combined frequently with red, the color of power. Without the aid of actual statistics and without forgetting that the medieval image is never a "photograph" of reality, we must recognize that from the ninth to twelfth centuries those two colors were the ones most often used by the illuminators to dress kings, princes, and important personages. The only exceptions are those manuscripts copied and illuminated in southern Italy and the Iberian Peninsula.[56]

This Germanic green is also a Scandinavian green. Many chroniclers have noted that the Normand pirates who attacked the coasts, ascended the rivers, and pillaged the churches and monasteries for almost three centuries often wore green tunics.[57] Dyeing in green was a relatively easy process in northern Europe. Nettle, fern, plantain, oak leaves, and birch bark provided a wide variety of shades. Nevertheless, the dyes did not easily penetrate fabric fibers, and most greens were not vivid or solid. But this color green, attested to in many documents, seems to have been a lucky one for northern pirates and sailors—whom tradition awkwardly refers to as "Vikings." When just prior to the year 1000 a troop of Icelandic colonists led by Erik the Red landed in Greenland, they declared the region habitable, founded two colonies there, and gave the country the name it retains today—not so much because vegetation then grew there in abundance but because for these men of the north, a green, verdant land was a sign of hope, happiness, and prosperity.[58]

GREEN SERPENTINE PATEN

This serpentine paten inlaid with fish of gold is a Roman work from the first century. The circle of silver garnished with stones probably dates to the second half of the ninth century. This composite object, kept in the treasury of the Saint-Denis Abbey was long used at the coronation of the queens of France.

Paris, Musée du Louvre, Département des objets d'art, MR 415.

Islamic green

The present volume concerns the social and cultural history of green in western Europe, not the history of this color on the global scale. For the historian the issues of a color are essentially social issues. That is why, in order to speak with relevance, one must limit oneself to a given cultural domain and not lapse into simplistic generalizations or a reductive scientism based on badly digested neurobiological observations. Humans do not live alone, they live in societies.

On the other hand, comparative studies can be fruitful, especially when they take into account neighboring societies in contact with one another. That is the case with Islam and the Christian West at the height of the Middle Ages. Before venturing further into the history of the color green in Europe, beyond the year 1000, let us look briefly at its history in the Muslim world. The Muslim world is extremely vast, extending from Morocco to central Asia and to the borders of India. Let us limit ourselves to its early Arab centers and to the period between and including the seventh and twelfth centuries: "Islam in its first grandeur" to echo the title of a famous work.[59]

The Quran, that is to say the whole of the divine revelations made to Muhammad through the archangel Gabriel, offers a fixed text only twenty years after the death of the Prophet, when the caliph Uthman had an "official" version of it established. Subsequently some changes occurred in it, but they remained minimal. The text is comprised of 114 suras (chapters) of varying length, with a total of 6,226 verses. Each sura constitutes a whole, independent of the others. Some correspond to the Meccan period of the Prophet's life and others to the Medinan period, which results in thematic fragmentation and sometimes repetition and contradiction.

MEDICINAL PLANTS

Ancient Greek medicine made use of many plants. Arabic medicine, its heir, added a great many more and compiled anthologies that circulated in the medieval West. Some were translated or adapted into Latin. Among the leading plants in the medieval pharmacopoeia: poppy, belladonna, hawthorn, valerian, mint, St. John's wort, willow, and linden.

Miniature from an Arabic medical treatise, 12th century. Paris, Bibliothèque national de France, ms. arabe 2964, fol. 5.

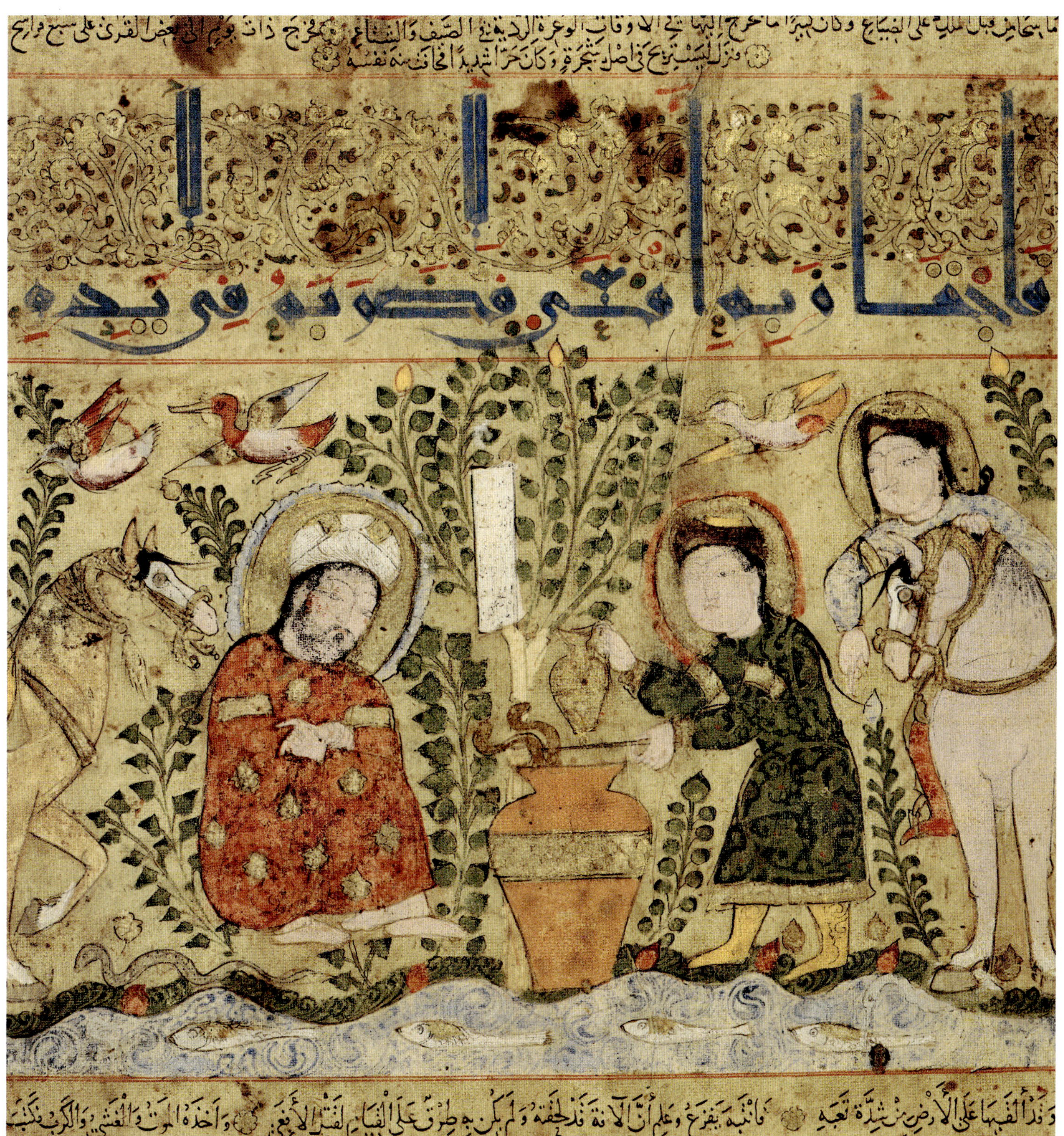

Like the Bible, from which it borrows extensively, the Quran says little of colors. With regard to the six basic colors, there are only thirty-three actual appearances: eleven for white, eight for green, seven for black, five for yellow, one for red, and one for blue.[60] Metaphors and comparisons—"the color of honey," "the color of dawn," and so on—are a bit more numerous but not so numerous as in the Bible. Green, which is our chief interest here, is always a positive color in the Quran, associated with vegetation, spring, the sky, and paradise. Never is it considered unfavorably, as black and yellow can be. Is that enough to make green a sacred color? Maybe not. To give green primacy over all the other colors and eventually make it the religious color of Islam, another tradition had to come together with the Quranic text.

That tradition, the traces of which are found as early as the seventh century, affirms that Muhammad showed a marked preference for the color green for a long period of his life. He liked to wear a green turban, and although he usually dressed in white, he enjoyed being surrounded by green fabrics. For wars he sometimes used a green and sometimes a black standard. The evidence is obviously scant and sometimes contradictory, but this taste for green was confirmed by many of the Prophet's companions and was gradually transformed into a truth no longer called into question.

After Muhammad's death in 632, it seems as though green became not so much the color of the new religion as the dynastic color of his family or at least of those who claimed to be his direct descendants. Thus it took on a political dimension, opposed first to the white of the Umayyad caliphate, a dynasty founded by one of Muhammad's companions, that reigned in Damascus from 650 to 749 (and in Cordoba from 756 to 1031), and then especially to the black of the Abbasid

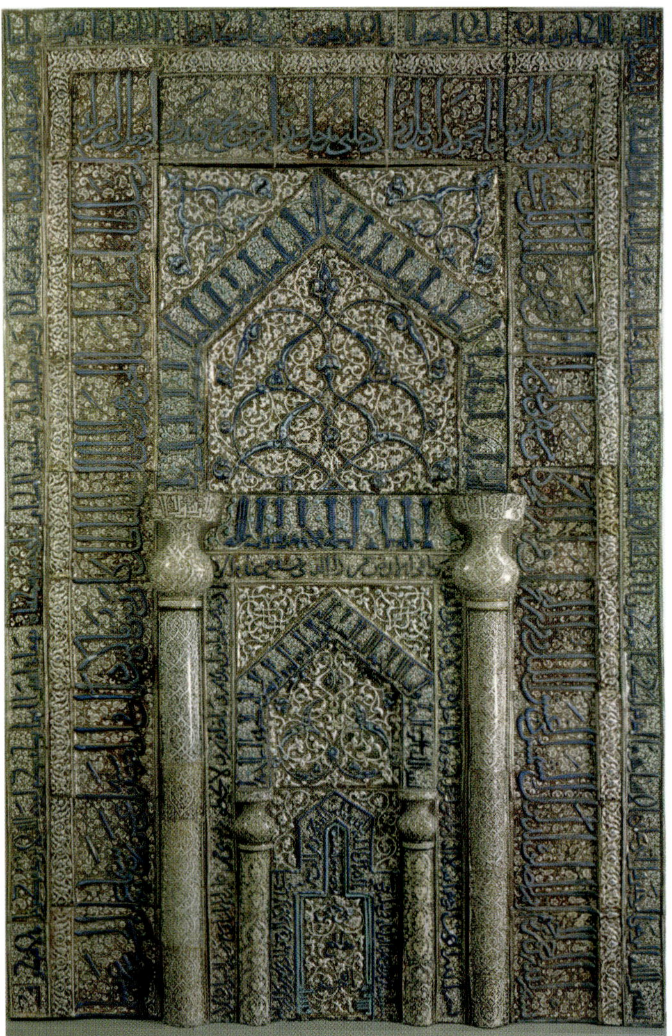

THE GREEN OF ISLAM

At first a dynastic color for the descendants of the family of the Prophet, green gradually became the religious color of Islam and, beginning in the eleventh century, ensured a certain unity in the Muslim world. A beneficial, venerated color, green adorns the earthenware tiles of many mihrabs, niches surrounded by columns indicating the direction toward which the faithful must turn.

Mihrab from the Kachan mosque, 1226. Berlin, Museum für Islamische Kunst.

caliphate, ruling in Baghdad from 750 to 1258. Later, in the tenth century, the Fatimids, who claimed to be descendants of Fatima, the daughter of the Prophet, broke with Baghdad, freed themselves from the tutelage of the Abbasids, settled in Egypt, founded Cairo, and chose green as their dynastic color.

Thus, around the year 1000 green was still not the sacred color of Islam but only a family color. Beginning in the twelfth century that changed. Gradually green took on a sacred quality, and after the fall of the Fatimids, it represented less a political color claimed by one particular dynasty than a religious color claimed by the whole of Islam. The black of the Abbasids, the white of the Almoravids, and later the red of the Almohads continued to oppose one another, sometimes violently, but green became a unifier. It united all the Arab peoples of the Islam world. There are various reasons for that, but the main one is perhaps linked to the Crusades. To the white and red of the crusaders' banners and uniforms, Islam had to oppose a different color, a single, unifying color throughout Spain, North Africa, and the Near East: it was green. We are permitted to venture that the view of the Christians themselves may have played a role in green's promotion in the ranks of their adversaries. Just as there were probably crusaders who drew the crescent out of the vast array of emblematic figures used by the Muslims and promoted it as the single figure to oppose to the cross, so they may have contributed to the promotion of green in the opposing camp: a single color to be emblem for the adversary. Throughout history, in the wars of emblems and symbols, the gaze of the other has always been a determining factor.

Whatever the case, beginning in the twelfth century, green seems to have definitively become the religious color of Islam. Although in every society each color possesses positive and negative aspects, in the Islamic world green is consistently considered good. It is almost unique in this respect. Its symbolism is associated with that of paradise, happiness, riches, water, the sky, and hope. Green became the sacred color. That is why many copies of the Quran from the Middle Ages had green bindings or covers, as they still do today. Similarly, a great number of religious dignitaries wear green clothing. By contrast, in carpets green gradually disappeared: one does not tread on so venerable a color.

The Turkish conquests and subsequent domination did nothing to change this chromatic primacy. Of course, relatively varied political and dynastic colors existed in the Ottoman Empire (blue even made its appearance there as the color of the Christian minority), red being the color of the central power. But green remained the religious and therefore unifying color. Contemporary flags in the Islamic world have retained the memory and the symbolism of it; nearly all of them include green, beginning with that of Saudi Arabia, adopted in 1983. Entirely green, its only decoration is the first verse of the Quran accompanied by the sword of the Prophet.[61]

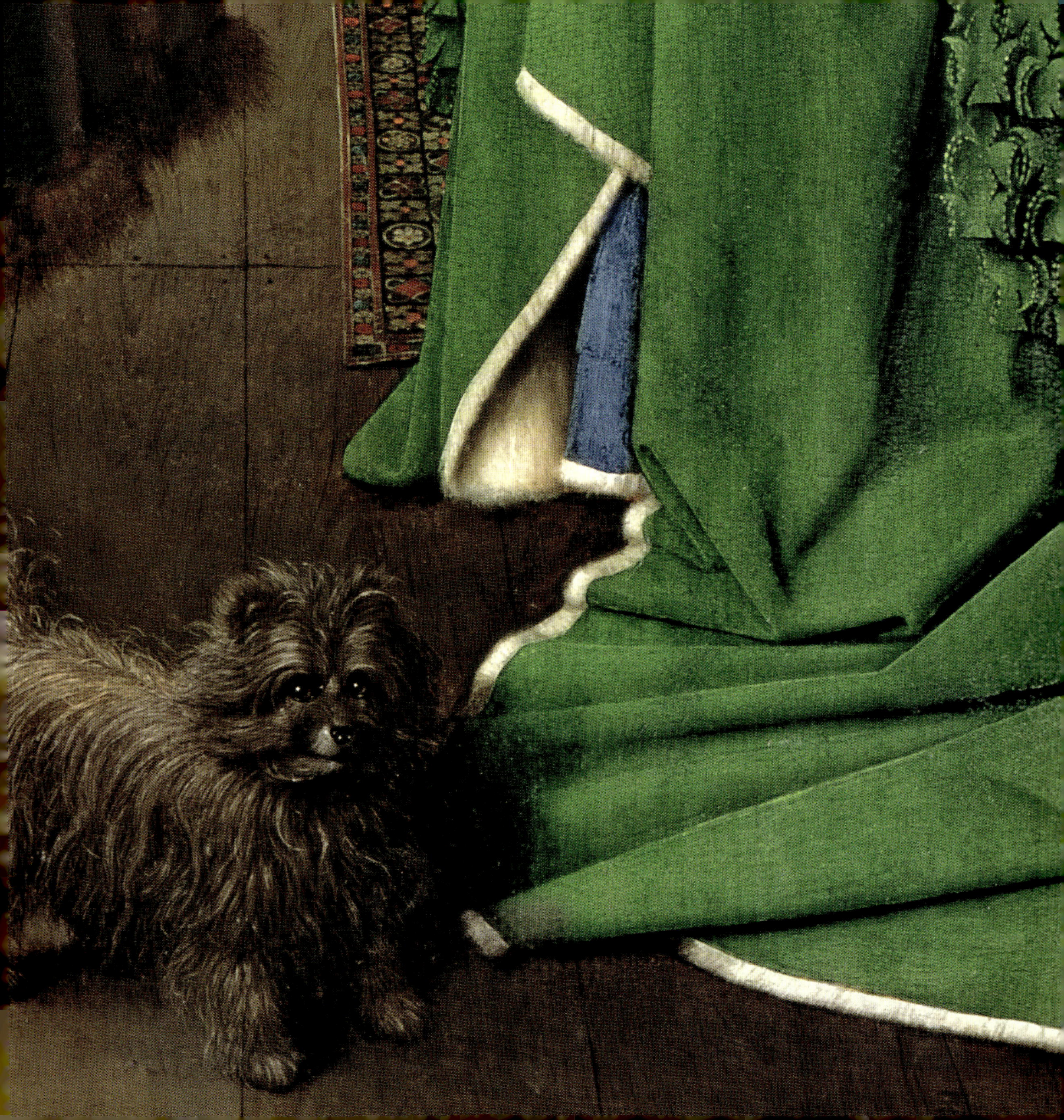

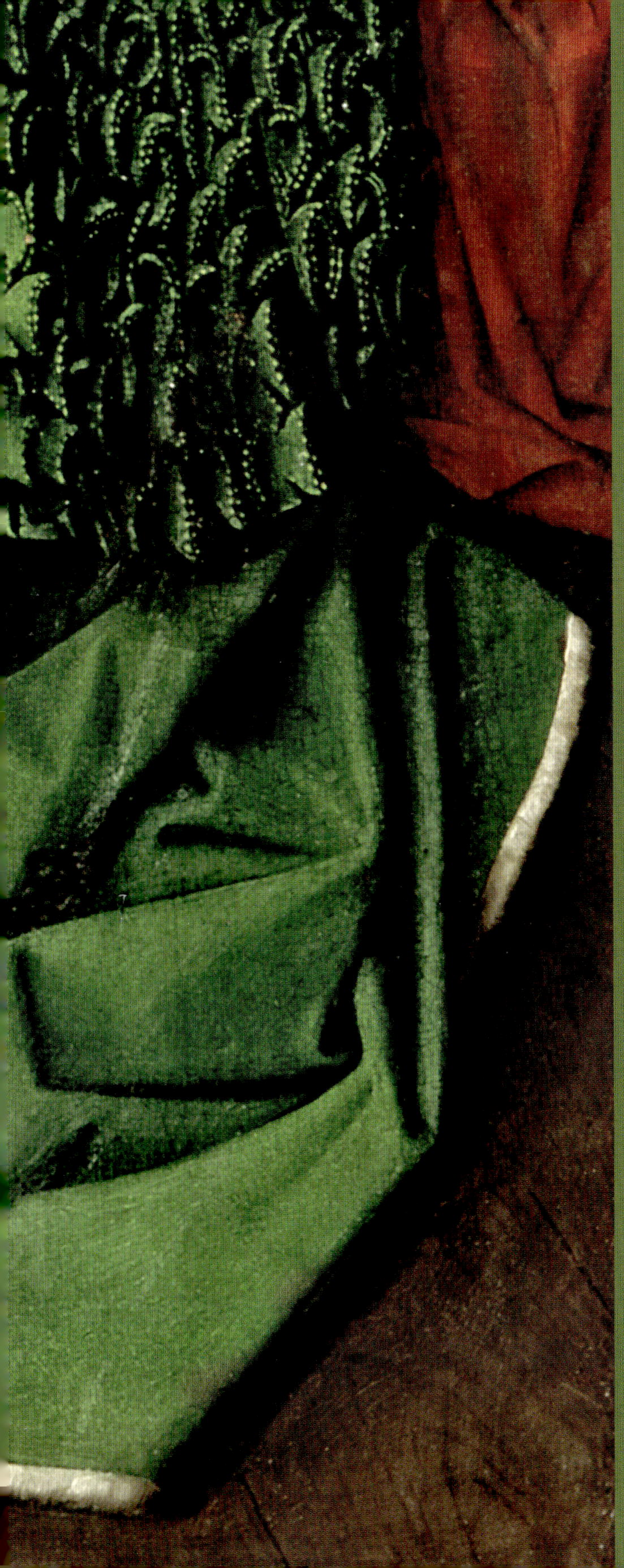

A **courtly** color

11TH–14TH CENTURIES

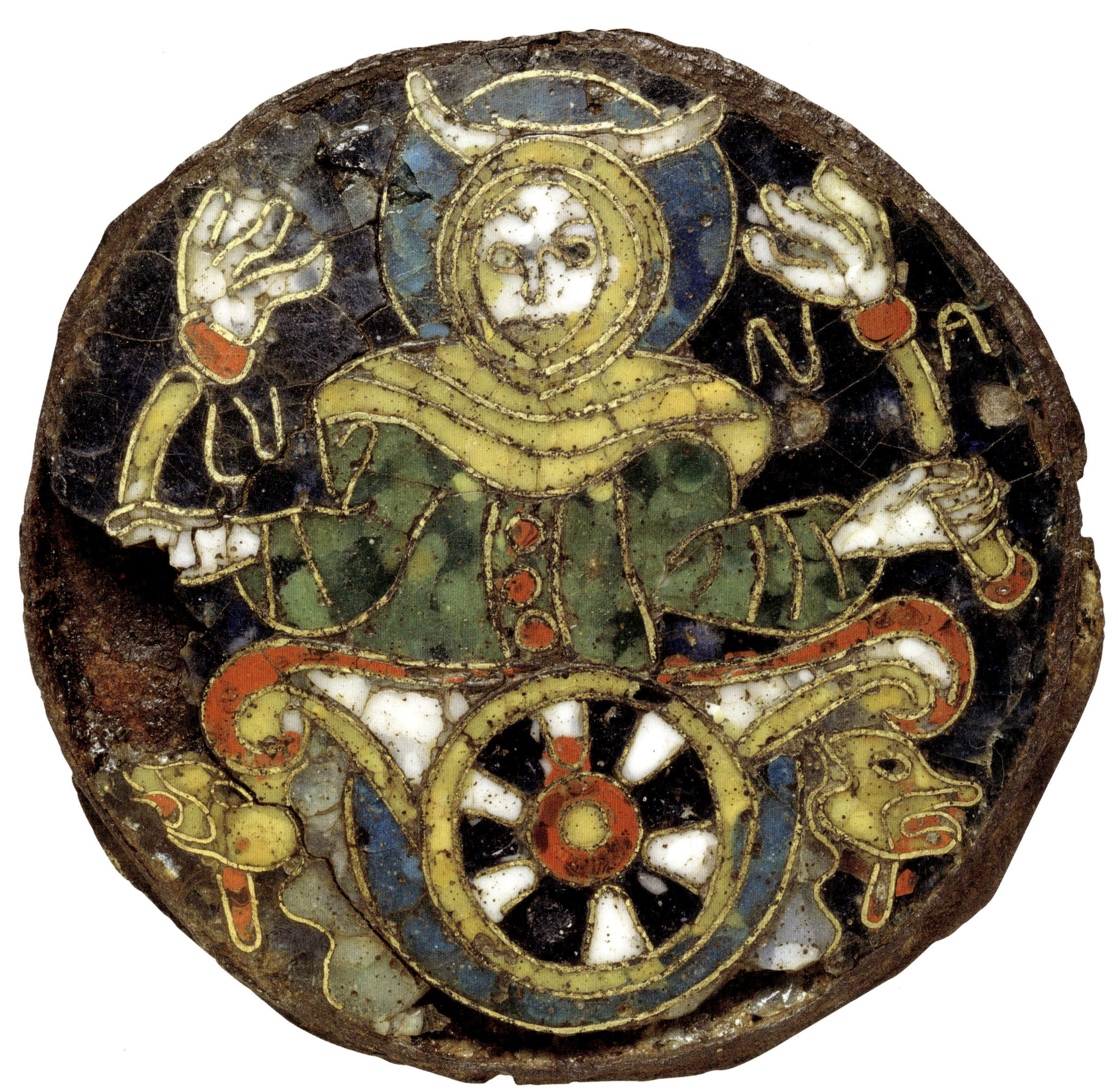

Inconspicuous and uncertain for many millennia, and by the same token resistant to historians' inquiries, green grew in presence and significance following the year 1000. Thus, in the world of representations, it played a role that it had never previously held, and even though—like all the other colors—it remained ambivalent, if not ambiguous, henceforth it was more often considered good than bad. Art and poetry frequently featured it and underscored how it was admired by princes and lords. Beginning in the twelfth century, stained glass, enamel, and the miniature brought it new attention, especially in the Germanic world, where the recent promotion of blue was felt less than elsewhere. A few decades later courtly literature made green not only the emblematic color for the plant world but also the color of youth and love, while chivalry reserved a novel place for it on the paths of adventure and the tournament fields. Only heraldry, then in its nascency, was still reluctant to grant it a primary role in its restrained and restrictive palette; there was much green in courtly decor but little in shields.

Under close examination it appears that the central Middle Ages was a period of undeniable promotion for the color green. Of course, its promotion was not as intense or pervasive as the one benefitting blue at the same time—to the point that we may speak of a "blue revolution" in the twelfth and thirteenth centuries.[1] But it was a very real promotion nevertheless, both quantitative and qualitative, that can be observed and studied through numerous field documents. Not only did the presence of green grow in daily life and in material culture, but in the world of images and symbols, it took on a significance it had never previously had.

THE MOON PERSONIFIED

In medieval images wearing green or yellow clothing is often a sign of disorder (clowns), mockery (minstrels), lunacy (madmen, the insane) or treason (Judas). This image of the moon personified constitutes one of the oldest examples. In medieval culture the moon was in effect a changeable star that, more than all others, influenced men's fate. Haloed here, it appears in a chariot and holds two torches that light up the night.

Cloisonné enamel, Limoges (?), late 11th century. New York, Metropolitan Museum of Art, Inv. 17.190.688.

The beauty of green

What was a beautiful color in the period of chivalry and courtesy? That is not an easy question to answer: not only because the dangers of anachronism lurk for historians here, but also because in conducting their research, historians are always the prisoners of words. The beautiful and the ugly are foremost a matter of vocabulary. Thus, between the actual color of beings and things, the true color perceived by an individual and the color named by one author or another, there can be considerable distance. Moreover, for this period the historian never has a window on individual sensibilities or tastes. Everything comes through the perspective of others and, what is more, through that of society and its values, either aristocratic or clerical. That is why judgments on the beauty or ugliness of a color reveal moral, religious, and social considerations above all.[2] Beauty was almost always what was suitable, just, temperate, and customary. Of course, the purely aesthetic pleasure of contemplating colors existed, but it involved primarily the colors of nature, the only truly beautiful, pure, lawful, and harmonious colors since they were the work of the Creator. Moreover, despite the testimony of poets, historians are badly equipped for studying that pure chromatic delight; here again, they remain a captive of the lexicon and clichés.

A WISE VIRGIN

On twelfth-century enamels green was often paired with blue, a pure light green, sometimes accentuated with yellow. That was no longer the case in the following century, when red became more dominant and green clearly less abundant.

Cloisonné enamel, Limoges, c. 1170–1180. Florence, Museo Nazionale del Bargello, Carrand 632.

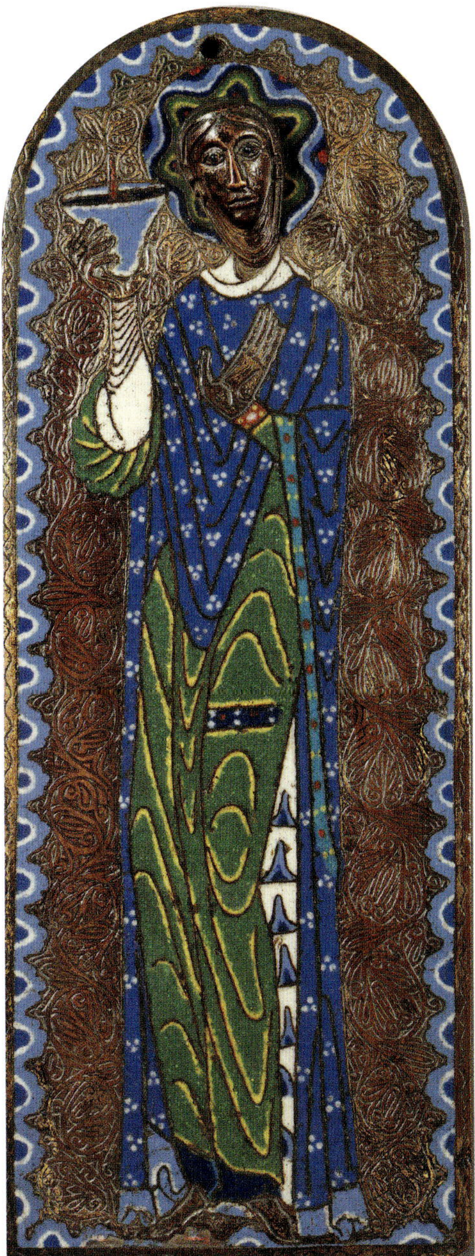

Notions of pleasure, harmony, and beauty in the Middle Ages were not what they are in the twenty-first century, very far from it. The very perception of color combinations and contrasts can vary from our own. To the medieval sensibility, for example, juxtaposing yellow and green produced the most violent contrast imaginable, whereas for us those two colors, as neighbors in the spectrum, are close to one another, and our eye is used to passing imperceptibly from yellow to green or from green to yellow without experiencing an impression of discontinuity, not to mention contrast. Conversely, contrasts like red/green or red/yellow, which are relatively strong for us, were not so to the twelfth- or thirteenth-century eye. Those colors were neighbors in the chromatic scales of artists and scholars.[3] Hence, how can we judge the colors that the central Middle Ages left us? Not only can we not see them in their original state but only as time has made them, not only do we look at them in lighting conditions that bear no relationship to those of the Middle Ages, but our eye does not fix on the same qualities or values or harmonies as theirs did. How can we differentiate today between bright and brilliant, dull and pale, smooth and plain, as they did in the twelfth and thirteenth centuries?[4] We tend to blur these notions that were not in the least identical then, not even similar. How can we learn to distinguish, as painters, heralds, and encyclopedists did, a saturated (*pleine*) color from a monochromatic (*plaine*) color, a dry from a moist color, a warm from a cool color? For the contemporaries of Saint Louis, green—the color of water—was cool, but blue—the color of air—was warm.[5]

Green was also a beautiful color, even a very beautiful color for some authors, not only because it dominates

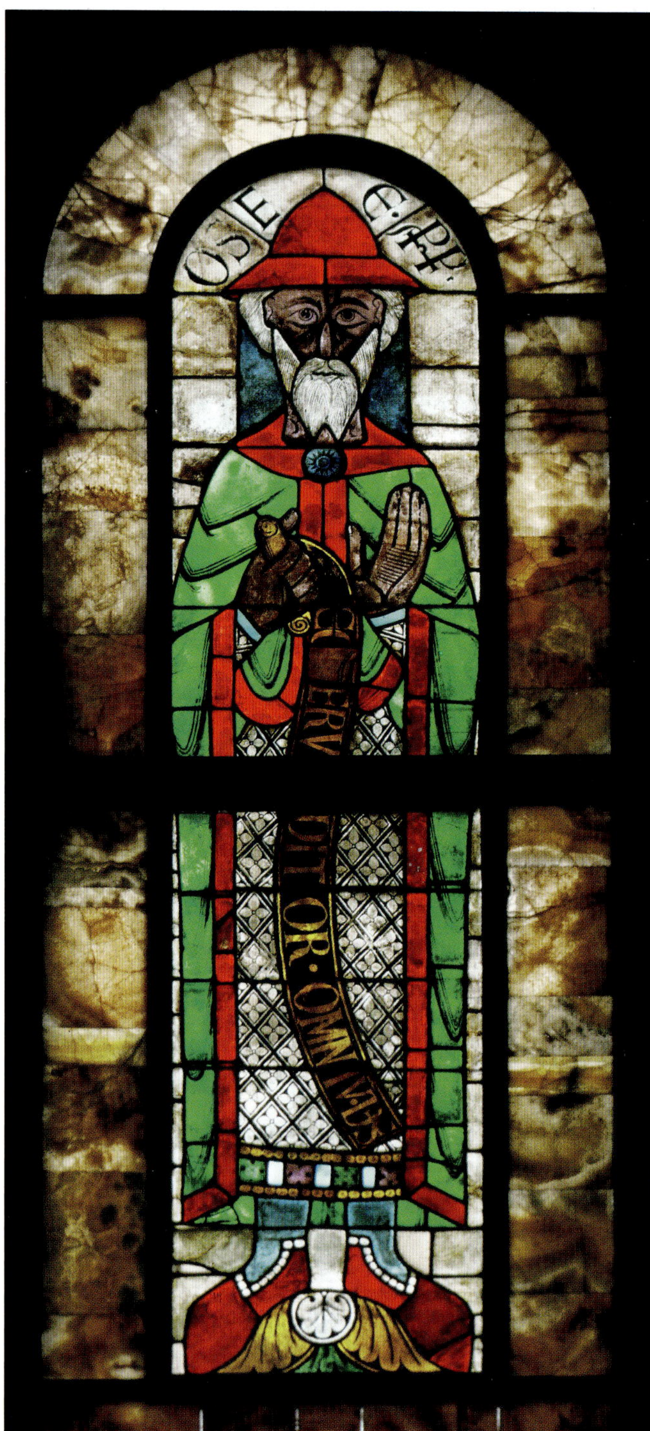

in meadows, woods, and gardens and thus delights the eye but also because it seems peaceful, because it quiets the eye and the gaze. Such ideas were not new; they were already present in Virgil, Pliny, and many Roman authors from the imperial period: green provides rest and comfort for the sense of sight. In Rome, emeralds were pulverized to make eye balms; green strengthened one's eyes and balanced one's vision.[6] Green's association with health continued through the centuries as green would gradually become the emblematic color for medicine and the pharmacopoeia.

The Middle Ages added another idea: green was beautiful because it was located in the middle of what we now call the "chromatic range." We saw in the last chapter that this was already the opinion of Cardinal Lothar (the future Pope Innocent III) by about the 1190s with regard to the liturgical colors: "green, the middle color between white, black and red, is proper for the holidays on which none of those three colors are chosen." Green was a middle color! That was

THE PROPHET HOSEA

Medieval stained glass provides much information for the historian of colors. There is little twelfth-century stained glass, unfortunately, that is still in place. Nevertheless, what there is allows us to observe the growing use of blue tones and, conversely, the diminishing use of greens. In this stained glass window from the Augsburg Cathedral, dating from 1110–1120, green is still dominant. It remained so in Germanic countries for a few decades, while in France, blue took over by the 1140s.

High window from the nave of the Augsburg Cathedral, c. 1110–1120.

not a fault but on the contrary a virtue, especially in the thirteenth century, a period that particularly cultivated temperance and the golden mean. Green was temperate, balanced, proper. Thus it was beautiful.

That was the position of Guillaume d'Auvergne, one of the greatest theologians of the time, the Bishop of Paris from 1228 to 1249.[7] We would expect such a prelate to glorify white or red, the two Christological colors. But no, he favored green because it was situated in the middle of the color axis, the one that Aristotle's followers proposed in 200 BCE and that ancient and then medieval scholars had never really questioned; they had simply increased it to seven colors: white, yellow, red, green, blue, purple, black. Let us note that this order of colors, which remained the basic order in the West until the discoveries of Newton, bears no relationship to the spectrum. In the thirteenth century—a century much preoccupied with light and vision—Guillaume d'Auvergne's opinion was shared by many men of science, all of them prelates or theologians (Robert Grossetête, John Peckham, Roger Bacon, for example). At the poles of the axis, white and black seemed too pregnant, too harsh, too remote, and thus strained the retina; white dilated it excessively while black strenuously contracted it. In the middle of the axis, on the other hand, green demanded no effort of it and allowed it to rest. Green was a soothing color. That is why in the early twelfth century, if we are to believe the poet and prelate Baudry de Bourgueil, green wax tablets were preferred to white or black ones for writing on. That is also why scribes and illuminators kept green objects beside them, even emeralds, which they gazed at from time to time to rest their eyes.[8]

For many authors green was also a joyous, "cheerful" color (*color ridens* is Saint Bonaventure's expression), meaning a color that cheered and lit up the surfaces on which it appeared.[9] Hence its early use in the arts in which light plays an essential role: stained glass, enamel, and the miniature. It was always a matter of a bright and relatively light green. Of course, little stained glass from before the mid-twelfth century remains for us today, but whether it is a matter of glass that is still intact or simple fragments, green is very present and even prized, especially in the Germanic countries. In the Augsburg cathedral, the large stained glass depicting the prophets offers impressive evidence; it dates from the years 1115–1120, and green covers much of the surface.[10] Similarly, green occupies a major place in twelfth-century enamels, where it was often paired with blue or white. In the following century it lost ground, both in stained glass and in enamel work, especially in France, where the spectacular rise of blue tones and the triumph of red/blue combinations in the period of Louis IX made it less noticeable in the precious arts. In the countries of the Empire, green retained some prominence, but until the first Romantic movement in the late eighteenth century, it never regained the place in the arts it had held in the Romanesque period.

A place for green: the orchard

ORCHARD FLORA

The medieval orchard was an organized space where fruit trees abounded and grape vines were also sometimes present. At the center was found the *prael*, a lawn surrounded by benches of greenery and banks of flowers, in which roses, lilies, and irises dominated.

Miniature from a manuscript of the *Livre des propriétés des choses*, illuminated by Évrard d'Espinques for Jean du Mas, central France, c. 1480. Paris, Bibliothèque national de France, ms. fr. 9140, fol. 289 v°.

Associating the idea of nature with the color green is commonplace today, obvious, almost a reflex. For us, nature is green. But that has not always been so. Our ancestors had a much wider conception of nature than our own, which is too often limited to the plant world. In the Middle Ages nature encompassed all of Creation; it was the work of God and involved all living beings. Some theologians defined it as what all individuals had in common. Others more grounded in the concrete, or "physics," considered nature the "complexion" of beings and things, all formed from combinations of the four basic elements: air, earth, fire, and water. Since each of those elements had its own color, nature was constructed around four colors: white (air), black (earth), red (fire), and green (water).[11] Medieval water, in fact, was conceptually green and not blue, as it would later be seen.

Thus the idea of nature in the Middle Ages was strongly polysemous and brought into play various complex notions.[12] That was true, at least, for the scholarly world because in the twelfth and thirteenth centuries in many less speculative areas, iconography and poetry for example, a more limited concept of nature seems to emerge, primarily associated with the framework of flora in which aristocratic society evolved: the garden, the meadow, the grove, the forest. Such a conception already existed in Roman antiquity, notably among poets singing the virtues or the beauties of the countryside (let us think here of Virgil). And it was not unknown among the authors and artists of the early Middle Ages, but in the feudal period courtly literature and customs gave it primary importance. Trees, plants, grasses, and flowers were the objects of a renewed curiosity and thus contributed to the evolution of the way green and all the feelings associated with it were seen. Later, much later, the Romantic period developed an

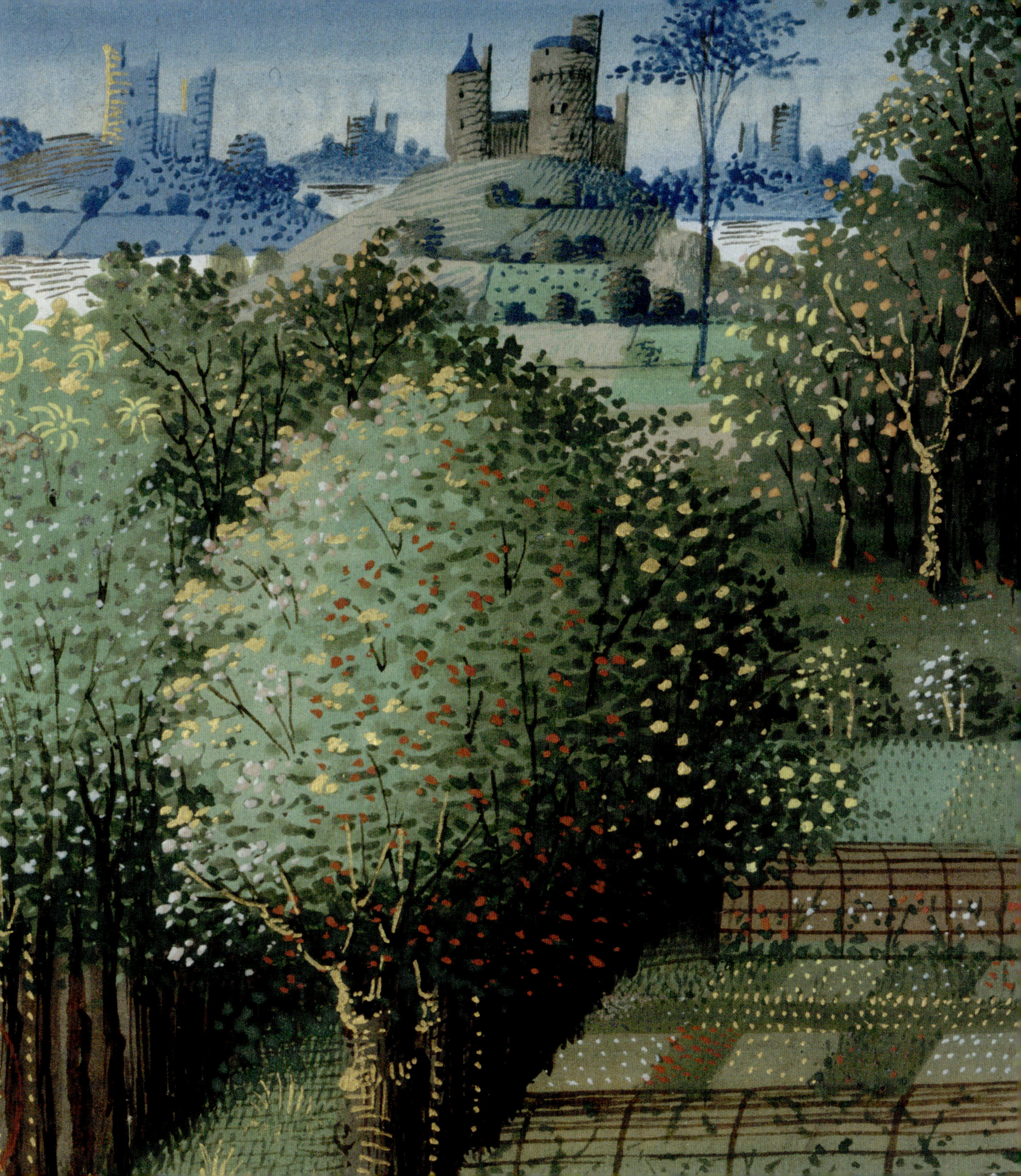

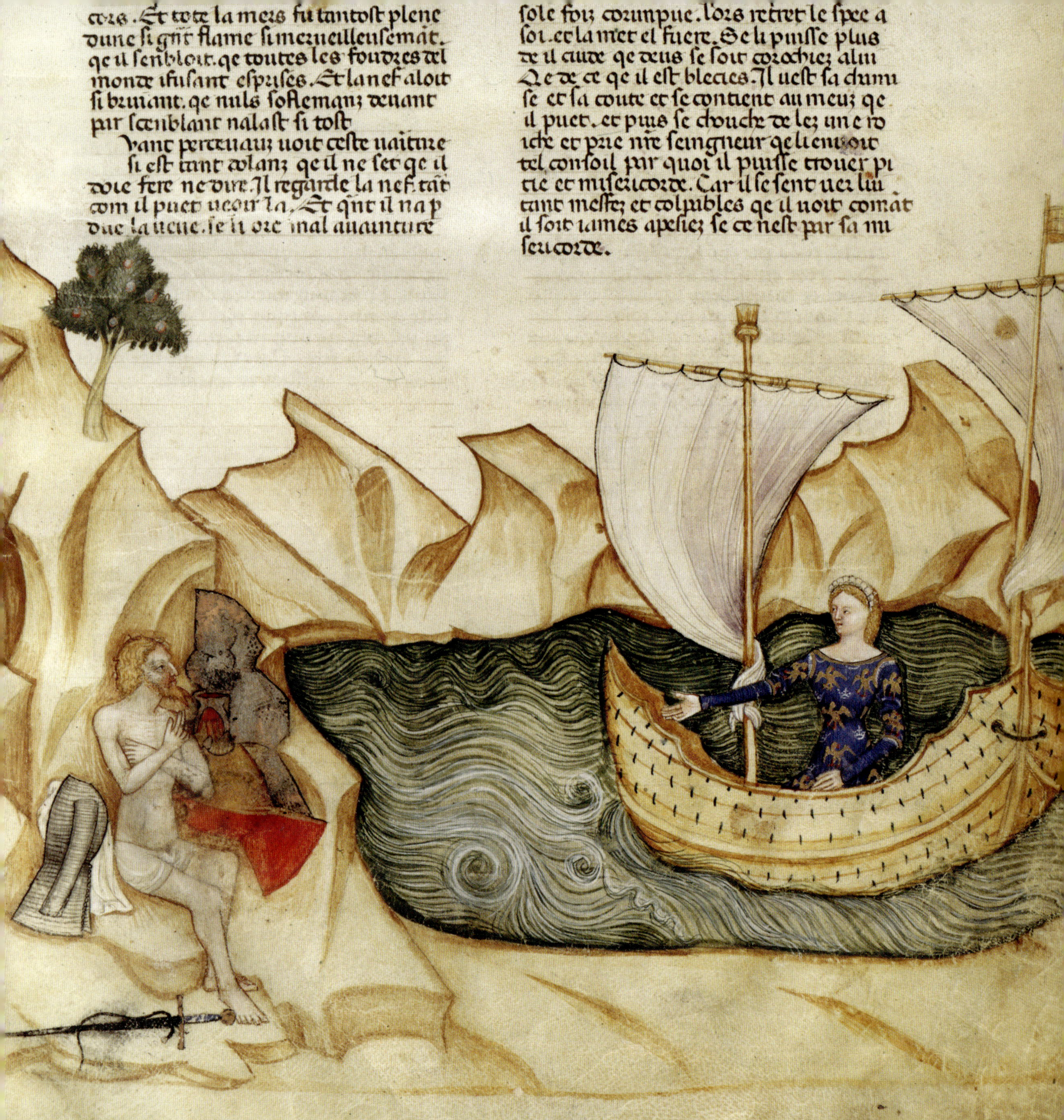

cors. Et tote la mers fu tantost plene
dune si grant flame si merveilleusemant.
qe il senbloit. qe toutes les foudres del
monde i fusant esprises. Et la nef aloit
si bruiant. qe nuls soflemanz devant
par senblant nalast si tost
Vant percevauz voit ceste vaiture
si est tant dolanz qe il ne set qe il
doie fere ne dire. Il regarde la nef. tant
com il puet veoir la. Et quant il na p
due la veue. se li ore mal avanture

sole foiz corumpue. Lors retret le spee a
soi. et la met el fuere. Se li puisse plus
de il cuide qe deus se soit corochiez a lui
Qe de ce qe il est bleciés. Il vest sa chami
se et sa coute et se contient au meuz qe
il puet. et puis se chouche de lez une ro
iche et prie nre seingneur qe li envoit
tel consoil par quoi il puisse trouer pi
tie et misericorde. Car il se sent vers lui
tant messez et colpables qe il noit comant
il soit iames apesiez se ce nest par sa mi
sericorde.

PERCEVAL ABANDONED ON AN ISLAND

The sea is frequently featured in medieval images. Its water may be green or blue, but until the fifteenth century green was most common. Wavy lines, more or less accentuated, indicate the calm or agitated movement of the waves. Sometimes a few sea monsters serve as iconographical symbols and help to distinguish the sea from lakes or rivers.

Miniature from a Lombardy manuscript of the *Queste del Saint Graal*, Milan or Pavia, c. 1380–1385. Paris, Bibliothèque national de France, ms. fr. 343, fol. 32.

even closer tie between "nature" and "vegetation" and definitively made green the color of nature.

In the central Middle Ages there was one place above all others where this new taste for green found expression: the orchard. It was a place of relaxation and pleasure, of rest and harmony, of expectation and meditation. Its very name made it the place of green par excellence. Old French *vergier* derives directly from the Latin *viridarium*, which belongs to the same family as the adjective *viridis*, which describes everything that is green or pertains to the color green. Before becoming a pleasure garden, and then a space planted with fruit trees, the *viridarium*, both in classical and medieval Latin, was a place of greenery where greens abounded, the place for all greens and even, at the risk of being anachronistic, the "museum" of the color green.[13]

The courtly romances of the twelfth and thirteenth centuries have provided us with many descriptions of the literary orchard.[14] Its constituent elements recur. First of all there was an enclosure; the orchard, like any garden, was a closed space often in the form of a square, the door of which played an essential symbolic role: to go through it required ritual trials (confronting a dragon, fighting a formidable knight). Next there were one or several areas where trees abounded, fruit trees or not; the vineyard itself was often present there. At the center of the orchard was the *prael* (small meadow), a kind of lawn, planted with flowers and surrounded by garden benches, where one could sit and enjoy the view and the scent of flowers. In the center of the *prael* was a lively, noisy, rushing fountain where the streams and channels that irrigated the periphery began. In all medieval orchards the presence of water—live water—was required. Added to all that were pavilions and bowers, paths and terraces, aromatic and medicinal plants. Everything was ordered, partitioned, positioned; the symbolism of the four cardinal points played an essential role. The presence of numerous animals was added as well: first of all birds that sang and, with the fountain, created the music of the place, but also rabbits, squirrels, the "little beasts" who played on the lawns and in the trees; sometimes deer and even the big cats—some orchards had menageries. More audacious than the texts, the images sometimes even introduced fictitious creatures into the orchards: unicorns, griffons, and phoenixes.

The model of these literary orchards was the garden of delights mentioned at the beginning of Genesis: "God planted a garden in Eden, in the east, and there he placed the man whom he had formed."[15] There are many representations of it in medieval documents. Most of the time it is a matter of a closed garden with crenellated walls surrounded by flames, at the center of which flow the four rivers of paradise. Vegetation is abundant there, animals as well. Among the many species of trees appears the Tree of Knowledge, the fruit of which is forbidden. In Mediterranean traditions this was a fig tree or vine; later in Spain it was an orange or pomegranate tree. In the temperate West it was primarily an apple tree that assumed the role, basically because of the name of its fruit: *malum*, a perfect homonym for the word that designates evil (*malum*). The forbidden fruit, the one that the tempter serpent induced Eve to pick and that Adam bit, was an apple; up to the modern period it would remain a fruit of pleasure and sin, the fruit of paradise and the Fall.

Actual orchards differed a bit from literary ones, but not entirely. They were also places of rest and pleasure before being utilitarian gardens. The models for them were Roman gardens, known in the Middle Ages through the texts of poets (Virgil and Ovid) and agronomists (Varro, Columella, Palladius), but also and above all Oriental gardens, discovered and admired in the period of the Crusades. Water and vegetation made them oases of greenery, where potted plants prevailed over plants used for cooking, dyeing, or medicine. Beginning in the twelfth century in Western Europe, princely gardens were clearly distinguishable from monastic gardens, where the vegetable plot and the cemetery continued to occupy a significant portion of the space.[16] They were closer to literary orchards, those of courtly romances or the one described at length in the *Romance of the Rose* by Guillaume de Lorris in about 1230–1235:

> The whole orchard was populated with great laurel trees and pines, olive trees and cypress, elms with trunks thick and branching, as well as hornbeam and beech, very straight hazel, aspen, ash, maple, very tall fir trees and oak. What good is it to continue this list: I would be very hard pressed to name all the trees. . . .
>
> In the orchard lived fallow deer and roe deer, and there was a great crowd of squirrels in the trees. All day long, rabbits came out of their holes and spent their time playing in the verdant grass. In places there were fountains of clear water, without insects or frogs, shaded by the trees. The water ran in little streams, producing a soft, pleasant murmur. Slender grass grew thickly beside clear, lively springs: you could have slept with your beloved there as on a bed, so sweet and tender was the earth. Thanks to the water, grass grew there in abundance.
>
> But what made that spot even more beautiful was the profusion of flowers that it sheltered, violets in all seasons, summer and winter alike, fresh new periwinkles, flowers of incomparable whiteness, others of yellow, others of vermilion.[17]

In the orchard all the colors were present, but green dominated: the green of trees and plants, the green of grass and water, but also the green of clothing that was worn there, objects that were brought there, fabrics

A PLACE TO DREAM

The medieval orchard was a place for pleasure and repose, for courtly strolls and flirtatious banter. But it was also a place of waiting and meditation, where it was not unusual to fall asleep and be transported to the land of dreams.

Miniature from a manuscript of the *Songe du Verger*, illuminated by Robinet Testard, western France, c. 1470–1480. Paris, Bibliothèque national de France, ms. fr. 537, fol. 4.

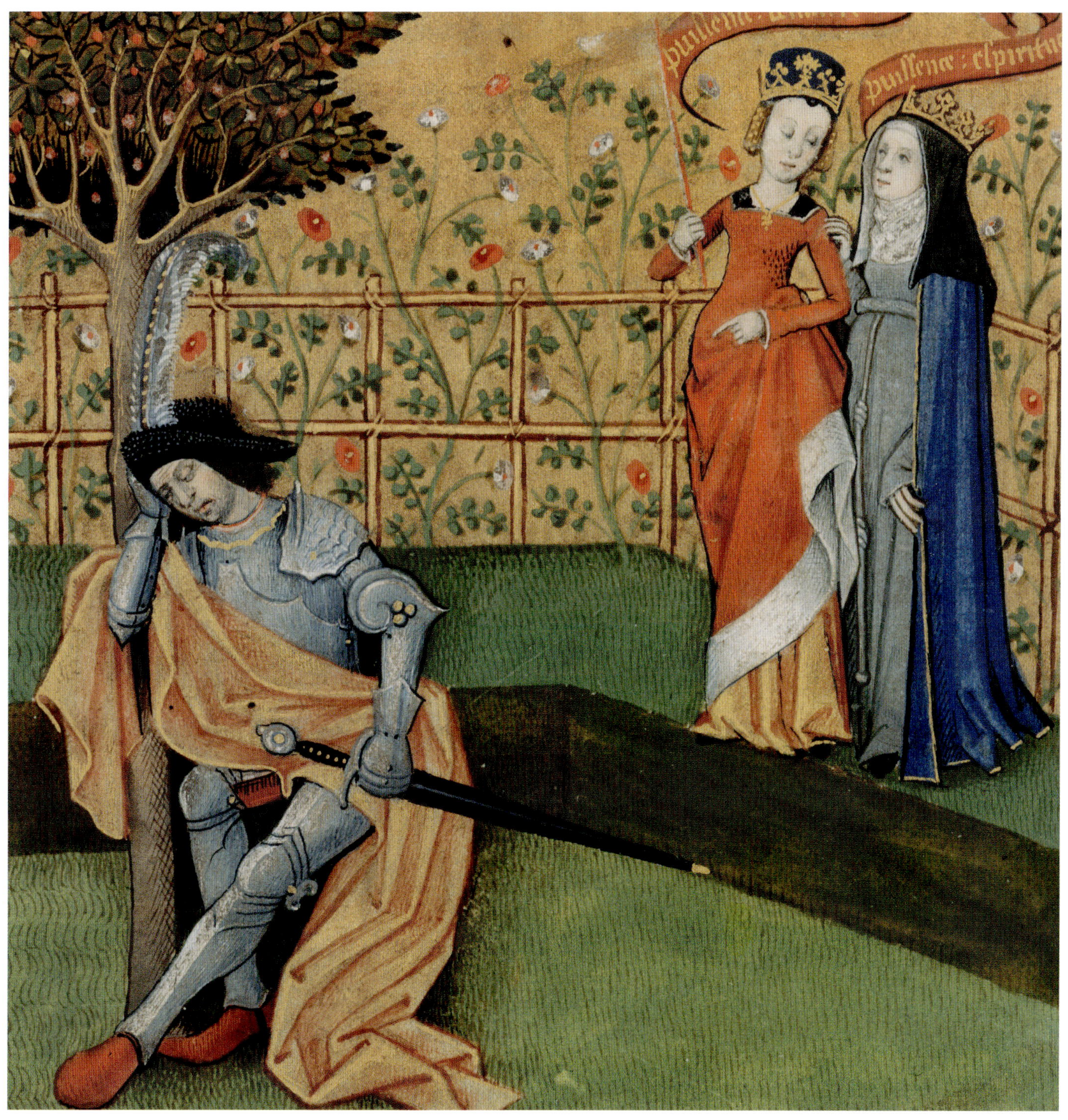

that draped the canopies and pavilions. This celebration of the color green seemed justified by two famous biblical verses, linked to the third day of Creation, when God separated the waters from the earth:

> Let the earth grow green with vegetation, plants yielding seed and trees bearing fruit, each according to its kind.[18]

Thus from the beginning of Genesis, green appears as a fertile, beneficial color, established by God, and the garden as a repository of multiple symbols. Further on in the Bible, the Song of Songs takes up that symbolism again by making the Shulamite fiancée (whom the Christian Middle Ages likened to the Virgin) "a lily of the valleys," "a locked garden," "a sealed fountain," "a basin of fresh water," "a cedar of Lebanon." Similarly in the New Testament, the theme of Christ the gardener, dear to the iconography of the late Middle Ages, seemed to legitimize all that was found or happened in the garden. Shortly after the Resurrection, Mary Magdalene weeps in the olive garden near the empty tomb; seeing a man standing near her, she does not recognize him and takes him for the gardener (in some later images he wears a straw hat and holds a spade) and asks him where he has taken the body of Jesus. The Lord reveals himself, and when Mary Magdalene throws herself at his feet, he orders her not to touch him (*Noli me tangere*).[19]

Every orchard was constructed as a symbolic space, and each plant found there possessed its own meaning. The meanings of flowers varied widely according to the period and region and took into account several characteristics: color, scent, the number of petals, the look of the leaves, the size of both petal and leaf, when they blossomed, and so on. A few general ideas emerge nonetheless for the central Middle Ages: the lily was the symbol of purity and chastity; the rose, beauty and love; the iris, protection and prosperity; the violet, humility and obedience; the lily of the valley, freshness and fragility; the columbine, courage and "sweet melancholy." Likewise, trees were always meaningful. The oak (rare in an orchard) was a tree of power and sovereignty; the elm, a tree of justice; the olive, a tree of peace. The linden—probably the favorite tree of medieval populations as it was already for the Romans and Germans—was the tree of love, health, and music; the pine, a tree of boldness and uprightness; the fig, a tree of fertility and protection. The yew and the cypress were associated with sadness and death; the hornbeam and hazel with magic; the service and mulberry with prudence; the ash with tenacity. Most trees were considered beneficial; a few were ambivalent (the poplar, cypress, and hazel). But only the yew, the alder, and the walnut were considered seriously evil: the yew because it was poisonous and because, being planted in cemeteries, it was associated with death; the alder because it grew in the marshes where no other tree would grow and because its glowing red wood resembled blood; the walnut because its shade was considered to be poisonous and its roots loved to grow toward stables to make livestock perish.[20]

A time for green: the spring

In the Middle Ages green not only had its preferred place, the orchard, it also had its season: spring. Encyclopedists, moralists, and authors of treatises on heraldry, who liked to establish correspondences between the colors and various elements drawn from the natural world, the calendar, theology, and medicine (metals, planets, zodiac signs, days of the week, deadly sins, human temperaments), were all in agreement in associating the color green with the first and most admired of the seasons. As for the other seasons, there was less consensus. Summer was often symbolized by red, sometimes by gold or orange; autumn by yellow or black (the color of Saturn and of melancholy), more rarely brown; winter by white or black.[21] The palette of the seasons was relatively unstable. Spring alone possessed only one lively and seductive color: green.

Such a link is not surprising. The reawakening of plant life saw nature adorning itself in green, a new, fresh, tender, gay green, all adjectives that the medieval sensibility applied not only to spring but also to everything associated with it: youth, joy, festivity, music, and above all, love. In the Middle Ages green was the color of love, or at least of secular love.

In old and middle French a word closely tied to the color green characterizes the whole of the beautiful season, the awakening of nature and the pleasure that results: *reverdie*. In its first meaning this term is synonymous with greenery or foliage. But applied to the calendar, it designates especially the beginning of spring that witnesses trees and plants "regreening." By extension it also describes the lightheartedness that everyone feels at that time of the year. As Guillaume de Lorris says so prettily, the spring *met el cuer grant reverdie*.[22] Finally, in its more technical meaning for lyric poetry, a *reverdie* is a piece of verse that celebrates all at once the return of good weather, the sense of happiness it inspires, and the birth of feelings of love.

By one of those tricks not uncommon to the lexicon and philology, there is another word that seems to link the color green and spring, but this time it is a Latin word rather than a vernacular one. In classical as well as medieval Latin, the most common term for naming spring is *ver*, a word that left a few traces in modern French (*vernal*, *primevère*).[23] Its etymology is debated, but there is great temptation to link it to the family of *viridis* and acknowledge that for Latin vocabulary, spring is the green season par excellence. Phonetic rules seem to argue against such a tie, of course, but for semantics, and even more for symbolism, the link seems almost natural.

The great thirteenth-century encyclopedists (Thomas of Cantimpré, Bartholomew of England, Vincent de Beauvais) and agronomists (Pietro de' Crescenzi, Walter of Henley) did not forego emphasizing this link. Moreover, they went on at length about the seasons and, with regard to spring, indulged in observations that could easily find a place in the works of modern authors. Reading them, we learn that in spring the sun becomes hotter, water is abundant, snows melt, rivers overflow, animals that hibernate awaken, and birds that migrate return. Above all, buds open, leaves multiply and grow, and flowers make their reappearance; everywhere, new, young grass sprouts, such a tender green that it "brings joy to the livestock freed from winter hay," as Pietro de' Crescenzi claims.[24] All our authors, all of whom lived in temperate regions, emphasize how spring is the season that witnesses man and beast moving from indoors to outdoors.

Illustrated calendars offer a slightly different story. They existed already in Roman antiquity, persisted more or less through the early Middle Ages, but did not really proliferate until the Romanesque period, especially in the decor of churches: sculptures, murals, stained glass, and even mosaics (in Italy). Later, they spread into liturgical books: psalters, books of hours, breviaries, and missals. Their iconography varies according to the period, climate, and region, but rather than emphasizing the cycles of nature, they all tend to feature the human activities that follow those cycles, especially agricultural chores. Each month is associated with a farming activity, its illustration constituting for us an important source of knowledge on techniques and tools: rest in January and February when farmers eat or warm themselves by the hearth; pruning the vineyard and the first chores in March; haymaking in June; harvesting and threshing grain in July and August; harvesting grapes and gathering fruit in September; wine making in October; letting the pigs forage for acorns in November; butchering a hog in December.[25]

With a few variations that was the rhythm of rural life and work in the fields. Two months however constituted the exception: April and May. To represent this season—spring—the calendars abandoned the activities of the peasants for those of the nobles: elegant young men holding small branches or flowers; a walk at the edge of the forest; falconry; a dance, procession, or jesting in a setting of greenery. This was the time of

ANIMALS IN THE ORCHARD

In the orchard fauna was as abundant as flora. Many animals could be found there, not only birds, rabbits, squirrels, and *bestelettes* (little rodents), but also stag, fallow deer, roe deer, sometimes foxes, and even unicorns.

Miniature from a manuscript of the *Dit du lion* by Guillaume de Machaut, c. 1350–1355. Paris, Bibliothèque national de France, ms. fr. 1586, fol. 103.

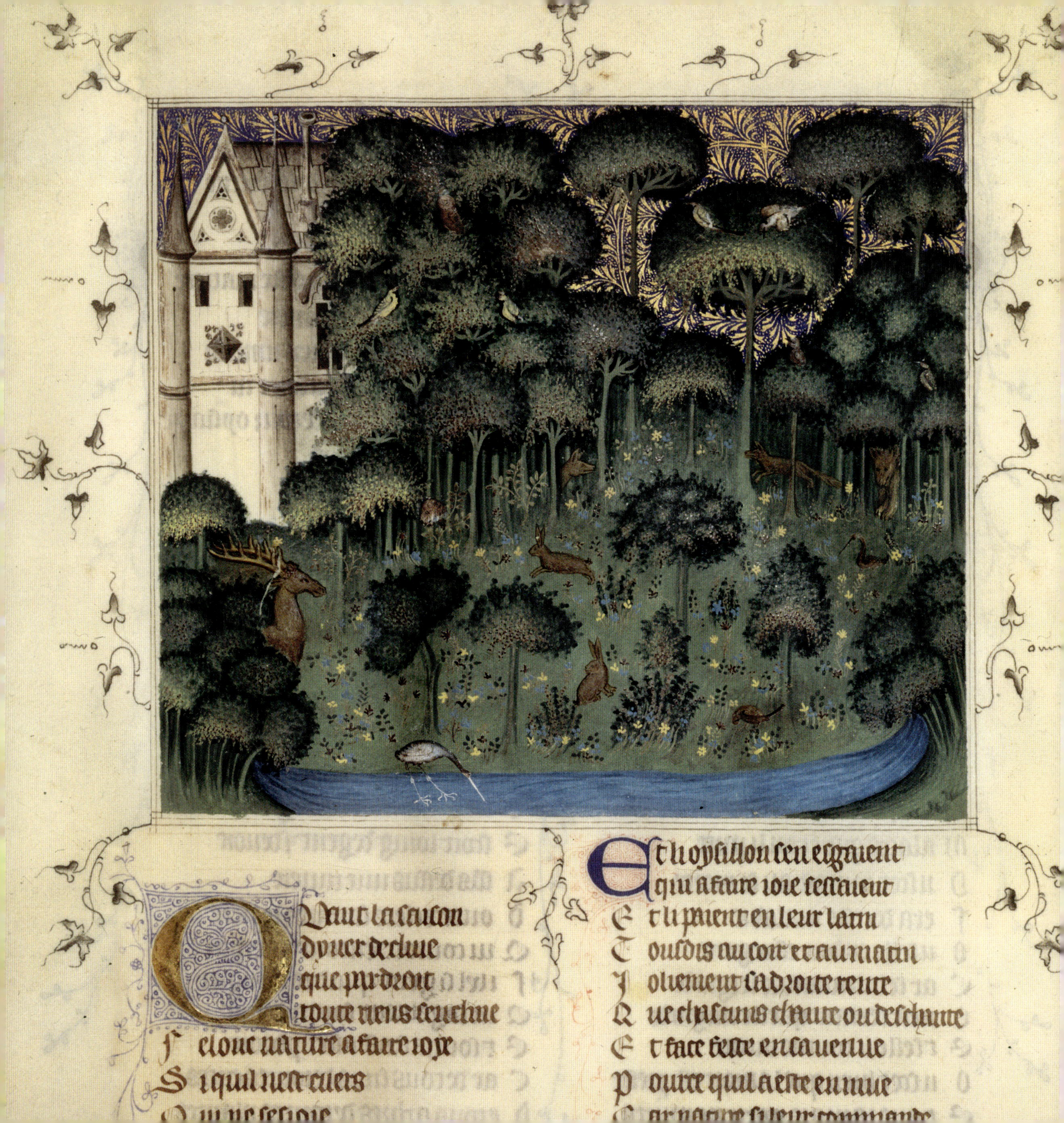

Quant la saison
dyuer decline
que par droit
toute riens sencline
selonc nature a faire ioye
Si quil nest cuers
Qui ne sesioie

Et li oysillon sen esgaient
qui a faire ioie sessaient
Et li paient en leur latin
Tousdis au soir et au matin
Joliement sa droite rente
Que chascuns chante ou deschante
Et face feste en sa venue
Pource quil a este en mue
Car nature si leur commande

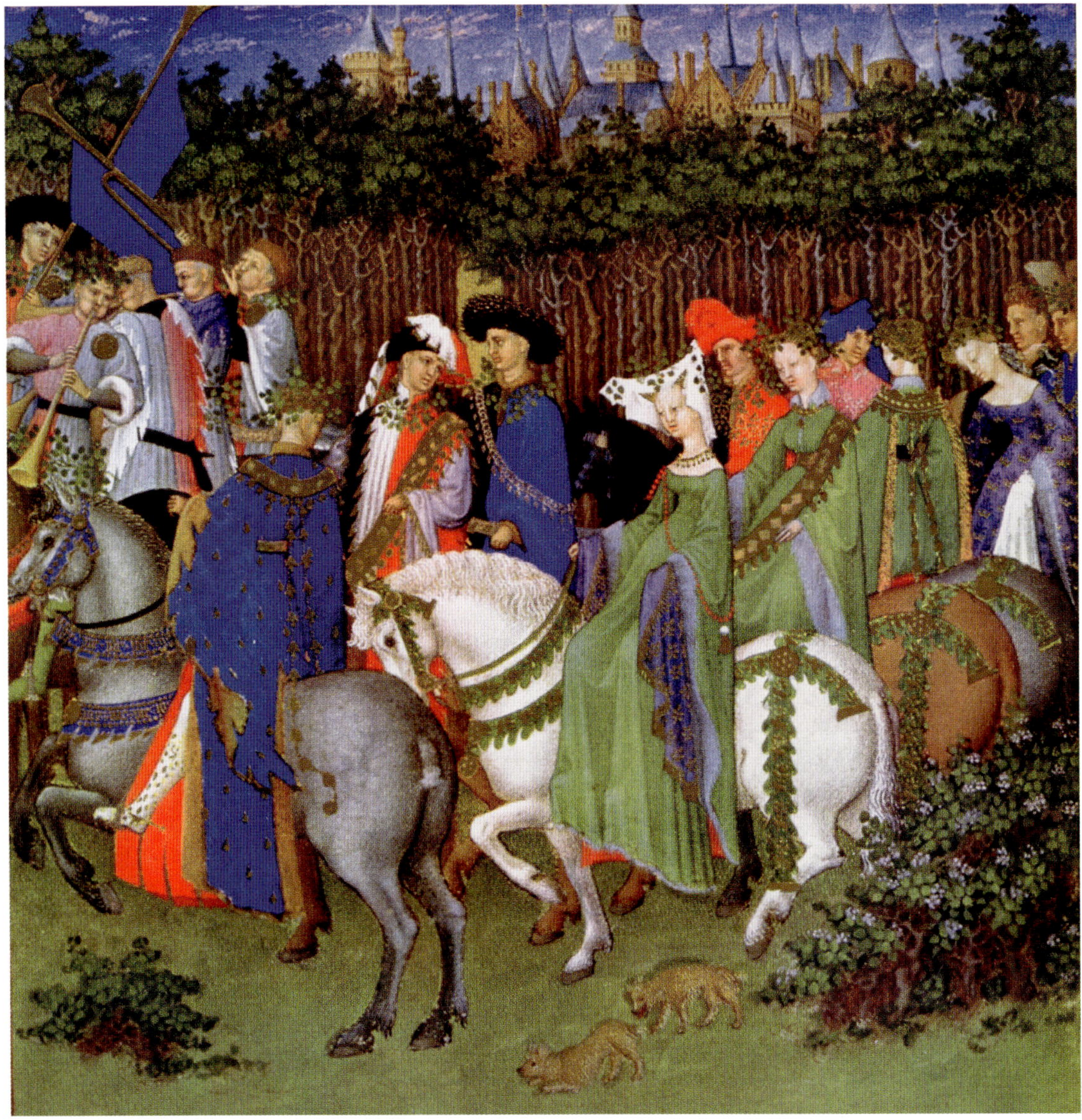

THE MONTH OF MAY

The calendar of the *Très Riches Heures*, copied and illuminated for the duke Jean de Berry in the early fifteenth century, represents each month of the year with an emblematic image: agricultural tasks, scenes of hunting or repose, wine making, letting pigs forage for acorns. For the month of May, the choice is a princely cortege. It is May first: three young women are dressed in green, and each of the sixteen figures "wears the May" in the form of crowns or necklaces made of leaves and small branches.

Miniature from the *Très Riches Heures* of Duke Jean de Berry, Paris, c. 1414–1416. Chantilly, Bibliothèque du musée Condé, ms. 65, fol. 5 v°.

festivity and leisure; it was also the time of courtesy and gallantry. As old French so graciously says, nature begins to *avriler* and the young men to *fleureter*, that is, to *conter fleurette*, murmur sweet nothings, to the young ladies.[26] In the images, the color green is ubiquitous, notably in the clothing, as if aristocratic society wanted to be in harmony with nature, both dressed in green to celebrate the return of good weather.

In this period full of lightheartedness and greenery, one day played a more important role than all the others: the first of May. On that day it was necessary to *s'esmayer*, that is, to wear and to plant the *mai* to celebrate the arrival of the most beautiful month of the year.[27] "To wear the May" consisted of attaching to oneself an element of greenery: a crown or necklace of leaves or flowers, a hat made of plants, ferns, or branches stuck to one's clothing. These elements had to be green or predominantly green. To be *pris sans verd*, that is, not to display on oneself a single element of this color, neither plant nor textile, led to becoming the object of mockery and harassment. Images from the late Middle Ages offer us many examples of this ritual. The most famous is found in the calendar of the *Très Riches Heures* by Jean de Berry, a splendid manuscript illuminated for that great patron of the arts and book lover in the years 1413–1416. The miniature representing the month of May shows a princely procession at the edge of a forest. Three young women are dressed in green, the pretty *vert gai* (light and bright) mentioned in wardrobe inventories and chronicles, and the sixteen figures are all wearing the *mai*: necklaces, crowns, leaves, branches.[28]

On the first day of the month of May, one had to dress in green and wear some bit of greenery. But there was another well-documented ritual that involved a greater portion of society: "planting the May," that is, going into the forest, uprooting a bush, and replanting it before the door or window of someone you wished to honor. Most of the time it was young men who planted a *mai* before the house of marriageable young women. Moreover, this planting was more symbolic than real; it was not a whole bush that was uprooted and replanted but a single branch that was cut and placed before the home of the beloved. The species in question could play a role: a linden branch constituted a declaration of love; a rose branch celebrated the young woman's beauty; an elder branch on the other hand discretely denounced her more or less fickle nature.

Many poets sang of this particular day for honoring love and greenery. Here is Charles d'Orleans in one of his most famous ballads:

> The god of love is accustomed
> To holding this holiday
> For loving hearts to celebrate
> Who desire to serve him.
> Thus the trees are covered
> With blossoms and the fields a gay green,
> To make lovelier the loveliest holiday
> The first day of May . . .
> Let us go to the woods to gather the May
> So that the custom continues.[29]

Lovers were not the only ones who went into the woods to bring back plants. A large portion of the rural and urban population did the same. On the first of May, houses were filled with flowers, trees were decorated and brought into the home, doors and windows were trimmed with leaves and branches. This was a matter of ancient practices already well attested at the turn of the twelfth–thirteenth centuries. Jean Renart, an author probably originally from Beauvaisis, left us this long description of them in his romance *Guillaume de Dole*:

> At nightfall, the inhabitants of the town went to the woods to do their gathering. . . . In the morning when the day was very bright and when all was decorated with flowers, gladiola and green, leafy branches, they brought in their May tree, carried it upstairs and displayed it before the windows, thus embellishing all the balconies. Onto the floors, onto the cobblestones, everywhere, they tossed grass and flowers to celebrate the solemnity and the joy of this day.[30]

All the rituals linked to the first of May are, to varying degrees, vestiges of paganism. Early on, the Church tried to Christianize them but with little success. Making that day the shared holiday of two apostles, Saint Philip and Saint James, was not sufficient. Spring and greenery were stronger than the Gospels and hagiography. It is true that the rituals celebrating the arrival of spring throughout Europe went back very far. Among the ancient Germanic peoples the period corresponding to late April and early May was marked by fire festivals, crystallizing in the Christian period in the famous night of Walpurgis (April 30–May 1), allegedly the grand sabbat of witches. Among the Celts, the same day was consecrated to Belenos, god of the solar light. His holiday (Beltaine) marked the passage from the dark season to the bright season and the return to outdoor activities: working in the fields, putting the livestock out to pasture, hunts, raids, wars. Among the Romans it was Flora, the goddess of flowers, who held the place of honor. For five consecutive nights floral games, the *Floralia*, were devoted to her: poetry and singing competitions, but also more or less lascivious dances and entertainment.[31] The goddess Maia was also honored at the beginning of May, one of the many divinities associated with fertility. She gave her name to the Romans' favorite month.[32]

Throughout Europe, pagan holidays exalting the awakening of nature and the return of good weather also took place at the equinox, around March 21. At that time the custom was to disguise oneself in plants, to appear as the "leafy man" or the "mossy man," or even the "green man" or wild man and, through transgressive behavior, create noise and disorder to disrupt the ordinary course of days and proclaim the end of winter. For a long time these pagan holidays survived Christianization. To eradicate them, the Church struck hard: not only did it move a few important Saints' Days to that time in the calendar (Saint Joseph, March 19; Saint Benedict, March 21; the archangel Gabriel, March 24), but it placed close to equinox one of the most important holidays of the liturgical year, the Annunciation (March 25), nine months after Christmas. But to no avail: pagan plant rituals endured into the modern period, until they were relegated to folklore in the nineteenth and twentieth centuries.

More effective than replacing pagan holidays with Christian ones was the Christianization of plants themselves. That is why a week before Easter, on Palm Sunday, the blessing of freshly cut branches commemorates the triumphal entry of Christ into Jerusalem as recounted in the Gospels (the crowds cheering him by waving palms) and continues the ancient pagan rites linked to the awakening of nature. In medieval France and Germany the branches were boxwood or laurel, whereas in Spain and Italy both olive and palm were used. In England it was most often willow that was called upon, and in Scandinavia, birch.[33]

Youth, love, and hope

Spring not only marks the reawakening of nature, it also witnesses the birth or rebirth of romantic passions. Moreover, the two events are linked, as plants have always played an important role in romantic rituals (even today, don't we give flowers to declare our love?). In this season the sap rises in young men and women as much as in trees and plants. By the same token, green, the color of springtime, is also the color of love. Or at least of new love, of young, hopeful love, and of impatient love as well.

All the same, in the Middle Ages love possessed a wide palette. The green of the uncertain loves of youth contrasted with the blue of lawful, faithful love, the gray of unhappy loves, the red of Christian love and charity. We could even add to this list the yellow of jealous love, the black of despair caused by the loss of the beloved, and the purple of incestuous or forbidden loves.[34] Red itself could be divided: on one side, Christological red, shed by and for Christ; on the other and at the opposite extreme, erotic red, the red of carnal affairs, luxury, debauchery, and prostitution. From the symbolic perspective it was absolutely not a matter of the same red. Nor from the artistic perspective: painters never used the same pigment to represent the red of divine love and the red of carnal love, even if the color effect produced on the panel or the painting seemed the same.[35]

Associated with feelings of love, green thus appeared to be the color of youth, impatience of the flesh, and inconstancy of the heart. It was very often a changeable color, fickle and frivolous, in the image of youth itself. Moreover, youth was associated with green not only in matters of love. Green was youth's color in many other areas as well, as conveyed by clothing: in noble circles, the adolescents who received their education at the court of a lord often dressed in green, while marriageable young women sometimes wore green dresses or more often some piece of clothing in this color (headdress, ribbon, belt, hood).[36] Similarly, in the system of correspondences between colors and times of life that the moralists and heralds delighted in establishing, childhood and adolescence (in the sense that we understand that word today) were both symbolized by green, while infancy was symbolized by white, the prime of life by red, middle age by blue, old age by gray, and senescence by black.[37]

The plant model explains in part this recurring link between green and youth. Like nascent vegetation youth is new and fresh; like fruit it is green before becoming red (cherries, strawberries, raspberries), then blue or black (plums, blackberries, blueberries). The idea of freshness is key for the medieval sensibility, and the adjective "fresh," which recurs constantly in literary texts from the twelfth and thirteenth centuries, is always meant in a good way. It underscores how courtly society—and even medieval society as a whole—did not fear cold and damp as much as heat and dryness. Contrary to the commonly accepted idea, people knew how to protect themselves from the cold in the Middle Ages, whereas against extreme heat they were defenseless. Hence the importance of the idea of freshness. Moreover, "green" and "fresh" were sometimes synonymous. Their common antonym was the word "dry," a term that often had bad connotations and that was sometimes associated with the color yellow.

Medieval youth was thus constantly symbolized by the color green.[38] It wore green clothing, symbolic of freshness and vigor, and was "green behind the ears," according to the colorful German expression already attested in the Middle Ages and still used today.[39] In the spring damsels and their beaux liked to meet in the orchard, the place for flirtatious banter, sensory delights, and secret rendezvous. That was where the god Love reigned, as presented in the *Romance of the Rose*, or the goddess *Minne*, the personification of the lyric poetry to which she gave her name in the German language: *Minnesang* (literally "song of love").[40] *Frau Minne*, as the poets called her, is a capricious and unpredictable goddess; her arrows strike whom she likes and when she likes. Iconography represents her armed with a bow and arrows that she aims toward the hearts of her victims. She is often wearing a green dress, symbolic of her inconstancy and the uncertain love she prompts. The poet's heart bleeds, and the red of his blood joined to the green of the goddess form the pair of colors that seem to constitute the banner of the *Minnesang* in Germanic countries.

However *Frau Minne*'s green dress was not the only green symbol that artists presented to convey love relationships. A tree and an animal played similar roles: the linden and the parrot. In images the parrot always displays perfectly green plumage; the lover offers it to his beloved as he would offer her a branch of greenery, and the bird's color is sufficient to express a declaration of love. The iconography here is faithful to a certain reality; in the last half of the thirteenth century and the first decades of the fourteenth century, the parrot was a favorite bird among nobility throughout Europe. It was fashionable to give parrots as presents and to own them, especially since they were rare and precious creatures imported from far away (India, Morocco) and endowed with a remarkable skill: they talked. Thus the parrot was considered a courtly bird, symbolic of beauty, speech, and love. Later, in the late Middle Ages and the early modern period, European painters represented parrots in all colors. The parrot became the colorful bird par excellence. Along with flowers, butterflies, and precious gems, parrots came to represent

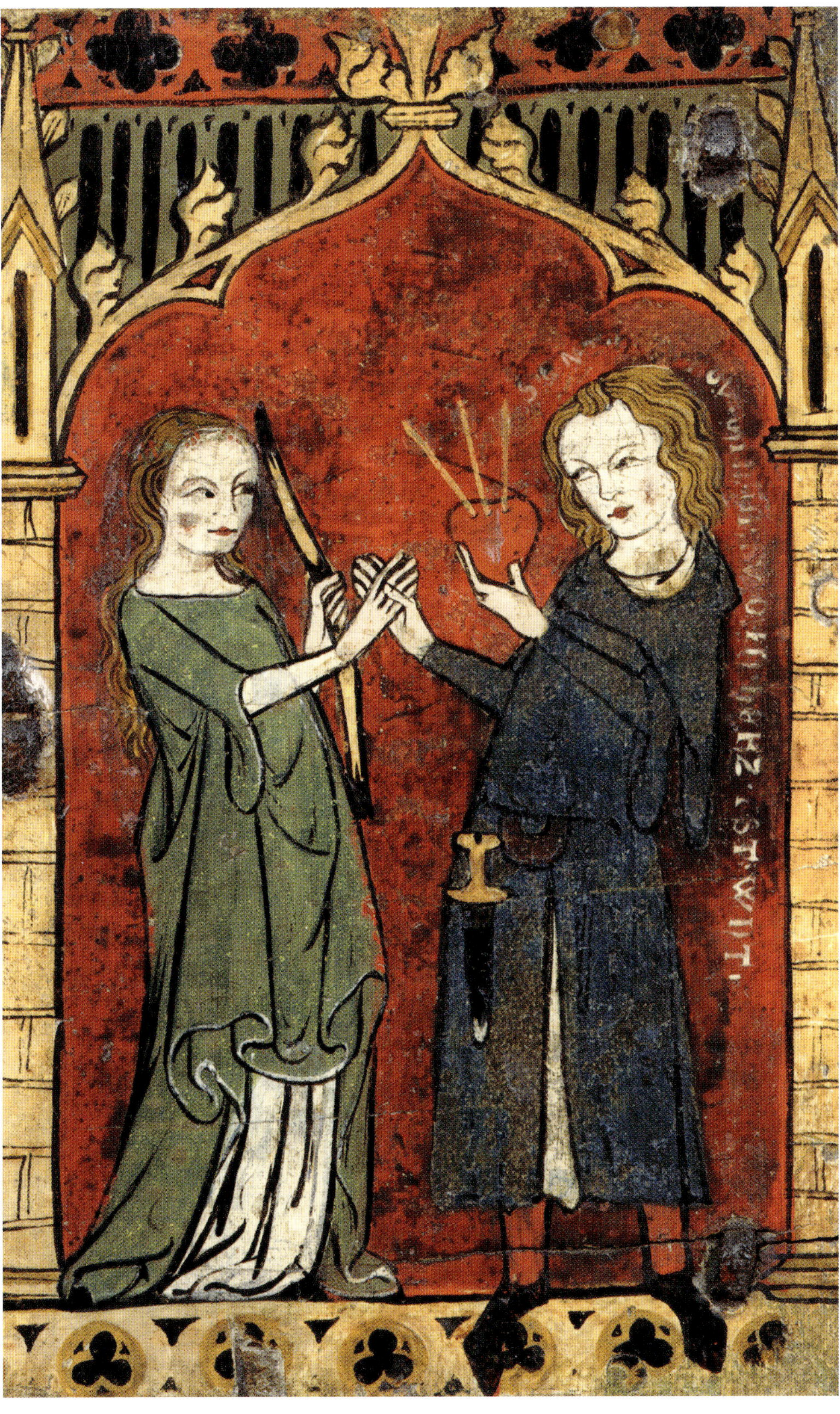

FRAU MINNE'S GREEN DRESS

In the twelfth and thirteenth centuries, lyric poetry in the German language sang of love, courtesy, and chivalry. It often featured *Frau Minne*, the goddess of love, whose fearsome arrows pierced the poets' hearts. Like Venus in the Roman period, *Frau Minne* is capricious and deceitful, strikes whom she pleases, and decides the fate of those who suffer "the sickness of love, delicious and cruel" (Walther von der Vogelweide). She is frequently depicted wearing a green dress, a sign of her inconstancy and the precarious fate of lovers. Here, nevertheless, the poet with his pierced heart offers the capricious goddess a small gesture of peace.

Painted wooden love box, southern Germany, c. 1320–1330. New York, The Cloisters, inv. 50.141.

LINDEN, THE TREE OF LOVE

Linden was the favorite tree of medieval men and women, especially in German-speaking countries. Poets attributed every virtue to it. It was simultaneously the tree of the pharmacopoeia, the tree of music (it resounded with the song of bees that gathered nectar from its blossoms), and the tree of love (its leaves were heart shaped). Under the linden young lovers met, kissed, exchanged pledges of love. Also under the linden, as in this famous painting from the *Codex Manesse*, one rested, took refreshment, and bantered with young ladies.

Miniature from the *Codex Manesse*, Zurich or Constance, c. 1300–1310. Heidelberg, Universitätsbibliothek, cpg 848, fol. 314.

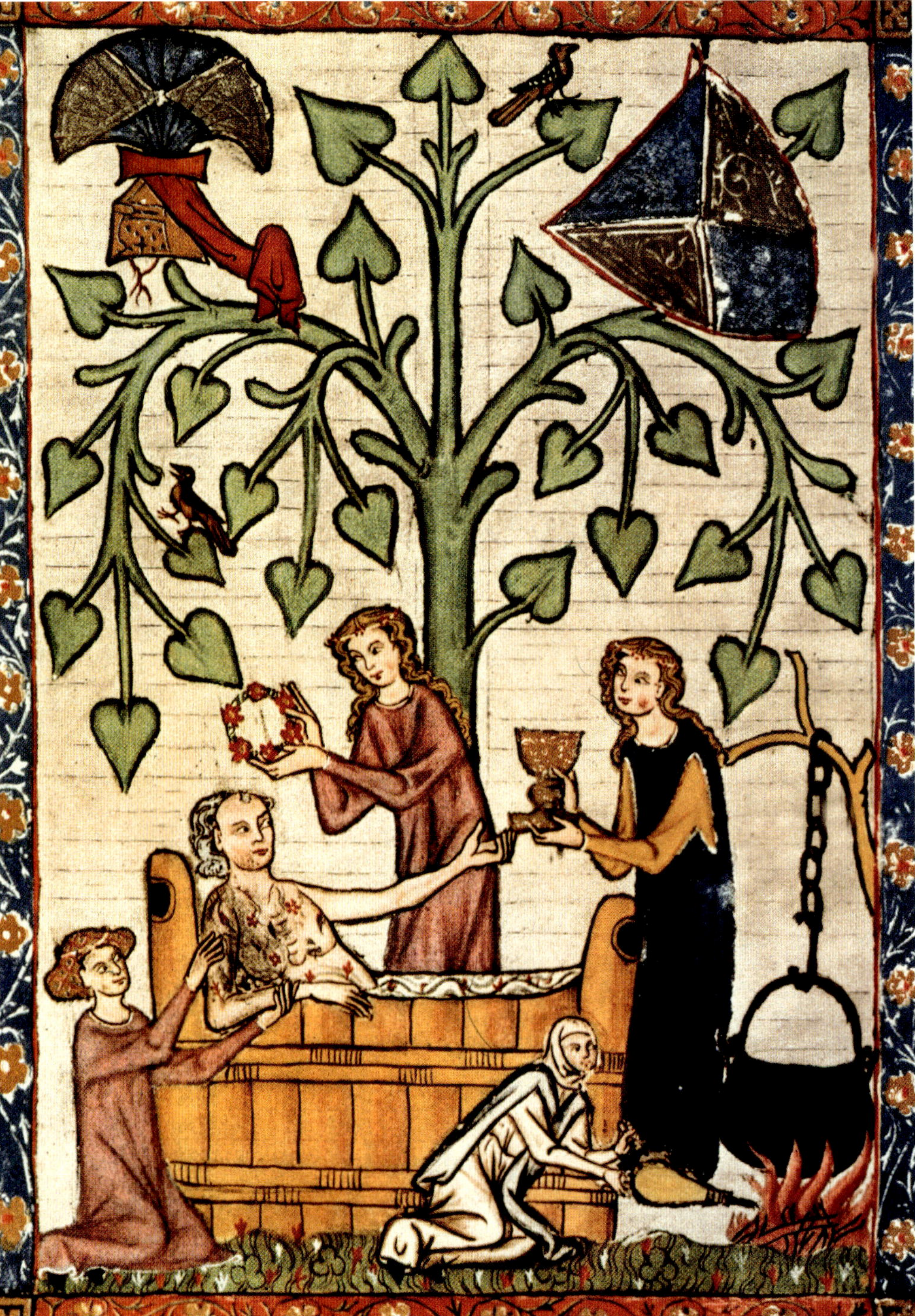

OPPOSITE PAGE:

A COURTLY BIRD, THE PARROT

To give a parrot, the green bird par excellence, was a gesture of love in courtly poetry and in thirteenth-century miniatures.

Miniature from an English bestiary, c. 1230–1240. London, Harley ms. 4751, fol. 39 v°.

nature at its most seductive in the area of polychromy. But earlier, in thirteenth-century miniatures, the parrot was always green; no doubt parrots of other colors were unknown at the time. Hence the not uncommon French expression for a very vivid green: "greener than a parrot," like the expression "blacker than a crow," which comes from that same period.

As for linden, it was the favorite tree of medieval men and women. Authors only ever attributed it with virtues, the only tree consistently presented favorably, to my knowledge. First it was admired for its majesty, opulence, and longevity, but even more for its scent, its music (the hum of the bees that gathered nectar from its blossoms), and the wealth of products that could be made from it. Linden was the prize tree in the medieval pharmacopoeia, to the point that its name in German (*Linde*) gave rise to a verb meaning to care for or soothe (*lindern*). Linden was also a musical tree (most of the instruments from the medieval period were made from its wood) and, once again, the tree of love.[41] It owed this symbolic dimension to its beauty, its scent, and its music, but even more to the form of its leaves; they are heart-shaped. Those in love met under the linden; the tree's leaves—sometimes exaggerated in size in images—were one with the hearts of the young. Thirteenth- and fourteenth-century illumination and fifteenth-century tapestry provide us with much evidence of this.[42]

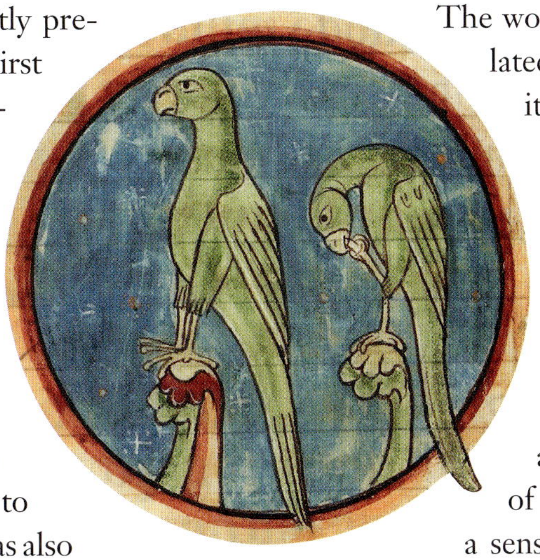

Let us return to the German *Minnesang*. It possessed many traits borrowed from the poetry of French troubadours and *trouvères* who, since the twelfth century, sang of a particular form of amorous feeling: "courtly love." The latter is all the more difficult to define since the expression did not exist in the Middle Ages but was coined in the late nineteenth century by the great scholar Gaston Paris. All that existed for the troubadours was the Occitan expression *fin'amor*, untranslatable with precision into modern French. "Courtly love" is a makeshift term to describe an amorous casuistry foreign to our modern sensibility, all the more so because the idea of courtesy is itself difficult to define. The word first of all describes anything related to court life, but in literary texts it refers more to the ensemble of virtues necessary to live in an exemplary manner in princely or lordly circles. Those virtues are numerous: frankness, loyalty, fidelity, politeness, elegance, generosity, distinction, courage. *Corteisie* (courtesy) assumed a high birth, a good upbringing, a knowledge of high society's customs and ways, a sense of honor, ease in conversation, a taste for appearance. It was opposed to *vilenie*, applied to those of low birth, ill bred, unrefined, greedy, avaricious, slander mongering, cowardly, slovenly.

By itself, green was not sufficient to portray all the qualities of the courteous man: honesty and frankness were better expressed by white; loyalty and fidelity by blue; honor, courage, and generosity by red. On the other hand, green was wholly the color for elegance, for youth, for singing a lady's praises, and for feelings of love. Here again, it was often paired with red, which embodied desire, that is to say, the hope of a carnal relationship.

In *fin'amor* the woman occupied the highest and most essential place; the poet was both her vassal and her suitor. He sought to serve her at the same time as conquer her. This conquest was long and difficult, all the more so as the lady was generally of a higher rank, often married, sometimes haughty and capricious. The question most debated by modern criticism is whether or not the poet's (or the knight's) true goal was possession of the woman's body, and thus the sexual act. Among the troubadours of the southern regions of the French realm, that seems to have been the case; the body is omnipresent and the erotic dimension undeniable. In this regard, red is very much the color of *fin'amor*. Among the *trouvères* of the northern realm and the *Minnesänger* of the Germanic countries, intentions are less clear, the lady less carnal and more distant. Ultimately the reader sometimes has the impression that the poet is in love with love, that he desires only desire; the hope of possible happiness is enough to make him happy. Here, the emblematic color of love is no longer red but green.

Indeed green is the color of hope in the West and has been for a long time. In Rome in the late Empire, newborns were sometimes swaddled in green to wish them long lives.[43] But it was in the Middle Ages that this important symbolic dimension of the color green—which survives to our day—came into its own. Marriageable young women, as we have said, frequently wore green dresses or a piece of green clothing. The famous green hat that the "Catherinettes" wear for the Feast of Saint Catherine, November 25, finds its distant origin here. But when the hope of finding a husband was finally realized, green clothing for young women then took on another meaning: awaiting a happy event. In effect, and especially in the late Middle Ages, green became the color for pregnant women. For example, Saint Elizabeth, pregnant with the future John the Baptist, sometimes wears a green dress in mural paintings and miniatures. Moreover, saints were not the only ones destined for green when they were expecting, ordinary women wore it as well. The painting by Jan Van Eyck traditionally titled *The Arnolfini Wedding* (c. 1435)—one of the most famous paintings in the entire history of painting—shows a pregnant young woman dressed in a vast and splendid green dress, symbolic of her state.

All the same, the late Middle Ages invented nothing in the matter. Two centuries earlier, green was already the color of hope for maternity; Saint Louis's chroniclers and biographers tell us that in 1238–1239, in order to conceive his first child, hopefully a son, the king of France forced himself to sleep for several consecutive nights in "the green bedroom" of the Île de la Cité palace with his young wife, Marguerite de Provence. We do not know what that "green bedroom" was exactly, but we know that it was located not far from the present-day Sainte-Chapelle (not yet built then), and we can guess that it was painted with foliage and greenery, motifs then in fashion in secular decor.[44]

THE ARNOLFINI WEDDING

This famous painting has raised many questions: subject? place? identity of the figures? Is the young woman pregnant? To this last question the green color of her dress and the image of Saint Margaret carved at the head of the bed allow us to answer in the affirmative.

Jan Van Eyck, *The Arnolfini Wedding*, 1434. London, The National Gallery.

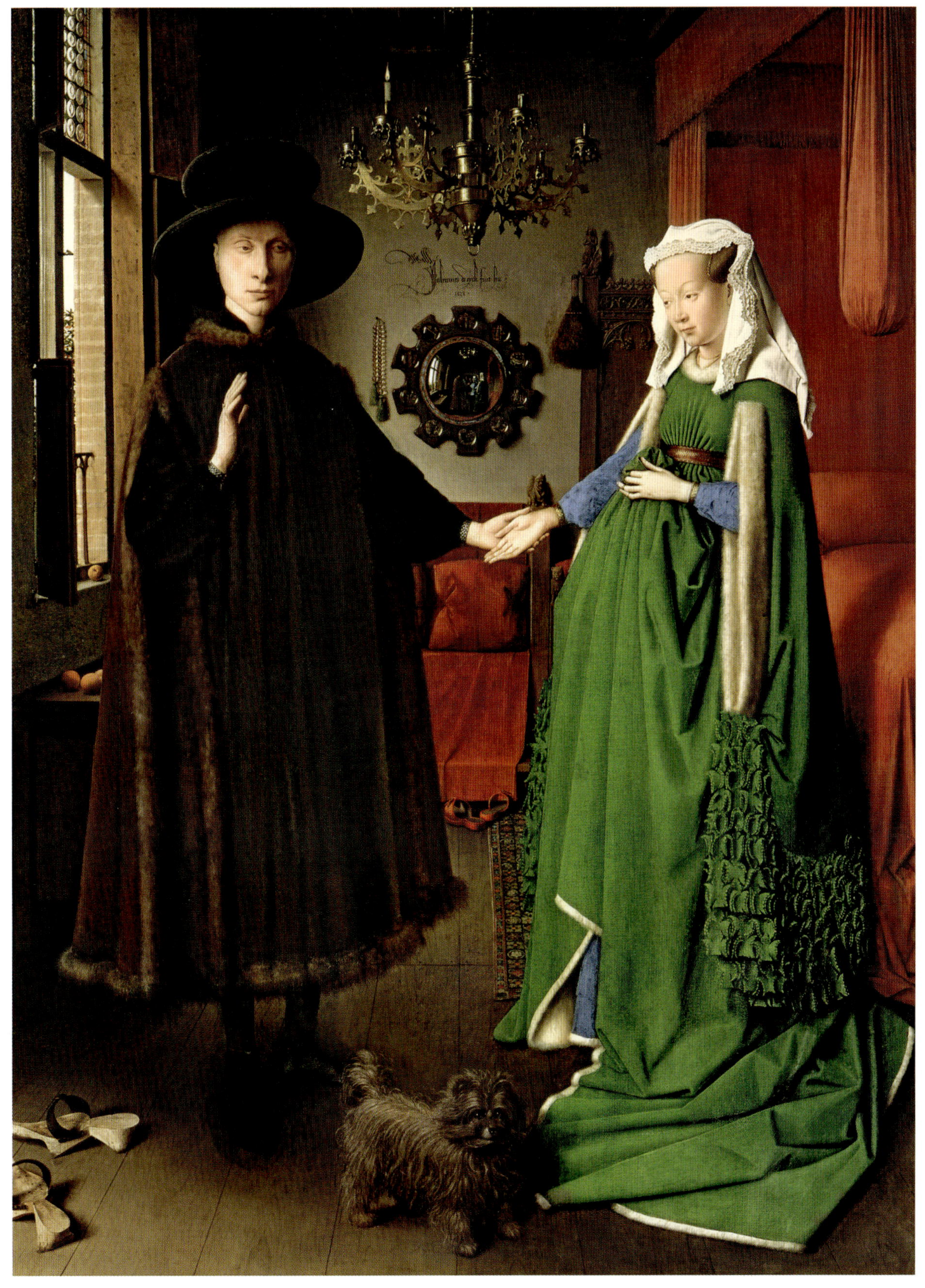

A chivalrous color

CHIVALRIC ELEGANCE IN THE LATE MIDDLE AGES

If green (*sinople*) was rare in coats of arms, it was nevertheless frequently featured in court and chivalric decor. It was the color of youth, beauty, and love. That was why horses—the only animals besides falcons that were dressed in the Middle Ages—frequently wore green quarter sheets in parades, jousts, and ceremonies.

Miniature from the *Codex Capodilista*, Basel, c. 1435–1440. Padua, Biblioteca Civica.

Beginning in the mid-twelfth century and until well into the thirteenth century, chivalry and courtesy went hand in glove. That is why the palette we find on the tournament fields is akin to the one featured in life at court. The colors are vivid and clear, creating strong contrasts in which red and green dominate, at least until the heraldic colors came to reorganize and then to control that palette, which had long been unrestrained. Even though the first coats of arms appeared over the course of the twelfth century, it was not until a century later that heraldry truly exerted control over the use of colors in courtly and chivalric decor.

Like all "sports" rituals, the medieval tournament was both a competition and an entertainment event in which colors played a major role, simultaneously deictic, aesthetic, emblematic, and symbolic. Green was ubiquitous there, not only because, unlike the joust, the tournament took place in an open space, at the edge of a forest or on the expanse of a moor or even a vast meadow, all places where vegetation constituted the main part of the decor, but also because in the stands—when there were stands—green fabrics and clothing were plentiful. Poets and romancers gave green a large place in their descriptions of tournaments. Moreover, in the francophone world many authors seem to have had a particular attraction to the word for green (*vert*), as well as for all the terms that echo it sonically: *vair* (the fur), *verre* (glass, the material), *ver* (springtime), and even the adjective *vere* (Latin *verus*, true) and the verb *voir* (to see) conjugated into various tenses. They did not hold back from playing with these phonic clusters to perform semantic shifts revolving around the symbolism of *vert, vair, verre, vrai*, and *vu* (green, fur, glass, truth, and seen).

Tournament competitors were happy to display this color, not so much on their shields or banners as

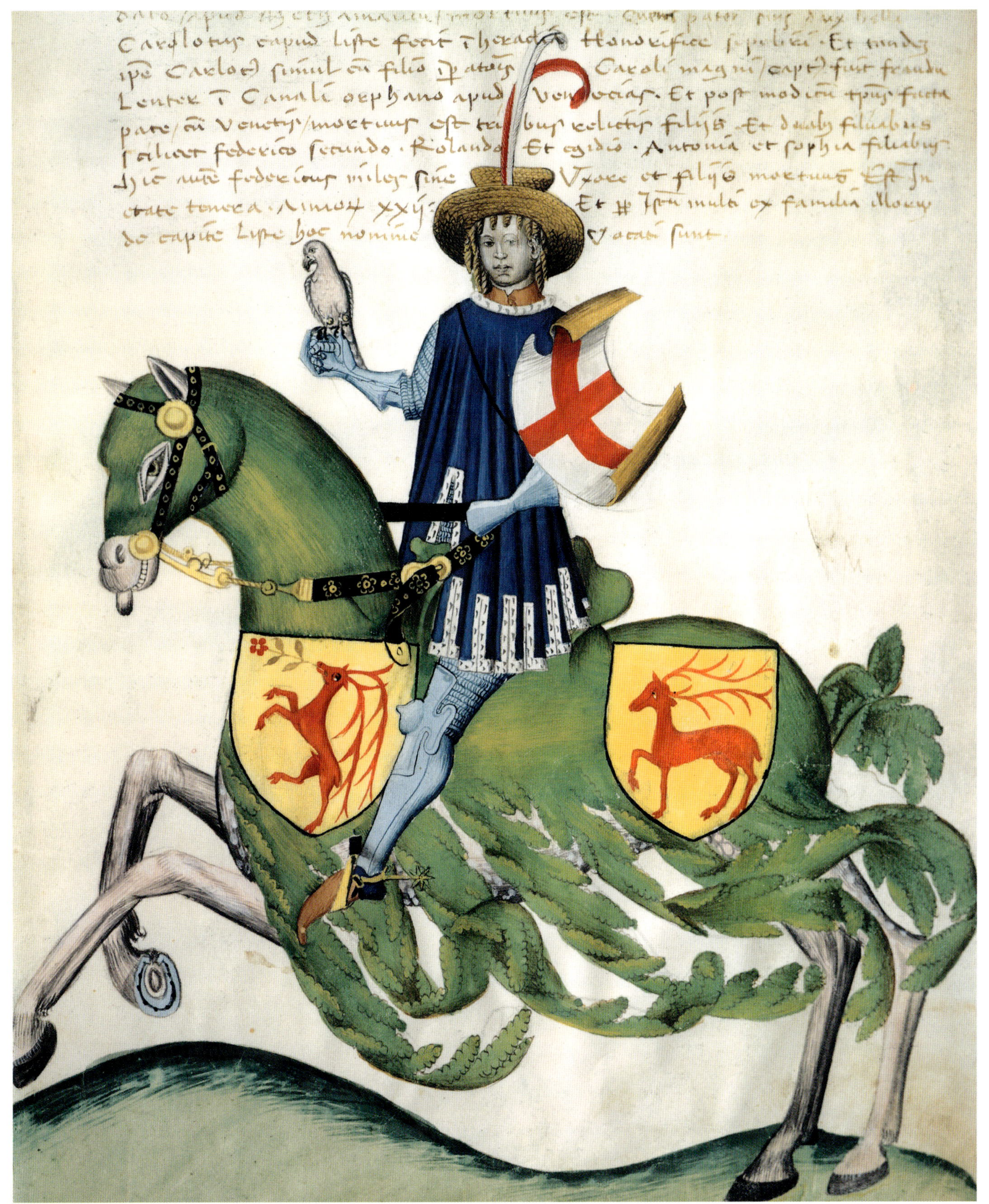

on their horses' quarter sheets, their coats of arms, or a piece of their equipment. It could be an occasional color, linked to the love of a woman whose sleeve or belt they wore, but it could also be a color chosen for the long term, even for their entire careers as tournament knights.

As early as the second half of the twelfth century, literary texts featured a few of those "green knights" who became more numerous in the following century. They were often young knights whose intrepid and spirited behavior was the cause of disorder. Thus, in the anonymous romance *Perlesvaus*, which dates to the first years of the thirteenth century, the hero Perceval is accompanied by his young brother Gladouin the Green, whose restless and careless behavior leads to perilous situations. That is almost always the case with "green knights" in Arthurian romances of this period. One chromatic topos is exemplary from this perspective: the appearance, partway through the story, of an unknown character bearing arms and equipment in a single color; he stands in the hero's path and challenges him.[45] This episode is always a delaying device: the color worn by the unknown knight is the author's means of letting the reader understand what the hero is dealing with or guess what is going to happen. A vermilion knight is a knight driven by bad intentions (he might also be a character coming from the Other World).[46] A black knight is a hero—sometimes of the highest order (Lancelot, Tristan)—who seeks to hide his identity; he can be good or evil as black is not always negative in this type of literature.[47] A white knight is generally seen as good; sometimes he is an older character, the hero's friend or protector. Finally, a green knight is a young knight whose audacious and insolent behavior will disrupt the established order. In the color code of Arthurian romances, blue and yellow are absent, the first because its full symbolic promotion has not yet taken place, the second because its close proximity to gold confines it to a very minor literary role.[48]

The "green knights" were not only literary figures, they existed in reality as well. The most famous of them lived in the fourteenth century: Amadeus VI, Count of Savoy, who was born in 1334 and died in 1383. During his lifetime he was given the nickname the "Green Count," which posterity has preserved for him. The reason for this was his habit of dressing in green to joust or compete in tournaments, and legend has it that he chose this color during a tournament in Chambéry in the spring of 1353. Green was supposed to have been the color of the dress of a lady with whom he was in love and whose sleeve he initially wore. The lady's name is unknown (did she ever exist?), but the link between the green sleeve and feelings of love is centuries old. A famous song considered by many music lovers to be the most beautiful of all times bears the title *Greensleeves*. It dates from the sixteenth century, the melody is that of an ancient Irish ballad, and the words are attributed to King Henry VIII of England, a cruel and jealous lover. In fact, in the song the author complains of the inconstancy of his beloved.

Let us return to the period of chivalry and courtesy, when the images tell the same story as the literary texts: green, the dominant color at the tournament, is also the color of love in them, especially in the Germanic countries. The *Codex Manesse*, a lavish manuscript produced in Zurich about 1300–1310, offers us a good example. It includes the work of 140 courtly poets writing in the German language from the twelfth and thirteenth centuries and is illustrated with 137 full-page paintings representing either the poet in question or a scene from one of his poems. The theme for most of the illustrations is love, and thus the color green is used constantly. Sometimes it is a matter of plant life framing the scene—linden, with its heart-shaped leaves, plays an important role in them; sometimes it is a matter of objects, buildings, and even animals (parrots) appearing in that color. But most frequently it is the figures' clothes that are green, either the lady's dress or the poet's coat of arms, sometimes both. The green of hopeful new love is often combined with the red of passion, two colors that recur throughout the manuscript. *Frau Minne* herself, represented many times in the process of shooting her arrows, wears both: a green dress and a red mantle.

The preeminence of green in courtly fashions and chivalric rituals should have been accompanied by this color's major presence in heraldic arms. But strangely enough, that is not the case at all. At no time and in no country in the Middle Ages did the frequency rating for green in heraldic arms reach 5 percent, whereas it often exceeded 50 percent for red, 45 percent for white and for yellow, and, according to the period and region, somewhere between 20 and 30 percent for blue and for black.[49] What accounts for this rarity of green in heraldry, that immense color system invented by European feudal society and still exerting considerable influence across the continents today (flags, logos, sports emblems, road signs, and so on)?

Coats of arms appeared in the mid-twelfth century on battle and tournament fields. Concealed under their helmets and covered in their great chain mail, the combatants became unrecognizable. In order to identify one another in the fray, they gradually adopted the custom of always having the same colors and figures represented on the large surfaces of their shields, which were then subject to a few consistent rules of composition. Thus a new sign of identity was born—the coat of arms—and with it, a new code of representation—heraldry. That is why, over the course of decades, the use of coats of arms was no longer limited to combatants and battlefields but extended to society as a whole. Beginning in the 1200s, they appeared on a great number of media: fabric, clothing, seals, coins, buildings, monuments, art objects, and objects from daily life. They were not only signs of identity but also marks of possession and ornaments. The churches themselves became veritable "museums" for coats of arms; they were found on the walls, floors, and stained glass, and on liturgical objects, vestments, and books. At the end of the thirteenth century, coats of arms were encountered everywhere: a large part of Western society made use of them, not only noblemen and knights but also women, clergy, patricians, bourgeois, artisans, civic and religious communities, towns and guilds. In certain regions, even the peasants had them.[50]

Medieval heraldry employed only six colors: white, yellow, red, blue, black, and green. In coats of arms they were not combined randomly but according to a few restrictive rules for juxtaposition and superimposition. Those rules were respected throughout, but they do not explain in the least why green always presents a frequency rating much inferior to those of the other five colors, no matter the owners, the number, the nature, or the whole of the coats of arms considered. Green was never absent but always rare, even very rare indeed.

What is the reason for its rarity? Heraldry experts have still not found an answer to this question. Is there a visual reason, linked to the very origin of coats of arms? On battle and tournament fields, where vegetation abounded, would the green in shields and banners have been less visible than other colors? That was the hypothesis of seventeenth-century scholars and is all the more convincing as green still predominated in the decor later when tournaments were organized in less rural places, within the walls of a fortress or even in the center of towns. There as well the green of shields and the green of the decor could have been confused.

Or, on the contrary, is the reason a technical one? Producing and fixing the color green was often a difficult task in the Middle Ages, both in dyeing and in painting. That is a strong argument promoted by various heraldry experts in the nineteenth and twentieth centuries. Or was there a symbolic reason? Since green had been the religious color of Islam since the ninth and tenth centuries, and sometimes the color of the devil in the West, was it rejected by combatants who had fought against the green emblems and standards of their adversaries during the Crusades? That is possible, but all historians are now in agreement that the Crusades played no part in the appearance of coats of arms.

Thus we are forced to recognize that there is no one explanation and also to note that in the Middle Ages green appears much more frequently in literary coats of arms—those of the knights of the Round Table, for instance—than in actual ones. Literary coats of arms do not need to actually be painted or dyed to exist; describing them is sufficient. The result is a greater statistical balance among the six colors of heraldry; in literature, heraldic green is no less rare than the other five colors and is often even more significant.

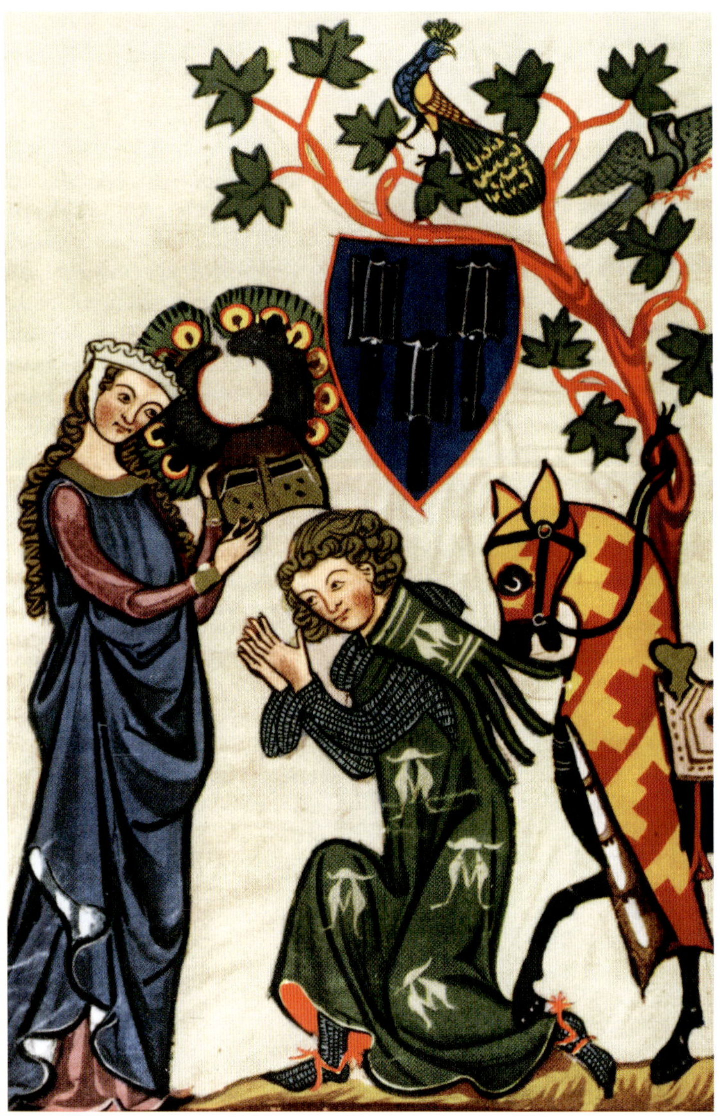

GREEN, THE COLOR OF LOVE

An archetypal courtly scene: before leaving for a tournament, the knight is dubbed by his lady. He is amply clothed in green, a symbol of his enamored state, which is also emphasized by the letter A (*Amor*) used as a decorative motif.

Miniature from the *Codex Manesse*, Zurich or Constance, c. 1300–1310. Heidelberg, Universitätsbibliothek, cpg 848, fol. 82 v°.

A green hero: Tristan

Among the literary heroes that the medieval imagination attributed with green or predominately green coats of arms, one stands out among all the others: Tristan. He was the favorite hero of the medieval public, the one whose unhappy love affair and tragic destiny seem to have most profoundly moved the aristocracy as well as the commoners, as is proven by his name, adopted as a given name by all the social classes. His legend, much older than the first written accounts of his story in the second half of the twelfth century, goes far back and seems to bring together various Scottish, Irish, and Cornish traditions. For a long time it belonged only to the oral tradition, recited by the Welsh bards and then sung by the trouvères of northern and western France. There are written versions that later spread into Germany, Italy, Scandinavia, and even beyond. Nephew of King Mark of Cornwall, Tristan is the victim of fate; when he returns from Ireland accompanied by the Irish king's daughter, the beautiful Iseult, engaged to Mark, the two young people accidently drink a love potion that was not meant for them. From then on, a tragic passion unites them that leads them from adventures into misadventures and finally to their deaths.

In many ways Tristan maintains special relations with the color green. He does so first by means of the plant world, always present in his story. Early on, he is healed of a mortal wound thanks to Iseult's knowledge of medicinal plants and her well-stocked pharmacopoeia. Then, on the boat that brings them to Cornwall, they both drink accidentally of the *vin herbé*, a magic potion prepared by Iseult's mother from plants. Twelfth- and thirteenth-century romances do not identify them, but the list can be easily reconstructed from well-known collections of recipes. In the Middle Ages four plants were indispensable for concocting love potions: vervain, artemisia, valerian, and St. John's wort. Other plant and animal products could be added, but the presence of those four plants was mandatory. Later in the story, when Iseult has become King Mark's wife, it is in the orchard that the young lovers meet at night, sometimes under a linden tree, sometimes under a pine. They use a linden leaf as a signal, floating on the surface of a stream or not, to communicate and to arrange or postpone these rendezvous.

But it is when Tristan and Iseult seek refuge in the forest that the presence of green reaches its height. Henceforth trees and plants constitute the setting for their daily lives. The leaves shelter them and serve as their clothing; Tristan becomes a hunter and even a magician. Like Merlin the Wizard, another literary hero who lives partly in the woods, he becomes expert in all the properties of plants and their uses, creating most notably the famous Unfailing Bow, a marvelous bow that never misses its target. When this outcast couple is forced to *s'enforester*, as old French so nicely puts it, Iseult is not the only one to resort to magic; Tristan does so as well and thus seems to change in nature. In fact, in courtly romances the forest is always a disturbing, mysterious place of strange encounters and temporary metamorphoses. One goes there to flee the world and society, to seek God or the devil, to restore oneself, be transformed, and connect with the beings and forces of nature.[51] All sojourns into the forest (*silva*) made human beings into unusual beings, "savages" (*silvaticus*).[52] Tristan and Iseult are no exception to this rule.

Later Tristan leaves his exile in the forest and adds to the green of the hunter and the magician other attributes linked to the symbolic function of that color. In order to return to King Mark's court and see his beloved again, he disguises himself first as a juggler, next as a musician, and then as a clown. The texts of the various romances give us no details on the costumes our hero wears on these occasions, but images, miniatures from the late Middle Ages in particular, often dress these three social types in green. In the general reader's mind, no doubt, Tristan disguised as juggler, musician, and then court jester was dressed entirely or predominantly in green. Without this color the disguise would have been neither effective nor complete.

Heraldry seems not to have been forgotten in all of that. Beginning in the 1230s, in the immense anonymous romance known as the *Prose Tristan*, the romance that definitively grafts the legend of Tristan to the legend of King Arthur and the knights of the Round Table, King Mark's nephew is attributed with a shield emblazoned with a green field and a yellow lion: *de sinople au lion d'or*. Henceforth this would be the coat of arms born by Tristan in all documents—text and image—until the end of the Middle Ages and even well into the seventeenth century. We have much evidence of this: miniatures, murals, tapestries, heraldic arms, accounts of jousts and tournaments, Arthurian feasts, and entertainment. Tristan too became a "green knight," but a green knight without peer. Of course, the color of his shield is very much the color of love and youth—that meaning is inevitable—but it is also the color of the hunt and the forest, music and madness, disorder and transgression, and no doubt greater still, the color of despair and tragic destiny.

A chemically unstable color, in the last centuries of the Middle Ages, green was in fact often associated with all that was symbolically unstable: not only childhood and youth, love and beauty, but also luck, hope, fortune, destiny. By the same token, it appeared as an ambiguous, disturbing, and even dangerous color.

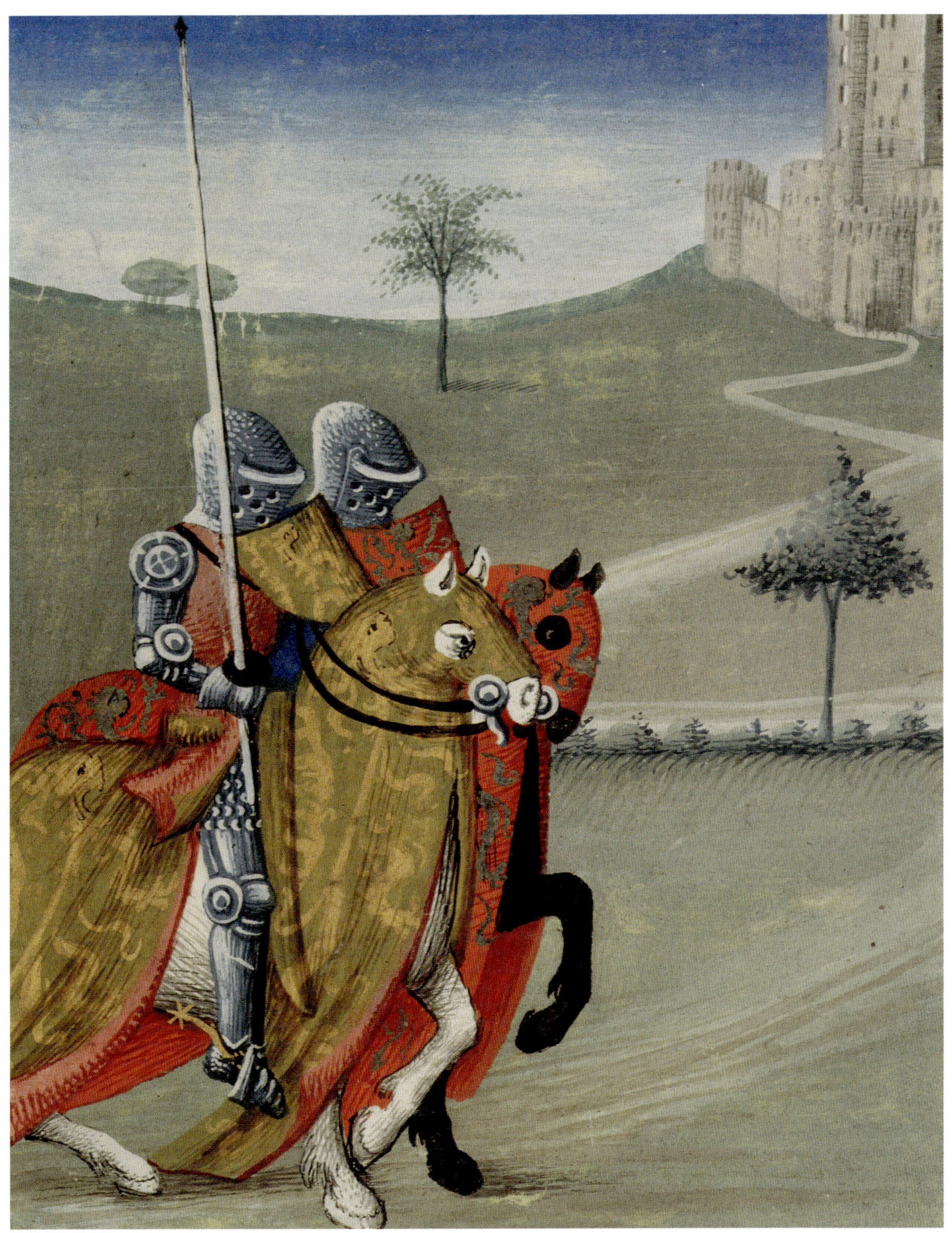

TRISTAN'S COAT OF ARMS

Tristan, the favorite literary hero of the Middle Ages, maintained close relations with green, the color of hunters and jugglers, of love and madness, and especially of fate. That is probably why, early on, he was equipped with a shield with a lion—the archetypal lion of Christian chivalry—posed on a field of green: *de sinople au lion d'or.*

Miniature from a manuscript of the *Prose Tristan*, illuminated by Évrard d'Espinques for Jacques d'Armagnac, 1463. Paris, Bibliothèque national de France, ms. fr. 99, fol. 633 v°.

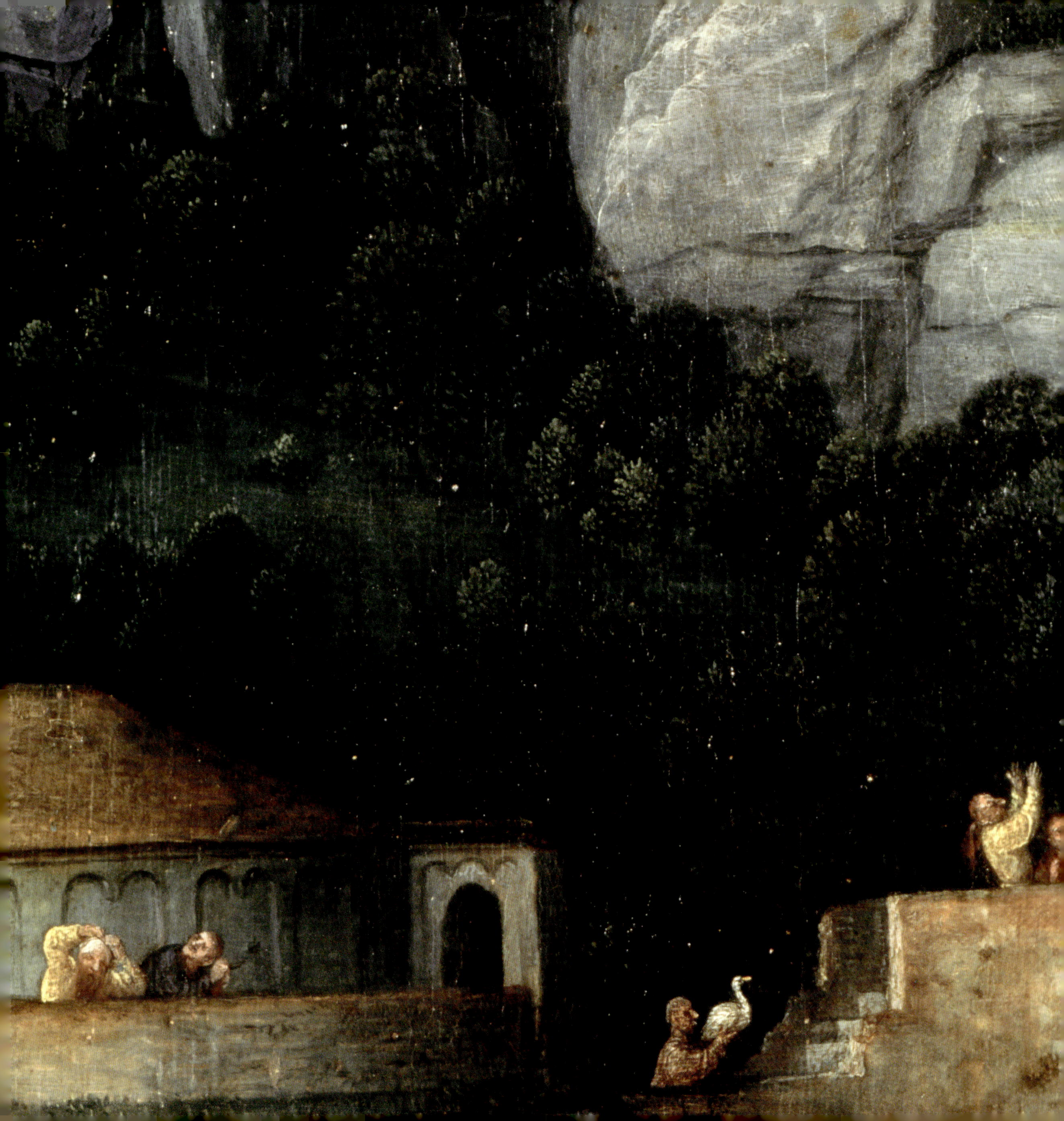

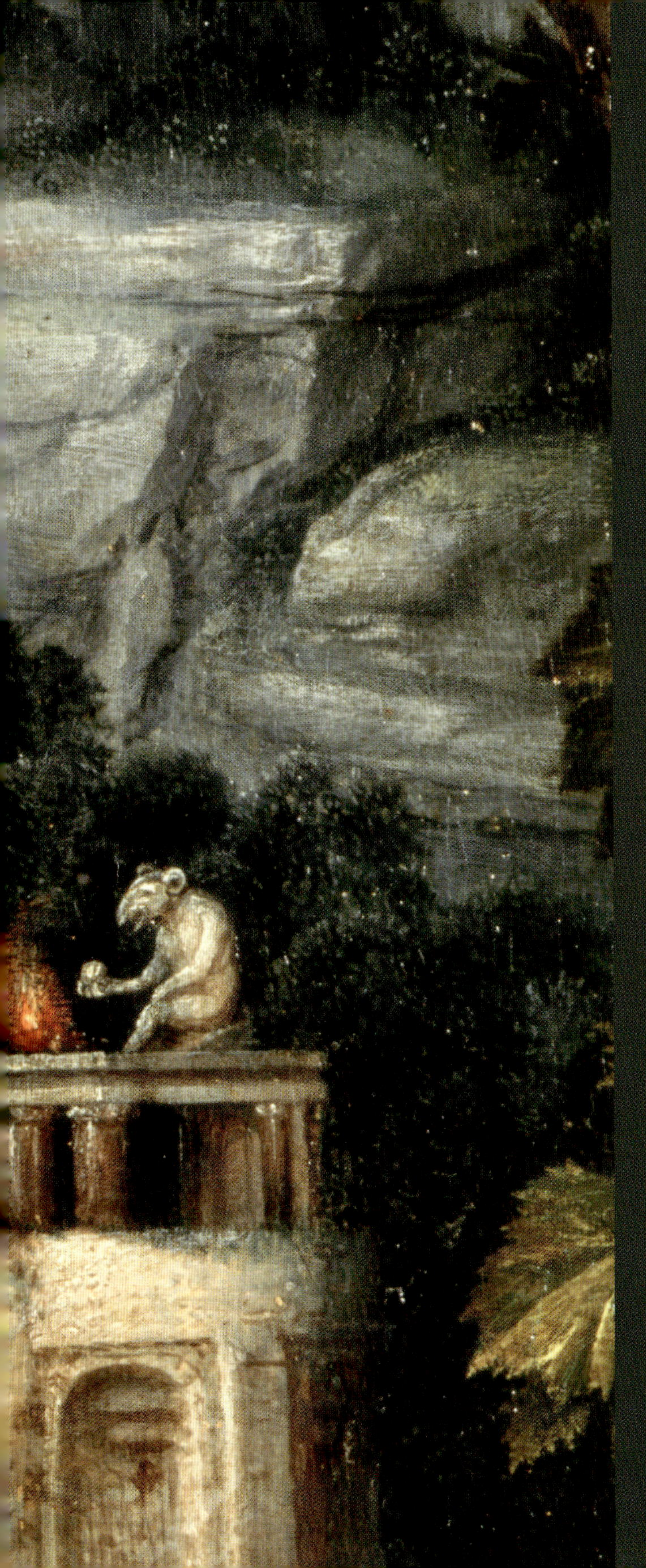

A **dangerous** color

14TH–16TH CENTURIES

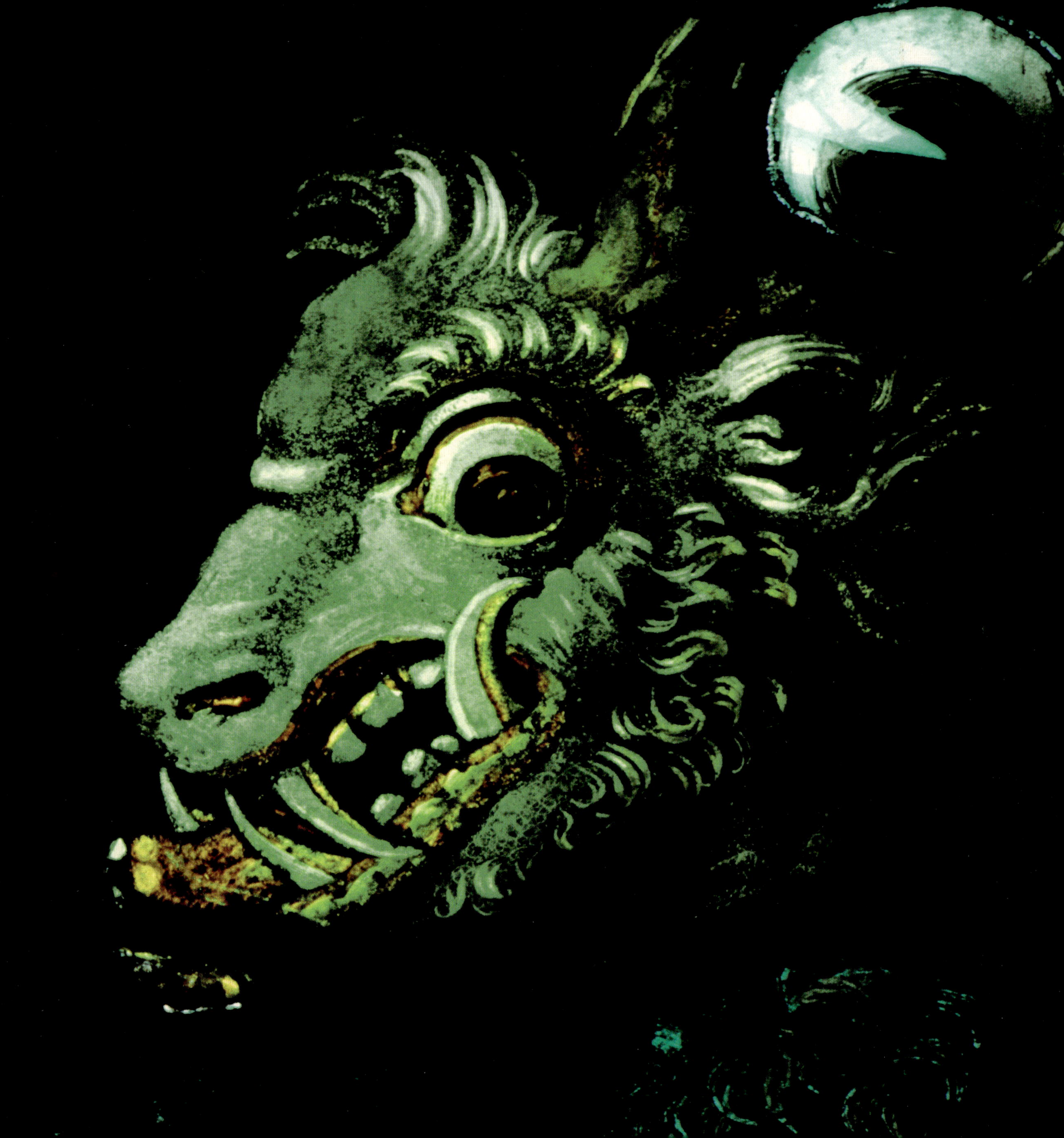

At the end of the Middle Ages, green, so admired in the time of chivalry and courtesy, began to lose standing. As a chemically unstable color, both in painting and dyeing, it was henceforth associated symbolically with all that was changeable or capricious: youth, love, fortune, fate. By the same token it tended to have a split personality. On the one hand there was good green, associated with gaiety, beauty, and hope, which had not disappeared but had become more subdued; on the other there was bad green, associated with the Devil and his creatures, witches, and poison, which had expanded its territory and henceforth brought misfortune into many domains. The vocabulary itself reflected this opposition and increasingly conveyed a greater sensitivity to the different shades of colors. New words appeared and expressions were created to better define the semantic or symbolic field of each color. Middle French, for example, frequently contrasts *vert gai*, light, lively, and appealing, with *vert perdu*, duller, sadder, more disturbing.

At the same time, the color codes that had appeared in the preceding period became more numerous and more specific. Civil and religious authorities henceforth distinguished honest colors from those that were less so. Perhaps falling victim to the immense promotion of blue, green had the misfortune of being assigned to the bad group. In many areas it lost ground, its stature diminishing as much in artistic creation as in daily life. Only a few poets continued to give it a place of honor in the color order.

GREEN, THE COLOR OF THE DEVIL

In medieval art works and images the Devil can be any color and is usually two or three colors rather than one. In the Romanesque period, however, black and red are the dominant colors. Later, at the end of the Middle Ages and in the early modern period, it is green that plays this role, especially in stained glass and illuminations.

Stained glass of the *Last Judgment* by Engrand Leprince, c. 1520. Beauvais, Saint-Étienne Church, Saint-Nicolas Chapel.

Satan's green bestiary

The Devil is not an invention of Christianity. Nevertheless he is almost unknown in Jewish traditions and does not appear in the Old Testament, at least not in the form that Christian traditions gave him. It is the Gospels that reveal his existence and the Apocalypse that grants him a primary role by foretelling his short reign just preceding the end of time. Subsequently, the Church Fathers made him both a demonic being who dared defy God and a fallen creature, leader of the rebel angels. His image developed slowly, between the sixth and eleventh centuries, and long remained unstable and polymorphous. After the year 1000 it tended to stabilize and to take on a hideous, bestial appearance. Satan's body was thin and withered to emphasize that he came from the realm of the dead; he was naked, covered with fur or pustules, sometimes spotted, always repugnant; from his back hung a tail and two wings recalling his condition as fallen angel; his cloven hooves resembled a goat's. His head was dark and enormous, with pointed horns and bristly hair standing on end, evoking flames. His face, sometimes adorned with a snout or a muzzle, was grimacing, his mouth stretched into a grin from ear to ear, his look convulsed and cruel.

Romanesque art, always more inventive in representing evil than good, offers proof of incomparable diversity and expressiveness in its representation of Satan. With regard to colors however, the palette was reduced. Either the Devil was all black (as is most often the case) or he was black and red: black body and red head, red body and black head, two-tone body and entirely black head. These two colors came directly from hell; the black of darkness was combined here with the red of infernal flames. The Devil bore them on his being, thus contributing to their negative reputations. Subsequently the diabolic palette gradually altered, and the first green devils made their appearance about the mid-twelfth century, first in stained glass, later in illuminations, murals, and the precious arts. Were they the result of increasing hostility between Christians and Muslims? Since, in the eyes of the former, green had become the religious color of the latter, the iconography of the period of the Crusades might have enjoyed painting devils and demons green. We cannot affirm this. The origin of these devils may lie elsewhere. It is difficult to say if it was the progressive depreciation of the color green that created green devils, or if it was those devils, increasingly numerous over the course of the decades, that contributed to green's disrepute.

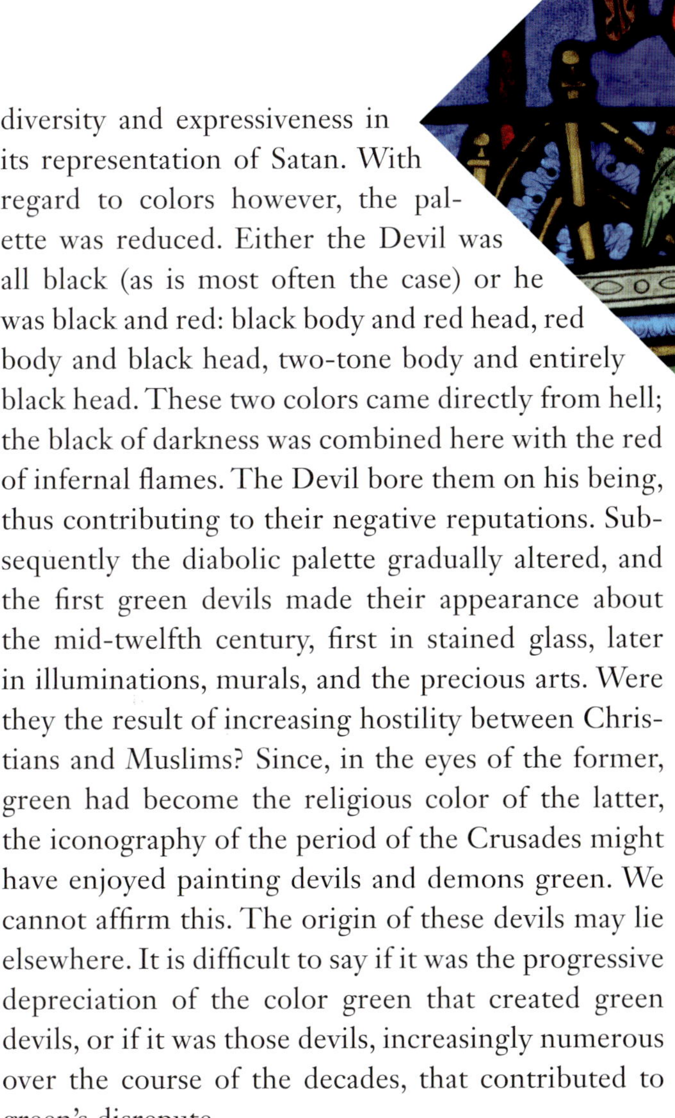

GREEN, THE COLOR OF DEMONS

In Gothic stained glass windows green is not only the color of the Devil, it is also the color of the demons, sorcerers, dragons, and all the infernal creatures that accompany him.

Stained glass of the life of Saint James the Greater, c. 1215–1220. Chartres, Notre-Dame Cathedral ambulatory.

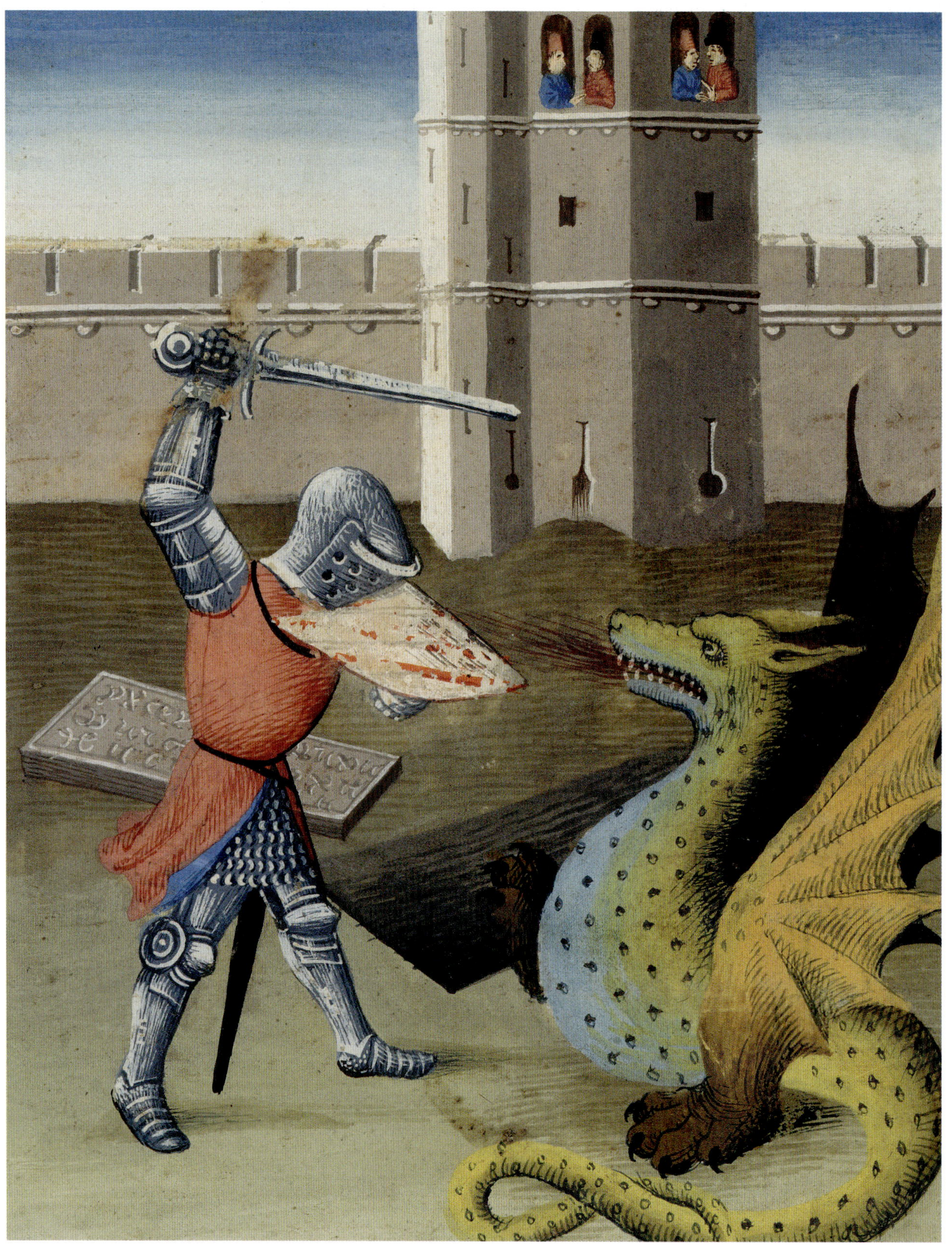

LANCELOT FIGHTING A PUSTULAR DRAGON

If we are to believe the bestiaries, dragons could change color at will. All the same, in miniatures they are usually green and yellow, or even greenish or yellowish, and covered with spots, scales, or swellings to emphasize their viscous, slimy, and pustular nature.

Miniature from a manuscript of the *Prose Tristan*, illuminated by Évrard d'Espinques for Jacques d'Armagnac, 1463. Paris, Bibliothèque national de France, ms. fr. 99, fol. 509.

The Devil did not live alone and did not appear by himself; he was accompanied by a retinue of animals and wicked creatures. At the end of the Middle Ages, many of them maintained close relationships with green, notably the demons who "are legion," who tormented humans, possessed them, and spread vices and cruelty. They especially watched for signs of weakness in the sick and feeble and tried to snatch the sinful soul of the dying at the moment when it was about to leave the body. Similarly, among the animals accompanying Satan, in whom he liked to incarnate himself, some were black or dark (bear, wolf, boar, goat, cat, owl, crow) and others green (dragon, serpent, crocodile, hydra, basilisk, frog, siren, locust). Let us pause to consider this second group, which makes up a particularly formidable "green bestiary," and let us read what the bestiaries and encyclopedias tell us about them.

Most serpents were green, and that color was a sign of their evil and dangerous nature. That was the case with the asp, viper, and dragon. The asp's venom induced sleep more than it killed, but it induced sleep for good; the man or woman bitten by it fell into a deep slumber and did not awaken. That was what happened to Cleopatra who committed suicide by placing an asp on her breast. The viper was more cunning and cruel; it hid in order to spring out and bite its unsuspecting victim. The female viper was especially hateful. Its union with the male was tragic for the latter: in order to mate successfully, the male had to put his head into his companion's mouth, but once he had deposited his semen, she immediately decapitated him with her teeth. From this deadly union were born just as pitiless young; immediately upon leaving their mother's belly, they killed her.

The dragon was even more appalling. For medieval culture the dragon was a real animal, the largest of the serpents, but a composite serpent, attributed with paws and often wings. Covered with scales much tougher than those of fish, its body extended into a long tapered tail, and a spiked ridge ran down its back. Its legs, similar to a lion's, ended in eagle talons; its head was small and elongated, with pointed ears and sometimes a beard. Its eyes were red, its gaze steady and paralyzing. Its mouth was not large, but it harbored cruel teeth and a tongue in the form of a trident. Dragons bit, ripped, devoured, swallowed, vomited, spit, and slobbered; they were ogres. Some dragons had more than one head. The amphisbaena had two, one on its neck, the other at the end of its tail; "the dragon from the country of the Amazons" had three, one large with two small ones on either side. Some even had seven, like the dreadful hydra, monster of the waters, enemy of the crocodile whose color she borrowed: green.

Green was also the color of the ordinary dragon. A few authors specify, however, that its back was green and its belly yellow. Others add that it was so very sly it could change color at will like the chameleon. Moreover, if the dragon was green or yellow and green outside, the inside of its body, gorged with blood and fire, was red. Its blood was collected to make a pigment used by painters and illuminators: *sandragon*. Recipe collections tell us that it had to be used to paint the face of the Devil, the punishment of the wicked, and the flames of hell.[1] Oddly, no bestiary associates the dragon with the color black, or even with somber tones; it was green, slimy, pustular, gleaming, and fiery. It maintained close relationships with the four elements (water, earth, air, fire) and with the five senses; it was terrifying (sight), noisy (hearing), slimy (touch), nauseating (smell), and ogre-like (taste). Its breath reeked; the flames emitted from its nostrils and mouth burned and destroyed; its venom, located at the end of its tail like a scorpion's, killed. But its sperm and spittle were considered fertile and fertilizing, and for those who bathed in it, its blood could harden to become a sort of shell that guaranteed immortality. Siegfried, the hero of the *Song of the Nibelungen*, did so, but an unfortunate linden leaf that fell between his shoulders prevented him from becoming completely invulnerable. Here the green of the favorite tree contrasts to the red of the animal most feared; those two colors are paired one more time.[2]

In the water lived other green creatures that were all negative as well. Here we find the frog, which for the bestiaries was not the little sympathetic creature we know. It was a "worm of dirty water, slimy and venomous, green on head and back, spotted under the belly, horrible to see and hated by all; like its friend the viper, it is full of poison."[3] Fortunately the frog was timid; at the least sign of danger, it sought refuge in water or a water vessel. Its cowardice was proverbial. There were countless recipes linked to witchcraft involving organs or secretions taken from frogs: tongue, spittle, venom, eyes, skin, legs. Many had to do with sexuality, the frog being one of the common symbols for lust. Many authors affirmed that frogs mated at night and indulged in orgies similar to those of the witches' sabbat.[4] These were demonic beings, as the color of their skin made clear.

The siren was one as well. This was a hybrid creature, half woman, half animal. In antiquity she was usually a bird; in the Middle Ages she was most often a fish. Her body, the upper half superbly feminine, ended in an unnerving "fish-like" tail of the color green. Sirens were hypocritical and cruel; they charmed sailors with their beauty and the sweetness of their songs, drew them into the high seas, and lulled them to sleep. Then they boarded their ships, abused the sleepers, and threw them into the ocean depths; some of them even devoured the corpses.

More ferocious still was the crocodile, the monster of the rivers. Even though its name evokes the color yellow (*croceus* in Latin, from which is derived *crocodilus*), in images it was always green and resembled a winged dragon or an enormous lizard with four very short legs and wide feet. Its body was covered with enormous scales, hard and sharp. Its head was a horrible sight, long and slit by an immense mouth, tongueless but all the more threatening because of the great number of teeth it enclosed. It did not use those teeth to chew but only to bite and to kill. The crocodile was extremely voracious, and since its bottom jaw remained immobile, it swallowed its prey without chewing it. Its very long intestine explained why its digestion was slow, obliging it to remain still for long periods, in the water at night, on riverbanks during the day. Like the fox and all sly creatures, it could pretend to be sleeping and then wake suddenly, rise all at once on its tail, and seize any animal that had come near it. It was treacherous,

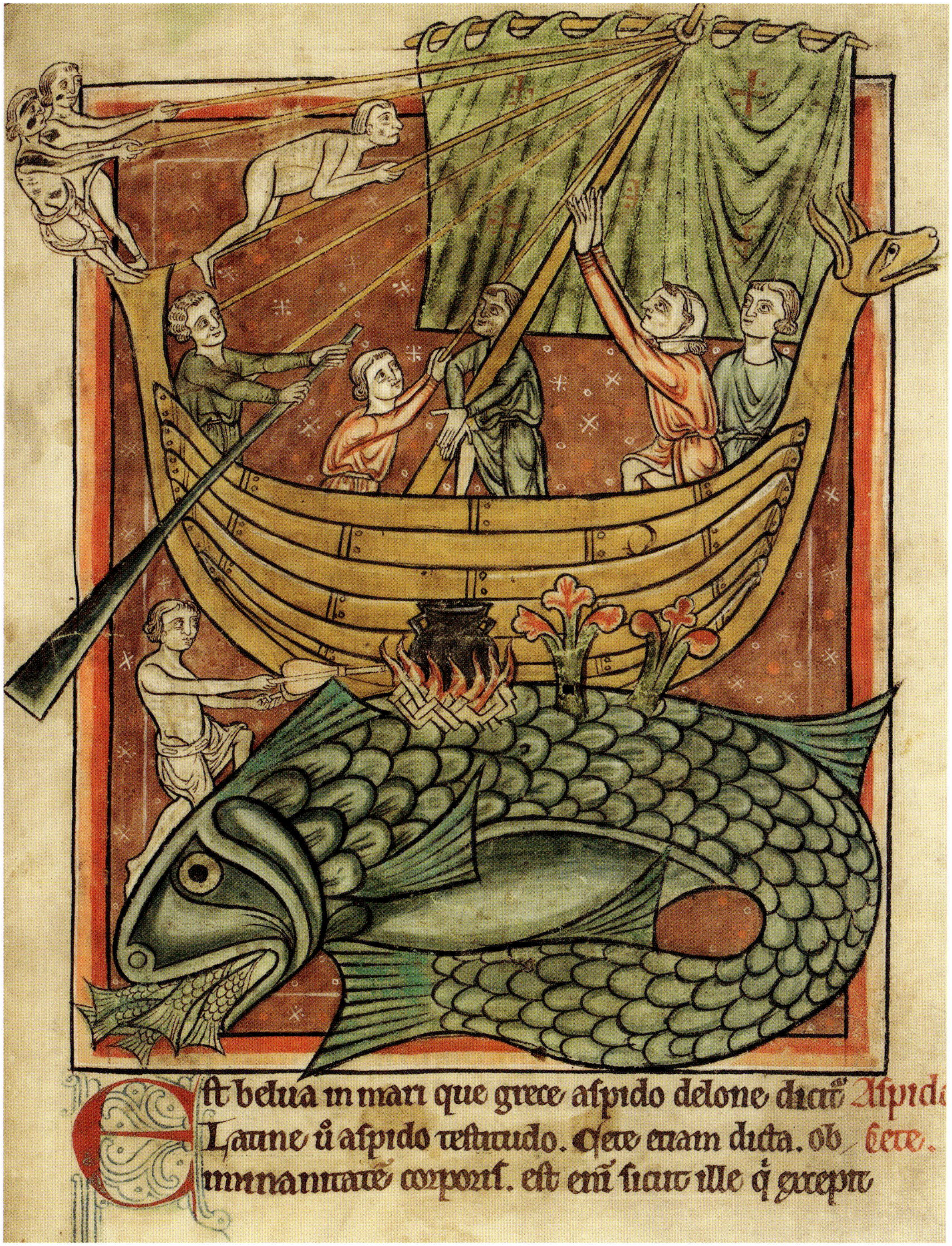

A GREEN MONSTER: THE WHALE

In the Middle Ages green was the color of water. That is why frightful or formidable creatures who lived there were often represented in this color: the dragon, the crocodile, the siren, the viper, and even its friend the frog, that "dirty and venomous worm." In the sea the most dangerous creature was the whale, who pretended to be an island; sailors berthed, rested, and built fires there. It would wake suddenly and hurl them into the ocean depths.

Miniature from an English bestiary, c. 1230–1240. London, British Library, Ms. Harley 4751, fol. 69.

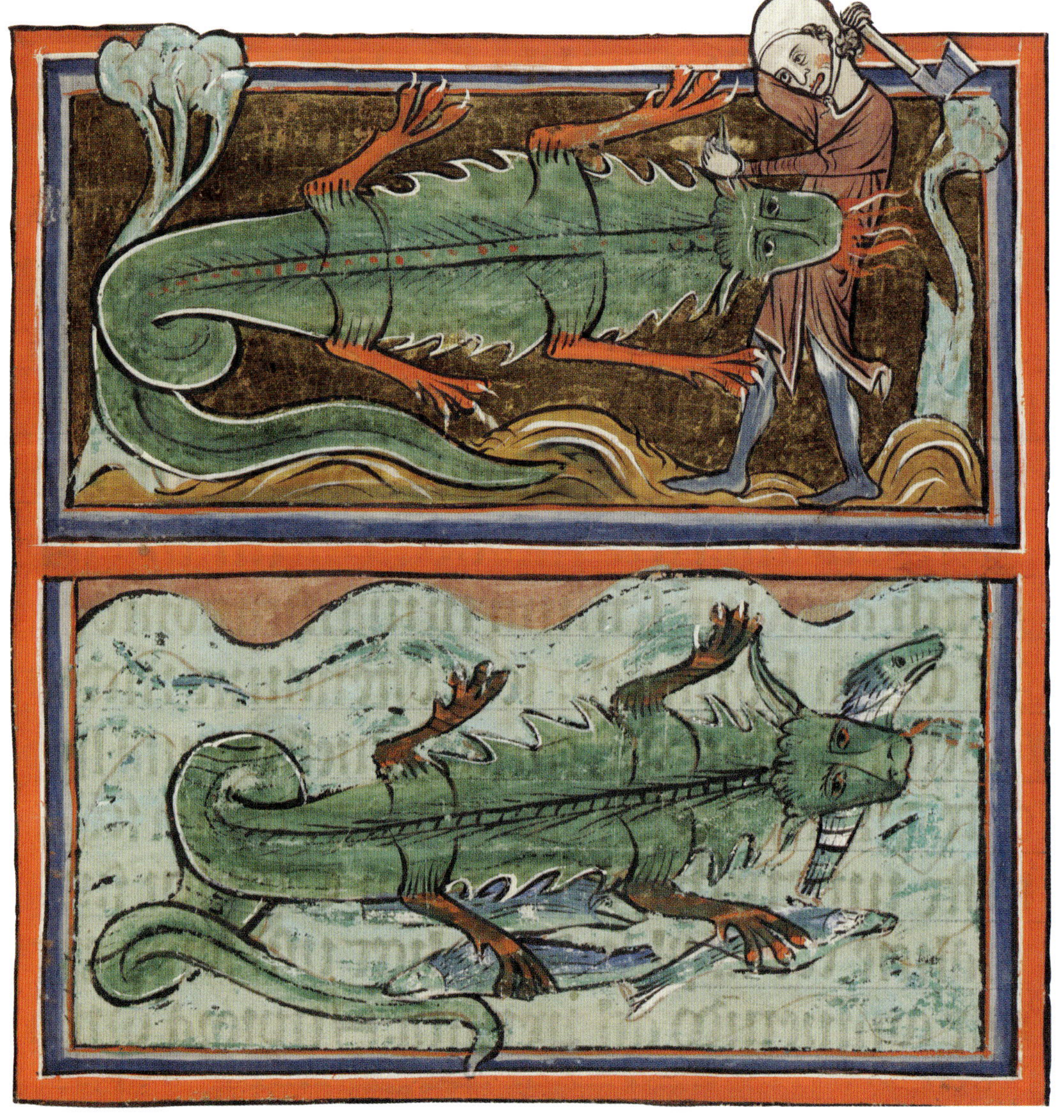

GREEN OR YELLOW: THE CROCODILE
Medieval bestiaries often maintain that the crocodile, a voracious and hypocritical animal, owes its name to its strange yellow color (*croceus/ crocodilus*), but pictures almost always show it as green, the color of water and creatures of the Devil.

Miniature from an English bestiary, c. 1230–1240. Oxford, Bodleian Library, Ms. Bodley 764, fol. 24.

violent, and voracious. But strangely, it seemed to experience remorse. All the bestiaries recount how the crocodile cannot help but seize and devour men when it sees them come near. But then it regrets what it did and cries for a long time: thick, abundant, greenish crocodile tears.

From green to greenish

Most of the green animals that appeared in the Devil's bestiary lived in water or frequented the watery world. It is possible that green evoked not only their evil natures but also this tie to the aquatic universe. In the Middle Ages water was generally considered and represented as green. As we will see in the following chapter, it would remain so in some cases until well into the modern period, notably on cartographic documents. Seas and oceans, rivers and streams, lakes and ponds would pass from green to blue very, very slowly between the fifteenth and seventeenth centuries.

This aqueous green of the demonic bestiary was also a viscous green. Attentive to the detailed rendering of bodily surfaces, the illuminators and painters of the Middle Ages proved skillful at conveying this idea of viscosity by using undulating lines, drawing compartments that fit together into scales, and employing various shades of green, especially of desaturated greens. On the bodies of sirens, dragons, and crocodiles, artists took the liberty of wetting the color and utilizing the nature of the binder to obtain a sleek and slimy green.

Aqueous, viscous, desaturated, this negative green is sometimes greenish as well—in which case the color is neither bright nor clear, but more or less gray, faded, blanched. In images as in real life, this greenish tonality—expressed in medieval Latin by the adjective *subviridis*—was always disturbing, if not deadly. It was the color of mold, disease, putrefaction, and especially decayed flesh. By the same token it was also the color of corpses, and through analogy—customary in the Middle Ages—it was the color of ghosts who left the land of the dead to come to earth to torment the living and claim their right to eternal life.[5] Sometimes they were white, as our modern phantoms are, but more often they were grayish or greenish, as were the specters, apparitions, and most of the spirits from the world of dreams or of night.

They must be linked to a certain number of small mysterious beings who lived in nature, sometimes in stables or even in houses: spirits of the fields and woods, leaf spirits of the trees and hedges, elves and sylvans of the forests, water nymphs, and even goblins of the mines, mountain trolls, Germanic kobolds, Breton korrigans, sprites, imps, and *nuitons*. In the Middle Ages they flourished, and many have survived in modern folklore. Some were benevolent, others harmful, still others changeable or mischievous. Even if their names and appearances differed according to period and region, they all belonged to the same world, a strange world halfway between the natural and the supernatural. Their bodies or their clothing were frequently green, and even as it emphasized their ties to the plant world and to various fertility rites, this seems to constitute the chief characteristic of that strangeness. These are the distant relatives of our "Martians," extraterrestrial humanoid creatures who appeared toward the end of the nineteenth century and were supposed to live on Mars; the contemporary imagination gave them thin bodies, enormous heads, and entirely green skin. Like his medieval ancestors and like many other unreal beings—fairies, for example, whom we will discuss further on[6]—the Martian is bound to be a "little green man."[7]

The green of witches falls into a related symbolic system, but unlike that of nymphs, elves, and leaf spirits, it is entirely negative. Moreover it belongs more to the modern period than to the Middle Ages. It is a mistake to believe that the business of witchcraft belonged to the medieval world and its supposed "obscurantism." In fact, the important cases and major trials only appeared in the fifteenth century and involved to an even greater extent the two centuries that followed.[8] By promoting a pessimistic conception of human existence, the Protestant Reformation furthered popular beliefs in supernatural forces and the possibility of becoming allies with them in order to get ahead in life, acquire certain powers (clairvoyance, the evil eye), cast spells, make potions, and harm one's enemies. Beginning in the 1550s, the printed book then took over by making widely available both collections of witchcraft recipes and treatises on demonology. These were nearly all bestsellers. Enlightened minds sometimes wrote them. That was the case with Jean Bodin (1529–1596), philosopher, jurisconsult, author of already quite modern works on law, economics, and political science. Nevertheless, in 1580 he published a book entitled *De la démonomanie des sorciers* in which he attested to the existence of evil forces and pacts with demons, described in detail witches and warlocks, and recommended torture and burning at the stake to eradicate such scourges.[9] His book, which was reissued several times, was imitated by many authors until well into the seventeenth century.

From this abundant and repetitive literature we can gather various facts regarding the color green: witches had green eyes and green teeth; they often wore green dresses; they concocted poisons and evil potions that were greenish in color. Moreover, when they went to the sabbat deep in the forest at night, they were surrounded by a double bestiary: black animals on one side (goats, wolves, crows, cats, dogs) and green animals on the other (basilisks, serpents, dragons, locusts, frogs, hybrids of all kinds). They themselves displayed both those colors; their green dresses, a sign of their evil nature, were smeared with soot, not only because they passed through chimneys before flying off to the sabbat, but also because black was the color required for participating in the infernal mass, in pacts with the Devil, and in sacrificial banquets.[10]

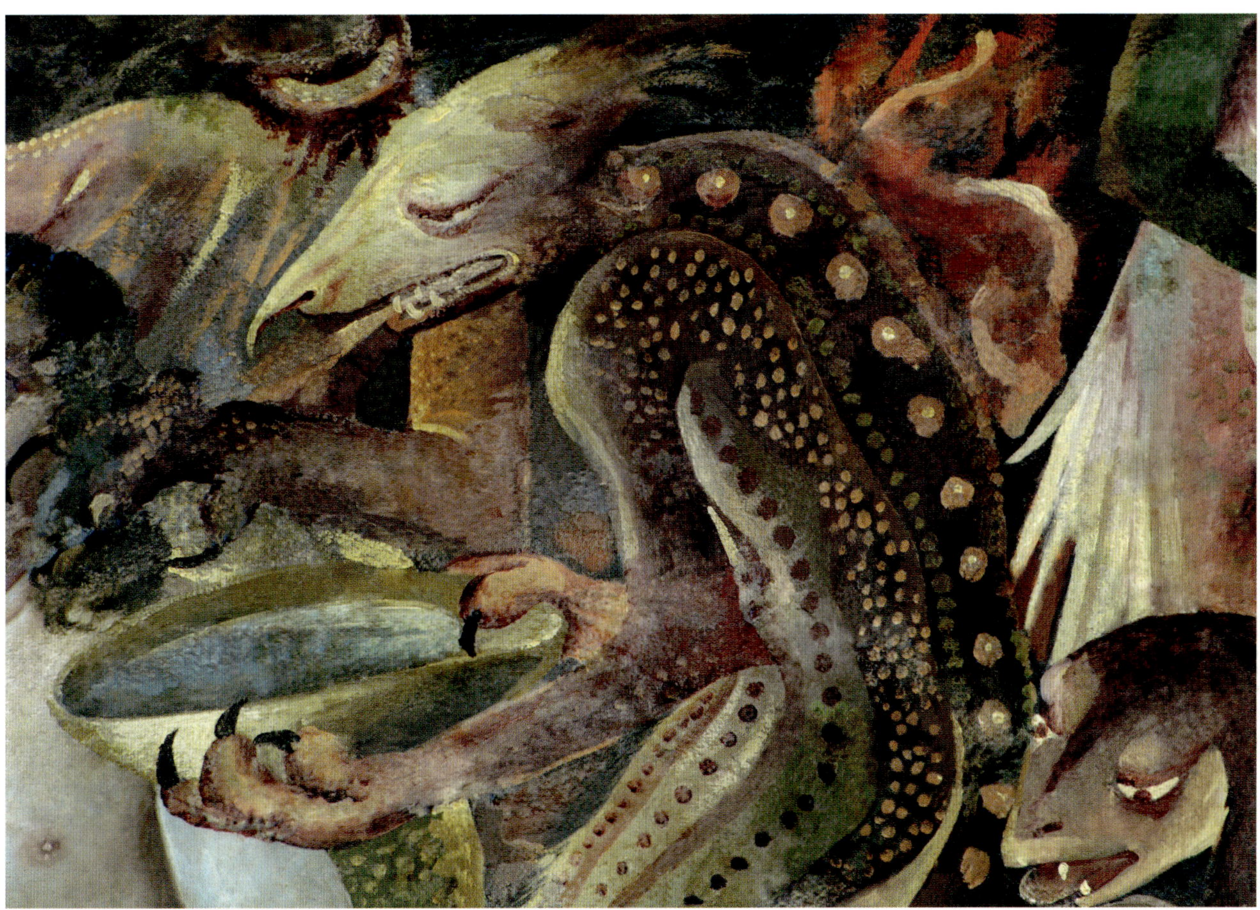

THE GREENISH AND THE VISCOUS

In medieval iconography greenish, aqueous, viscous, and pustular are often linked. Artists used them to represent infernal creatures with serpentine bodies and dragon heads who snatch up the damned to take them to hell.

Detail from *The Last Judgment*, chancel wall painting, late 15th century. Albi, Sainte-Cécile Cathedral.

The bad reputation of green eyes is not exclusive to the late Middle Ages or the modern period. It was already well attested in ancient Rome (the poet Martial, for example, saw in them a perverse and debauched nature) and was present throughout the medieval period.[11] Treatises on physiognomy, which tended to reestablish the value of blue eyes (discredited by the Romans) beginning in the thirteenth century, were not so kind to green eyes. Green eyes revealed bad character, a false and deceitful spirit, a life of pleasure and debauchery. Especially if they were small and deep-set, green eyes belonged to traitors, false knights, Judas, prostitutes, and witches.[12] They also belonged to the basilisk, a monstrous reptilian serpentine rooster whose body was

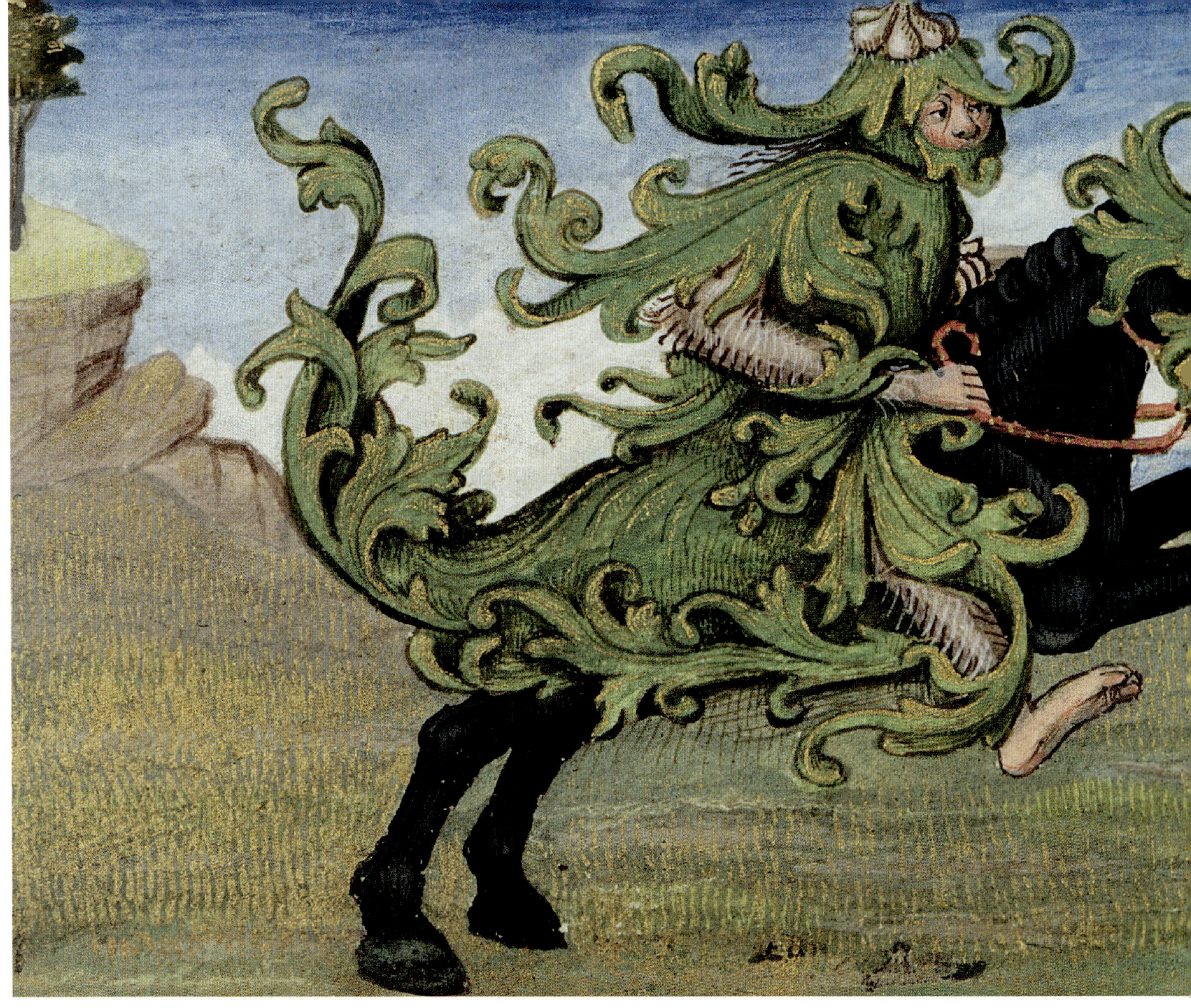

entirely filled with venom and whose gaze was fatal. The Devil himself was sometimes represented with green eyes. A common saying in the sixteenth century proclaimed that men and women who had green eyes were destined to join him in his infernal lair: "grey eyes to paradise, black eyes to purgatory, green eyes to hell."[13]

In the bestiaries green eyes belonged not only to the basilisk but to all the serpents (the French wordplay, "*yeux verts, yeux de vipère*"—green eyes, viper eyes—dates only to the nineteenth century nevertheless) and to some of the dragons. However dragons often had eyes of two different colors: one yellow, the other

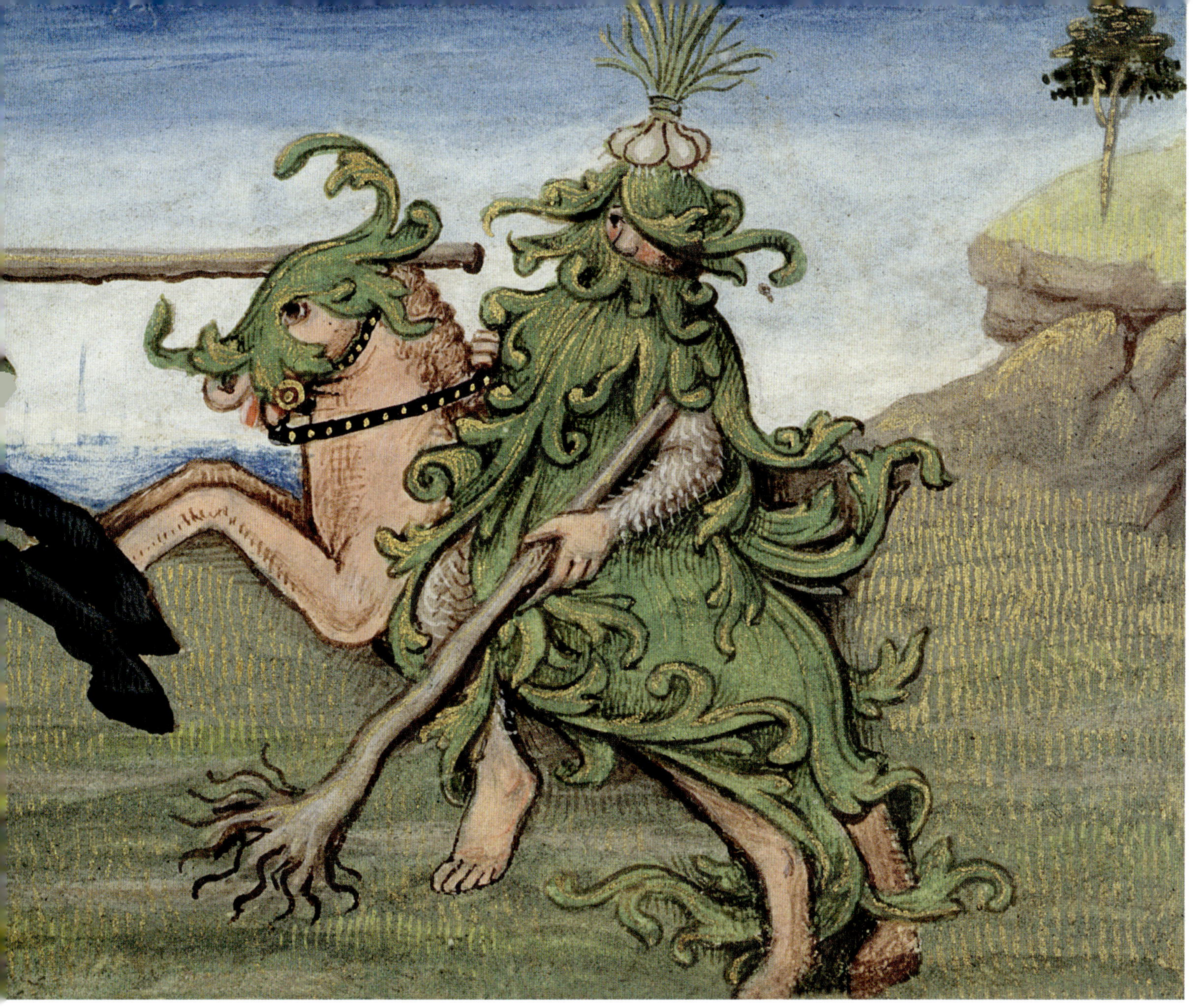

green. Such "wall-eyes" (yellow and green, but also blue and green, or brown and green) were considered particularly negative and disturbing in the medieval value systems. One should never, for example, mount a horse with two different-colored eyes; out of pure treachery it would throw its knight in the middle of a tournament

TWO SYLVANS JOUSTING IN THE MONTH OF MAY

Medieval folklore is rich in small beings associated with plant cycles and fertility rituals: spirits of the fields and woods, leaf spirits of the trees and hedges, elves and sylvans of the forest.

Miniature from the *Hours* by Charles d'Angoulême, illuminated by Robinet Testard, c. 1490. Paris, Bibliothèque national de France, ms. latin 1173, fol. 3.

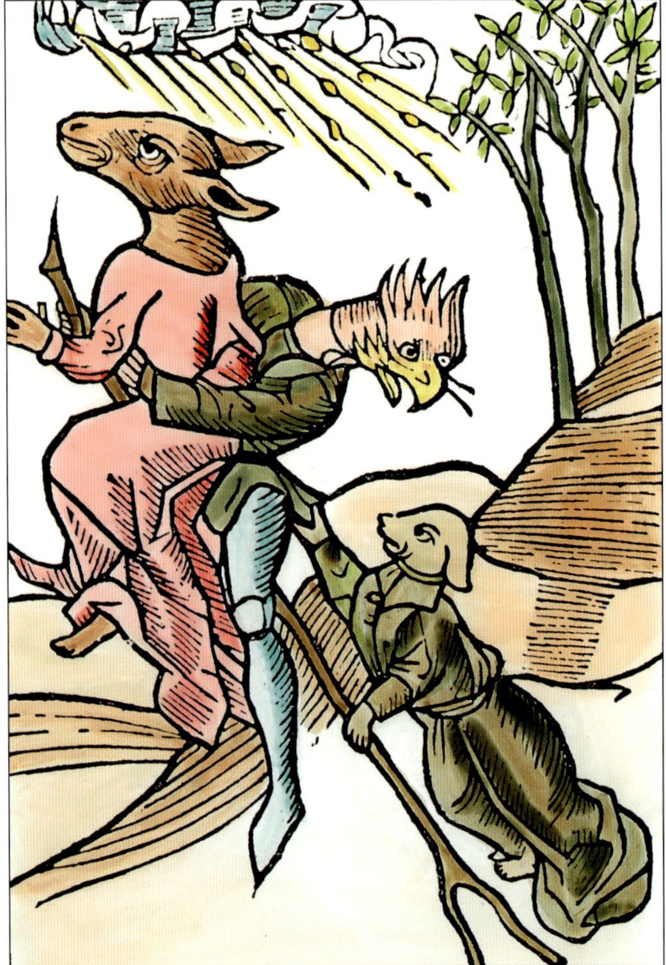

WITCHES AND WARLOCKS LEAVING FOR THE SABBAT
Witches maintain a variety of relationships with the color green; not only do they have green teeth and eyes, but they also often wear robes of that same color.

Wood engraving from a Latin edition of a treatise on demonology by Ulrich Molitor, *De lamiis et pythonicis mulieribus*, Cologne, 1499. Paris, Bibliothèque du musée des arts décoratifs.

or battle.[14] On the other hand a *cheval vair* (as opposed to *vairons*—wall-eyed), that is, a dapple-gray, was a good and beautiful horse, much sought after by princes in the late Middle Ages.[15]

The greenish color of witches' and warlocks' eyes was found again in the potions and poisons they concocted. Liquid or solid, the color here was poisonous, in the image of the ingredients that went into the composition of such products: toxic plants (yew, hemlock, belladonna, digitalis) and venomous animals (toad, frog, scorpion, viper). The toad was the star of the poisonous bestiary. Medieval culture disliked it and considered it "a frog condemned by the Lord to live underground."[16] All the bestiaries emphasized its ugliness, its foul nature, and its link to witches and sorcerers. A hypocritical creature, it participated in the sabbat dressed in green livery, whereas its natural color was gray, and it indulged in orgies with its cousin the frog, whom it detested and envied for living in the water.[17] Above all, its spittle, urine, secretions, and venom went into the composition of many potions and drinks meant to harm or even to kill. On the other hand, when dried and reduced to powder, the toad could have prophylactic virtues, attracting to itself the forces of evil and thus protecting the one who carried it enclosed in a small cloth or leather sack.[18]

The color green for poisons was relatively rare before the late Middle Ages. In the feudal period poisonous drinks or food were red or black instead. Hence the apple bearing venom that we encounter in many tales of chivalry (Gawain, nephew and heir to King Arthur, almost falls victim to it twice) and that we find again in the modern period in various fairy tales (*Snow White*, for example) is perpetually red. A green apple was not a poisoned apple, it was simply a sour apple. The dark or black brews concocted by the Devil's henchmen lost ground in the late Middle Ages and henceforth gave way to green potions and greenish ointments. Here, as elsewhere, the period was one of increasing value for black tones and depreciation for greens.[19]

The green knight

In truth, this negative dimension of the color green was not an invention of the late Middle Ages. It already existed much earlier. Green eyes, as we have just said, had long had a sinister reputation. Satan's green bestiary was already well established in representations from the Romanesque period, and witches and sorcerers did not have to wait until the fourteenth century to be dressed in green (let us recall here the figure of Merlin the Enchanter, an ambiguous character to say the least, who maintains close ties with green and greenery).[20] Nevertheless, as the Middle Ages came to an end, negative green seemed to extend its empire and enter domains where it had hardly exerted influence before. That was the case with Arthurian literature. In thirteenth-century romances, a green knight, that is to say a knight whose shield, tunic, or horse's quarter sheet were green, was often a young knight whose hotheaded behavior would be the cause of disorder. But, for all that, he was not seen in a bad light. On the contrary, recently dubbed, he sought to prove his worth, to earn a heraldic figure with which to decorate his shield—it was customary for young knights to bear monochromatic shields for a year after they were dubbed—and then to be admitted to the company of the knights of the Round Table.[21] That character disappeared in the following century. Henceforth, green knights became less common or turned into strange, disturbing figures and bringers of death.

The most famous example is found in an English romance from the late fourteenth century, *Sir Gawain and the Green Knight*. The text, written in alliterative verse, survives only in a single manuscript, and the author has remained anonymous. At most, a dialect from the Midlands region can be recognized in his language. The story begins at King Arthur's court at Camelot one week after Christmas. A green knight of gigantic

THE GODDESS FORTUNE AND HER TWO BROTHERS
Inconstant, capricious, unpredictable, the goddess Fortune wears a striped or *mi-parti* dress in images from the late Middle Ages. Here she is seen between her two brothers, as described by Christine de Pizan in her famous *Mutation of Fortune*. To the left, Heur (Happiness) is an elegant young man dressed in green and crowned with leaves. To the right, Meseur (Unhappiness) is a short-skirted rustic peasant whose raised club, ready to strike, is a bit unnerving.

Miniature from a manuscript of the *Mutation of Fortune* by Christine de Pizan, c. 1420–1430. Chantilly, Musée Condé, ms. 494, fol. 16.

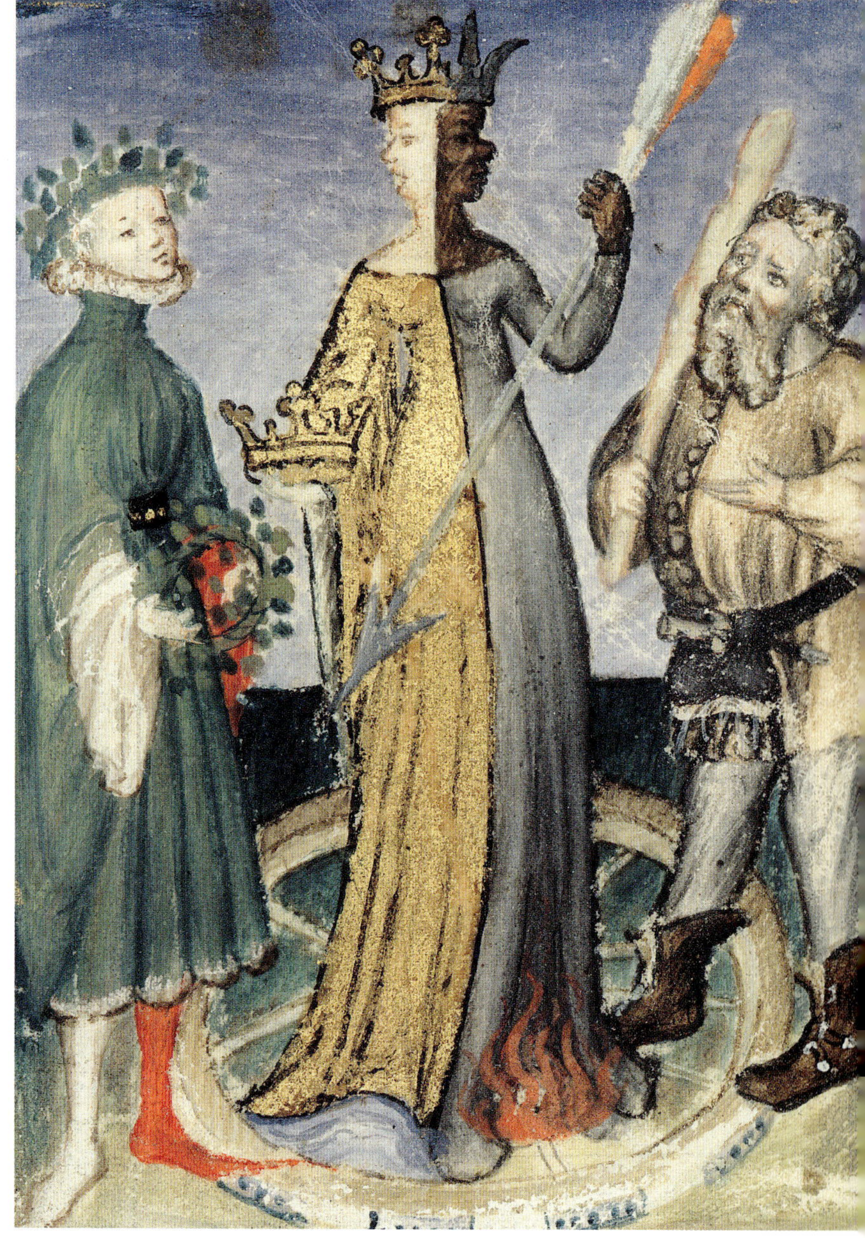

stature, armed with a battle-ax, presents himself and proposes a game: that someone take his battle-ax and strike him a blow, only one; he himself will return the blow a year and a day later. Gawain accepts this strange challenge. With a strike of the ax, he decapitates the Green Knight. But the knight retrieves his head and leaves, reminding Gawain of his promise: to meet in a year and a day at a place called the "Green Chapel." A year passes. Gawain starts out in search of the chapel and meets with various adventures. In a mysterious castle the wife of a lord who gives him lodging tries to seduce him. Gawain resists the temptation, accepting only three kisses as a token of love and an enigmatic green belt endowed with magical powers; the one who wears it is protected from death. Led to the Green Chapel, Gawain finally finds the Green Knight again. The knight is armed with a scythe, the instrument of death par excellence. Three times he pretends to decapitate Gawain, stopping his arm just in time and leaving only a small nick on the neck of Arthur's nephew, who is terrorized by what is happening to him. The knight then explains to him that he is the husband of the lady temptress and that this entire, cruel scene was dreamed up by Morgan le Fay in order to test the best knight of the Round Table. If he had been loyal and courageous to the end, Gawain would not have accepted the green belt. Disconcerted and a bit ashamed, Gawain returns to King Arthur's court, recounts his adventure and confesses his lack of courage at the moment of receiving the fatal blow. His companions pardon him and decide to wear green belts as a reminder of this adventure.

The reader is disconcerted as well. Everything in this story is strange and at odds with traditional tales of chivalry. A certain savagery and vestiges of paganism even surface at various points. They lead us to guess that the author combined many earlier legends and traditions to create an Arthurian work. The omnipresence of green poses a problem: what does it mean? We can perhaps understand the choice of this color for the chapel, isolated and inaccessible in the heart of the forest, and for the belt, a magic object and token of love. But what about the Green Knight, old, married, gifted with supernatural powers, and seemingly a victim or lackey of Morgan le Fay, enemy of King Arthur (her half-brother) and the knights of the Round Table? This knight is both terrifying and benevolent, violent and friendly, tempter and forgiver. His appearance especially is most unusual; not only are his weapons, clothing, and equipment entirely green, but even his skin is green, making him a supernatural being. Is he the Devil incarnate or one of his representatives? But in that case we have to acknowledge that he is not entirely negative. Alternatively, does he represent Christ—Christ the Judge—and the green belt is the crown of thorns? That interpretation would be going a bit too far. Must we thus see in him the more or less Christianized remains of an ancient Celtic divinity, a kind of spirit of the woods and forests charged with testing mankind? Is this the green of nature, vegetation, strangeness, magic, madness, witchcraft, or alchemy? Or all of that at the same time? The color has caused much ink to flow and, despite a considerable bibliography, has still not revealed all its mysteries.[22] In any case we have come a long way from the green of youth, beauty, and courtesy discussed in the previous chapter.

For my part I would like to see in this strange and threatening green the color of the goddess Fortune, often represented in late medieval images wearing a green or striped dress. By accepting the challenge proposed by the Green Knight, Gawain wagers not only his reputation but also his life. It is probably the green of fate that is presented here, a risky and capricious green that can reverse any individual's destiny for better or for worse. This "existential" dimension of the color green is very much present in fourteenth- and fifteenth-century documents, especially in literary works and illuminated manuscripts. Christine de Pizan, for example, in her *Livre de la mutacion de Fortune*, a long, octosyllabic, allegorical poem, dresses the goddess in a green and yellow robe—a two-color combination was itself a sign of changeability—and her brothers in two contrasting colors: green for *Eur* (chance, luck) and gray for *Meseur* (sadness, misfortune).[23]

The Green Knight of the English poem *Sir Gawain and the Green Knight* is not the only one of his kind. Other works originating in Great Britain present heroes of the same color and just as enigmatic. Thus, *The Greene Knight*, an English romance from the fifteenth century, also composed in the Midlands region, tells a

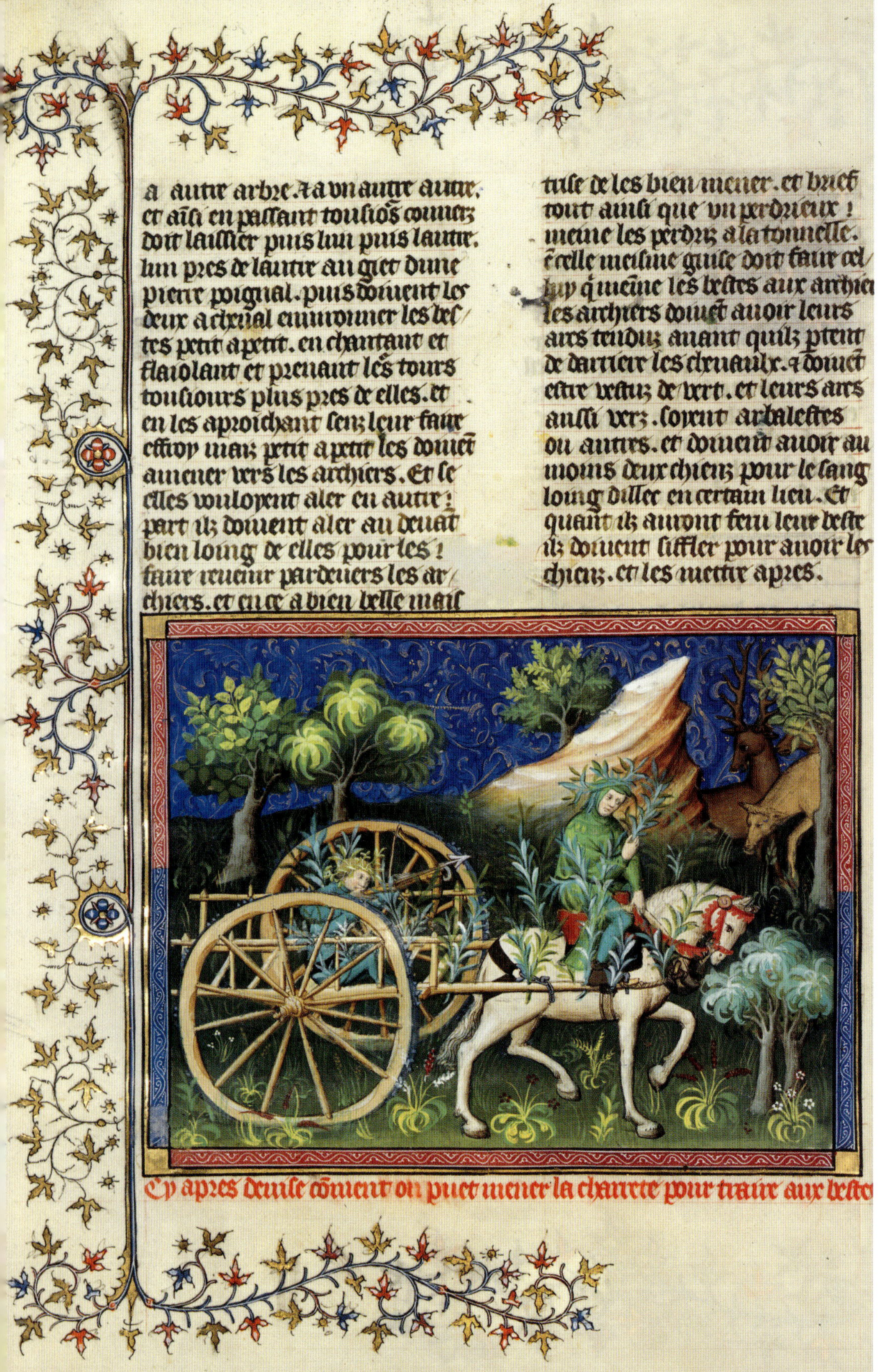

THE SLYNESS OF HUNTERS

Hunters often tended to be dressed in green, not only because green was the emblematic color of the hunt in the Middle Ages but also because it allowed them to hide in the vegetation. That was indispensable for approaching game as sensitive and fearful as the stag.

Miniature from an illuminated manuscript of the *Livre de la chasse* by Gaston Phoebus, c. 1410. Paris, Bibliothèque national de France, ms. fr. 616, fol. 114.

OPPOSITE PAGE:

INSTALLING TRAPS AT THE EDGE OF THE FOREST

In medieval images the forest was not always green. It became so at the end of the Middle Ages, and the illuminators endeavored to vary the shades of green by resorting to various pigments (earth greens, malachite, artificial greens from copper) and playing with the saturation of the color.

Miniature from an illuminated manuscript of the *Livre de la chasse* by Gaston Phoebus, c. 1470–1475. Paris, Bibliothèque Mazarine, ms. 3717, fol. 91 v°.

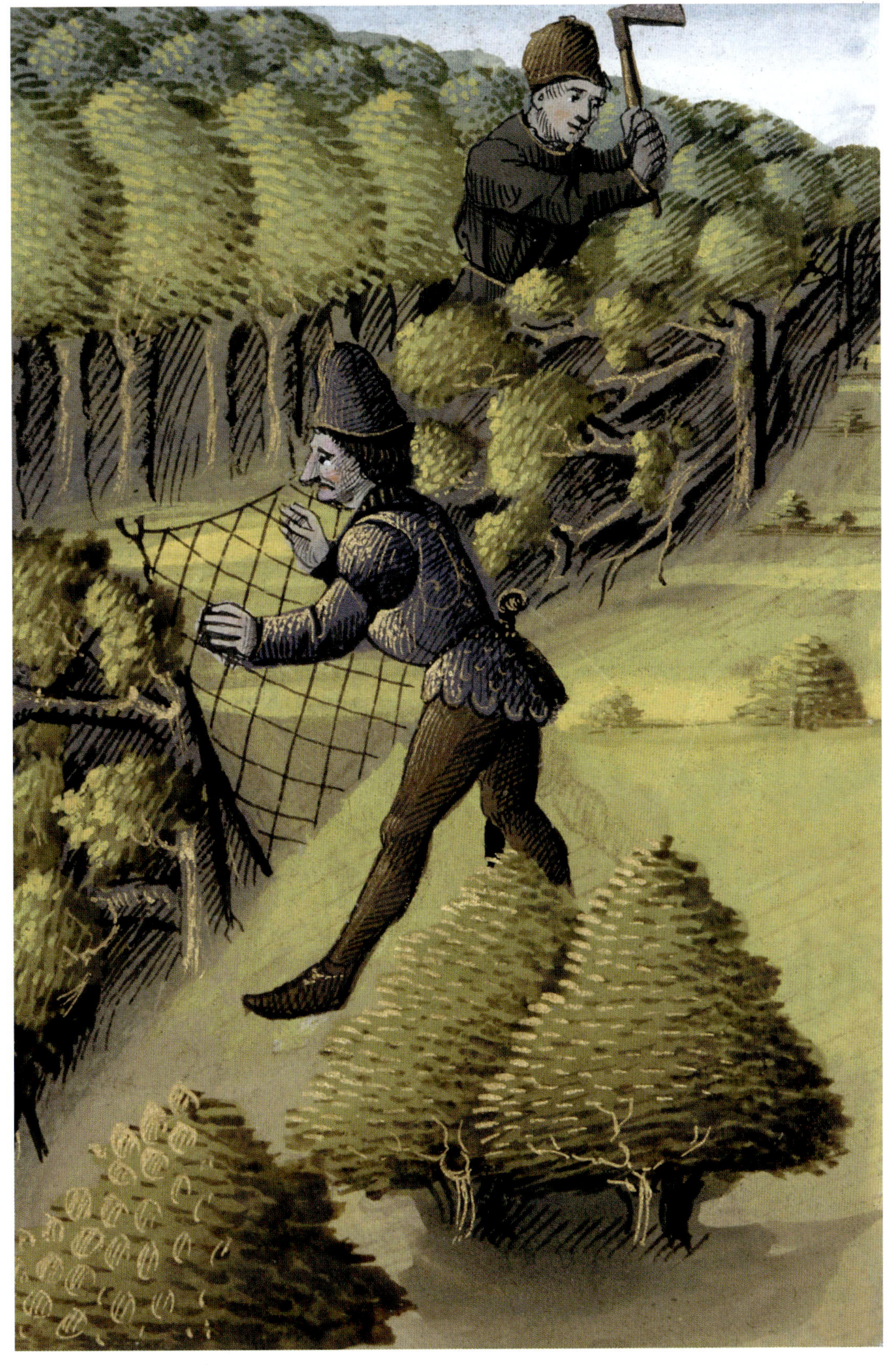

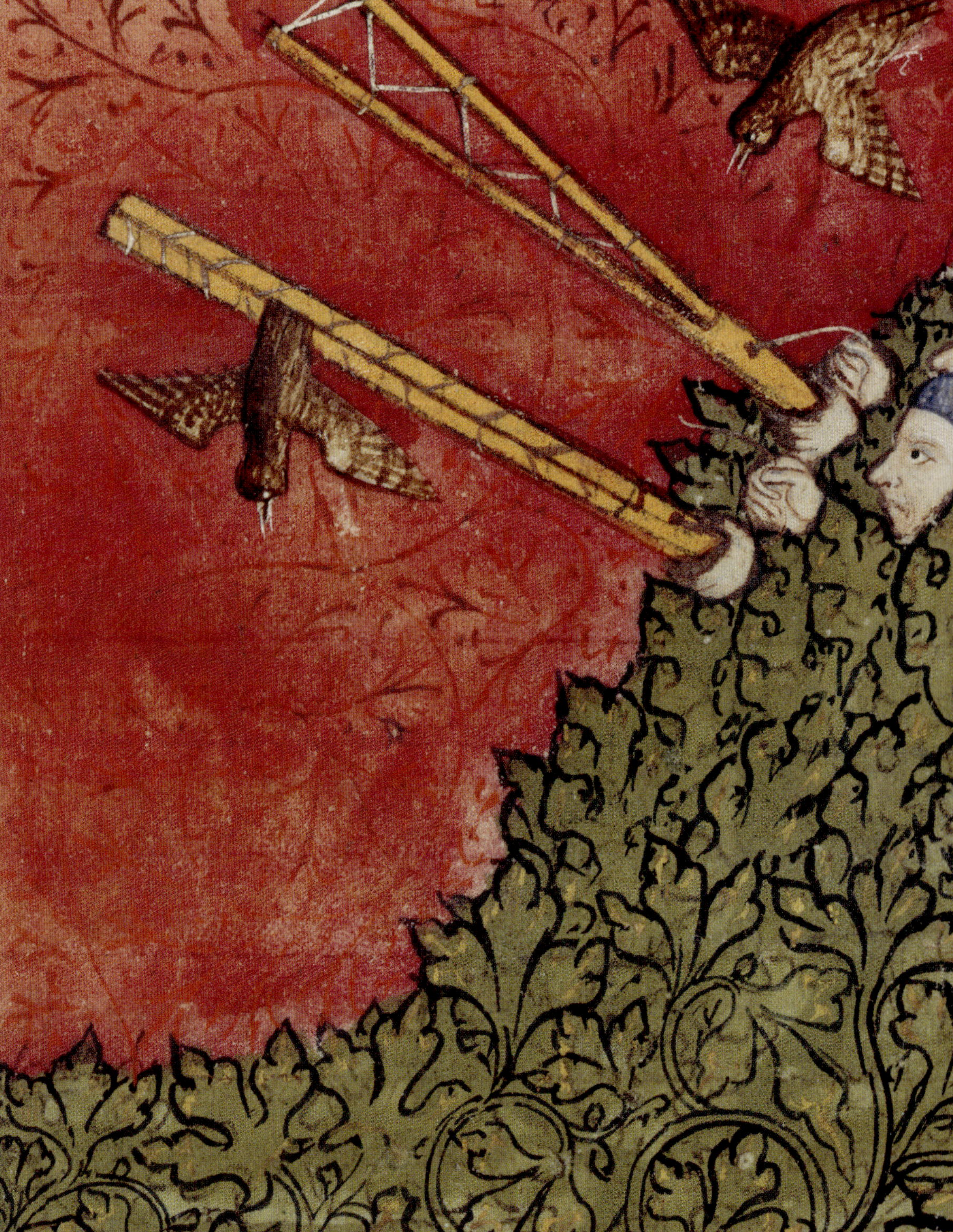

THE BIRD HUNT

In princely circles the bird hunt was limited to falconry; it was not the man who hunted but the falcon, the favorite animal of medieval aristocracy. Lower down the social ladder, traps and cunning were used to catch thrush, partridge, and turtledove. Here we see how hunters hid in a blind of greenery to snare birds with sticks smeared with birdlime. An owl itself has been caught.

Miniature from an illuminated manuscript of the *Livre du Roy Modus et de la Reine Ratio* by Henri de Ferrières, 1379. Paris, Bibliothèque national de France, ms. fr. 12399, fol. 93 v°.

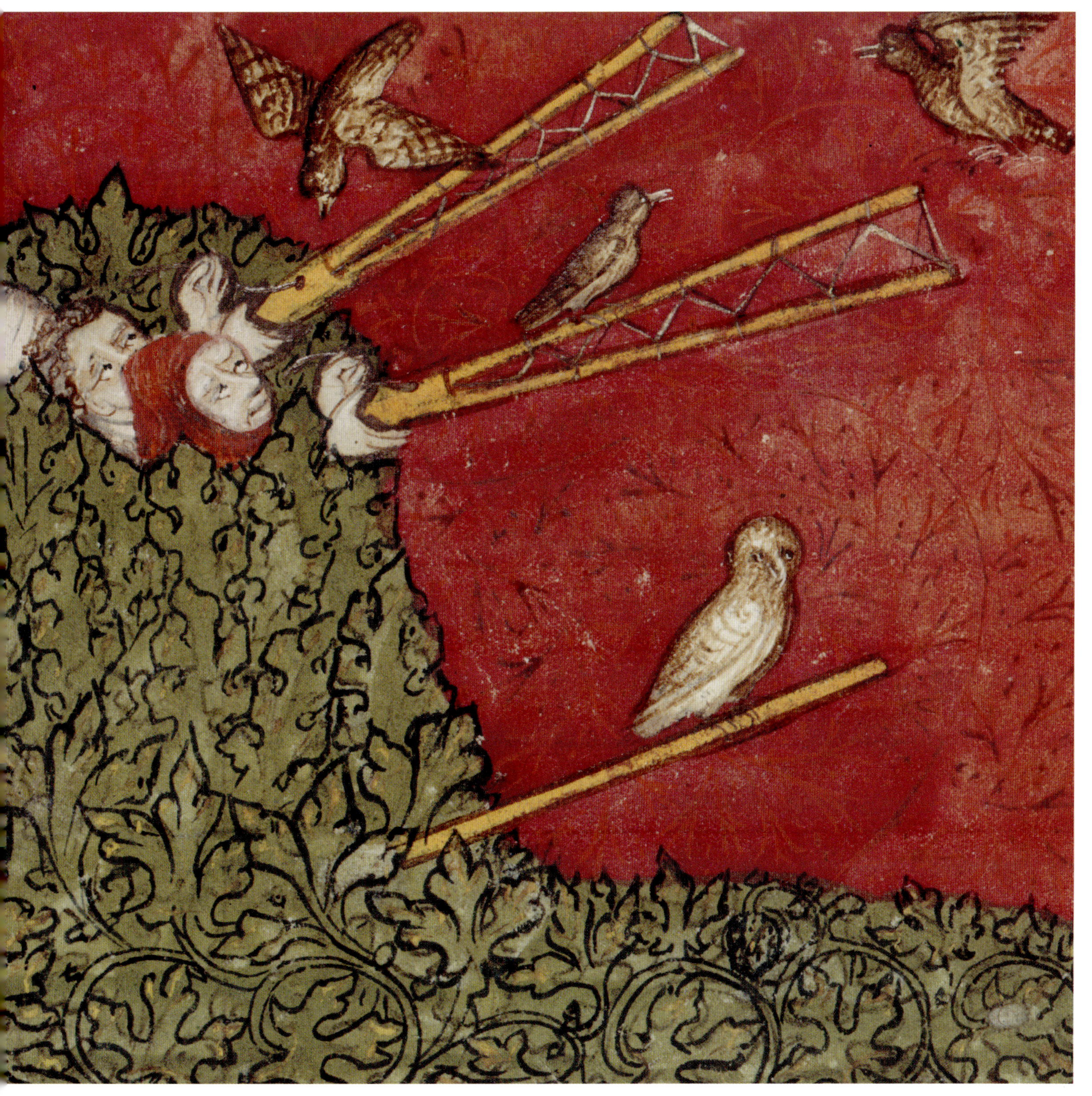

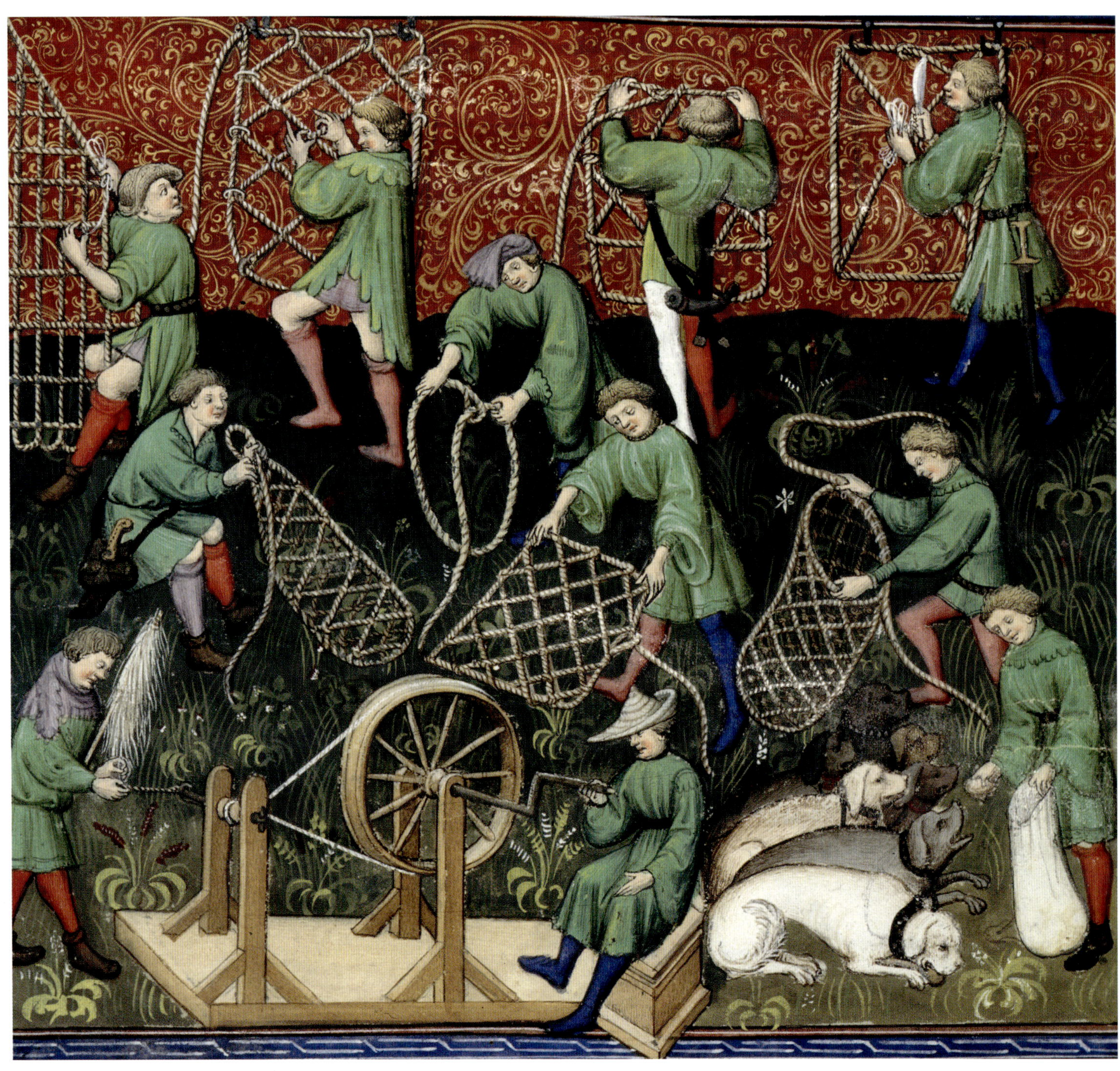

THE GREEN OF VENERY

Green was the color for huntsmen and their valets. It is present in every miniature of this manuscript of the famous *Livre de la chasse* by Gaston Phoebus, even when it is a matter of installing traps and not just chasing game.

Miniature from an illuminated manuscript of the *Livre de la chasse* by Gaston Phoebus, c. 1410. Paris, Bibliothèque national de France, ms. fr. 616, fol. 53 v°.

story similar to that of *Sir Gawain*. Also there are the fragments of a ballad, difficult to date and surviving in a single manuscript from the seventeenth century, *King Arthur and King Cornwall*. In both these cases the Green Knight is endowed with supernatural powers but is nevertheless the victim of a woman's treachery. Later, in the vast compilation by Thomas Malory, *Le Morte d'Arthur*, put together in the mid-fifteenth century and printed as early as 1485, we encounter another, even more formidable, Green Knight (*The Grene Knyght*). He is a false knight, the enemy of Gareth, younger brother of Gawain. His relative and companion is a mysterious Red Knight (*The Rede Knyght*) who is just as cruel and disloyal.

Among the distant cousins of all these green knights from literature, we must cite the strange and recurring "Green Hunter" (*der grüne Jäger*). This character drawn from the medieval imagination participates in disturbing nocturnal escapades in which the dead hunt side by side with the living, and infernal creatures with men who have committed grave sins or signed pacts with the Devil. These nocturnal hunts, which probably derive from Germanic mythologies, are attested throughout much of Europe as far back as the early Middle Ages. They are known by various names: "Wild Hunt," "Artus's Hunt," "Household of Hellequin," "King Herla's Hunt," "Wodan's Army."[24] Accompanied by howling dogs, the participants, dressed in black or green, pursued obscure game that they would never catch throughout the night. Their appearance was terrifying and the din that they caused unbearable. It was better never to encounter them if one did not want to be carried off toward death.

These dreamlike wild hunts, whose echo could still be heard in modern Europe—Goethe's famous poem *Der Erlkönig* ("The Alder King") is one of the last literary resonances (1782)—remind the historian how the medieval hunt was not so much a quest for food as a ritual in which loud racket was the essential element. That was equally true for literary hunts and for actual hunts. Any huntsman was a lord; it was his duty to make noise in the forest, to make his dogs howl, his horses whinny, his valets hoot, his hunting horn ring. None of this was permitted to the commoner. Similarly, he had to dress in green, or green and red, as these two colors combined formed a kind of chromatic music proper to the ritual of the hunt. Late medieval illuminations have provided us with much evidence of this, like those decorating the splendid manuscripts of the famous *Book of the Hunt*, composed in 1387–1388 by Gaston Phoebus, Count of Foix. Green is present there in all its shades in all the miniatures; it is the color of the trees and forest, the hunters and their men, the traps and disguises. It is a color simultaneously enticing and disturbing.

The dyer's vats

It is not easy to locate the reasons for green's depreciation in the late Middle Ages. They are probably multiple. One material cause, however, can be put forward: the difficulty of dyeing in green. What was possible to do in the feudal period no longer seemed so in the late medieval period. Dyeing had become a large-scale industrial enterprise and increasingly restrictive professional regulations hindered the production of certain colors. That was the case with green, which had formerly been obtained quite easily: in villages, with inexpensive plant colorants that produced dull, nonresistant tones; in towns, by immersing fabrics first in a vat of blue and then in a vat of yellow, a mixing technique unknown or unpopular with the Romans but common among the Germans and that remained in use in the West until the feudal period. By the end of the Middle Ages, everything had changed. Not only did customers demand solid, pure, luminous colors, but also in the cloth industry in large towns the dyeing trades were reorganized in such a way that mixing blue and yellow to make green was henceforth forbidden.

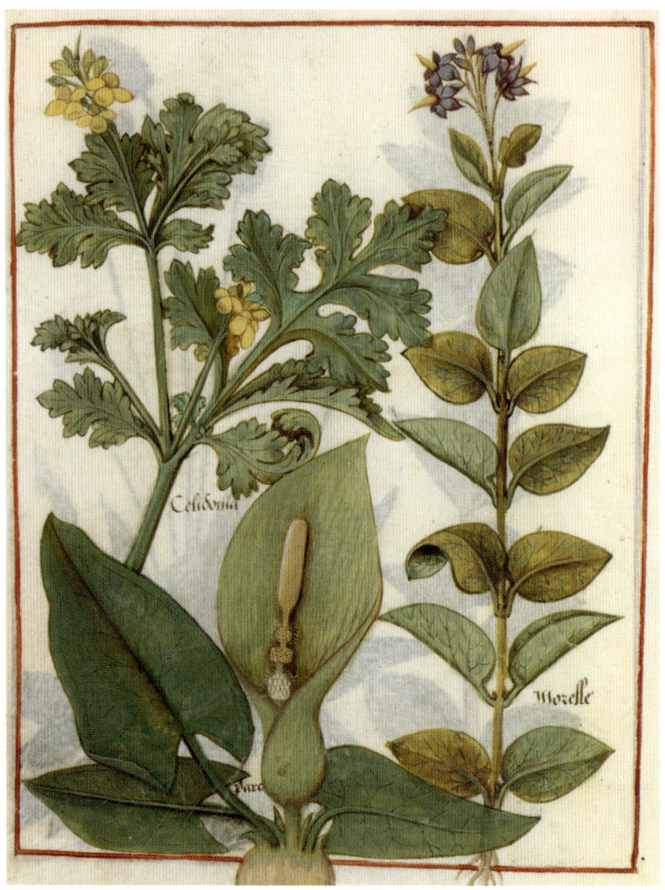

MEDICINAL PLANTS

Plant guides and herbaria became numerous in the late Middle Ages. Unlike bestiaries, which focused on the symbolism of animals, they were less concerned with the meaning of plants than with their medicinal, culinary, or tinctorial properties. Here we see a few leading plants in the pharmacopoeia: celandine, arum, and solanum (left); hemp, cabbage, and cardoon (right).

Miniature from *Livre des simples médicines*, illuminated by Robinet Testard, early 16th century. Paris, Bibliothèque national de France, ms. fr. 12322, fol. 138 v° and 171.

Canapa

Caules

Cameleunta
nigra

Indispensable to the textile industry—the only true industry in the medieval West—the dyeing profession was very much compartmentalized and strictly regulated. Many texts describe in detail how it was organized, where it was located in the city, the rights and obligations, the list of legal and illegal colorants. They demonstrate how this powerful, unruly guild was carefully supervised.[25] There were frequent conflicts that pitted dyers against other trade associations, especially the cloth makers, weavers, and tanners. Throughout, the extreme division of labor and strict professional regulations retained the monopoly on dyeing practices for the dyers. But other professions that did not have the right to dye did so nevertheless, resulting in lawsuits and court proceedings, hence providing rich archives of information for the historian.

Moreover, the dyeing trades were specialized and compartmentalized according to textile (wool, linen, silk) and color. Regulations forbade working in a range of colors for which one was not licensed. With regard to wool, for example, a dyer of red could not dye it in blue, and vice versa. On the other hand, blue dyers were often responsible for green and black shades, and red dyers for the range of yellows and whites. This strict specialization in the dyeing occupations hardly comes as a surprise to the historian of colors. It must be seen in the context of that aversion to mixtures, inherited from the biblical culture, that deeply permeated medieval sensibility and symbolism.[26] Its repercussions in social life and material culture were numerous.[27] Mixing, blurring, merging, combining were often considered demonic operations because they infringed upon the Creator's desired order. All those whose professions required them to do so (dyers, smiths, alchemists, apothecaries) prompted fear or suspicion; they seemed to be cheating with matter. Dyers were the primary targets, as is evident from the French play on words, common in the 1500s, that connects the verbs *teindre* and *feindre*, "to dye" and "to pretend." We find it again in English a few decades later (in Shakespeare, for example), where there is a thin line between "to dye" and "to lie."[28]

Thus dyers in the late Middle Ages rarely mixed two colors to make a third—and especially not blue and yellow to obtain green[29]—not only because of the taboos just noted but also because of professional compartmentalization: since blue vats and yellow vats were not found in the same facility, it was materially impossible to mix those two colors. A similar impossibility existed with regard to shades of purple; they were never obtained by mixing blue and red because the blue dyers were not licensed to dye in red, and vice versa. Medieval purple was usually obtained by

THE FEET OF SAINT ANTHONY THE MONK

Even in the seventeenth century, dyeing in green was still not an easy exercise; either the color did not deeply penetrate the cloth and gave it a faded appearance, or it held up badly to the effects of air, sun, and washing and turned yellow, brown, or gray. Some painters, such as Lorenzo Lotto here, tried to convey with their pigments the instability of the green colorants used by dyers and to emphasize how their use was limited to the least valued pieces of clothing.

Lorenzo Lotto, detail from *Reredos of the Holy Spirit*, 1521. Bergamo, Church of the Holy Spirit.

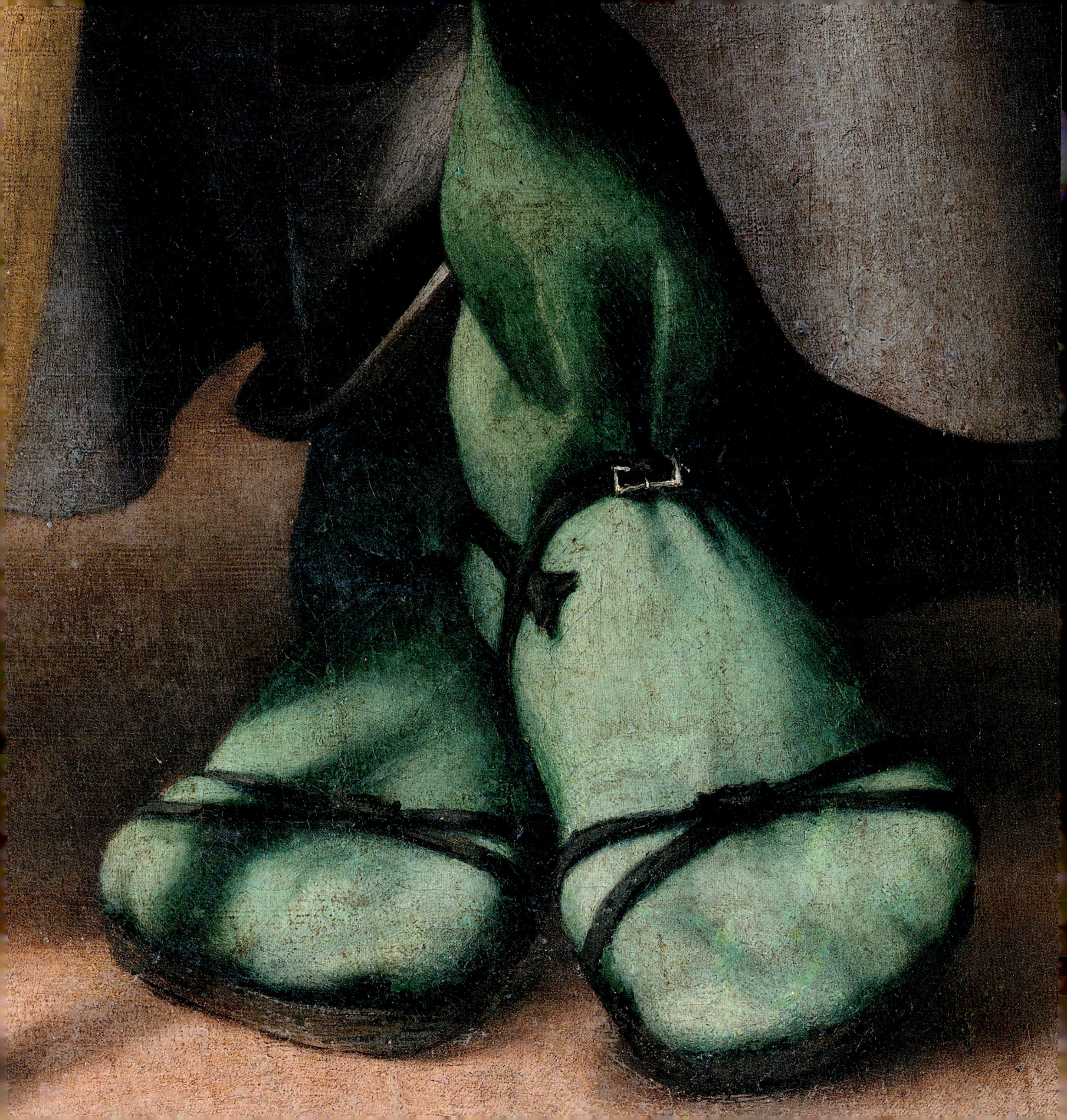

mixing blue and black. This color did not have a good reputation.

Despite all these difficulties, simultaneously ideological, regulatory, material, and topographical, medieval dyeing was able to be effective, more effective than Roman dyeing, which for a long time was only able to dye in red and yellow. Although the secret of true purple was lost, progress was made over the course of the centuries, especially in the ranges of blues and blacks. Only the whites and greens continued to pose delicate problems. Dyeing in a true white was almost impossible except in the case of linen, and even so it was a complex operation. For wool one often had to be content with natural shades, "whitened" outside with the highly oxygenated water of dew and sunlight. What is more, the white obtained in that way was not truly white and sooner or later turned yellowish or grayish.[30]

As for green, it was even more difficult to produce and to fix. On fabrics and clothing green tones were often faded, drab, and nonresistant to washing and to light. Making colors deeply penetrate cloth fibers, rendering them pure and luminous, and keeping them from quickly discoloring remained difficult undertakings for a long time in Europe. For most ordinary dyeing plant products were used: greens like ferns, nettle, or plantain, flowers like foxglove, branches like broom, leaves like those of the ash or birch, bark like that of alder. But none of those plant products provided a pure, rich, and stable green. The green hardly took, dissipated, and even disappeared on some fabrics. Moreover, the need for a powerful mordant tended to kill the color, which was often faded, never lively. That is why green was reserved for ordinary clothing and the common people. Sometimes for special occasions (a holiday or tournament), mineral dyestuffs with a copper base (verdet) were used to obtain more vivid and stronger tones, but, as in painting, those materials were corrosive, toxic, and did not produce a lasting dye. Following this process, which the theater continued to use until the seventeenth century, fabrics were more painted than dyed.

All these difficulties explain the lack of interest in green for noble and princely attire in the late Middle Ages. Barring a few exceptions ("the May," for example, which we have already discussed), this color was ordinarily reserved for servants and peasants. In the village, where small-scale artisanal dyeing was practiced using native plants as a base and mordants of mediocre quality (vinegar, urine), green was less rare than in the castle or the town. It could be light or dark, but it often had a washed-out look. Moreover, the light of candles or oil lamps sometimes added grayish or blackish tones to it, which made it a color not in high demand.

Geographical differences accompanied these social differences. In Germany, for example, beginning in the late fifteenth century, green clothing seemed no longer to be limited to the peasant class. Henceforth, the bourgeois and patrician classes enjoyed wearing it, as the great Protestant scholar Henri Estienne humorously noted, returning from a fair in Frankfurt in autumn 1566:

> In France, if one sees a man of quality dressed in green, one might think that his brain was a little off; whereas in many places in Germany, such dress seems to indicate his worth.[31]

This remark has not only social and cultural significance. It has a technical and professional dimension as well. It reveals that in Germany, earlier than in France, Italy, or the rest of Europe, the dyers ignored the prohibitions of the trade and resorted to a technique that their Germanic ancestors used: first soaking cloth in a blue bath and then in a yellow bath. This did not yet involve mixing blue and yellow in the same vat, but it was a dual operation to superimpose two colors. Professional regulations expressly forbade it, and the rigid specialization of the dyeing workshops prevented it. Nevertheless, German dyers did it, and not only in the 1500s, as proven by the analyses of preserved textile fabrics, but probably earlier, as attested by an interesting lawsuit involving a dyer in the late fourteenth century.

This dyer was named Hans Töllner. He practiced in Nuremberg as a *Schönfärber* (a "large-scale" dyer) and was licensed to dye wool in blue and black. In January 1386, probably denounced by several colleagues jealous of his success, he was discovered to have yellow dyeing vats at his facility, a color for which he was not licensed. Legal proceedings were brought against him, over the course of which he defended himself very badly, denied the evidence, claimed that the vats did not belong to him and that he did not understand why they had been transported to his premises. He was heavily fined, exiled to Augsburg, and banned from the dyeing profession, which his father and grandfather had practiced before him.[32]

No expertise in dyeing is needed to understand that this Hans Töllner, a specialist in blue tones—whose new popularity hit Nuremberg as early as the late thirteenth century—also worked in the green range. And not only did he dye according to the usual, often disappointing, processes using traditional products but also according to a much more successful method: immersing the cloth first in a vat of woad and repeating the operation several times in order to give it a solid *pié*—"foot" of blue; then immersing it in a vat of weld so that the yellow would combine with the blue to transform it into green. Depending upon whether one wanted a light or a dark green, the weld bath was strengthened or reduced, and a mordant was then used. This process seemed new at the end of the fourteenth century (it was described for the first time in a Venetian dyeing manual published in 1540), but it was, in fact, very old.[33] In 1386, the year of the lawsuit, it necessitated not only bypassing or violating professional regulations—as Hans Töllner did—but also knowing that blue mixed with yellow produced green. Such knowledge was not yet widespread at the end of the Middle Ages outside the circles of painters and dyers.[34]

"Gay green" and "lost green"

In the fifteenth and sixteenth centuries these technical changes were reflected in unequal results on both fabric and clothing. The old and most widespread processes still consistently produced dull, grayish greens. The new, less common processes sometimes resulted in very beautiful, rich, vivid, luminous greens. French vocabulary conveyed these distinctions with two colorful expressions: *vert gai* for the shades that were pleasing to the eye; *vert perdu* for those that were displeasing. These two phrases are frequently encountered in wardrobe inventories, accounts, and notarized documents, and sometimes in chronicles and poetic texts as well. Today they are often misunderstood or mistranslated: "light green" for *vert gai* and "dark green" for *vert perdu*. That is not exactly what is at issue here. *Gai* must be understood in its primary sense: "joyous," "lively," "dynamic." As for the adjective *perdu*, it expresses a dim, faded, unsaturated shade, but not necessarily a dark one.

On fabric, it was not unusual for a *vert gai* to become a *vert perdu* in a matter of weeks, as the color faded or discolored with time. For dyers, even for those who superimposed blue and yellow, the great difficulty remained that of fixing the color green. Whatever process was used, it was a color that "kept" badly—and that would keep badly until the eighteenth century. Hence the negative reputation that was often associated with it. It was a "false color," that is to say, an uncertain, changeable, deceptive color, simultaneously appealing and disappointing. *Il n'y a pas de fiance*—one could have no confidence in it—as an anonymous poet tells us at the end of the fifteenth century.[35]

Chemically unstable, green was associated symbolically with all that was changing and ephemeral—youth, love, beauty, hope, which we have already discussed—and with all that was false, treacherous, and hypocritical.

THE CHANGERS

At the end of the Middle Ages, green was the color of money, not only that of the coins themselves but also that of the baize on which they were counted, checked, or arranged.

Quentin Massys, *The Changer and His Wife*, 1514. Paris, Musée du Louvre.

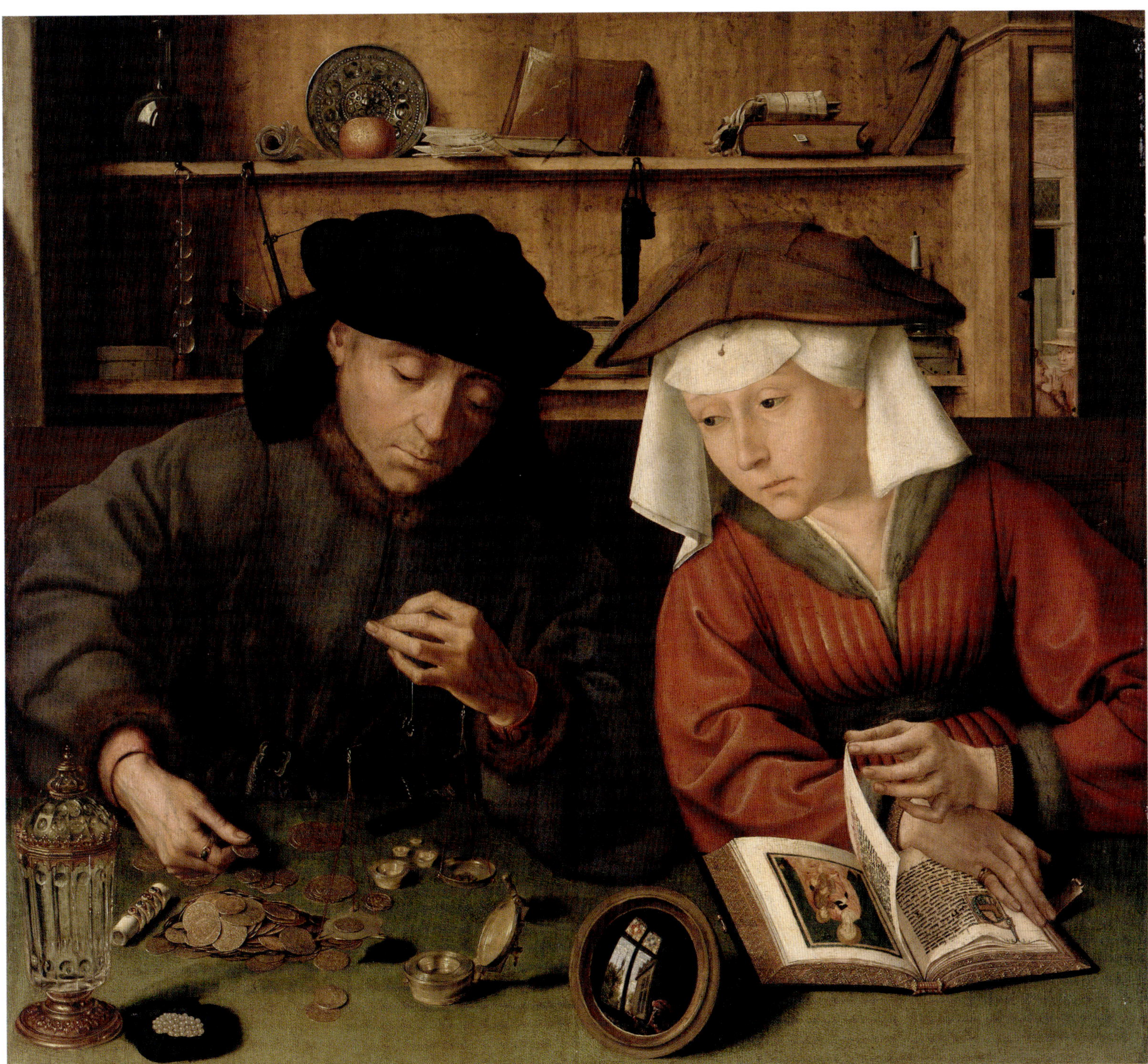

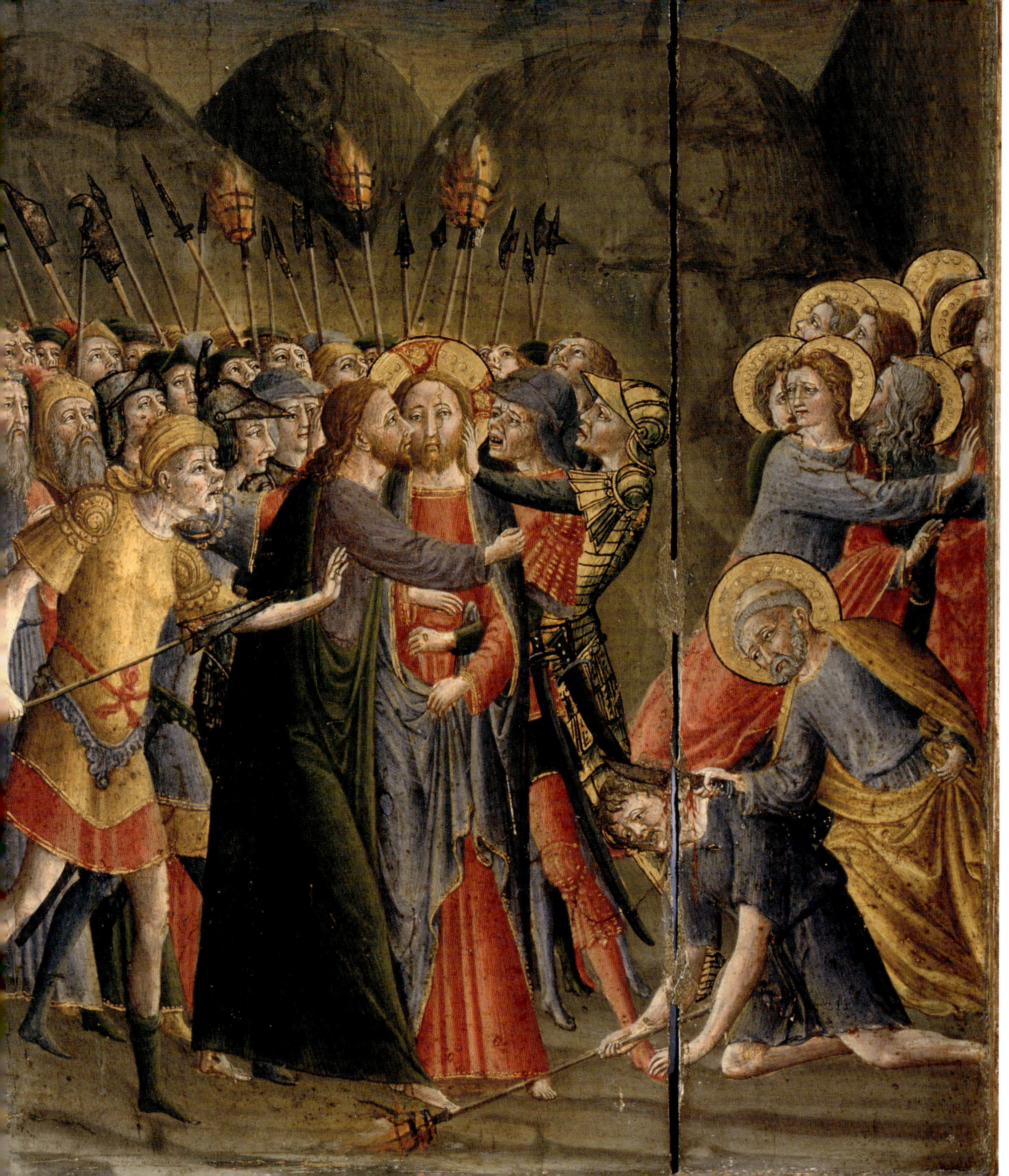

THE KISS OF JUDAS

The Gospels do not speak of physical appearance. But over the course of the centuries, medieval iconography gave Judas a repertoire of more or less numerous attributes: short stature, low brow, bestial or convulsed features, red hair, thick beard, black lips, absent halo. Added to them were the purse with thirty silver pieces, the stolen fish, and green, yellow, or green and yellow clothing. Artists drew as they liked from this abundant repertoire.

Lorenzo di Pietro (Vecchietta), *The Arrest of Christ*, 1445–1446. Siena, Santa Maria della Scalo Hospital, church treasury, inner panel of large reliquary armoire.

In late medieval images many negative individuals are thus dressed in this color. All of them have to do with inconstancy, duplicity, and betrayal. Middle French liked to characterize them as *divers*, a pejorative term that makes a pun of the name of the color. The thin line between *vert* and *divers* in terms of sound was even thinner in terms of symbol. To be dressed in green was to be ready to betray, to be a "turncoat" in the common modern French—or English—expression.

Judas is the most emblematic of all these traitors. In paintings and illuminations he wears either a yellow robe, a green robe, or a piece of yellow and green clothing.[36] But he is not the only one of his kind; other just as detestable biblical figures are sometimes similarly dressed (Cain, Delilah, Caiaphas), as well as some false knights from courtly romances (Agravain and Mordred, the traitors in Arthurian legend). These same colors are sometimes also found in the dress of various figures located at the margins of the social order or engaged in more or less lawful occupations: executioners, prostitutes, convicts, simpletons, buffoons, and even jugglers or musicians. They are not all systematically dressed in green or green and yellow, but they frequently are, especially in Flanders and the Germanic world.[37] In the case of prostitutes, their green clothing survived until the twentieth century in the form of the "low greens," ascribed by certain painters (Toulouse-Lautrec, Schiele, Matisse, Beckmann) to women who were free with their bodies and professionals in debauchery.

Falseness and treachery were not the only vices associated with the color green in the late Middle Ages. Within the system of the seven deadly sins, often present in texts and images, avarice was portrayed as green and would be for a long time. The palette for this group of seven was relatively stable beginning in the mid-fourteenth century and hardly changed in the modern era, as attested by iconology manuals and numerous color treatises printed in Italy. Pride and lust were red; anger, black; sloth, blue or white; envy and jealousy, yellow; avarice, green. Sometimes jealousy and envy could also be green, but that has more to do with language ("to be green with envy") than with color symbolism.[38]

The link between the color green and avarice is old and enduring. It offers the historian a long-standing record of the relationship between green and money.

FOLLOWING DOUBLE PAGE: AVARICE

From the fifteenth to the seventeenth centuries, in the systems of correspondences between colors and deadly sins, green was associated with avarice, and more rarely with envy. Envy was often yellow, while pride and lust were red, anger was black, and sloth was white or blue.

Enameled window in the graveyard cloister, early 17th century. Paris, Saint-Étienne du Mont Church.

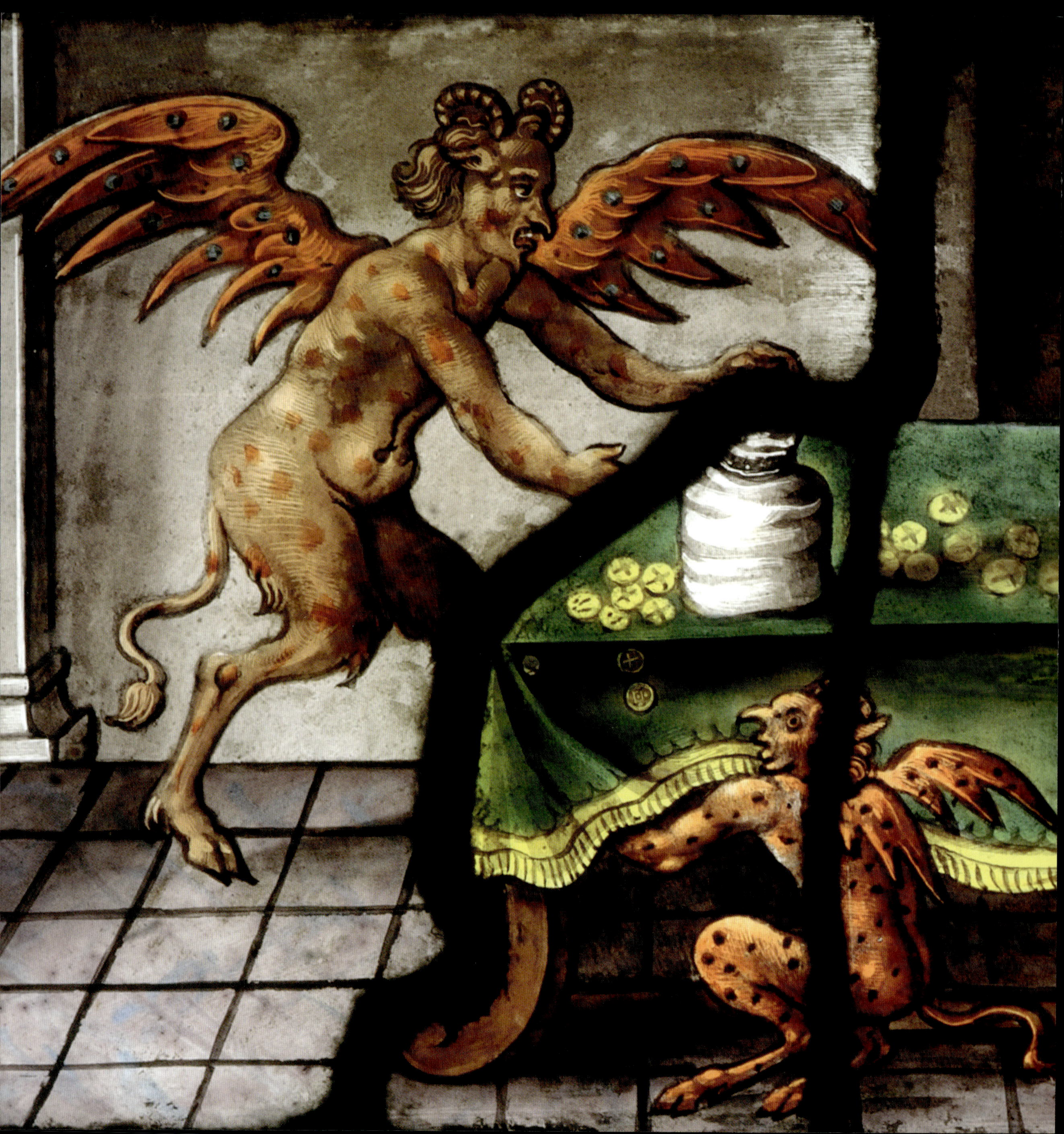

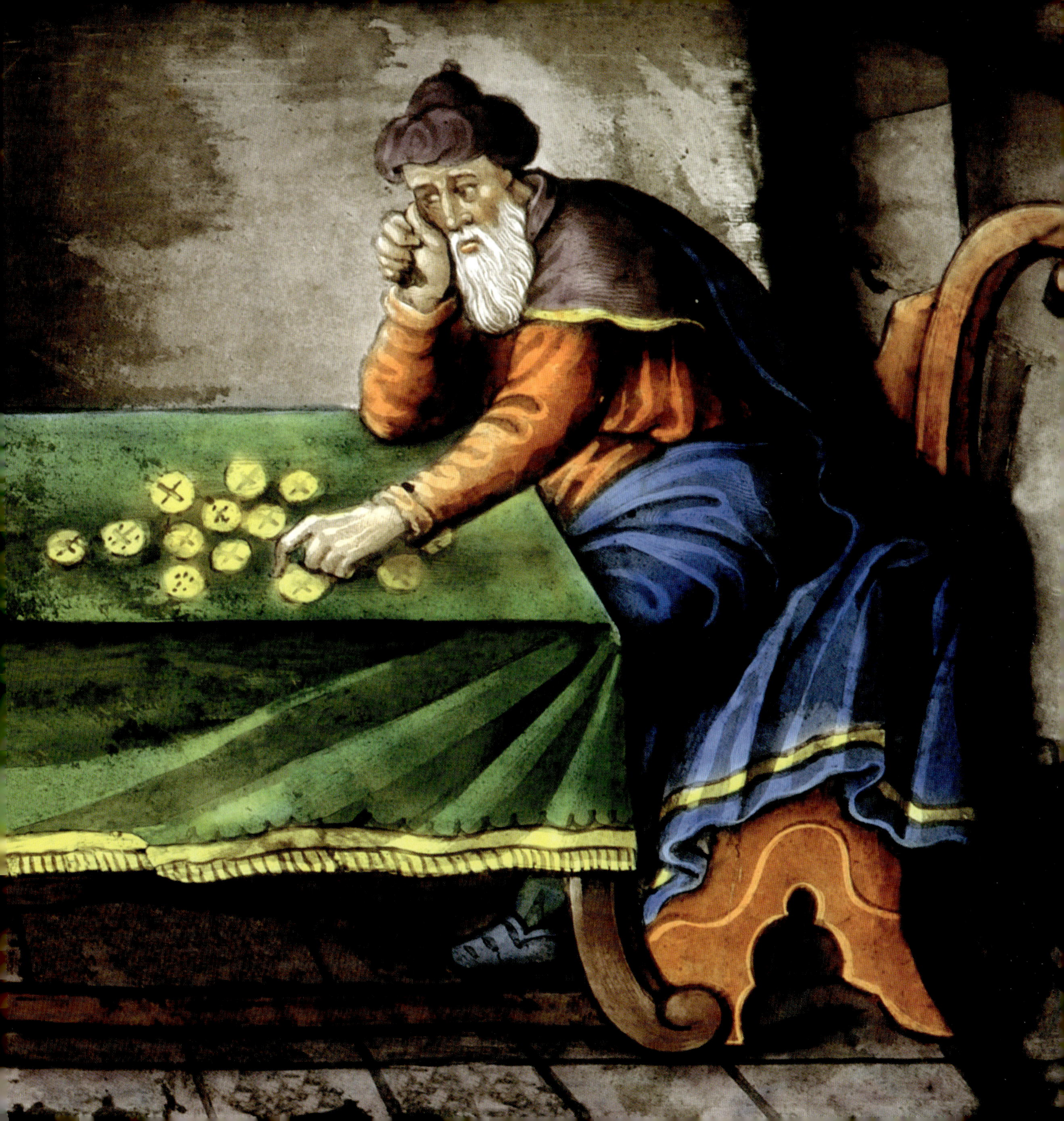

Well before the famous "greenback," the American dollar, appeared in 1861, green had long been the color of money and money matters. The dollar invented nothing in this domain; it only reinforced age-old symbolism. Consider the odd, infamous "green bonnet" worn by dishonest debtors and merchant or bankers who fraudulently declared bankruptcy. Its traces can be found as early as the fourteenth century; in many northern Italian towns it was the custom to put in the stocks dishonest debtors wearing the *cornuto verde*.[39] Subsequently, this custom was exported beyond the Alps (into southern Germany notably) and then dematerialized to give way to expressions for fraudulent or real bankruptcy: "to take the green bonnet," "to wear the green bonnet," "to don the green bonnet." La Fontaine provides an amusing example of this in his fable *La Chauve-souris, le Buisson et le Canard*, published in his third and last collection of fables in 1693–1694. This unlikely trio, the bat, the bush, and the duck, decide to pool their resources, venture into business, and "trade long distance." Unfortunately these are bad business ventures and soon

> There they are without credit, without money,
> without resources,
> Ready to wear the green bonnet.
> No one will lend them money . . .[40]

Many explanations have been offered to account for the color of this bonnet. For some, it is supposedly the color of madness; one would have to be mad to venture into such risky enterprises, break the laws, not pay one's debts. For others, on the contrary, the green bonnet is supposed to be a sign of hope; after failure and punishment the man who has gone bankrupt regains his freedom, bounces back, "turns green again." For still others green is the color of the wax seal and silk ribbons on the letter sending the debtor to prison; it is a "judicial" green. None of these hypotheses stands up to analysis, and it is simpler and more relevant to see this green once again as that of the inconstant goddess Fortune, mentioned earlier. Her wheel turns and takes with it all those who put their trust in her. The leap from Fortune's green attire to money matters was taken in the late Middle Ages or the early modern period, and green gradually became the color of money, debts, and gambling. From the sixteenth century on, in Venice and elsewhere, gaming tables were covered with green baize, the color symbolizing chance, the stakes, the ante, and the money to be won or lost. In the following century the rough, colorful language of card players, seated around a green table, was called *langue verte* in French. Later in the nineteenth century, that expression was also applied to various forms of slang, underscoring the link between the color and sauciness, even coarseness. *Verdeur*—tartness—henceforth belonged not only to the plant world but also to people, their behavior, and ways of expressing themselves. It became the antechamber of the uncouth.

Heraldic green

Let us return to the end of the Middle Ages and the beginning of the modern era. Despite its connections with a great number of vices and sins, the color green was not always seen as negative. Poets continued to celebrate the greens of nature, the works of the Creator, and "gay" greens: lively, radiant, admirable sources of joy and pleasure. They sometimes contrasted them to the greens that humans clumsily tried to make: pale, sad, unreliable, and more or less "lost."

That was the opinion of a herald well known in his time, Jean Courtois, nicknamed "the Sicily herald" because of his position, who lived until about 1437 or 1438. After having served various princes, he became the chief herald for King Alfonso V of Aragon. Toward the end of his life, he composed in French a curious treatise on heraldry, in which colors occupy almost the entire text, *Le Blason de toutes armes*. For the historian of colors, this is an important document, as are most of the heraldic works from the fifteenth century. Here is what Sicily writes regarding green:

> The last color found in coats of arms is green, which is called *sinople*. Because it does not have a place among the four elements, some authors say it is less noble than the others. . . . But if green is deemed less noble, that applies only to the green found in dyeing and painting, not the pure, natural green found in the fields, on the trees and in the mountains. Nothing is more beautiful, nothing so delights the eye and the heart. . . . There is nothing in the world more pleasant than the beautiful verdure of fields in blossom, broad-leafed trees covered in foliage, banks of the rivers where the swallows come to bathe, stones that are green in color, like precious emeralds. What is it that makes April and

May the most pleasant months of the year? It is the verdure of the fields, which prompts the small birds to sing and to praise spring and its delightful gay green livery.

It would be hard to better glorify the greens of nature. For our herald they were the opposite of the greens produced by dyers or made by painters. The green of the countryside, of meadows and woods delights the eye and the heart. Such an opinion was not remarkable of course; it was already present in Virgil and Horace, flourished again in the courtly lyric of the twelfth and thirteenth centuries, and reached its height in Romantic poetry. Similarly, making green the last heraldic color was not exclusive to the Sicily herald. All the manuals and treatises from the fifteenth and sixteenth centuries presented the colors in this hierarchical order and gave them their heraldic names: *or* (yellow), *argent* (white), *gueules* (red), *azur* (blue), *sable* (black), and *sinople* (green). This last color was "the least noble," as our herald says, but also the least common, those two characteristics perhaps being linked. Its frequency rating in coats of arms varies according to region and country, but it rarely reaches 5 percent, while it is close to 50 percent for *or* and *argent* and is even higher for *gueules*. All the same, *sinople* is not always listed last; when they wanted to make a group of seven, some authors added a supplementary color, *pourpre*, which they put at the end of the list after *sinople*. This heraldic *pourpre*, very rare in authentic coats of arms, bears no relation to the crimson of antiquity and had little value. It was not a sumptuous red but a mix of many other colors, a kind of violet or slightly dirty gray.[41]

Let us pause to consider the term *sinople* that designates the color green in the language of French heraldry from the second half of the fourteenth century on. It is a most unusual word and presents nearly insoluble questions for the philologist and heraldist. Until that time to name the color green heraldry simply used the word "green." But about the years 1350–1380 its lexicon changed. In documents composed in French (armorial documents, heraldry manuals, accounts of tournaments), the term *vert* gradually disappeared, to be replaced by the word *sinople*. The reasons for this change, which took place over less than two generations, remain mysterious. Perhaps we can understand how heralds, the first specialists in the language of heraldry—which they often sought to enrich or to complicate to make themselves indispensable—may have wanted to align the color green with the other colors and thus designate it as well with a special term, different from ordinary language. Perhaps too we can recognize that there was a possible confusion between *vert* (the color green) and *vair* (the gray fur); to change one of those terms would avoid that confusion.[42] So far so good. But why seek out the word *sinople*, a color term long used in literary language but that designates red, not green? The word's etymology leaves no doubt on this subject: the French *sinople* comes from the Latin *sinopis* or *sinopensis*, adjectives constructed from the name of a town in Asia Minor located on the shores of the Black Sea, *Sinopa* (Sinop today, in Turkey). In antiquity there were clay pits surrounding it that provided a red ocher of good quality and put to various uses: pigments, dyes, cosmetics, balms.[43] Sinop was the port of exportation for that ocher to the Roman world, and all the Latin terms derived from its name evoke the color red. Moreover, in modern French the term *sinopia* survived and is still used today in the fine-arts lexicon to designate a drawing or sketch done with red ocher chalk, producing effects similar to those of blood.

Why did the word *sinople* take on the meaning of "green" in the language of heraldry about 1350? Was some ignorant, priggish herald responsible for this

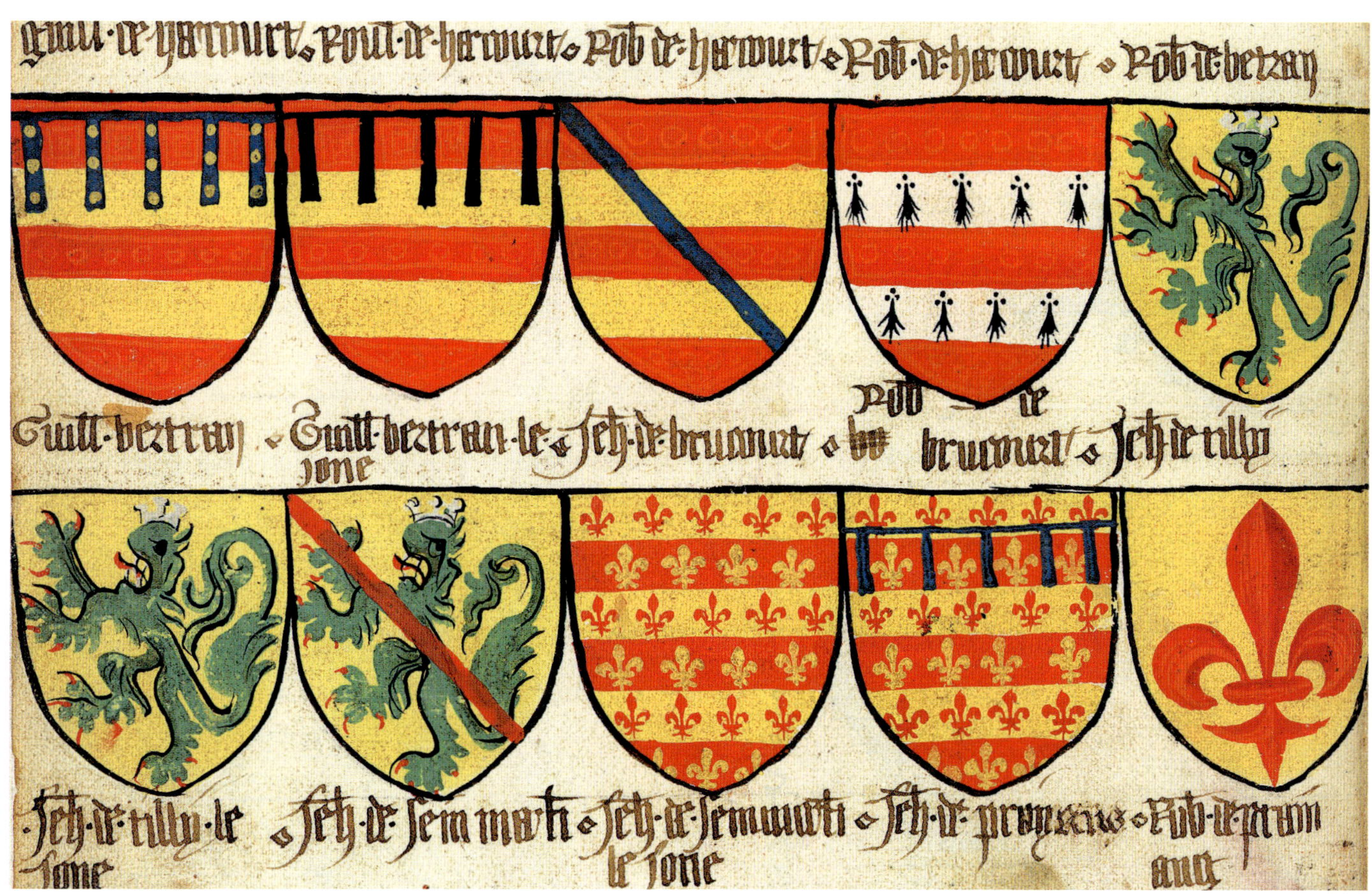

LIONS OF *SINOPLE*

Norman coats of arms in the *Grand armorial équestre de la Toison d'or et de l'Europe*, c. 1435. Paris, Bibliothèque de l'Arsenal, ms. 4790, fol. 64 v°.

change in meaning, immediately adopted by all his colleagues? Or must we look beyond heraldry for the reasons for this astonishing semantic mutation? Given the current state of our knowledge, we cannot answer that question.[44]

The Sicily herald did not know the old meaning of the word *sinople*. He always uses it in the sense of "green," never "red." It is true that he was writing in the years 1430–1435, nearly a century after the change in meaning. That does not prevent him from going on at length about the color green and trying to present it in all its most favorable aspects. According to the customs of his time, he thus proposed to his readers many correspondences between the seven colors of heraldry and other entities that also form groups of seven: the metals, the planets, the precious stones, the days of the weeks, the virtues. Green was associated with lead, Venus, emeralds, Thursday, and strength. This last association is somewhat surprising since we know the difficulty of making a dense, solid green. But perhaps it is the vigor of plants that was being evoked here? Hope, which we might expect to find corresponding to green, was linked to white according to Sicily; faith to gold, charity to red; justice to blue; prudence to black; temperance to purple. These correspondences may perhaps be understandable. On the other hand the link between the color green and Thursday remains inexplicable. Why was Thursday thought of as green at the end of the Middle Ages? And why was Monday white? Or Tuesday blue? Or Wednesday red? It is difficult to say. Monday was sometimes associated with the deceased, Tuesday with all the saints, Wednesday with the Holy Spirit. In contrast, it is easy to understand why the color black was attributed to Friday; the black of Black Friday was extended here to all Fridays.[45]

The treatise on heraldry by the Sicily herald enjoyed great success throughout the fifteenth century. So much so that in the years 1480–1490 an anonymous author added a second part to it, more elaborate and no longer focused on heraldic colors and the composition of coats of arms but rather on liveries, dress, and the symbolism of colors in clothing. The work then took on a more complete name, *Le Blason des couleurs en armes, livrées et devises*. It too enjoyed considerable success; printed in Paris in 1495, it was still in print in 1614. In the meantime it was translated or adapted into various languages (first Italian, then German, Dutch, Castilian). It had great influence in many domains, notably literature and art. Certain authors and artists followed it to the letter and presented characters dressed according to the color code proposed by this small work. Others, on the contrary, made fun of its simplistic symbolic system, which did not seem to be founded on anything. Hence, here is Rabelais on Gargantua's livery:

> Gargantua's colors were white and blue. I know well that reading these words you will say that white signifies faith and blue steadfastness. . . . But what tells you that white signifies faith and blue steadfastness? A book, you say, very little read, that is sold at bookstalls under the title of *Le Blason des couleurs*. Who wrote it? Whoever it was, it was prudent of him not to put his name on it anywhere.[46]

Sicily's successor did indeed propose colors for every social state and life circumstance; his choices depended upon the "virtues, properties and meanings" of those colors. He recommended certain combinations and advised against others. Green, which is "delectable to the eye" and which "signifies gaiety and pleasure" was supposed to be worn by "joyous and free" young men "in memory of the knights who in days of old went off to lead their adventures under this color" and by young women who were "betrothed but not yet newlywed." Once they were married, they were no longer supposed to wear green except on "belts, garters and other nothings." As for the very old, they were never to wear green, the color of youth, but rather tan, purple, and black. If one wished to combine green with another color, it was better to avoid red and blue: "blue with green and green with red are very common liveries and hardly at all beautiful." On the other hand "gray and green is a beautiful livery" and "green and incarnadine (pink) more beautiful still." Combined with purple, green signified hopeful love disappointed; with yellow, disorder and madness; with black, the sorrows of the world.[47]

Those are a few of the meanings our author attributed to colors and the relationships between them. His remarks did not rely on actual observation of practices so much as on heraldic, aesthetic, and purely symbolic considerations. That being the case, he is wholly of his time.

The colors of the poet

The end of the Middle Ages and the beginning of the modern era did indeed witness a flourishing of works devoted to the beauty, harmony, and symbolism of colors. Many of them remained manuscripts, sleeping silently in the libraries. But those that were printed, especially in Italy, became bestsellers. As an example, let us cite the strange *Del significato dei colori* by Fulvio Pellegrini Morato, published in Venice in 1535 and continually reissued until the end of the century.[48] Or again, the more classical *Dialogo dei colori* by the prolific Ludevico Dolce—a relative of Titian—published in the same city in 1565 and immediately translated into several languages.[49] Like others, those two works were authored by writers who were close to artists and were part of the great debate then raging in painters' circles: which was primary, line or color? In Venice, whether one was a painter or a writer, primacy was always given to color. Venetian to the tip of his pen, Morato explains that the eye is more important than the mind and that the beauty of colors prevails not only over the perfection of the line but even over the meanings attributed to them. Thus he recommends to his painter friends many combinations specifically meant to produce pleasure for the eye and the senses. According to him the most beautiful combinations were black with white, blue with orange, gray with fawn, light green with flesh color, and dark green with "Sienna brown."[50]

In France in about the 1500s, the discourse on colors remained more theoretical than aesthetic. The symbolism of heraldry and devices still exerted a strong influence on artistic and literary works. The colors constituted language more than harmony. Always *senefiantes*—meaningful—they were associated with vices and virtues, feelings and emotions, age groups and social categories, moral intentions and rules for living. Literature and painting were subject to the codes that governed them.

An elegant poem by Jean Robertet (circa 1435–1502), completed at the end of the fifteenth century and entitled *L'Exposition des couleurs*, provides us with both a key and exemplary evidence. The author was a senior civil servant; after first serving the dukes of Bourbon, he then served the kings of France, Louis XI, Charles VIII, and Louis XII, filling various diplomatic and administrative positions. But he was also a first-rate writer, a friend of Charles d'Orléans, Georges Chastellain, and Jean Molinet, a translator of Petrarch, and a poet himself, participating in most of the literary ventures of his time. He was considered one of the most skillful rhetoricians of the French court.[51] *L'Exposition des couleurs* is not his most original work, but it is a well-written poem that is relevant to our subject on many accounts. Made up of ten quatrains and an envoi, it reviews nine colors, sets out their principal characteristics, highlights the links between them, lists the vices and virtues attributed to them, and concludes by connecting them with a moral or social type. In order, these nine colors are: white, blue, red, gray, green, yellow, purple, tan, and black. The tenth quatrain is devoted to the *riolépiolé*, a pattern of red, black, and white stripes. It was the color of the "*Faux-Semblant*," that is, of hypocrites.

The order in which the colors are presented is not insignificant but hierarchical. First comes white, symbolic of humility and modesty; then blue, which signifies loyalty and thus must be placed very close to white. Red—formerly the most beautiful of the colors, the color "par excellence"—only ranks third here; it is the color of victory and glory but also of pride; unlike white and blue it is not entirely positive. Gray in fourth place seems surprising unless we consider that the fifteenth century was a period of great promotion for gray; often presented in contrast to black, the color of affliction, it was always seen as positive and the bearer of hope.[52] At the end of the Middle Ages, many poets composed verses expressing their high regard for it, beginning with Charles d'Orléans, who wrote a lovely poem entitled *Le gris de l'espoir* about 1430 when he was a prisoner in England.[53]

After gray comes green. Jean Robertet placed it in the middle of his palette and made it not a color of hope but of joy:

> Vert:
> À l'esmeraulde ressemble precieuse,
> Me delectant en parfaicte verdeur;
> Mal seant avec noire couleur,
> Et n'appartiens qu'à personne joyeuse."
>
> (Green:
> I resemble the precious emerald,
> Finding my pleasure in the greatest verdure;
> It is not suitable to combine me with black,
> And I only belong to someone joyous.)

Proposing the emerald as a referent for green is obviously a great cliché. In the first century CE, Pliny's *Natural History* had already done so. But here it is a referent that bestows value, perhaps more so than grass or leaves would have. At the end of the Middle Ages, precious stones were held in high esteem, the emerald and the diamond in particular. Similarly, to underscore that green used in livery or devices was only suitable for someone joyous is not at all original. That allows us to understand that green is a young, lively, gay, dynamic color, all very commonplace characteristics. On the other hand to maintain that green and black is not a good combination is more unusual. Nevertheless,

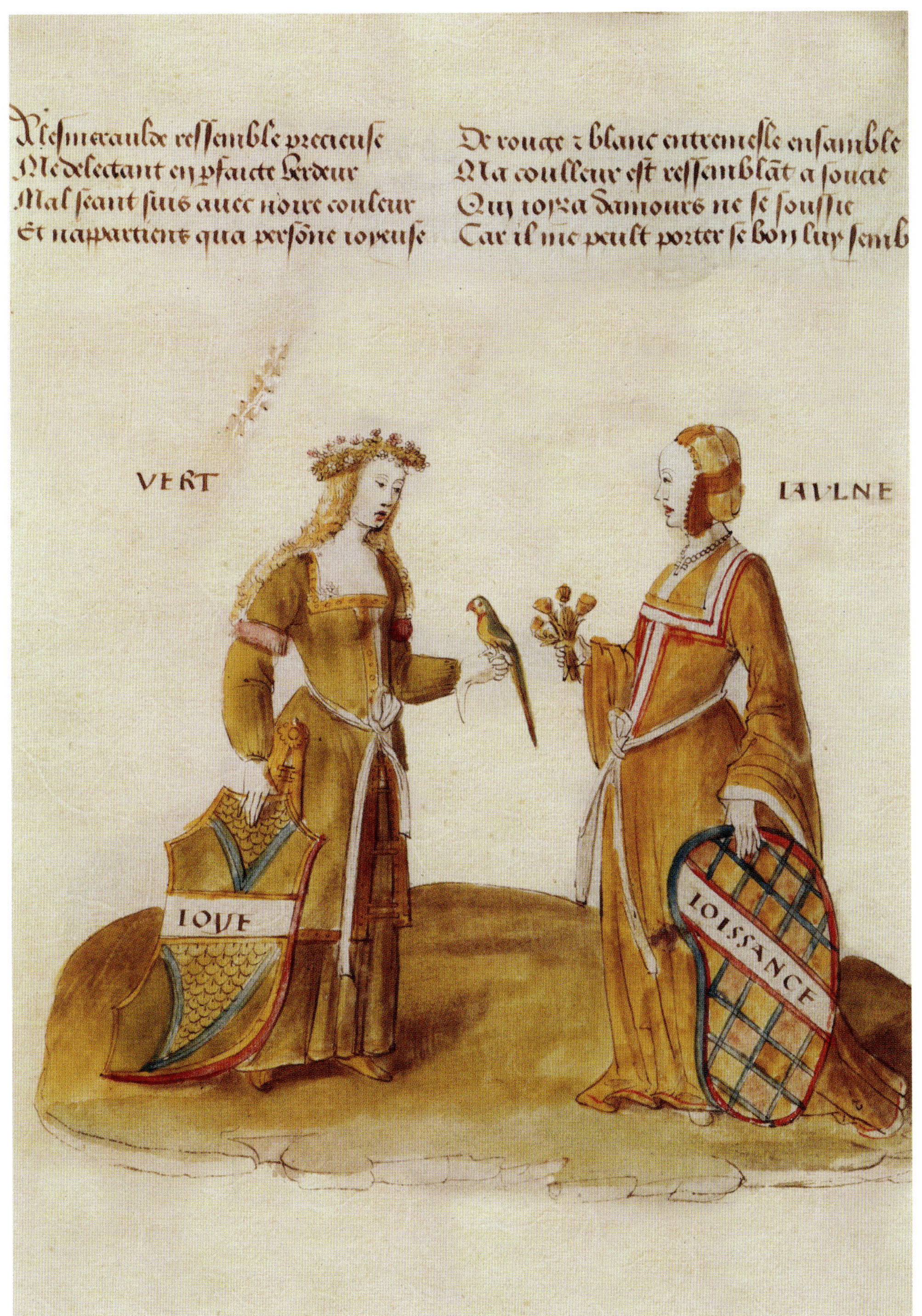

ALLEGORICAL PERSONIFICATIONS OF GREEN AND YELLOW

In literary symbolism in the 1500s, all colors were ambivalent and sometimes associated with vices, sometimes with virtues. When it was seen as positive, green embodied joy, beauty, love, and hope. For its part yellow represented prosperity, riches, and pleasure in the worldly possessions.

Watercolor illustration accompanying the poem by Jean Robertet, *L'Exposition des couleurs*, from an early 14th-century manuscript. Paris, Bibliothèque national de France, ms. fr. 24461, fol. 111.

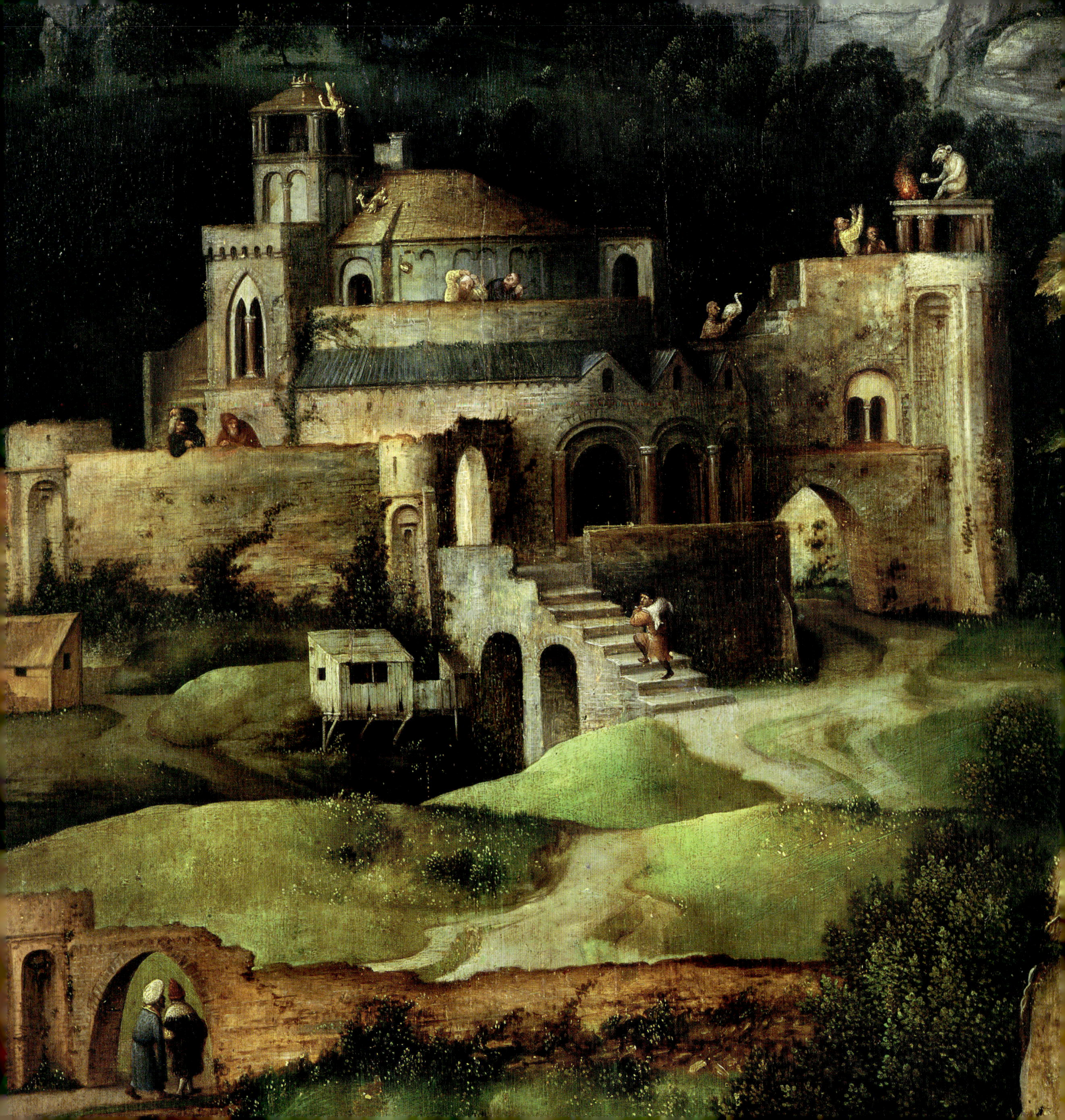

Robertet is not the only one to make such a remark. In the same period the Sicily herald's successor saw in the juxtaposition of green and black the expression of all the sorrows of the world. But neither he nor Robertet specify the reasons for its bad reputation. Why would green and black not go well together? Located at the center of the color axis, is green too distant from black to be superimposed or juxtaposed with it? Or, on the contrary, from the heraldic or emblematic perspective, is it too close? It is difficult to say, as the casuistry of color symbolism at the dawn of the modern era is very far removed from our own logic.

After green come four colors that are more negative than positive. Yellow, a sign of pleasure and unconcern, was ambivalent or even ambiguous; purple, worn by traitors, in the image of Ganelon in *The Song of Roland* ("*Vestu en fut le traistre Ganellon*"), was the color of infamy. Like most of the authors of his time, Jean Robertet considers these two colors mixed colors; yellow was a mix of red and white ("*De rouge et blanc entremeslez ensemble*") and purple, a mix of black and blue. Such definitions may surprise us, but we must remember that in the 1500s the spectrum was unknown (and remained so until Newton's discoveries) and that the Aristotelian order of colors still consistently constituted the basic classification: white-yellow-red-green-blue-purple-black. Green, as in our poem, was located at the center of the axis, and yellow found its place between white and red. Robertet invented nothing here.

After purple came *tanné*, fawn colored or dark russet, which the Sicily herald's anonymous successor presented as "the ugliest of all the colors." Robertet does not go that far but he considers *tanné* a changeable, unreliable color, full of uncertainty and worry ("*je porte ennuy en couverte pençée*"). Finally, black, assigned the next-to-last position, just ahead of the strange "*riolépiolé*," is completely negative; unpleasant, sad, obscure, violent, a sign of mourning, anger, or melancholy (then considered a disease), it was disliked by everyone. We are very far here from the majestic, luxurious black that was generally in fashion in the courts of the late Middle Ages.

Jean Robertet ends his poem with an envoi; he invites each prince to construct his "device" according to the colors of his choice, and we learn that he himself has opted for white and blue . . . as Rabalais did for Gargantua a few decades later.[54]

PATINIR'S DREAMLIKE GREENS

Joachim Patinir was a tremendous painter of blues, of strange, distant blue waves that he put in the background of his paintings, inviting the viewer into travels, dreams, or melancholy. But he was also a great painter of greens that are just as mysterious and sometimes disturbing.

Joachim Patinir, *The Rest of the Holy Family*, detail, c. 1520. Madrid, Museo del Prado.

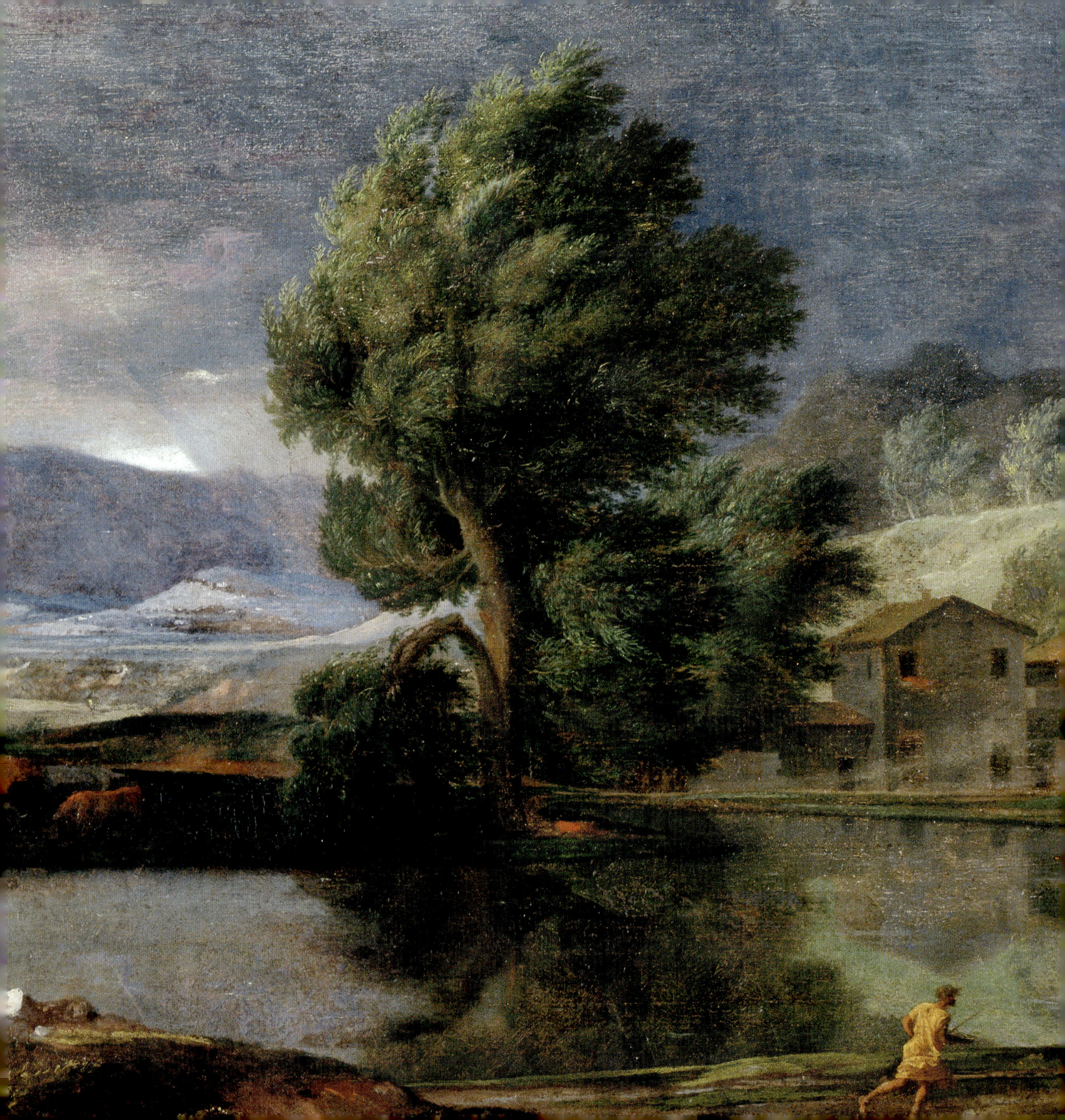

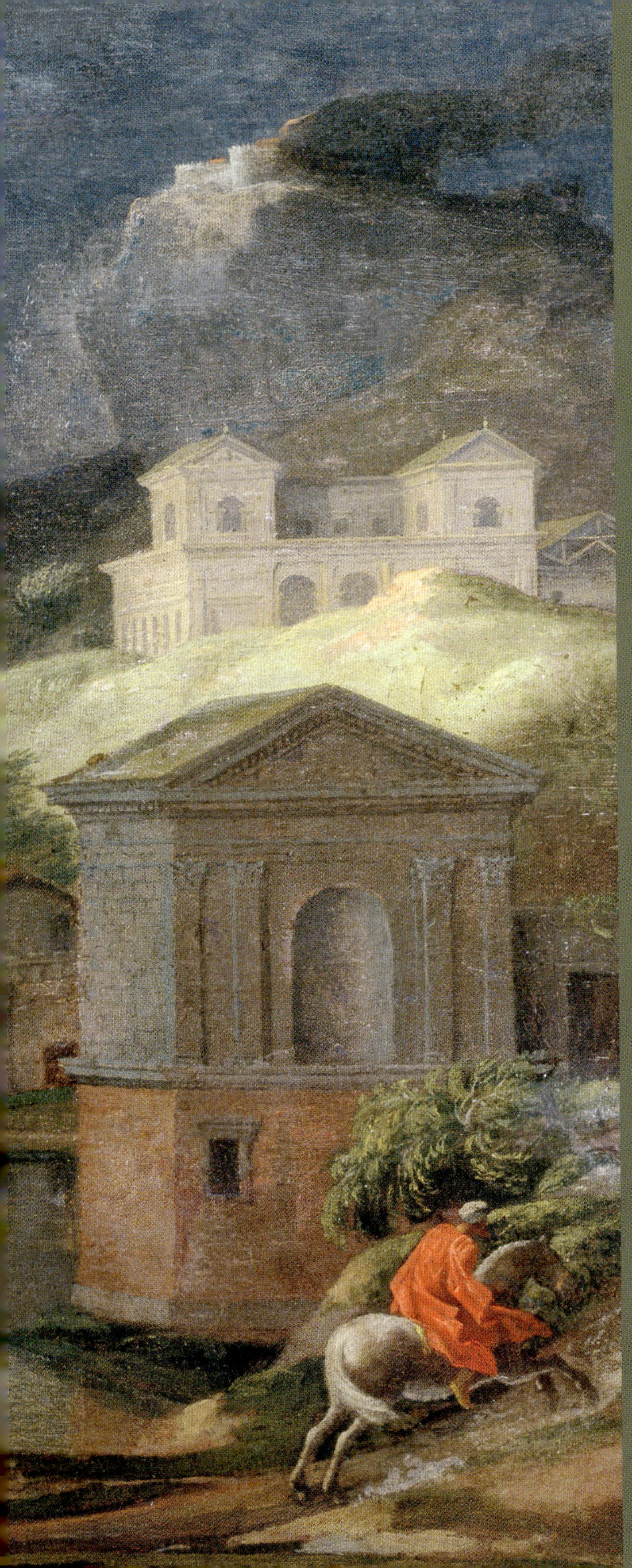

A **secondary** color

16TH–19TH CENTURIES

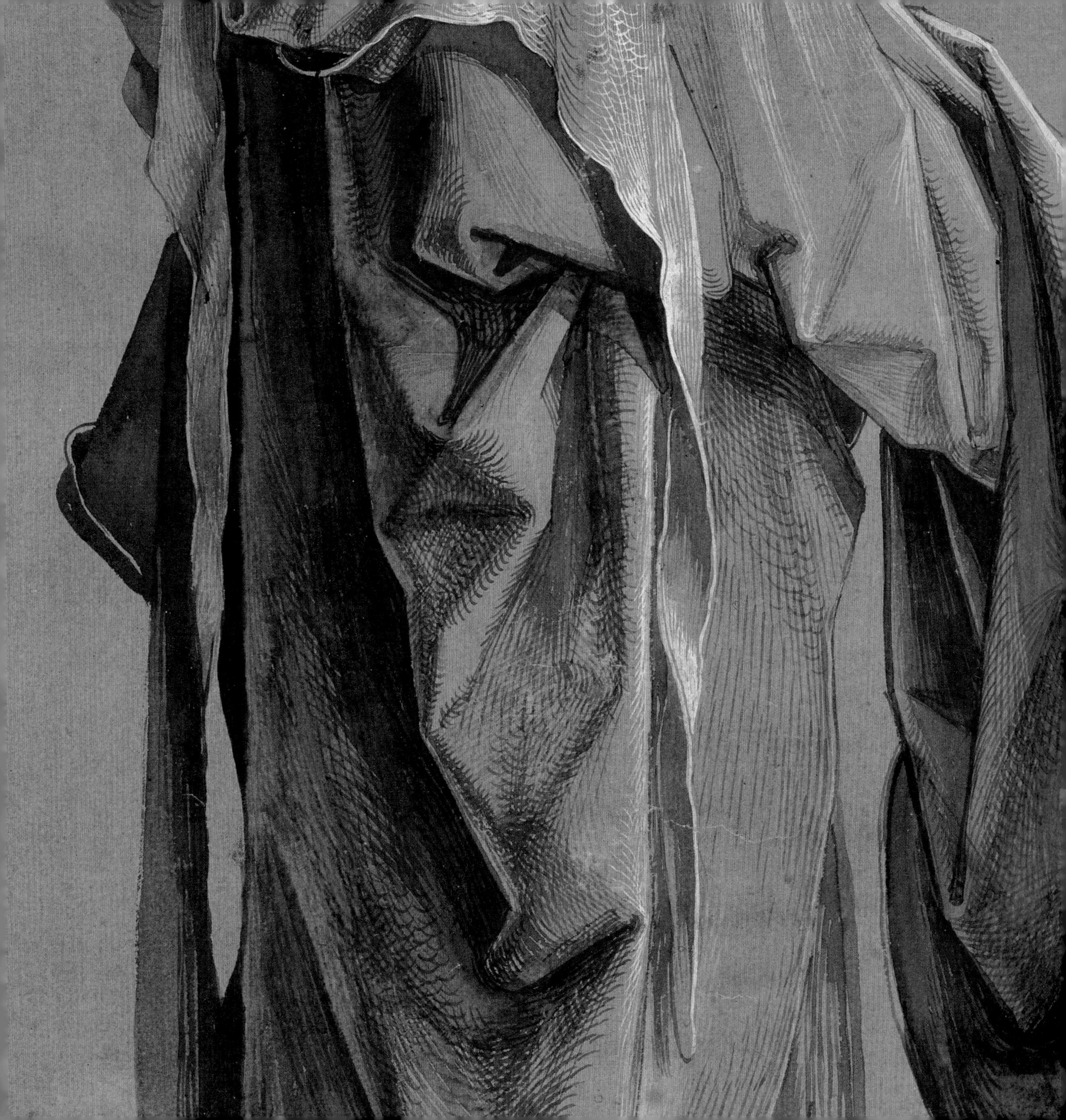

The depreciation of green, already very real at the end of the Middle Ages, continued into the modern era. First on the moral and religious planes, as much for the vestimentary decrees handed down by civil authorities as for the moralizing sermons of the great Protestant reformers, green was a frivolous, immoral color that all good citizens and all virtuous Christians had to avoid. Only the green of nature was dignified and respectable because it was the work of the Creator; all other greens were more or less condemnable. Next on the artistic level, there were many painters who abandoned or scorned green, relegating it to landscape and genre painting. Great painting, whether religious or mythological, used it only sparingly, always peripherally and never centrally. And finally on the scientific plane, the old color order inherited from Greek antiquity henceforth gave way to new classifications in which green was no longer a basic color but a secondary one, a mixed color, the product of blue and yellow. This downgrading of green in the scholarly chromatic genealogy reflected its decline in everyday life and in the world of arts and symbols.

It was not until the second half of the eighteenth century and the awakening of Romanticism that the color green regained a certain dignity. Tastes changed, nature became appealing again, people loved to walk in the woods and meadows, into the depths of the forests, along mountain paths. Herbaria and landscape painting came into fashion, melancholy became a virtue, and tormented souls found in green and greenery restorative peace and quiet and new aspirations.

DRAPERY ON GREEN PAPER

At the turn of the fifteenth to the sixteenth centuries, many German artists liked to draw or engrave on colored paper, especially on green or blue.

Albrecht Dürer, *Study of Drapery*, detail, chalk and graphite drawing on green paper, 1508. Berlin, Kupferstichkabinett.

Protestant morals

Heir to the sumptuary laws and religious moral codes of the late Middle Ages, the Protestant Reformation early on declared war on the colors it judged to be too lively or too loud and gave priority in all domains to a black-gray-blue axis, more dignified than the "papist polychromy" and more in keeping with the civilization of the printed book and engraving, then in full expansion.[1]

This Protestant chromoclasm first of all involved the church. For the great reformers, the place of color was excessive there; it had to be reduced or eliminated. In their sermons, they repeated the biblical words of the prophet Jeremiah railing against King Joachim and "the princes who construct temples like palaces, cutting windows in them, paneling them with cedar and painting them with vermillion."[2] Red—the most vivid color for the Bible and the one that symbolized the height of Roman luxury in the sixteenth century—was particularly targeted, but yellow and green were as well. They had to be driven from the temple. Hence the violent destruction—of stained glass windows in particular—and strategies for decolorizing walls: stripping, whitewashing, plain black or gray drapery to hide paintings and representations. Chromoclasm went hand in hand here with iconoclasm.[3]

SERMON IN A CALVINIST CHURCH

The favorite theme of many seventeenth century Dutch painters was the representation of churches with walls devoid of color and only coats of arms or funeral scenes for images. As Calvin stipulated in the preceding century, "The most beautiful ornament in the church must be the word of God." The devout themselves avoided lively colors and dressed in black, gray, and white.

Emanuel de Witte, *Interior of a Calvinist Church*, c. 1660. Hamburg, Kunsthalle.

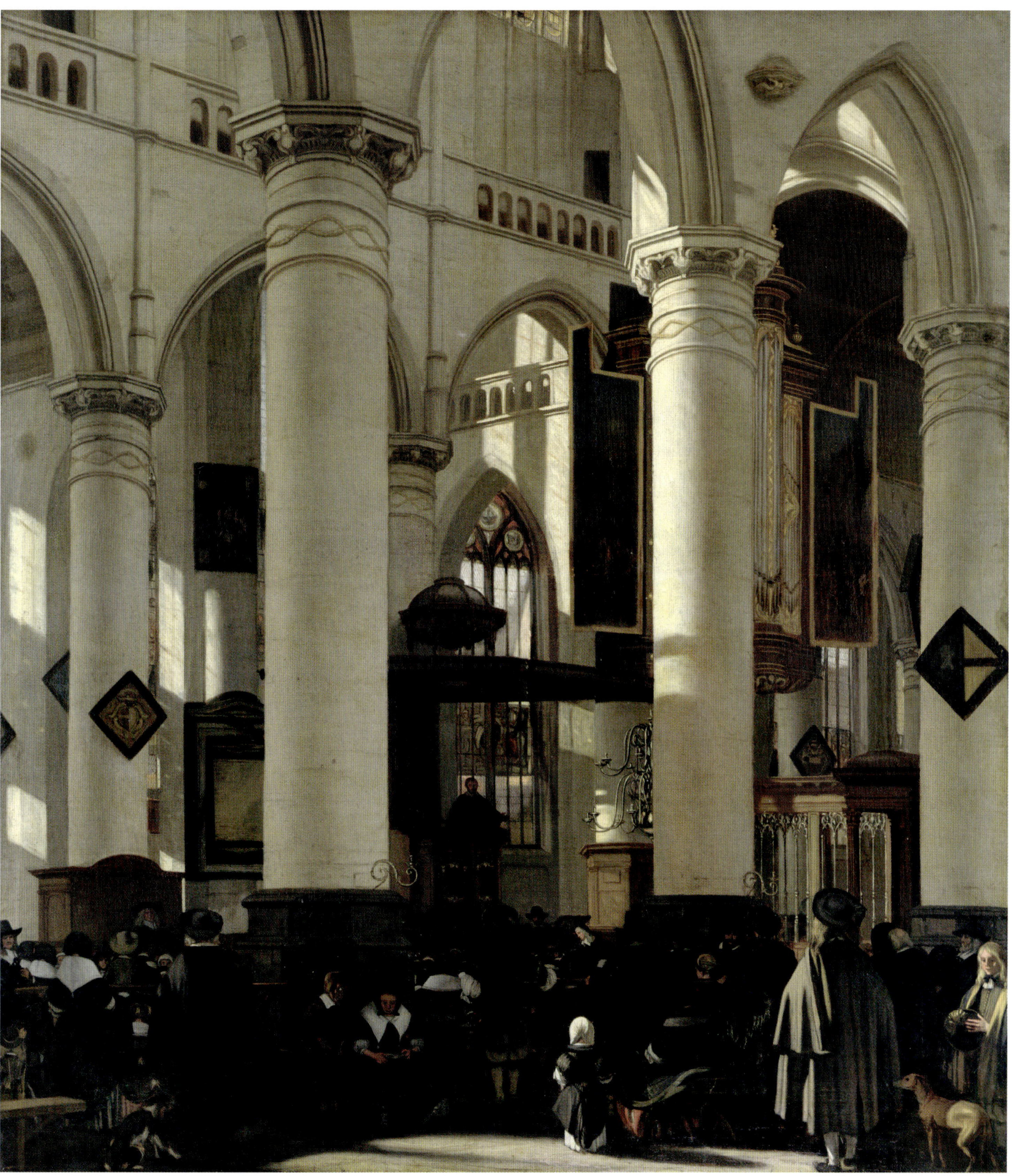

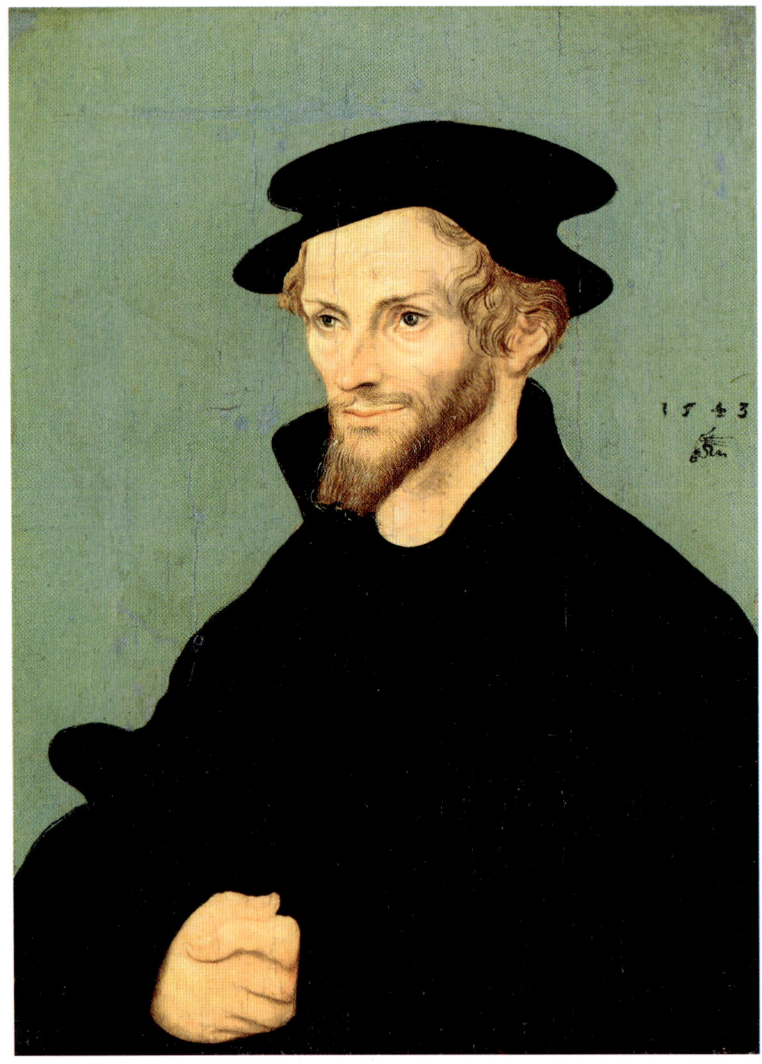

PHILIPP MELANCHTHON
Among the great Protestant Reformers of the sixteenth century, Melanchthon was the most severe with regard to colors. In a famous sermon from 1527, he railed against men and women "dressed like peacocks."

Lucas Cranach, *Philipp Melanchthon*, 1543. Kassel, Gemäldegalerie, Alte Meister.

More drastic still was the Reformation's attitude toward liturgical colors. In the ritual of the Catholic mass, color played an essential role; the vestments and articles of worship were not only coded by the calendrical color system but they were also coordinated with the lighting, the polychromatic architecture and sculpture, the painted images in the holy books, and all the precious ornamentation in order to create a veritable theater of color. Henceforth, all of that had to disappear: "the temple is not a theater" (Luther), "pastors are not players" (Melanchthon), "rituals that are too rich and gaudy falsify the sincerity of worship" (Zwingli), "the most beautiful ornament in the church is the word of God" (Calvin). Thus the system of liturgical colors was abolished. Even green, a color for the ordinary days, was considered improper. It had to give way to black, white, and gray.

All the same, even if churches gradually became as stripped down and drab as synagogues, it was probably in habits of dress that Protestant chromophobia exerted its strongest and most enduring influence. For the Reformation clothing was always symbolic of shame and sin. It was linked to the Fall; Adam and

Eve lived naked in their earthly paradise, but having been disobedient, they were expelled. Clothing meant to hide their nakedness was then given to them. This clothing was the symbol of their sin, and its primary function was to remind man of his fallen state. That was why all clothing had to be somber, simple, plain, adapted to the climate and occupations. Protestant morality had the deepest aversion to luxurious clothing, make-up and finery, costumes, and changing or eccentric fashions. Hence their extreme austerity in dress and appearance and the elimination of all useless accessories and artifices. The great reformers set the example, both in their personal lives and in the painted or engraved representations they left of themselves. They all had themselves portrayed in somber, severe, monochromatic clothing.

Vivid colors, considered dishonest, were absent from the Protestant wardrobe: red and yellow above all, but also pinks, oranges, all the greens, and even the purples. On the other hand, dark colors appeared in abundance, blacks, grays, and browns ranking first. White, a pure color, was recommended for children's and sometimes for women's clothing. Blue was tolerated to the extent that it remained subdued. Any colored pattern, which dressed up "men like peacocks"—the expression used by Melanchthon in a famous 1527 sermon—was severely condemned.[4] Green even seems to have been particularly targeted; it was the color of buffoons, players, and parrots, talkative and useless birds.

We find the same rejection of vivid colors again in artistic creation, notably painting. The Protestant palette was not the Catholic palette, that is undeniable. In the sixteenth and seventeenth centuries it was heavily dependent on the discourse of the great reformers with regard to artistic and aesthetic matters, a sometimes wavering or changeable discourse (Luther's is an example) that varies according to religious persuasion. It is undoubtedly with Calvin that we find the greatest number of consistent dictates and considerations regarding art and colors, and his positions on green seem rather favorable.

Calvin did not condemn the plastic arts, but they were to be exclusively secular and strive to be instructive or to honor God. They were to represent not the Creator (which was an abominable practice) but Creation. Thus the artist had to avoid artificial, gratuitous subjects that invited intrigue or lasciviousness. Art had no value in and of itself; it came from God and was to aid in better honoring him. By the same token, the painter had to work with moderation, seek harmony in forms and tones, find his inspiration in creation, and represent what he saw. The most beautiful colors were those of nature; the blue tones of the sky and water and the green tones of plants were his preferred colors because they were the direct work of the Creator; they had "more grace."[5] Green, banished from the church and prohibited in clothing, regained a certain legitimacy here. Calvinist painters, who loathed polychromy, who sought the somber tones and vibratory effects of grisaille, granted green a greater role than Catholic painters did. Not only great artists like Franz Hals or Rembrandt but also the minor masters of northern Europe turned to landscape painting and tried to convey on canvas or panel the silences of nature and the harmony of the plant world.

The green of painters

When did European painters adopt the habit of mixing blue and yellow to obtain green? It is not easy to answer that simple question, especially since art historians never seem to have considered it. Perhaps they thought that such a practice, now taught in kindergarten, existed since time immemorial. Nothing could be further from the truth. No recipe, document, image, or art work from antiquity or the early Middle Ages attests to mixing blue and yellow to make green. On this point the texts are silent and analyses done in laboratories are almost all negative. On the other hand such a process was well known by the eighteenth century; most of the manuals and treatises on painting mention it in the recipes they propose, and pigment analyses confirm that those recipes were in fact put to use by a great number of artists. In that period, however, such practices seem relatively recent; in about the 1740s, we find a few French painters (Oudry for example) railing against their colleagues in the Royal Academy who settled for mixing blue and yellow rather than using traditional green pigments (earth greens, malachite, artificial greens from copper). In their eyes, it was a matter of an easy and deviant process, unworthy of a true artist.[6]

Such a position, however, only represented a minority opinion and no longer the general one. It is even certain that as early as the preceding century, both in France and in neighboring countries, most painters were already obtaining their greens by mixing blue and yellow.[7] The problem is knowing when this way of working, originally empirical and circumstantial, became general and systematic. Was it necessary to wait for Isaac Newton, his experiments with the prism, and his "discovery" of the spectrum for such a mixture to be conceivable?[8] In 1665–1666 when the young English scientist succeeded in breaking down the white

PRODUCTS USED BY ALCHEMISTS AND PAINTERS

Medieval painters used various binders and pigments of animal, vegetable, and especially mineral origin. This miniature shows a certain number of them. The block of green in the third row resembles a block of malachite (natural copper carbonate that produced a magnificent green pigment), but in fact it is solidified vitriol called for in certain recipes for making artificial pigments.

Miniature from *Livre des simples médicines*, illuminated by Robinet Testard, early 16th century. Paris, Bibliothèque national de France, ms. fr. 12322, fol. 191 v°.

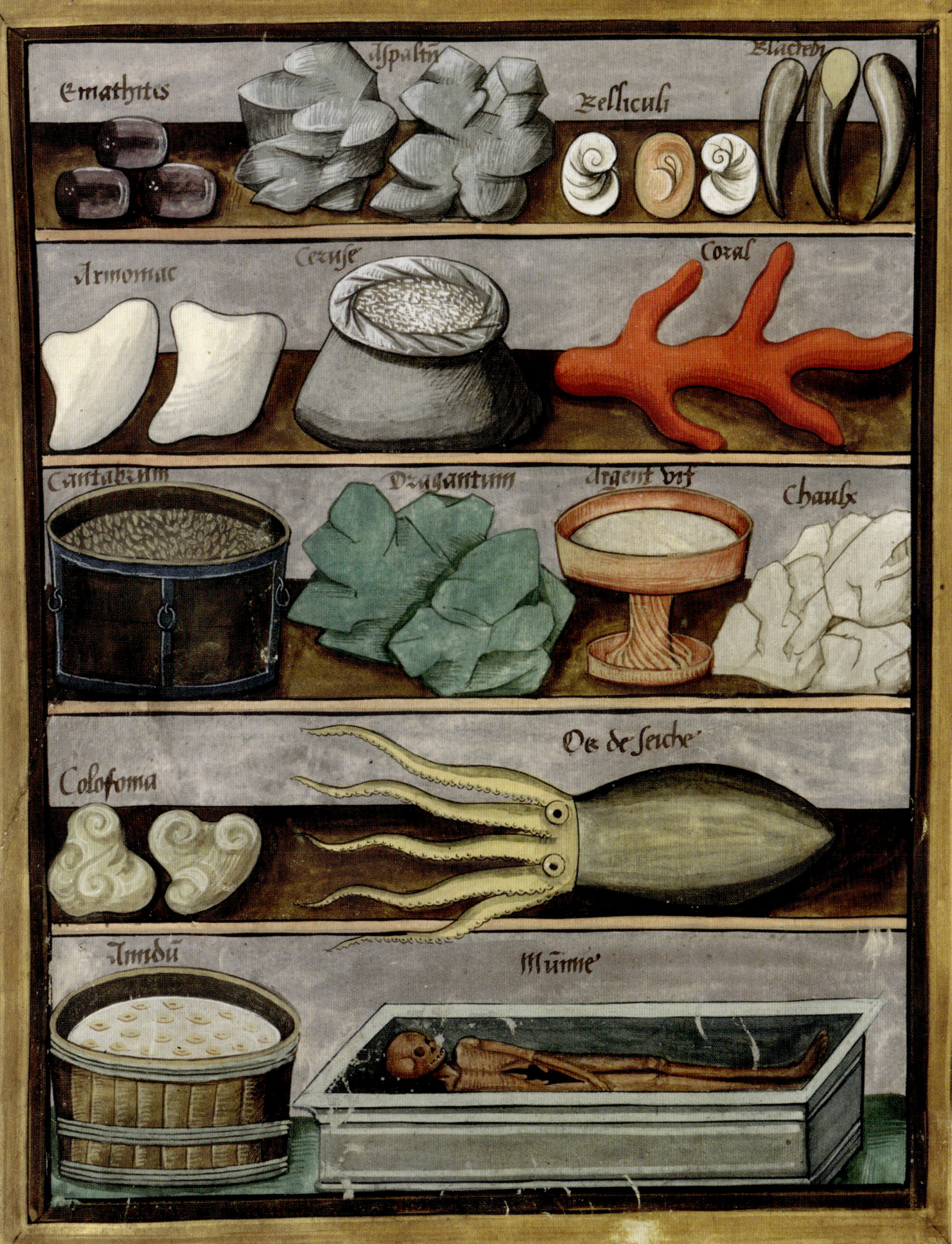
Emathites
Armoniac
Ceruse
Coral
Dragantum
argent vif
Chaulx
Os de seiche
Colofonia
Mumie

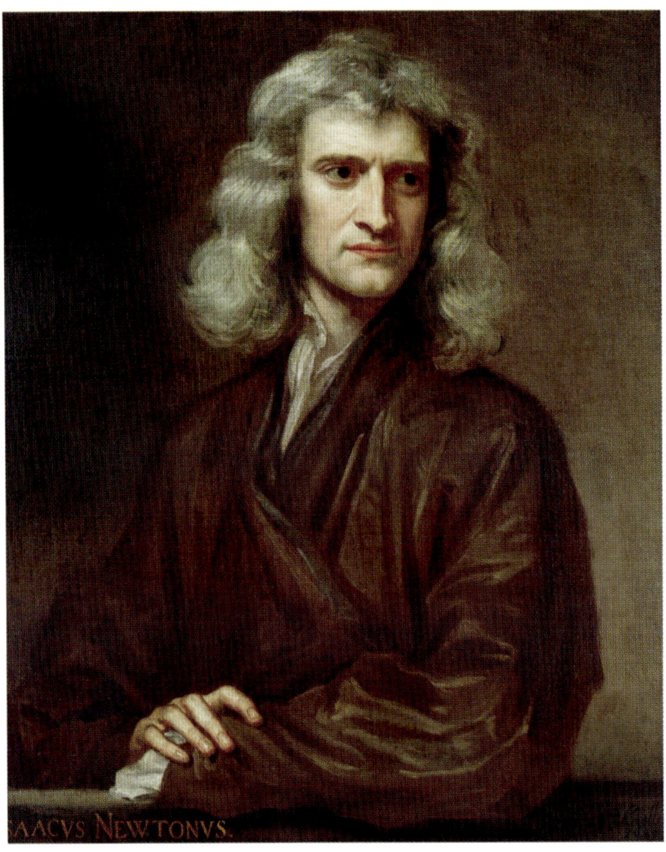

ISAAC NEWTON
By dispersing sunlight through a glass prism, Newton discovered the spectrum (1666). He kept his discovery secret for sometime before proposing to the scientific world a new order of colors within which neither white nor black had a place henceforth.

Godfrey Kneller, *Isaac Newton*, 1689. Uckfield, Great Britain, Uckfield House.

OPPOSITE PAGE: THE GREEN OF THE GREAT PAINTERS
Early on, medieval illuminators mixed blue and yellow to make green. Panel painters, on the other hand, only followed their lead quite late, and the very great painters even later still. In the mid-seventeenth century, making green by mixing blue and yellow remained a practice for minor masters. Neither Poussin nor Vermeer, for example, stooped to such crude methods. Earth greens, malachite, artificial copper greens, and the use of glazes sufficed for them to produce magnificent green tones.

Nicolas Poussin, *Stormy Landscape with Pyramus and Thisbe*, 1651. Frankfurt, Städel Museum.

light of the sun into different colored stripes, in effect he proposed to the scientific world a new color order, an order within which green finally found its place between blue and yellow: purple, indigo, blue, green, yellow, orange, red.[9] But prior to that date green was never located halfway between blue and yellow in the various color classifications. It was close to blue certainly, but far away from yellow. That was the case in the sequence most frequently chosen by late medieval artists to order their colors: white, yellow, red, green, blue, purple, black.[10] In such a sequence green was separated from yellow by red. On the theoretical level, then, it hardly made sense to mix blue and yellow to obtain green.[11] As long as the spectrum remained undiscovered, unknown, or unaccepted, yellow and blue were too far apart to have green as an intermediary.

That said, the discovery of the spectrum did not overturn the color order for painters from one day to the next. Moreover, Newton's experiments concentrated on light, not on matter; the new order of colors that he proposed to the scientific world was a matter of physics, not chemistry, whereas pigments were more firmly grounded in the chemistry of colors than in their physical properties.[12] Of course, it is difficult to separate completely the two domains, but pigments, like colorants, have first to do with matter and only afterwards with light. It is thus probable that the discovery

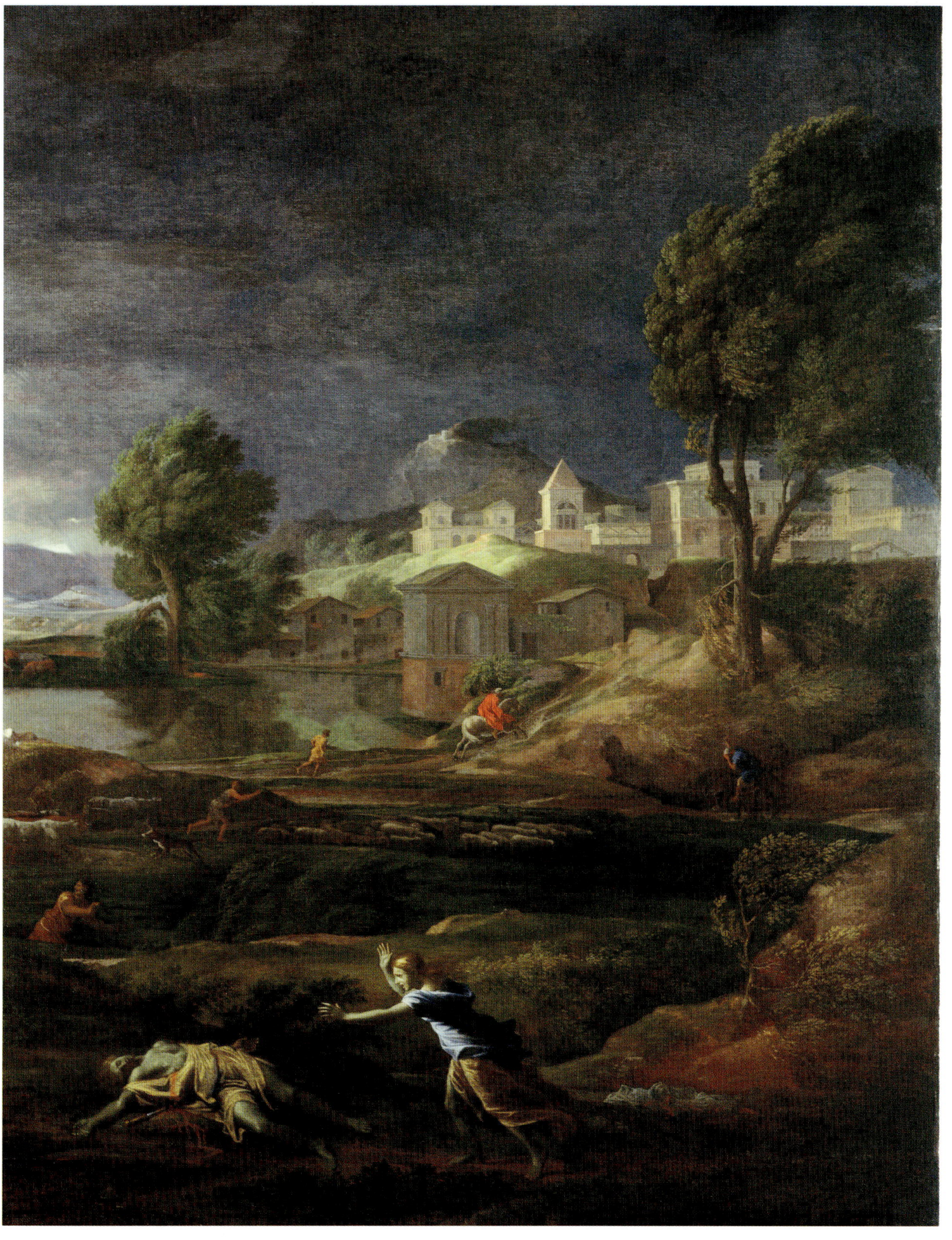

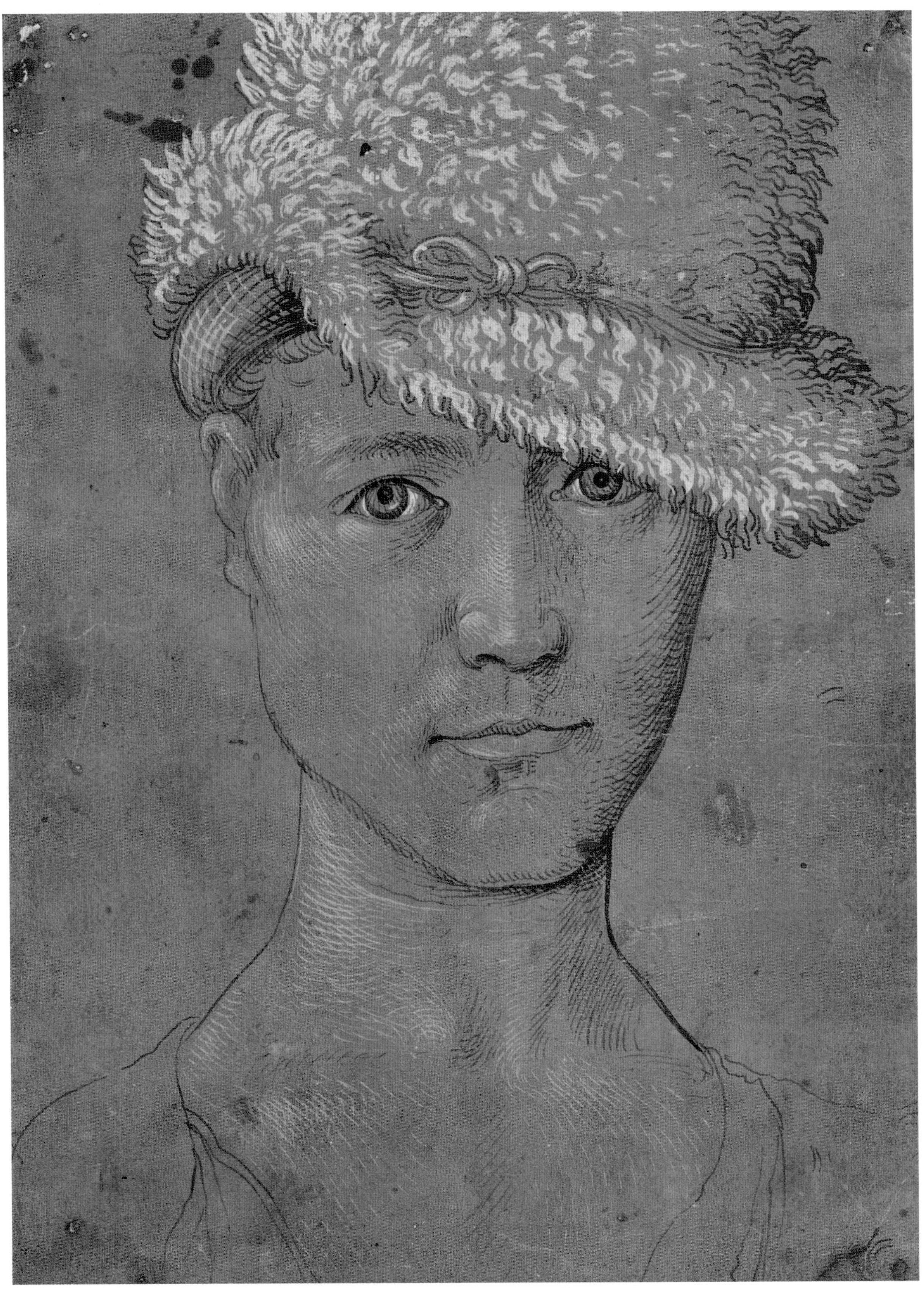

HANS BALDUNG GRIEN

In the early sixteenth century certain artists resorted to using dyed papers, different colored inks, and white gouache to give colored effects to drawings and engravings. Dürer and Baldung Grien excelled in this particular technique, most often using blue or green paper.

Hans Baldung Grien, *Self-portrait*, c. 1502–1503. Basel, Kunstmuseum.

of the spectrum only really concerned painters fairly late.[13] Conversely, it is also probable that well before this discovery, painters had empirically observed that green could be obtained by mixing blue and yellow.

Indeed for painters the experiment was easy to do and to reproduce. No doubt they tried it early on, even before dyers did, perhaps as early as the twelfth or thirteenth century,[14] especially since traditional green pigments, already in use in Roman painting, were not always satisfactory. Either they were expensive (malachite, which moreover tended to blacken as it aged), or they did not cover well (the earth greens, used especially as undercoat), or they held up badly (plant greens: black plum, iris, or leek juice), or they were corrosive and attacked neighboring colors and the support on which they were painted (artificial copper greens). There must have been great temptation to find other materials and processes for producing the color green.[15]

Among these processes the simplest consisted of mixing blue and yellow. Nevertheless, we can observe that among the great Italian painters of the sixteenth century (Leonardo da Vinci, Raphael, and Titian, for example), whose pigments have been analyzed many times, the green tones were never obtained from such a mixture. Only Giovanni Bellini, Giorgione—one of the

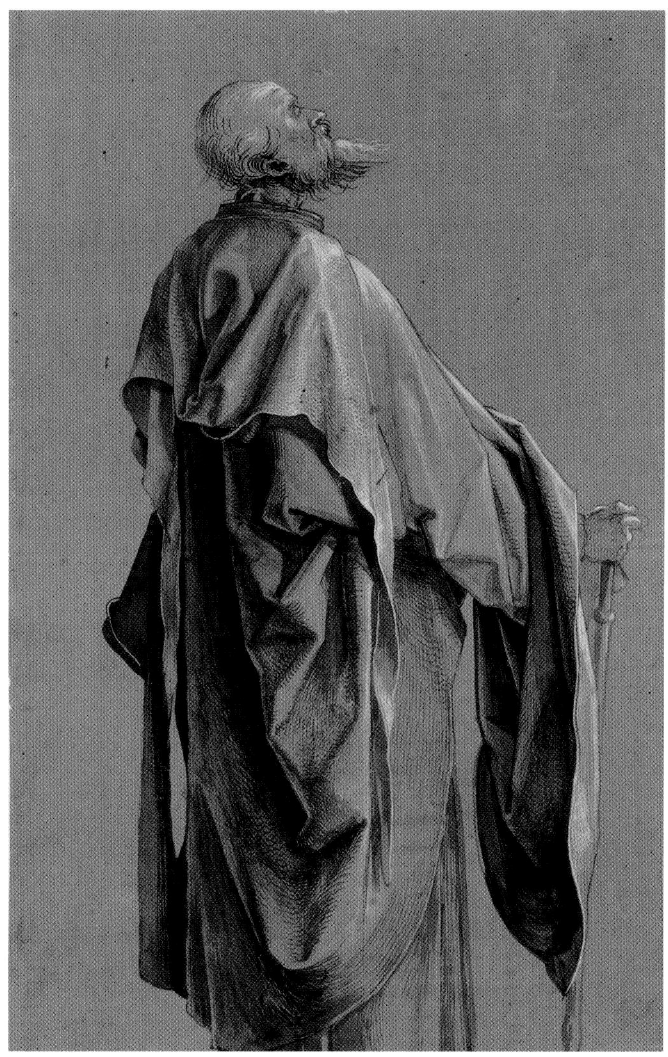

DRAWING ON GREEN PAPER

Albrecht Dürer, *Apostle*, study of drapery, chalk and graphite drawing on green paper, 1508. Berlin, Kupferstichkabinett.

THE GREENS OF VERMEER

Many analyses have studied pigments to learn Vermeer's secrets regarding light and color. In vain. The great Dutch painter used the same pigments as his contemporaries and proved to be even more sparing and traditional than many of them. For greens, he used earth greens, malachite, and artificial copper greens softened with honey. Though he frequently resorted to glazes to obtain greenish effects, he never really mixed blue and yellow to make green. His secrets lie elsewhere.

Johannes Vermeer, *Christ with Martha and Mary*, c. 1655. Edinburgh, National Gallery of Scotland.

all-time great painters of green—and a few minor Venetian masters were the exceptions.[16] Earlier, the same absence of mixing practices can be observed among the great artists of the fifteenth century, whether they were Italian (Pisanello, Mantegna, Botticelli) or Flemish (Van Eyck, Van der Weyden, Memling); none of them resorted to combining blue and yellow to make green.[17] That was not the case, on the other hand, with the illuminators. Many recent analyses have shown that it was not unusual for some of them to use this process in the last decades of the fourteenth century, not only by superimposing blue and yellow coats on the parchment—which they had done for a long time—but even by crushing blue and yellow materials in the same mortar or mixing them in the same receptacle. Certainly at that time this was far from being a general practice, but neither was it an exceptional one, as laboratory studies demonstrate. Usually it was a matter of two ores: azurite and tin yellow; lapis-lazuli and orpiment; but it could also be a matter of two plant products: woad and weld, or even one plant and one mineral material: indigo and orpiment.[18]

A collection of formulas intended for both painters and illuminators confirms the use of similar mixtures at the beginning of the fifteenth century. It was compiled by Jean le Bègue, a royal chancellery clerk connected to the Parisian circle of artists and humanists in the 1400s. Conserved as a single manuscript, this collection dates to 1431, but it includes various earlier recipes, some of them many centuries old, as well as others more recent or almost contemporary.[19] All the same, there is one recipe unknown from earlier collections: the mixture of indigo (*indicum*) and orpiment (*auripigmentum*). The text makes it clear that this method is valid for painting not only on parchment or paper, but also on canvas, wood, or leather.[20]

Here we have a very important piece of evidence, but we must be careful not to generalize and confuse the technical discourse of such compilations with actual workshop procedures. We must also distinguish between individual or circumstantial experiments and general practices. And finally we must recognize that the collections of formulas for making colors, whether meant for painters, illuminators, or dyers, are difficult documents to study and to date—not only because they were all recopied, and each new copy changed the state of the text, adding or removing recipes, altering others, transforming the name of the same product or calling different products by the same name, but also because the instructions appeared side by side with allegorical or symbolic considerations.[21] The same sentence could include glosses on the symbolism of colors or the properties of the four elements and specific advice on how to fill a mortar or clean a receptacle. Moreover, the notes on quantity and proportion were often imprecise and the cooking, decoction, or steeping times

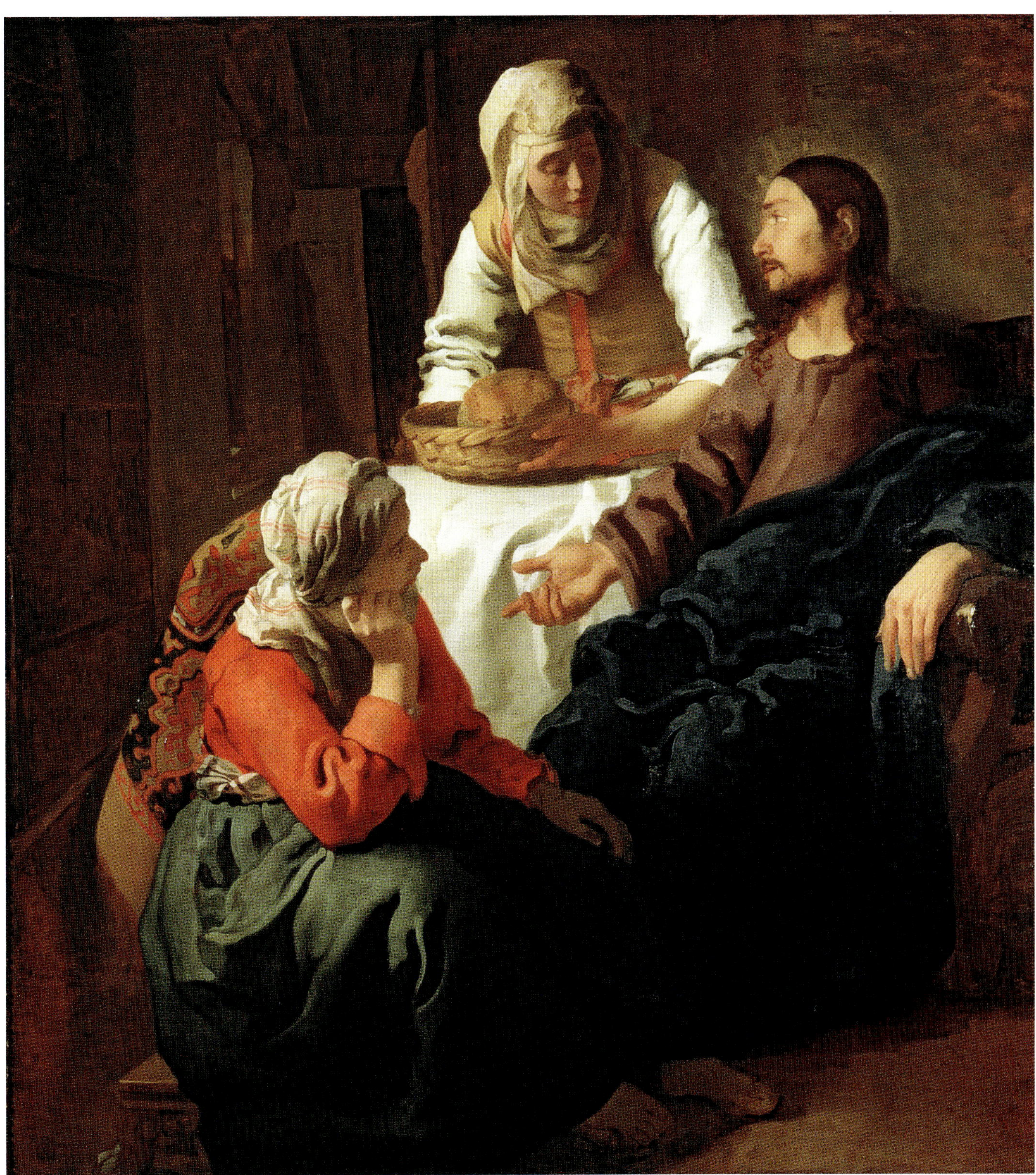

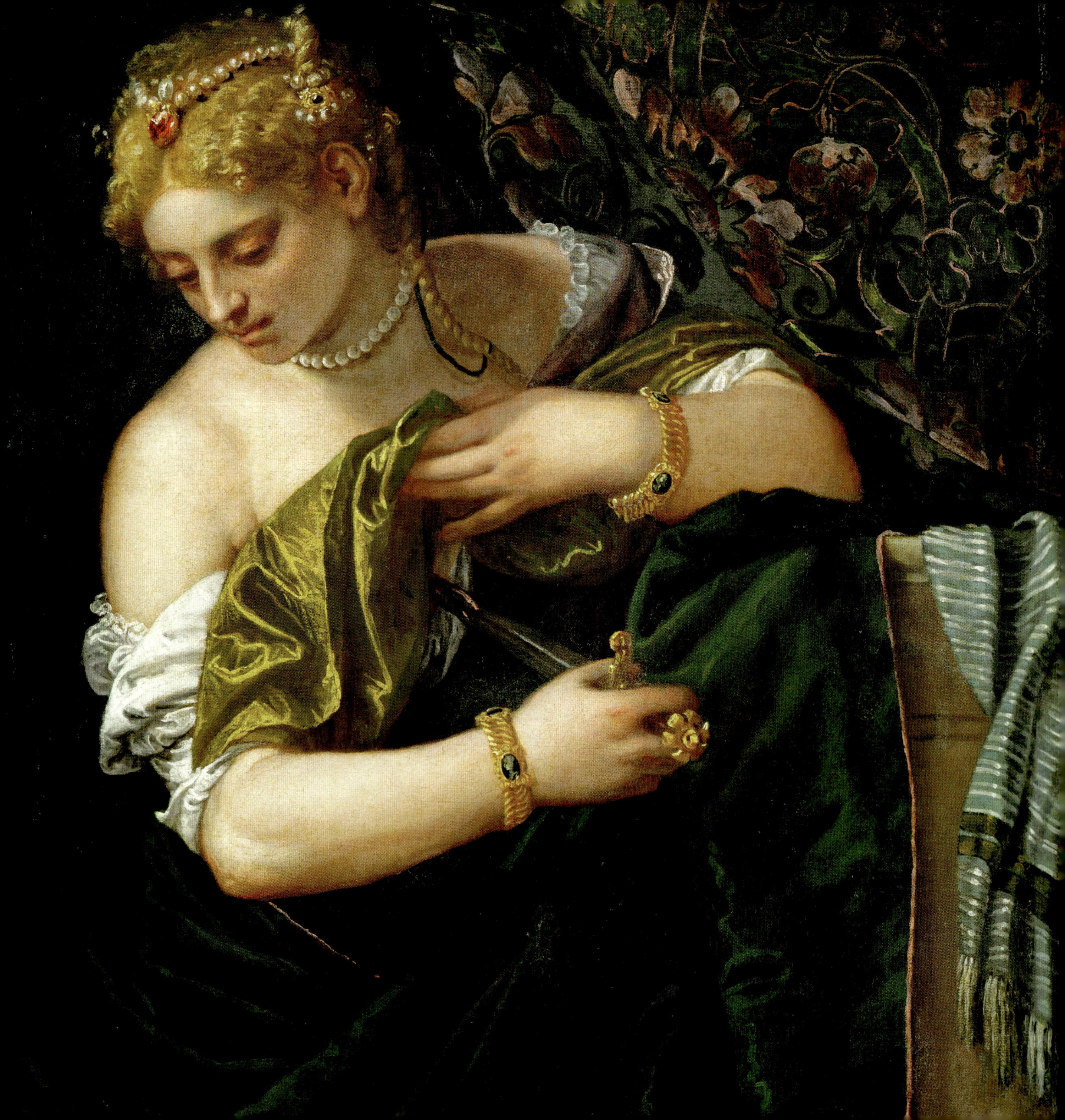

rarely indicated, or even disconcerting. Thus a late thirteenth-century text explains that to make a "good green paint," copper filings must be steeped in vinegar for either three days or nine months![22] As was often true in the Middle Ages, the ritual seems more important than the result, and the numbers are more qualities than quantities. For medieval culture three days or nine months represented almost the same idea, that of a period of waiting or gestation.

Manuscripts of recipe collections and printed manuals meant for painters present the historian with the same questions: what use did artists make of these texts, which were often more speculative than practical, more allegorical than functional? Were the authors also practicing artists? If not, for whom were their formulas intended? Some are long, others very short: must we conclude that they were aimed at different audiences, that some were truly read in the workshops and others had an independent existence? Given the present state of our knowledge, it is difficult to answer. But in a general way we must recognize that before the eighteenth century, there was little relationship between the writings of painters or meant for painters and their work. The most famous case is that of Leonardo da Vinci, creator of a treatise on painting, both compilation and speculation, and of paintings that do not put into practice what that unfinished treatise says or recommends.[23]

As an aside, the great painters seem not to have resorted to mixing blue and yellow to obtain green until quite late, later than the illuminators and the minor masters. In the seventeenth century, for example, Poussin and Vermeer, two artists of great prestige, refrained from doing so and seem to have been quite the traditionalists with regard to green pigments. They made abundant use of malachite—a natural carbonate of copper, related to azurite—and various earth greens—clay stones rich in ferrous hydroxide from Cyprus or the Verona region. Poussin also loved artificial metallic greens, obtained by oxidizing strips of copper with acid, lime, or vinegar; pigment obtained in this way was splendid but unstable, corrosive, and highly toxic. Vermeer avoided using it and preferred more reserved, mellow, refined colors to vivid, saturated tones.[24]

Generally, the seventeenth century, which engaged in lengthy discussions on the nature of light and colors, including within artists' circles (let us recall Rubens here, whose Anvers studio was a veritable laboratory), made few innovations in the area of pigments. For the range of greens, the discovery of America, the great transatlantic trade, and the products imported by various companies in the East Indies provided nothing really new.

VENETIAN GREEN

Venetian painters in the sixteenth century were stupendous colorists. Two of them particularly excelled in range of greens: Giorgione and Veronese. Nevertheless, the pigment we usually call "Veronese green" is an artificial pigment (copper arsenate) only perfected in the nineteenth century.

Paolo Veronese, *The Suicide of Lucretius*, c. 1583. Vienna, Kunsthistorisches Museum.

New knowledge, new classifications

THE GENEALOGY OF COLORS

In the first half of the seventeenth century, many diagrams were proposed to classify colors and show how they can mutually produce one another. One of the boldest was the one proposed in 1613 by the Jesuit scholar François d'Aguilon, a friend of Rubens and part of the painters' circles. Green clearly appears here as the product of combining yellow and blue.

François d'Aguilon, *Opticorum libri sex*. Anvers, 1613, p. 8.

With regard to science, on the other hand, this same seventeenth century constituted an important period of change for green—as for all the colors. Intellectual curiosity evolved, experiments multiplied, and new theories came to light, as did new classifications.

That was the case with the physical sciences, especially optics, which had hardly made any progress since the thirteenth century. Speculations regarding light proliferated in the 1600s and led to speculations on the colors and their nature, hierarchy, and perception. Nevertheless, at that time the standard order for colors arranged along an axis was still invariably Aristotle's (or allegedly so) of which we have just spoken: white, yellow, red, green, blue, purple, black. White and black remained full-fledged colors; green was not between yellow and blue, nor was it the opposite of red; as for purple, it was usually considered a mixture of blue and black, not red and blue. The spectral order of colors was still far off, even though many scientists tried to challenge this age-old classification system. A few of them proposed replacing the axis with a circle, others with branching diagrams often of remarkable complexity. One of the most audacious of those diagrams was the one reproduced by the famous Jesuit Athanasius Kircher (1601–1680)—a scholar and voluminous author who was interested in everything, including the colors—in his great work on light, *Ars magna lucis et umbrae*, published in Rome in 1646. This subtle diagram attempts to translate into image the entire web of relationships that the colors form among themselves.[25]

Other more pragmatic men of science observed and theorized about the know-how of artists and artisans. That was the case with Parisian doctor Louis Savot, who questioned dyers and master glass artists and then constructed his classifications based on their practices.[26] Or the Flemish naturalist Anselme

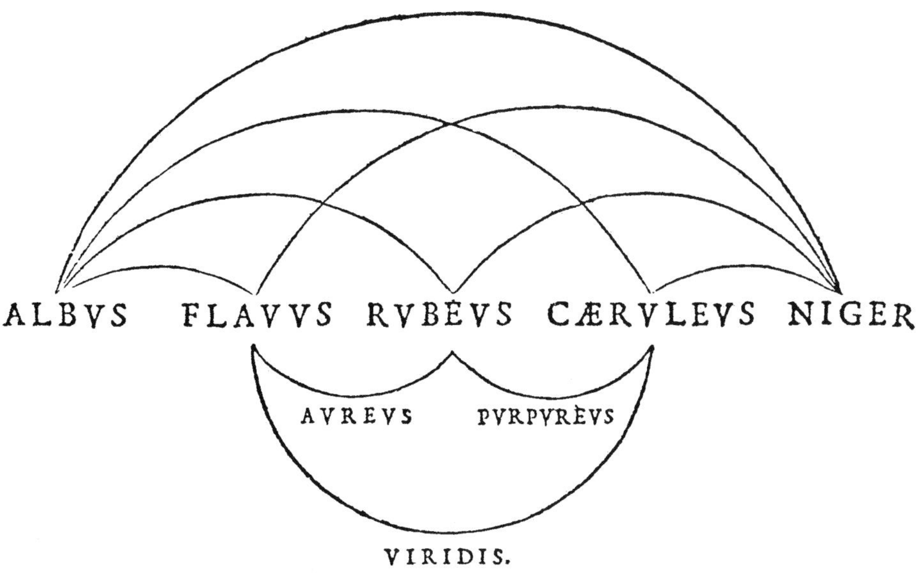

De Boodt, a regular visitor to the court of Emperor Rudolf II and his cabinet of curiosities; he focused his research on gray and demonstrated how mixing black and white was sufficient for obtaining it.[27] But above all there was François d'Aguilon, Jesuit writer of many and various works, friend of Rubens, who beginning in 1613 formulated the clearest theories and had the most influence on authors in the following decades. He distinguished the "extreme" colors (white and black) from the "moderate" colors (red, blue, yellow) from the "mixed" colors (green, purple, orange). In an elegant diagram similar to those of musical harmony, he showed how the colors combined to create other colors.[28]

In the same period painters were doing the same thing on their palettes. Empirically they sought ways to obtain a great number of tones and shades by simply mixing a small number of basic colors, either by mixing them before applying them or by superimposing them on the canvas, juxtaposing them (an optical mixing), or using colored mediums. In truth, this was hardly new, but in the first half of the seventeenth century, research, experiments, hypotheses, and controversies took on an intensity they had never before known. Throughout Europe artists, doctors, apothecaries, chemists, and dyers were asking the same questions: how many "basic" colors are necessary for creating all the others? How to classify, combine, and mix them? And even how to name them? On the last point the proposed vocabulary was extremely varied, no matter which language was concerned: "primitive," "primary," "principle," "simple," "elementary," "natural," "pure," "capital." In Latin the expressions *colores simplices* and *colores principales* were the most frequently used. In French the lexicon was more faltering and ambiguous. An expression like "*couleur pure*"—"pure color"—for example, was equivocal and designated a basic color as well as a natural color, or even a color to which neither white nor black was added. As for the adjective "*primaire*"—"primary"—already used at the end of the seventeenth century, it would not establish itself definitively until the nineteenth century.

How many basic colors were there? Three? Four? Five? Here, opinions varied widely. Some authors looked to the distant past and followed the ancient tradition, notably the opinion of Pliny who cited only four of them in his *Natural History*: white, red, black, and the enigmatic *sil* (*silaceus*), identified sometimes as yellow, sometimes as blue.[29] Understanding this term, an extremely rare one in classical Latin, is all the more difficult because Pliny spoke more about pigments and colorants than about color. That is why other authors did not refer to his *Natural History* or to classical antiquity but to the experience of contemporary artists and affirmed that five "primary" colors existed: white, black, red, yellow, and blue. Later, when Newton scientifically excluded black and white from the order of colors, most men of science accepted no more than three: red, blue, yellow. This was not yet the theory of primary colors and complementary colors, but it was already the modern subtractive triad that allowed Jakob Christoffel Le Blon to invent color engraving in the years 1720–1740 and then allowed other experimenters to make considerable progress in the areas of printing and reproduction over the course of the decades.[30]

Let us remain for the moment with the seventeenth century. Whether there were three primary colors or five of them, green was not in that number, and that was a very new thing. Whatever the system or diagram proposed before that time, green was always on the same plane with red, yellow, and blue. That was the case in all areas where the color green was concerned. Henceforth, it was no longer true: green, which many painters and dyers obtained by mixing blue and yellow, had become a second-rank color, a "secondary" color (the expression "complementary color" did not make its appearance until the nineteenth century). This new idea was soon shared by most artists and scholars. In a general work on the colors, *Experiments and Considerations Touching Colours*, the versatile Irish chemist Robert Boyle (1627–1691) expressed it very clearly in 1664, less than two years before Isaac Newton's discovery of the spectrum:

> There are very few simple or "primary" colors, the various combinations of which somehow produce all the others. Because even though painters can imitate the shades—but not always the beauty—of the countless colors one encounters in nature, I do not believe that they need to use colors other than white, black, red, blue and yellow to bring out this extraordinary variety. Those five, variously combined—and also, if I may say so, uncombined—are sufficient for creating a considerable number of colors, a number that those unfamiliar with the painters' palette cannot even imagine.[31]

By about the 1660s Robert Boyle's position was becoming widespread. There were only five basic colors, and green was not one of them. In the chromatic genealogy, it had fallen to second or even third rank, and we may wonder if its decline in the arts and sciences was the cause or the consequence of its withdrawal from daily life, material culture, and the world of symbols. Everywhere at the end of the century, green seemed to be in retreat. Its place in clothing and furnishings shrank, as did its place in coats of arms, emblems, poetry, and literature. It entered a new phase of its history, a long, regressive phase that lasted until the twentieth century. Henceforth—and for a long time to come—green was a "secondary" color.

Alceste's ribbons and the green of the theater

In the seventeenth century, however, artists' speculations and scientists' discoveries had not yet had an immediate effect on the colors of everyday life. It was not until the beginning of the next century, the Age of Enlightenment, that scientific and technical progress had concrete repercussions in the domain of colors for the material culture and the common run of people. For the moment, practices and tastes continued to evolve slowly, even in the area of clothing. In princely and royal courts black remained in fashion until mid-century, at least for ceremonial attire; ordinary dress was a bit more colorful. Women wore a wider variety of colors than men did but often in a very somber range. Greens especially were almost always dark. A few kings and princes exhibited a personal taste for this color, but that was not enough to make it fashionable. Henri IV, for example, king of France from 1589 to 1610, liked to dress in green, as did his predecessor Henri III and his son Louis XIII. But in Europe, they were the exceptions.

Moreover, it was not his personal taste for green that gave the good Henri IV his nickname of "*Le Vert Galant*." It was given to him shortly after his death, and posterity used it in a flattering way. Nevertheless, originally in middle French the expression "*vert galant*" designated first of all a bandit who hid in the woods to rob those who walked there or to attack women. Subsequently, the meaning was modified to characterize a womanizer, forward with the ladies, but a seducer rather than an attacker or rapist. Green here evoked sexual vigor and the turbulence of love. In the symbolism of lovers, blue was often good and faithful, and green fickle and carnal. In this use the expression "*vert galant*" may allude equally to the month of May, the *galant* month par excellence, the month of flirtatious banter, of *galanteries* and nascent love. At the beginning of May in many areas of Europe, the young man in love planted a *vert galant*, that is, a vigorous, leafy shrub, before his sweetheart's door or window; its growth would accompany their common destiny.[32]

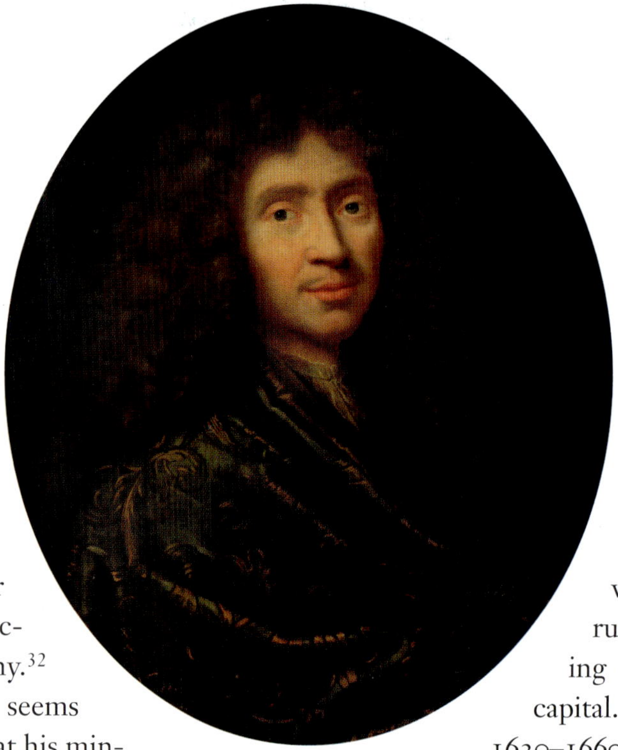

Like his father, Louis XIII seems to have loved green, a color that his minister, Cardinal Richelieu, detested. Extremely superstitious, Richelieu maintained that the color brought bad luck and worried when the king wore it.[33] Moreover others shared that superstition. Thus Catherine de Vivonne, marchioness of Rambouillet, one of the most famous noblewomen of the period, received her guests in her celebrated "blue room" and would not tolerate the presence there of anyone wearing green. In her eyes green was sad and harmful. At the Rambouillet mansion, where conversation was the great pleasure, it was not uncommon to discuss the colors: blue was "tremendously likable," red "terribly glorious," pink "brazenly gracious," and green "appallingly tiresome."[34] Such was the opinion of the refined nobility who loved the adverbs of manner, pushed superlatives to excess, and considered everyday expressions vulgar.

For many poets and contemporary novelists (Voiture, Scarron, Furetière) and for men of intellect, green was especially out of place, if not ridiculous; it was the color of the nouveau riche, eager to advance without knowing the ways of the world, or ignorant, rustic provincials, awkwardly trying to imitate the fashions of the capital. In French theater in the years 1630–1660, to present a character dressed in green was often to present a strange or burlesque hero and thus to prompt laughter.

A good subtle and subdued example is provided for us by Molière's play *Le Misanthrope*, performed for the first time in June 1666 in the Théâtre du Palais-Royal. Alceste, the main character, wages war on fashionable society, hypocritical manners, dishonest compromises, scandal mongering, fickle feelings, and general mediocrity. In truth, he seems to detest all of humanity. That does not prevent him from frequenting the salon of a cold-hearted coquette, Célimène, and from courting her in vain. He is both pathetic and ridiculous in the image of his costume that the play describes repeatedly: gray adorned with green ribbons.

Much ink has flowed as a result of these ribbons, and their color has prompted multiple interpretations. Some interpreters have seen the adornments as clearly comical, underscoring for the audience the caricature-like nature of the character. They have noted that in

Molière most ridiculous heroes wear green in their costumes: Monsieur Jourdain, the nouveau riche who wants to act the man of quality; Monsieur de Pourceaugnac, a peasant upstart led astray in Paris; Argan, the hypochondriac who tries to marry his daughter to the grotesque doctor Thomas Diafoirus; Sganarelle, a doctor despite himself, deceived by his wife and beaten by his valets. Sganarelle's costume adds yellow to this green; thus, he appears on stage wearing the traditional dress of buffoons and fools. As for Alceste, he is not really a buffoon; the brusqueness of his manners and the intransigence of his judgments is more irritating than laughable, and his simple green ribbons are enough to underscore his singular character.

Others have interpreted the green of the ribbons as a color gone out of fashion. Alceste is not dressed according to the tastes of the day but as if he were from one or two generations earlier. He is old-fashioned not only in his manners and his sentiments but also in his appearance; his chances for seducing Célimène are nil. In fact, in 1666, the date of the play's creation, green

ALCESTE, THE MAN WITH THE GREEN RIBBONS

A stubborn myth holds that Molière died on stage dressed in green, playing the role of Argan in *The Hypochondriac.* That is not entirely true; although he was indeed playing Argan at the time of his death, Molière was not wearing anything like a green costume. It is another role, the role of Alceste in *The Misanthrope*, that required him customarily to wear a green outfit, trimmed with ridiculous ribbons of the same color.

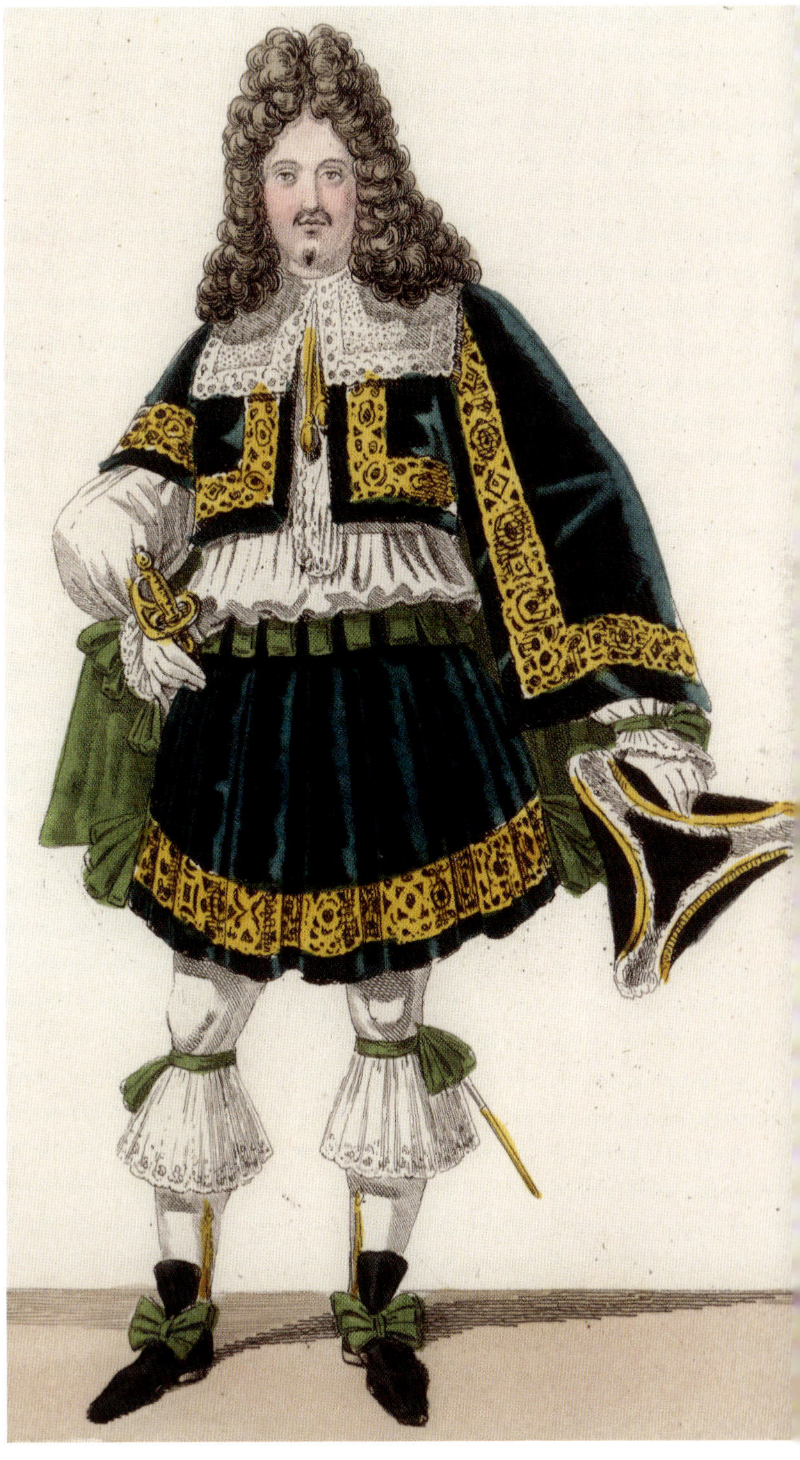

Costume of the actor Périer, playing the role of Alceste at Versailles in 1837. Paris, Bibliothèque national de France, Département des estampes et de la photographie.

Pierre Mignard, *Portrait of Molière*, 17th century. Paris, Comédie-Française.

was no longer a fashionable color, either at court or among provincial nobility, or even with the bourgeois. No doubt it had been—tentatively—in the 1620s or 1630s,[35] but that was no longer the case. Thus, to wear green could only be a cause for laughter. To this flaw of old-fashioned tastes, many critics add the one of social discredit. Unlike other Molière plays, *Le Misanthrope* takes place in noble circles. Many minor marquises frequent Célimène's salon, and Alceste himself is an aristocrat. Since he wears a color of commoners, that is not only laughable but out of place. In the eighteenth century a simple touch of color was enough to say who you were, to what class, rank, religion, or circle you belonged. That was true in France but perhaps even more so in the neighboring countries of England, Spain, and Italy, where green was not just a commoner's color but even more a peasant's color.

This social distinction by color or colors also appeared in literary works and began to form a sort of code that may have inspired Molière, sometimes very directly. In *Don Quixote* by Cervantes, for example, the hero—much more unreasonable and extravagant than Alceste—wears antique armor the various pieces of which are attached with green ribbons. These ribbons are not only unseemly but impossible to remove; hence the "knight with the sad face" must pass the night in an inn entirely dressed in his armor.

All these interpretations of the green color of Alceste's ribbons are relevant, and far from being exclusive, reinforce one another to make our misanthrope into a burlesque and disturbing character. Shakier, it seems to me, is the often advanced hypothesis that sees green as Molière's favorite color. Many rooms in his Paris residence were supposedly hung in green, his two companions, Madeleine and then Armande Béjart supposedly possessed many green dresses, and he himself supposedly wanted to play the roles mentioned above (Monsieur Jourdain, Monsieur de Pourceaugnac, Sganarelle, and so on) in green clothing. He was even supposed to have died thus dressed, February 17, 1673, while he was playing the role of Argan, the hypochondriac. Of course. But is that enough to justify those strange ribbons that quickly became symbolic of a role, a work, and a color? I do not think so, but obviously with regard to preferences, it is impossible to be certain.

The difficulties in locating the reasons for using one color or another for clothing are not limited to the theater or to literature. They also pertain to works of art and images and even more importantly to actual society and the actual clothing worn. For a long time historians were not interested in dress or clothing practices. They left those domains to "minor history" and the work of amateurs or were content with archeological studies of forms, totally neglecting colors. Fortunately, for several decades now under the influence of sociology and anthropology, the history of clothing has become a true historic discipline, reinvigorating its problematics and its methods and considering clothing practices as full-fledged social phenomena. This is cause for celebration and the hope that in the works to come, color will no longer be the great omission. There is still an immense gap between the wealth of documentation, the importance of color in all the social codes, and the too rare studies we have at our disposal. That is true for the seventeenth century but also for every other period.

Superstitions and fairy tales

Let us stay with the theater and mention here the contemporary taboo surrounding the color green among actors. Not only do they refuse to wear green, but they do not tolerate its presence on stage, whether it is a matter of fabrics, furniture, or objects. Green supposedly brings bad luck to the show, the play, and the actors. Moreover, wasn't Molière himself a victim of this color?

This superstition is very old. There was already much evidence of it in France in the Romantic period, prompting the fury of an author like Musset. In 1847, when a famous actress refused to wear the green dress the playwright wanted for the role of Mathilde in *Un Caprice*, he threatened to withdraw his play from the Comédie-Française program.[36] According to many theater historians, green's disrepute may be linked to lighting; the devices used at that time may have left fabrics and costumes dyed that color in the shadows. Hence its rejection by actors, especially women actors, since green did not show them to best advantage. That is not false, but taking a closer look, the suspicion regarding green seems to go back further. It can already be spotted in England in the Shakespearean period, when some actors were reluctant to wear the green—or green and yellow—costume of clowns on stage (to play the famous role of Bottom in *A Midsummer Night's Dream*, for example).[37] By about 1600 the idea that green in the theater brought misfortune seems to have already been well established.

But we must undoubtedly go back further still, perhaps to the mystery plays of the late Middle Ages. Legend recounts how many actors supposedly died after having played the role of Judas, traditionally dressed in green, yellow, or green and yellow.[38] Thus it might not have been a matter of lighting but of dye. To dye in a true green, as we have seen, was a difficult endeavor for

GREEN, THE COLOR OF FAIRIES

Fairies are very present in the work of Burne-Jones. They are often dressed in green, the color of strange creatures and supernatural beings. The bright, silky green differs here from the darker, more matte green of the vegetation, and contrasts strongly with the delicate flesh tones of the fairies' faces and the blond, red, or brown of their abundant hair.

Sir Edward Burne-Jones, *Green Summer*, 1864. Private collection.

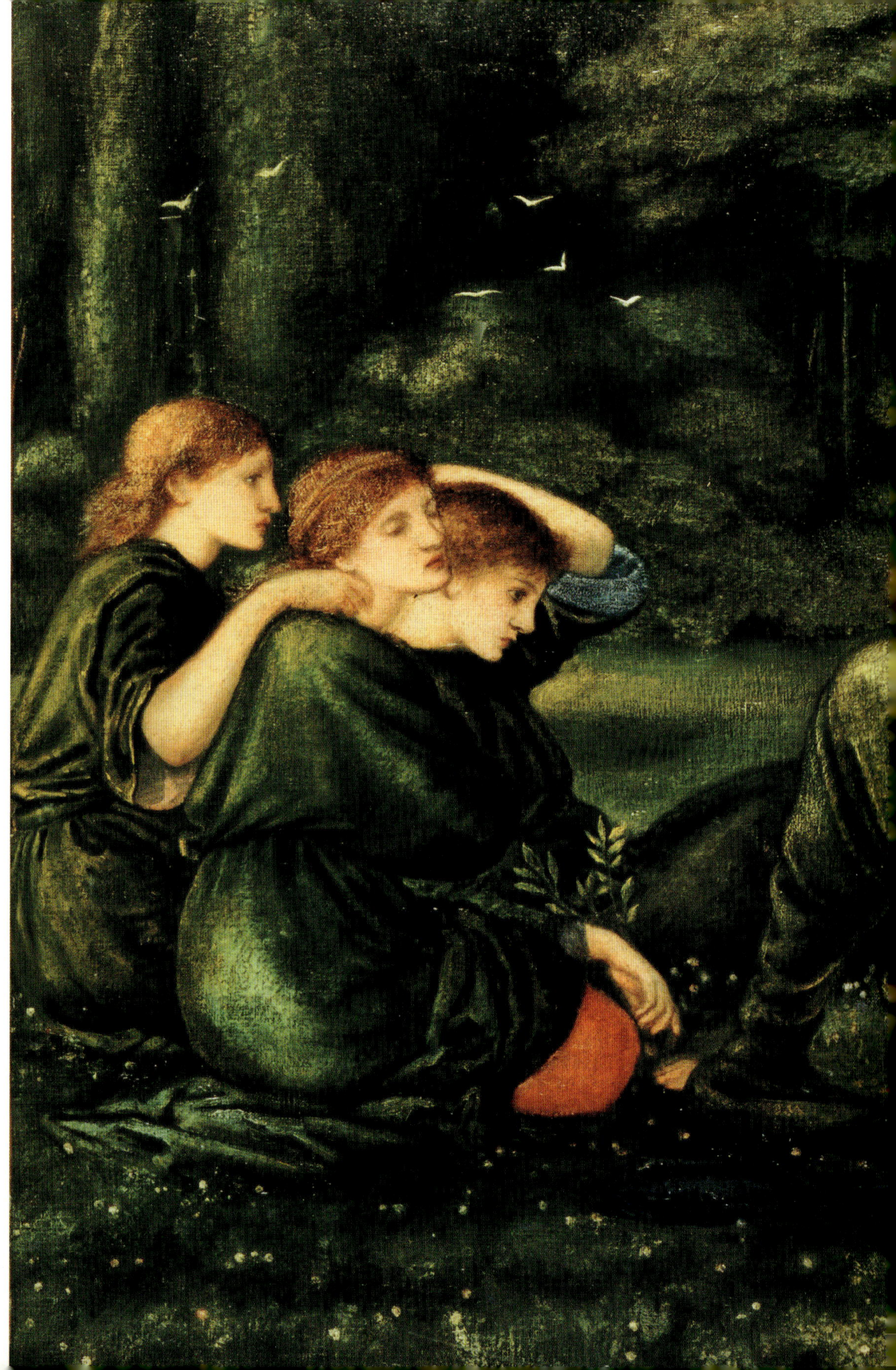

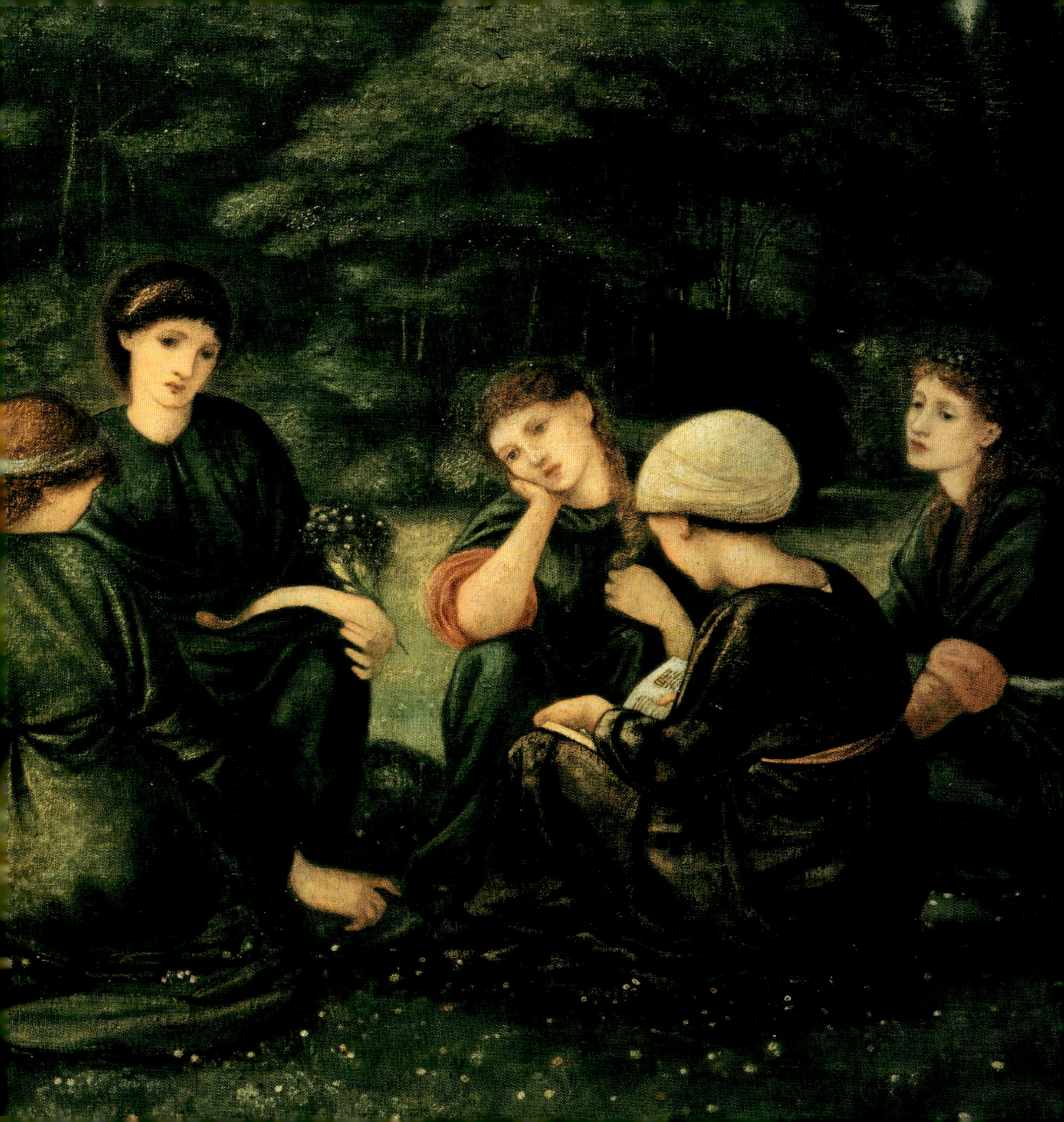

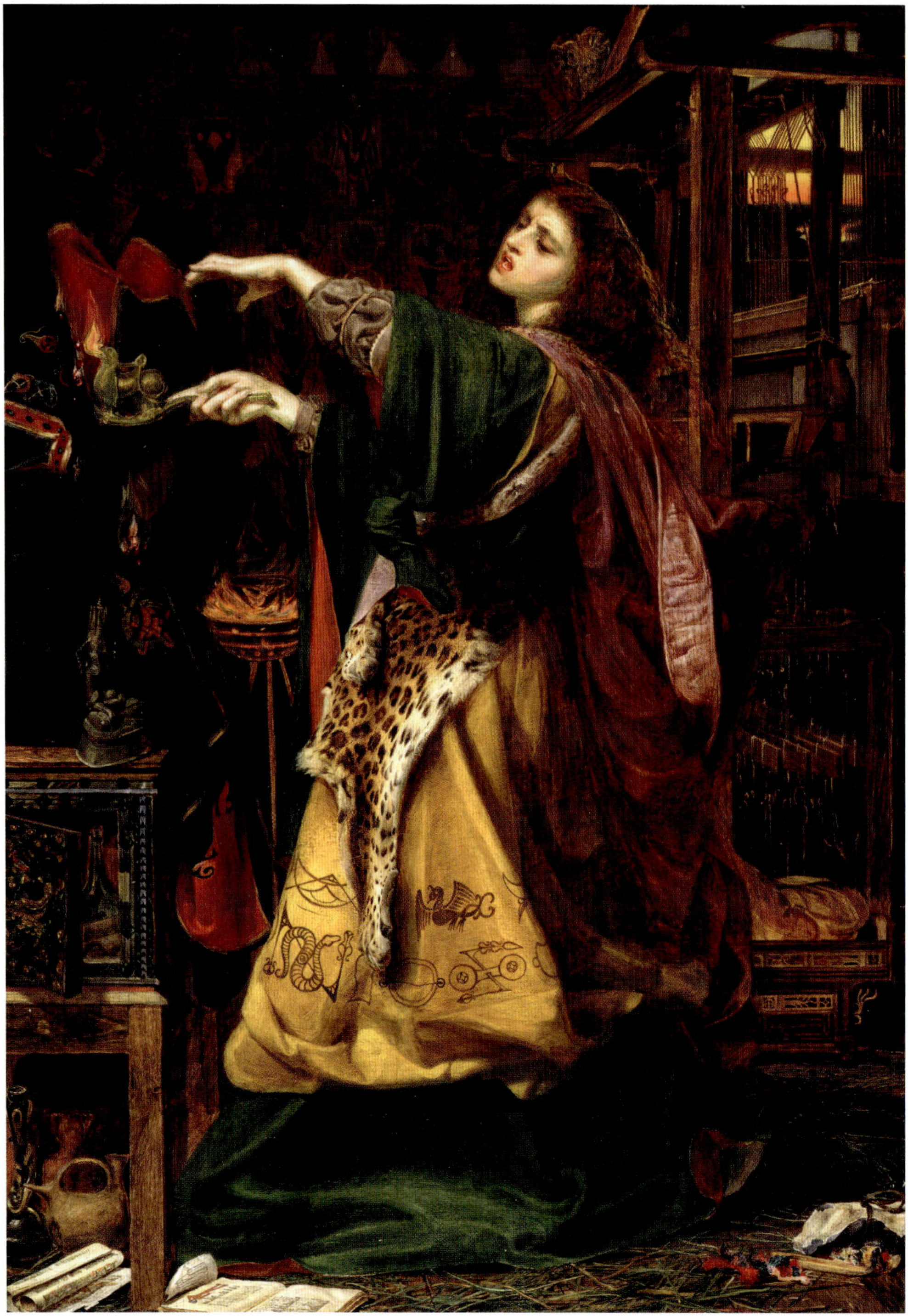

MORGAN LE FAY

In Pre-Raphaelite painting, as in medieval illumination, green was the color of fairies. All the same, wicked fairies—such as Morgan, the sister of King Arthur, shown here—generally combined green with yellow. This color combination was long considered an attribute of false, deceitful, or traitorous characters. Judas, Ganelon, and Morgan are archetypes.

Anthony Frederick Sandys, *Morgan le Fay, Queen of Avalon*, 1864. Birmingham, Museums and Art Gallery.

OPPOSITE PAGE: **THE GLASS SLIPPER**

In French there is much wordplay in medieval literature between *vert*, *verre*, and *vair*. It lasted into the modern period in tales and fables. That is why Charles Perrault, in his version of Cinderella, transforms the ordinary fur (*vair*) slipper into a dreamlike glass (*verre*) slipper, but he could just as well have called it a green (*verte*) slipper, dyed the color of destiny.

Théodore Lix, *Cendrillon*, colored engraving for an edition of Perrault's *Contes*, Paris, 1880.

a long time. In the theater, to identify characters, the colors of their clothing had to be vivid and pure. It is possible that *verdet* was preferred to ordinary vegetable dyes that produced grayish, faded shades. *Verdet* was a highly toxic colorant obtained from various copper acetates. On fabric and clothing, more painted than dyed, the color was brilliant but dangerous, the fumes and deposits from the *verdet* (a kind of verdigris) capable of causing asphyxiation and then death. Tragic accidents must have occurred, for which the reasons were not clearly understood. Hence, the sinister reputation of the color green in acting circles and its gradual banishment from the stage.

That said, the case of green is not unique because there are many taboos with regard to the theater. In France, certain words must not be uttered: "rope," "hammer," "curtain," "Friday." Performing on that day is considered risky moreover. In Great Britain *Macbeth* gained a reputation early on for being a cursed play, and a great number of taboos are associated with it (notably, its title must never be uttered—it must be referred to as "the Scottish play by William Shakespeare"). In Italy it is not green but purple that is banished from the stage, a color frequently associated with death. A similar ban exists in Spain, but it involves yellow, probably influenced by bullfighting. The bullfighter's cape is two-tone, red outside and yellow inside; if he is gored, the yellow will be his shroud.

Green's fate in the theater, then, must not be seen in isolation but as part of a whole set of beliefs and taboos for which the history largely has yet to be written. It would be particularly nice to have better dating for the evidence in order to establish precise chronologies, especially since the theater does not have a monopoly on superstitions surrounding this color.[39] On board boats, for example, it has long been undesirable, supposedly

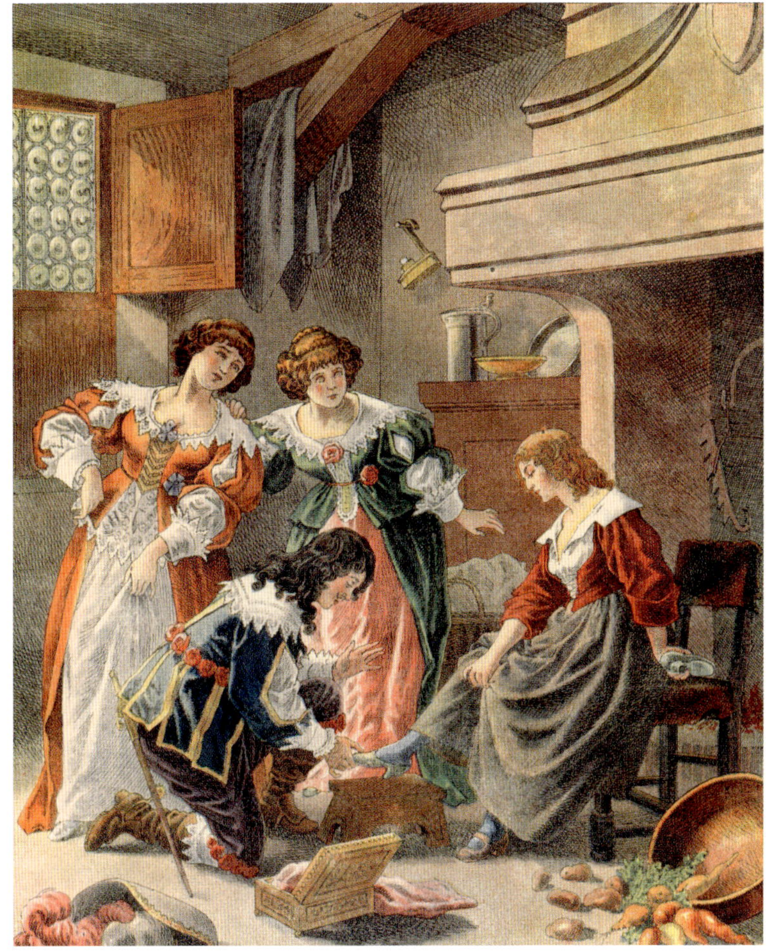

attracting thunder and lightning.[40] That is undoubtedly why green is missing from the international code of maritime signals, which developed slowly between the late seventeenth and mid-nineteenth centuries. That was also the reason why, in 1673, Colbert issued a strange edict requiring officers to have any ship destroyed if all or any of its hull was green.[41] In the same period Michel Le Tellier, secretary of state for war and then chancellor of France, probably the most powerful French figure after the king, had such a fear of green that he banished it from all his residences, changed

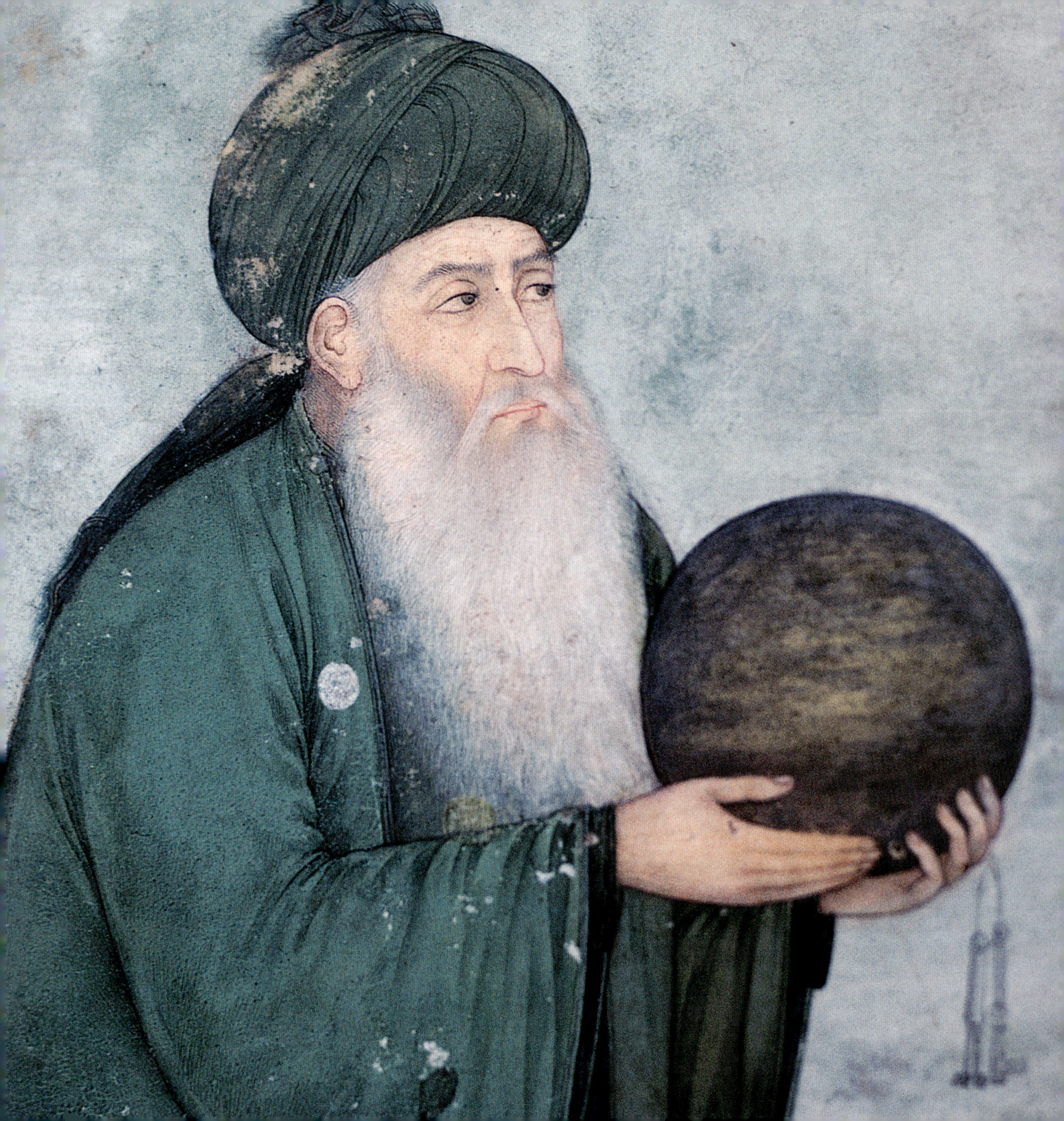

the color of his coat of arms (the heraldic figure had featured three lizards *en sinople*) and forbade it to be worn by the various regiments fighting for Louis XIV, including foreign regiments.[42] His son Louvois abolished this measure and reestablished *sinople* in the family coat of arms.

Nevertheless, if green was often assumed to bring bad luck, it also sometimes had the opposite reputation, for keeping away the forces of evil. In Germany and Austria, for example, the custom began very early of painting stable doors green to protect livestock from lightning, witches, and misfortune. Similarly, in many parts of Europe (Bavaria, Portugal, Denmark, Scotland), green candles were long believed to keep away thunder storms and evil spirits. Elsewhere, on the other hand, they attracted them. In fact, in the area of beliefs and superstitions, green was ambivalent, sometimes unlucky, sometimes beneficial.[43] That is still the case today in contemporary societies. Currently in Scandinavia, Ireland, and a large part of Germany, there are a great number of people who believe that green raincoats and umbrellas offer better protection from the rain than those of another color. Meanwhile, in rural areas of western France, wearing green for a wedding is still considered bad luck; inevitably, it will bring harm to the young couple or their descendants. Similarly, on the day of the wedding, it is advised not to serve green vegetables for meals—except for artichokes, considered lucky and an aphrodisiac—or to allude to the color green in any way.[44]

The same ambivalence can be observed in fairy tales, a favorite literary genre of the seventeenth century, which was responsible for essentially reviving if not creating them. Of course, there are not frequent references to color, but they are always significant. Less often than red, white, or black, green was the color of supernatural beings, notably fairies. In the modern era in many parts of Europe, they were called the "green ladies" (*die grünen Damen*). There were several reasons for this: sometimes their clothing or shoes were green; sometimes they had green eyes or hair (like witches); sometimes they lived in green surroundings that evoked their primal ties to plant cycles, water worship, trees, and forests. In northern Europe, when fairies dressed in green, they were not very happy if simple mortals did the same. If one wanted to gain their favor, it was better not to borrow this color from them nor use the plants from which they drew some of their magic powers: hawthorn, service tree, hazel, and a few others. Green was the color of fairies. Now, whether she was godmother or lover, guardian angel or evil spirit, a fairy was often capricious and, like the color itself, could quickly change mood, appearance, or meaning. She was to be feared and respected.

Western culture has no monopoly on green fairies or greenish genies. We also encounter them in various forms in Eastern cultures. The Islamic tradition, for example, features a curious character belonging to the supernatural world whose very name evokes the color green: Khidr (or Khisr), which means "green

AL KHIDR

Islamic traditions sometimes feature a character who, in certain respects, resembles the enchanters of the Middle Ages, notably Merlin: Al Kidhr, "the green man." He is at once a visionary prophet, a mischievous magus, and a good genie who protects sailors and travelers, saves the drowned, extinguishes fires, and wards off the forces of evil.

"Al-Khidr," figure from the Quran, Mughal miniature, detail, 18th century. Rampur, private collection.

man." His identity is difficult to pin down. Some consider him to be the son of Adam, others an angel or a saint, still others a visionary prophet or a guide sent by fate. Everyone sees him as a good, sometimes mischievous genie who protects sailors and travelers, fends off storms, puts out fires, saves the drowned, keeps away demons and serpents. The Quran mentions him only once, but he plays a role in many tales and legends.[45]

Let us return to the European tradition and fairy tales from the modern era. Like the tales of chivalry from the Middle Ages, fairy tales enjoy playing with the sound and spelling of certain words to create a strange or supernatural atmosphere. In French the word *vert* lends itself better to this than any other color term, maintaining phonic relations with words such as *vair*, *verre*, *ver*, and *vers*, and even with syllables with the same sound. Many semantic confusions and uncertainties in interpretation result, to the delight of the exegetes. The story of Cinderella, as it was formulated by Charles Perrault at the end of the seventeenth century, constitutes a good example. The origin of the tale is ancient and its versions multiple. But the framework is always the same: a poor young girl attracts the love of a prince and then disappears; her shoes, lost (or stolen) during a ball, help the prince find her again. Charles Perrault's version was published in 1697 in a collection entitled *Histoires ou Contes du temps passé avec des moralités* (*Stories or Tales from the Past with Morals*).[46] Here it is not a matter of shoes but of slippers, that is, dancing shoes.[47] The title of the tale moreover is formulated in this way: *La Petite Pantoufle de verre* ("The Little Glass Slipper"). What could a "glass" slipper actually be? Might Perrault have been mistaken and confused *verre* and *vair*? The slipper might have been richly lined with vair or even entirely made of vair, fur from the Siberian gray squirrel species. That is Balzac's hypothesis, commenting on Perrault's text in 1841, a hypothesis taken up again by Littré and many French language historians.[48]

But Charles Perrault (1628–1703) was not just anyone; a member of the Académie Française, writer of the preface to the first edition of the great dictionary compiled by that body (1694), leader of the *Modernes* against the *Anciens* (Boileau in particular), specialist in language and spelling, he could not have been mistaken. If he wrote *verre* and not *vair*, he had his reasons. Many critics have noted that glass and crystal play an important role in fairy tales. Others have stressed that in Perrault's version, a pumpkin is transformed into a carriage, rats into coachmen, lizards into valets; in a world as strange as that, slippers can certainly be glass. More recently, psychoanalysis has joined in and seen the glass slipper, a fragile object easily broken, as the young woman's virginity, lost during a ball as is often the case.[49] For three centuries there has been heated debate over Perrault's intended (or not) spelling. Failing to find definitive proof on the side of *verre* or of *vair*, a few critics have gone so far as to call upon the color *verte*.[50] The slippers could be green, offered by Cinderella's godmother (a fairy!), and the wording could be borrowed from the language of heraldry: slippers "of green" as one would say in heraldry "of *sinople*." This could be the color of youth, love, and hope; the prince hopes to find Cinderella again, and the reader hopes the story will have a happy ending.[51]

That all seems a little specious but confirms how green is a polymorphous color. Its semantic richness and dreamlike power are such that they cannot be contained in a single vocable; they encroach upon neighboring vocables and take on an exponential dimension in doing so, a symbolic richness that no other color can offer.

Green in the age of the enlightenment

The seventeenth century was a dark, often gloomy, sometimes very black age; the eighteenth century, on the other hand, was bright and colorful, vivid and rainbow-hued. The Enlightenment did not shine only on the domain of the mind, it was a presence as well in daily life; doors and windows grew larger, lighting improved and cost less, oil and wax were consumed more slowly. Henceforth, the colors were easier to see and given more attention; the fashion was for shades and variations of the whole range of colors, and all the more so as the chemistry of colorants was making quick decisive progress, especially in dyeing and textile production. All of society profited, including the less wealthy classes. Tones diversified, notably the half-tones, beiges, browns, pinks, and grays, while the vocabulary grew and sought to name precisely new shades, sometimes resorting to highly imaginative expressions (thus, in French, about mid-century, "*gorge de pigeon*," "*boue de Paris*," "*cuisse de nymphe émue*," "*pluie de roses*," "*caca-dauphin*"—pigeon's throat, Paris mud, excited nymph's thigh, rain of roses, dauphin's poop.)

Now measurable by physics, technically produced and reproduced at will, captured in all its nuances by the vocabulary, color appeared, for the first time in its history, as more or less mastered. That was why it lost a share of its mysteries. The relationship humans had with it, not only scientists and artists but also philosophers and theologians, even simple artisans and the common run of people, gradually changed. Attitudes changed, and dreams as well. Some questions regarding color, debated for centuries—its customs, symbolism, use in heraldry—faded into the background. New preoccupations, new fancies occupied center stage, like the interest in colorimetry that took over the sciences and the arts, or more simply the interest

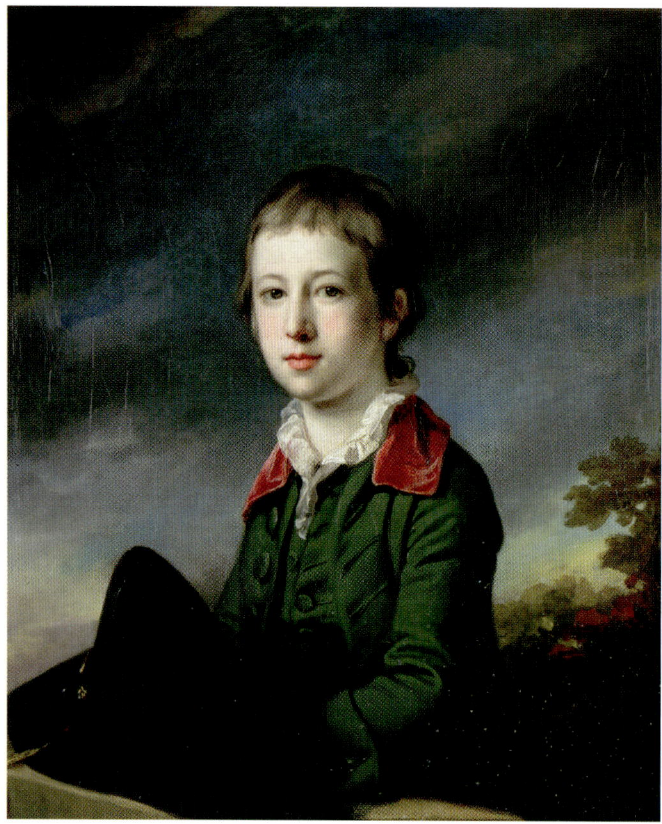

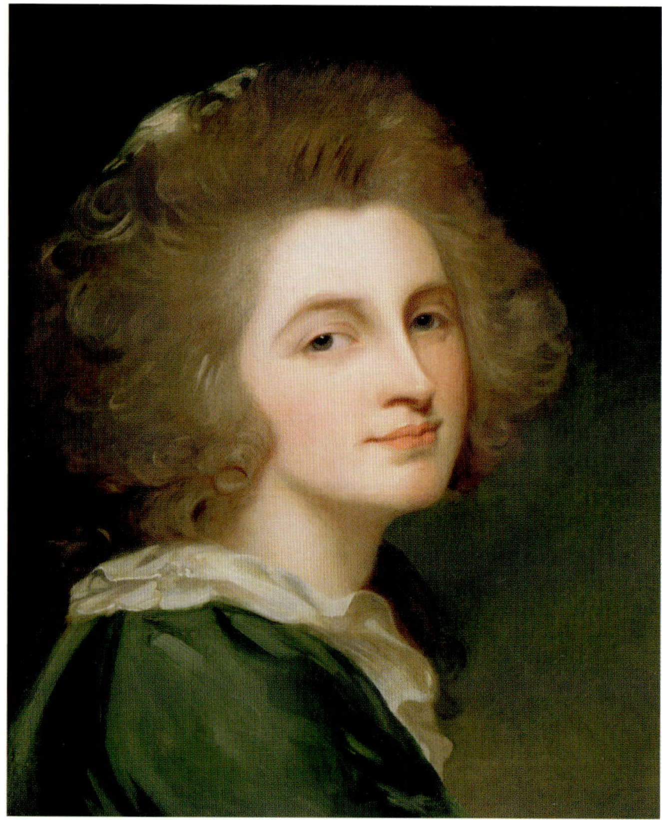

in fashion and the color "taste of the day" that henceforth involved quite a large portion of society.[52]

This progress and these transformations were of little use to the color green. The age of the Enlightenment was a great century for blue, but not in the least for green. It was undoubtedly in the eighteenth century that blue replaced red as the favorite color of Europeans (as it still is today, far ahead of all the other colors) and that its presence definitively expanded in everyday life, henceforth diversifying into countless shades, as much on walls and objects as on fabrics and clothing.[53] There were various reasons for this, but the main one was probably linked to the use of two new and effective colorants: Prussian blue and American indigo. Unlike at other moments in history (the thirteenth century, for example), this time chemical and technical progress preceded and engendered aesthetic and symbolic transformations.

Prussian blue (also called "Berlin blue") was perfected by chance in 1709 by a Berlin pharmacist, Heinrich Diesbach, and then marketed by a questionable chemist but a wise businessman, Johann Konrad Dippel. In painting its coloring power was very strong, and mixed with other colors it produced clear and admirable tones. Contrary to a stubborn myth—perhaps due to Dippel's bad reputation—it was not toxic and did not change into prussic acid; on the other hand, it was unstable in light. From the mid-eighteenth

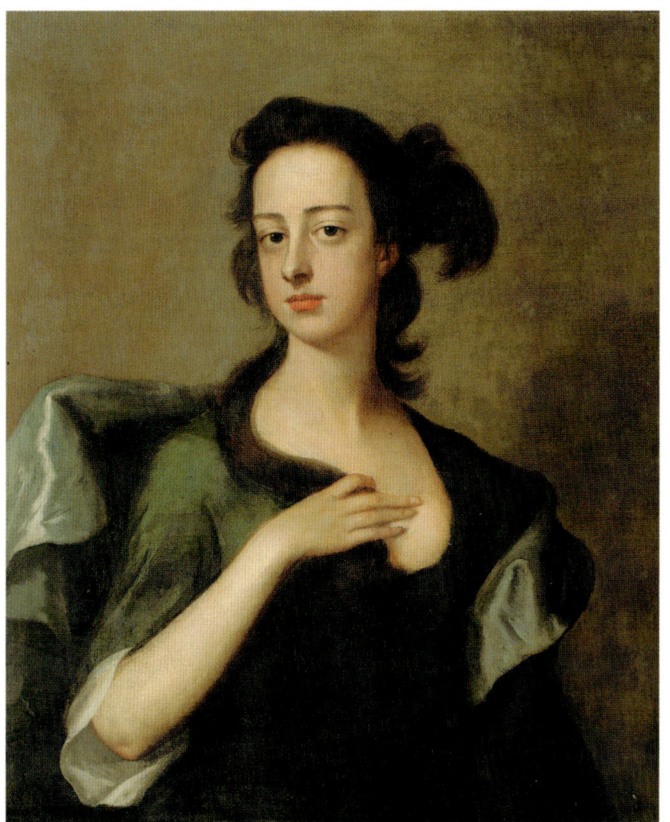

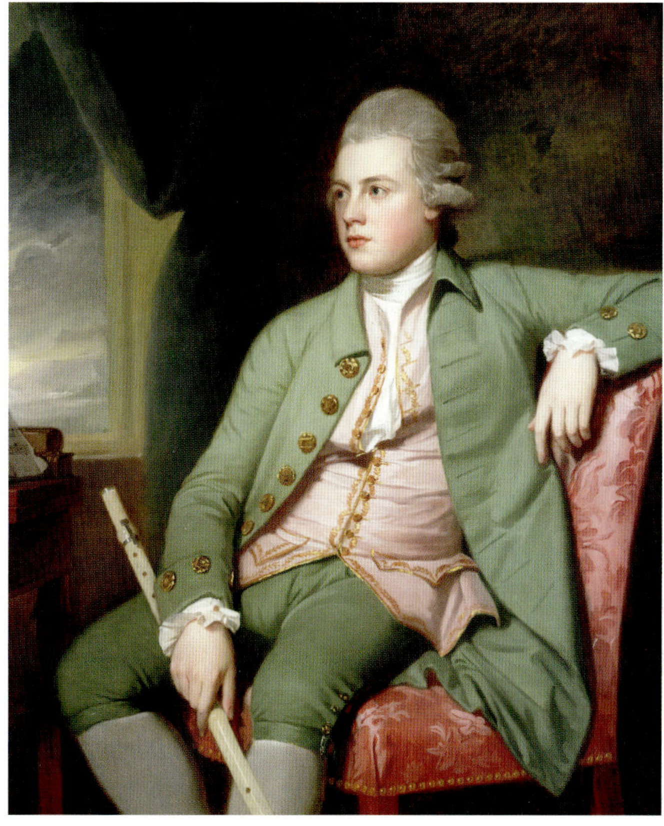

century, scientists tried to adapt this new blue to the techniques and constraints of dyeing in order to attain brighter, more vivid, and less costly tones than those obtained with traditional dyestuffs. Many societies and academies launched competitions to this end, but the results were for a long time disappointing.[54] The second material, indigo, was known for ages, but in the eighteenth century it was imported in vast amounts from the New World and no longer from Asia. Indigo from the West Indies was much more effective than Asian indigo, and despite the Atlantic crossing, it was less expensive than European woad because it was grown and made into dyestuff by slaves. That was why the protectionist measures attempting to save

THE GREEN OF THE AGE OF THE ENLIGHTENMENT
In eighteenth-century dress, green was not a very common color. Nevertheless, it was more common in England, Germany, and northern Europe than in France and Italy. And the more green was promoted toward the end of the century, the larger its place would grow.

FROM LEFT TO RIGHT:

Francis Cotes, *Boy in Green Coat*, c. 1750. Private collection.

George Romney, *Ann Barbara Russell*, c. 1780. London, Rafael Valls Gallery.

Michael Dahl, *Margaret Cavendish Bentinck, Duchess of Portland*, c. 1720. Private collection.

George Romney, *Francis Lind*, c. 1785. Private collection.

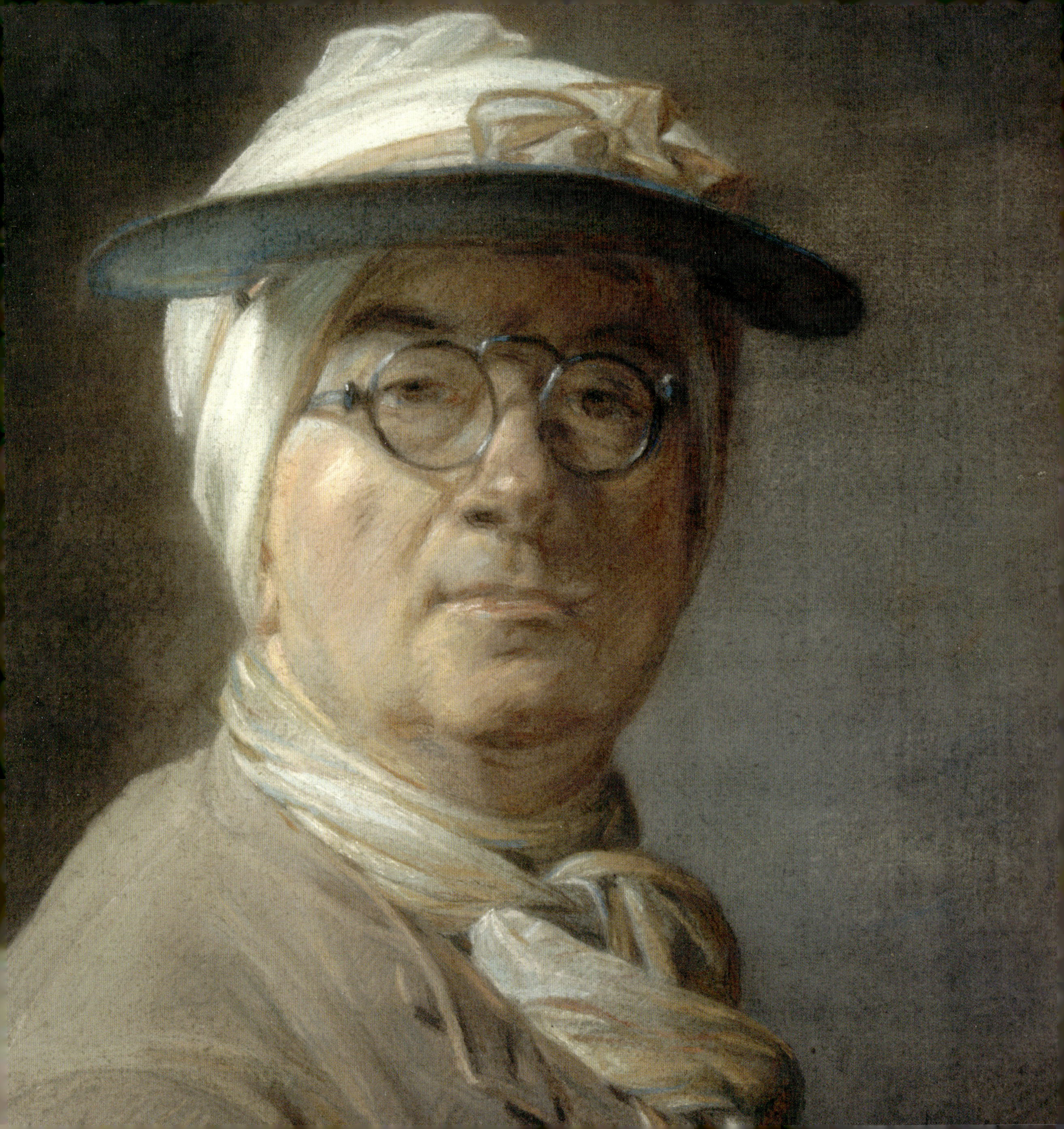

JEAN-BAPTISTE SIMÉON CHARDIN

An admirable painter of grays, Chardin was also good with greens, which he knew how to render in all shades: grayish or bluish, saturated or watered down, tending toward yellow or toward white.

Jean-Baptiste Siméon Chardin, *Self-portrait with a Green Eyeshade*, drawing on paper, 1775. Paris, Musée du Louvre.

European woad collapsed one after the other, leading to the ruin of certain cities (Amiens, Toulouse, Erfurt, Gotha) and the good fortune of a few ports (Nantes, Bordeaux).

From the 1730s until the 1780s, thanks to Prussian blue and American indigo, blue tones were all the rage. Their range diversified into a considerable number of shades, more than for any other color. Blue's progress did nothing for the greens, however. Of course by using new pigments and colorants it became possible to make beautiful tones of green more easily, notably dark greens, but that was not enough to establish or reestablish a taste for that color. And this was even more true because, as we have seen, there were still artists who were hostile to mixing blue and yellow, and with regard to dyeing, professional regulations were still strict and discouraged processes that merged those two colors. It was not until the end of the century that green began to become a fashionable color, first for furniture and later for clothing.

For the time being, mid-century, green remained neglected, inconspicuous, and unpopular. The fashion for blue tones was detrimental to it, especially as the idea circulated that green and blue went badly together (an idea still widespread today). An English proverb destined to great popularity in the following century made its appearance in the 1740s: "blue with green should never be seen." This echoes a slightly earlier German expression: *Blau oder Grün muss man wählen* ("blue or green, one must choose"). In the mid-eighteenth century throughout Europe, one chose blue and relinquished green. High-society women were especially hostile to the color because in the evenings, in the glow of lamps and candles, green tones turned dull and tended toward a more or less dirty brown. As in the theater it was better to avoid wearing them if one wanted to appear to best advantage. Moreover, many people continued to believe, as in the Middle Ages, that wearing green brought bad luck. First, it was supposedly dangerous, both in dyeing and in painting; second, it was still forever closely linked to demons and witches.

Later in the century, when dyeing had made great progress, especially with regard to the dark tones, green gained a little ground but more among the bourgeois than the aristocracy. Goethe echoed this in his famous *Treatise on Color*. Associating each color with a social category, he made green the color of the bourgeois and merchants, reserving red for nobility, black for the clergy, and blue for artisans and workers. It is true that we are now in 1810 and no longer in 1750. In that same treatise, which had some influence on dress and furniture fashions in Germany before being roundly rejected in the second half of the nineteenth century, Goethe sees green as a soothing color and recommends its use for decorating places of rest and conviviality. In his home in Weimar, his bedroom had dark green hangings. He died there in 1832, and his last words were, "More light."

A romantic color?

YOUNG GOETHE IN A GREEN COAT

In his epistolary novel *The Sorrows of Young Werther* (1774), one of the greatest bestsellers of the eighteenth century, Goethe dresses his hero in a blue coat and yellow breeches. For two or three decades all the young men of Europe would dress "à la Werther," all except Goethe whose favorite color seems to have always been green.

Georg Melchior Kraus, *Portrait of Young Goethe*, 1775. Weimar, Goethe Nationalmuseum.

There is great temptation to make green into a Romantic color, linking its growing popularity in the last years of the eighteenth century to a renewed attraction to nature. That is not false. Painters and poets delighted in celebrating trees and greenery, featuring walks in the meadows and woods, glorifying nature as a place of peace and contemplation, far from fashionable circles and the upheavals of society. Nevertheless, looking a bit more closely, we can see that green was not a particularly emblematic color for Romantic creation. That was much more true of other colors. First of all, the spectacle of nature was not limited to vegetation: water, the sea, the sky, the moon, and night played at least as great a role in it. Secondly, nature was only one of Romanticism's many themes: love, death, revolution, dream, travel, infinity, nothingness, to cite the principal ones. Consequently, the palette of the Romantic soul was not at all limited to the color green, and if it were necessary to highlight two colors, they would certainly be blue and black.

Blue, the color of dream and daydream, of sky and infinity, is especially associated with the beginnings of Romanticism. It is the color of Werther's famous morning coat, a blue coat with tails worn over yellow breeches, that Goethe describes in his epistolary novel, *The Sorrows of Young Werther*, published in 1774. The extraordinary success of the book and the "Wertheromania" that followed launched the rage for blue morning coats throughout fashionable Europe. But blue was also the color of the marvelous, inaccessible flower seen in a dream by the poet Novalis, a flower that embodies all at once the beloved woman, pure poetry, and the ideal life. It quickly became the symbolic figure of German Romanticism and, in the first years of the nineteenth century, reverberated throughout all of Europe.[55] A bit later it was black,

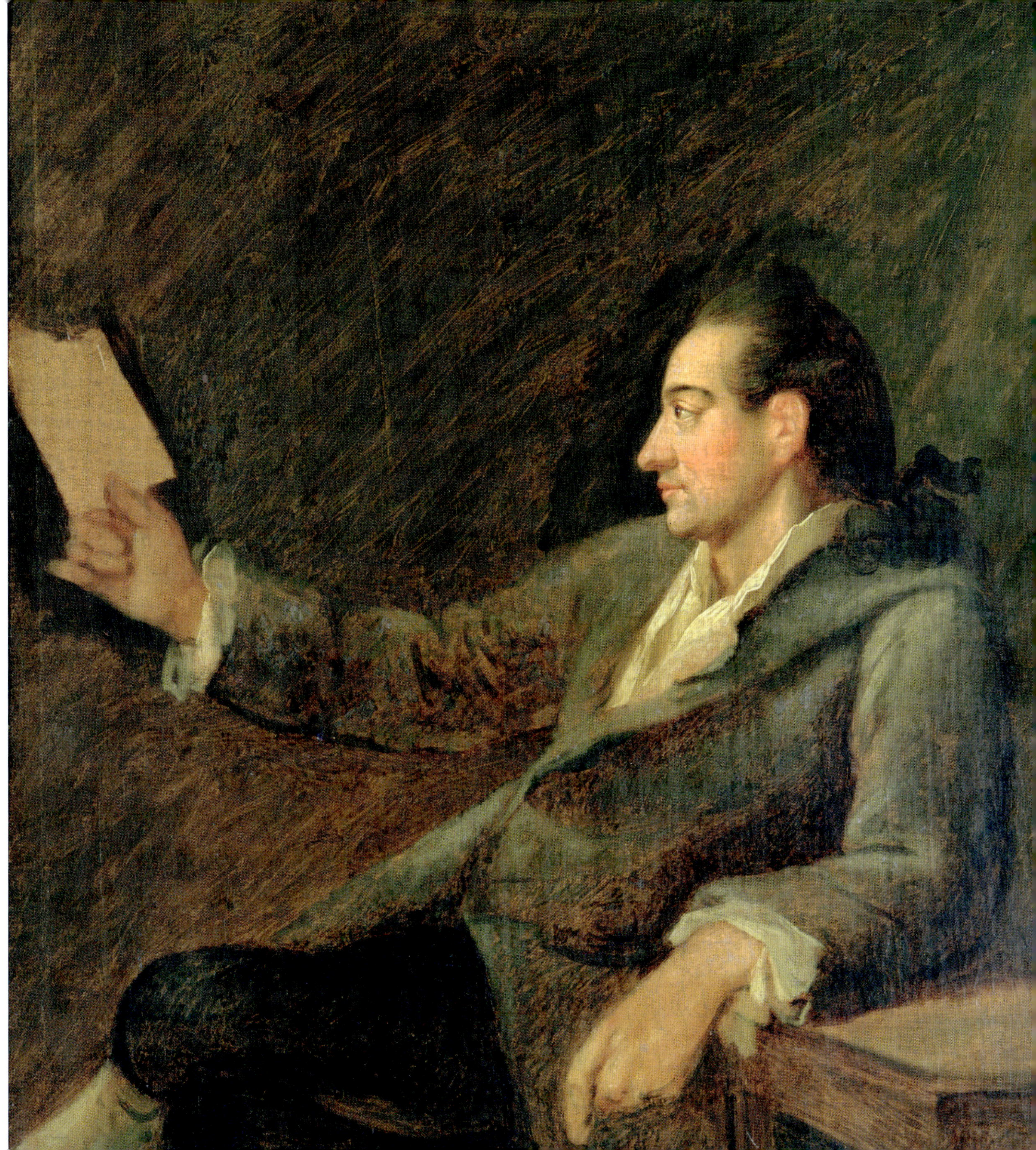

the color of night and death, that became the emblem of the second Romantic movement. Love then gave way to melancholy, day dream to nightmare, ecstasy to despair. Henceforth, no more blue flower seen in dreams but macabre hallucinations, witches, morbid and frenetic terrors. If statistics were meaningful and if one could count the color terms used by poets in the 1820–1850 generation, no doubt the adjective "black" would be the most common and the most significant, in the image of the bewitching "Black Sun of Melancholy" by Gérard de Nerval.

Blue, black, but not much green among the Romantics, unless we look further back, among their precursors, the pre-Romantics, in about the 1760s. Then green did capture the attention of poets and artists. It was the green of nature, or rather that of the plant world, which sensitive souls liked to contemplate and solitary hearts to confide in. That soothing and protective green was itself a refuge, a source of inspiration, and a divine color that offered the poet lessons in wisdom and infinity. It is delicately presented by Jean-Jacques Rousseau in *The New Heloise* (1761) and *Reveries of a Solitary Walker* (1776–1778) and then by his imitators or followers until the end of the century. It did not disappear with the next generation but became more subdued and ceded its place to blue and then to black.

On the other hand another green made its appearance a bit later and played an important role in the ideological movements of the 1800s: the green of liberty. It was also, in its way, a Romantic green, even if it is difficult to name its precise origin. Of course, in the ancient symbolism of green, a color that was unstable, agitated, and rebellious, there was always a transgressive and libertarian dimension, but that is not enough to make it the color of the new ideas and the revolution underway in the 1790s and 1800s. The Christian virtue of hope, associated with this color since the Middle Ages, would be better suited to the role. But perhaps we must look elsewhere, to color theories and classifications. The gradual distinction between "primary" and "secondary" colors, made first by painters and then by scholars, had gradually led to considering green one of red's opposites. As red had long been the color of prohibition, green, its opposite, had naturally become the color of permission over the course of decades. The two-color signal system in some ports in the North Sea and the Baltic constitutes one of its first applications; a beacon's green signal gave ships access to the port, red denied it.

This code for maritime signals, which became widespread in the first half of the nineteenth century, not only on land but also on sea, soon influenced railway signals, which in turn influenced roadway signals. In towns the earliest two-color traffic lights were installed in London in December 1868, on the corner of Palace Yard and Bridge Street. It was a matter of a pivoting gas lamp, operated by a policeman to produce a light that was sometimes green and sometimes red. It was a dangerous system since the following year an explosion mortally wounded a policeman who had come to light the lamps. London nevertheless proved to be the great pioneer in this area since Paris did not follow its lead until 1923, Berlin until 1924.[56] In the meantime, two-color lights had taken over the United States: Salt Lake City, 1912; Cleveland, 1914; New York, 1918. Henceforth, to be free to go was to "have the green light."

Whatever its origins, the green of freedom just missed being the color of the Revolution in France in 1789. On July 12 in Paris, in the Palais-Royal gardens, the young lawyer Camille Desmoulins harangued the

THE UNION OF BLUE AND YELLOW

In his famous *Treatise on Color* (1810–1811), Goethe made the combination of blue and yellow the perfect model of a chromatic couple. From this "union of opposites" was born green, a "medial, calm, and soothing" color that he recommends using in rooms meant for rest.

Illustration for an edition of the *Farbenlehre* by J. W. von Goethe, Tübingen, 1827, plate 5.

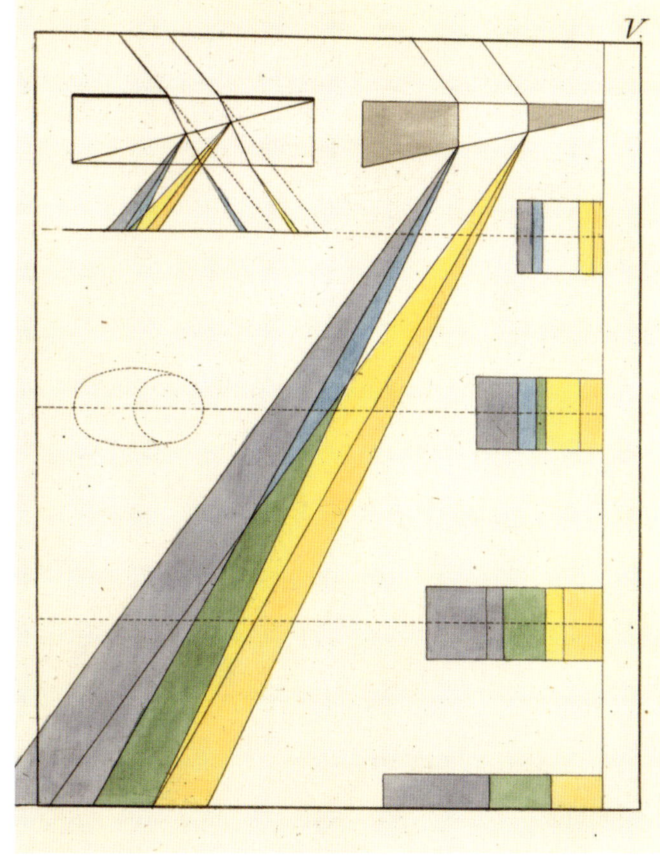

masses and urged insurrection. He picked a linden leaf, stuck it onto his hat and invited all the patriots who shared his mission to do the same as a rallying sign. The leaf became a cockade, the first revolutionary cockade; it was the color green.[57] The next day—unfortunately for green—the insurgents, heading toward the Invalides barracks to find guns, learned that green was the color of the livery of the Count of Artois, younger brother of Louis XVI (and future King Charles X), and that most of his men already wore green cockades or scarves. The Count of Artois was the fiercest enemy of reforms and new ideas; it was unthinkable to share this color with him, even if it was the color of liberty.[58] The green cockade was thus abandoned, even before the storming of the Bastille on July 14. Three days later, the tricolored cockade appeared, destined for a glorious future; the national flag would grow out of it. But we are allowed to dream here: if the Count of Artois had not had green livery (documented in 1784), perhaps the French flag would have been entirely green, the color of freedom and hope, and green might have become the national color of republican France, its palaces and monuments, its ceremonies, its soldiers, its sports teams. . . .

Although it was quickly dropped by the insurgents of July 12, 1789, Camille Desmoulins's green cockade remained famous and had a few heirs in neighboring countries. That was the case in French-speaking Switzerland. In January 1798 Vaud, which for centuries had been under Savoyard and then Bernese protection, declared itself independent, taking the name of the "Lemanic Republic." Adhering to the ideas of the French Revolution, the new state chose for its emblems a green flag and a green cockade, as reminders that green was the color of liberty. The existence of the Lemanic Republic was brief (three months), that of the Helvetian Republic that subsequently incorporated it not much

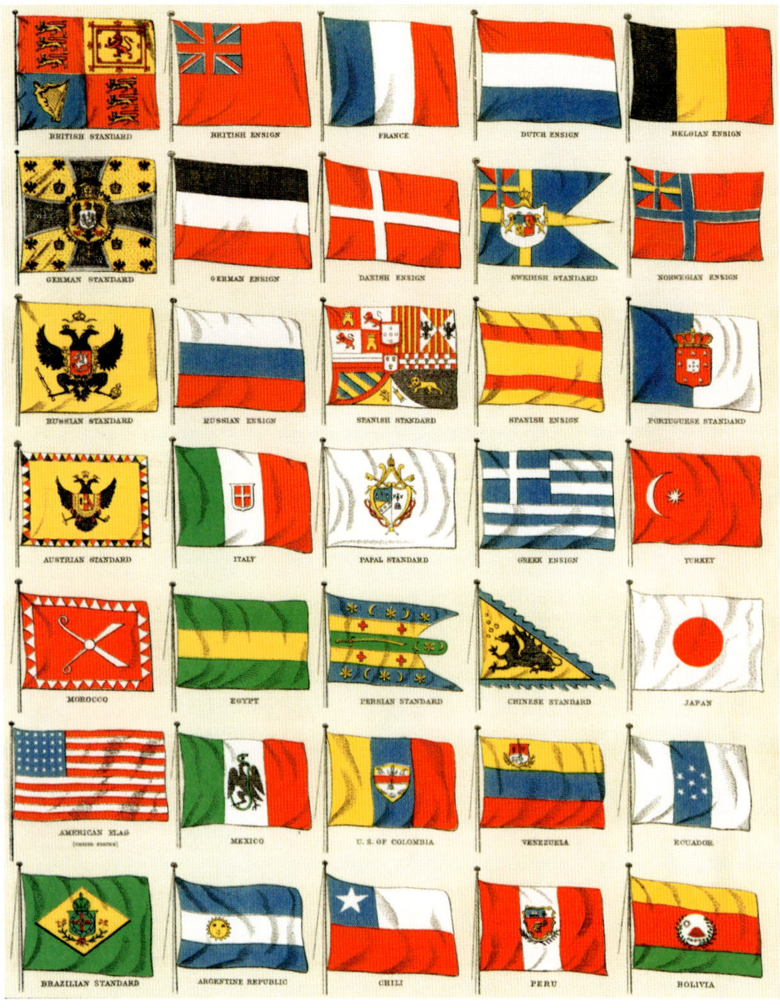

NAUTICAL FLAGS OF THE LATE NINETEENTH CENTURY

Rare in medieval coats of arms, the color green appears more frequently in the nautical flags of the modern period and even more often in contemporary flags. When it is not the religious color of Islam, it expresses ideas of liberty, hope, or prosperity.

Nautical flags, anonymous lithograph, c. 1880. Paris, Bibliothèque du musée de la Marine.

longer (five years). But in 1803, when Switzerland became a confederation again, henceforth composed of nineteen cantons, the new canton of Vaud adopted the emblems it still uses today: a bicolor white and green flag, a coat of arms *coupé d'argent et de sinople*, and a simply formulated device "*Liberté et Patrie.*" Here again, green and freedom are closely associated.

Today there are many flags throughout the world that include green. When it is a matter of a Muslim country, this green is the religious color of Islam, of which we have spoken at length in the first chapter of this book. When it is a matter of west African countries (Senegal, Mali, Ghana, Cameroon), green is one of the three pan-African colors (the other two being yellow and red), adopted at the time of independence. Elsewhere, the significance of green is more varied and uncertain. Often, moreover, it is a matter of a posteriori interpretations rather than true historical explanations. Rediscovering the reasons for the colors in a given flag is always a difficult exercise, as though to "function" well, that is, to be endowed with great symbolic power, a flag must always be surrounded with a certain air of mystery regarding its origins. Many countries associate the green in their flags with their vegetation, essentially their forests, and the riches they draw from them (Brazil, Gabon, Zaire). Others see it more simply as the color of hope (Jamaica, Togo). Still others see it as the symbol of freedom won from a tyrannical or dominant power (Mexico, Bolivia, Bulgaria, Portugal); in this case green is often combined with red, independence having been acquired through bloodshed. On the Irish flag the meaning of green is different; it represents the Catholic community while orange stands for the Protestant community, and the white that separates them signifies the peace that must reign between them.

The green of the Italian flag—green, white, red—is more difficult to interpret, despite the massive amount of literature that has been devoted to it. The vertical tricolor design was clearly inspired by that of the French flag, especially since it first appeared in 1796–1797, at the time when the short-lived Cispadane Republic was established. Legend has it that Napoleon Bonaparte was its creator. Although it is true that he showed a certain attraction to green even up until he died, it is doubtful that would explain the green in the Cispadane and then the Italian flag. The idea of liberty, of newly won freedom, might be more relevant here. Unless the green-white-red more mundanely represents the colors of the uniforms of Milan's civilian guards, who played an important role in the events of 1796–1797. That explanation would be solid historically, if disappointing symbolically. Later, after the establishment of the Italian realm and the definitive adoption of the tricolor flag in 1861, the colors were interpreted either as those of the Savoy (the *gueules* and the *argent* of coats of arms and the green of the dynastic livery), or as those of the three cardinal virtues of Christian theology: faith (white), hope (green), charity (red). Later still, more or less fanciful exegetes saw in the three colors those of the Italian countryside, or even of pasta sauces.[59] A flag is always a place of memory and an invitation to dream. But it is also an object that lends itself to all interpretations, aberrations, and trivialities.

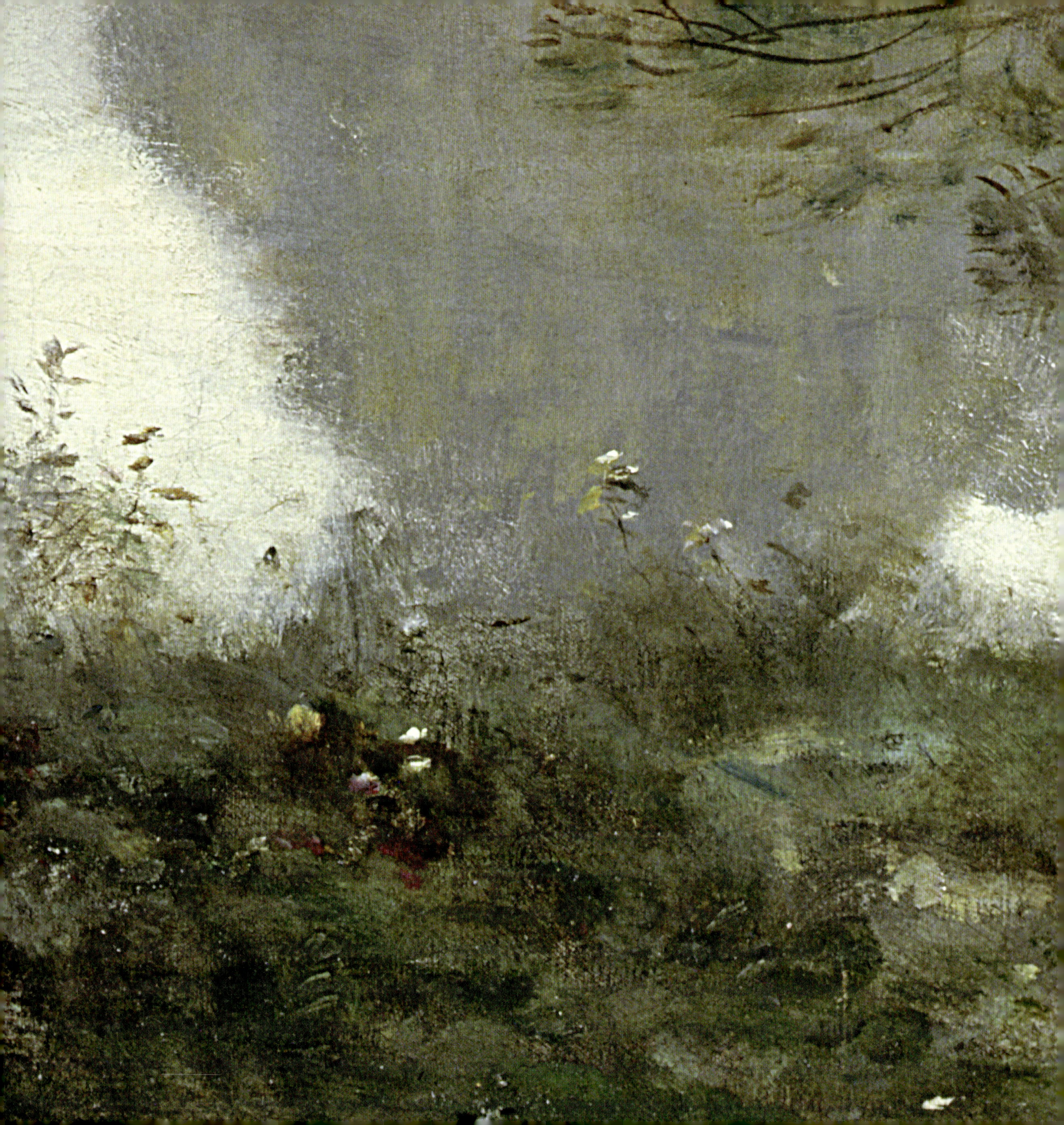

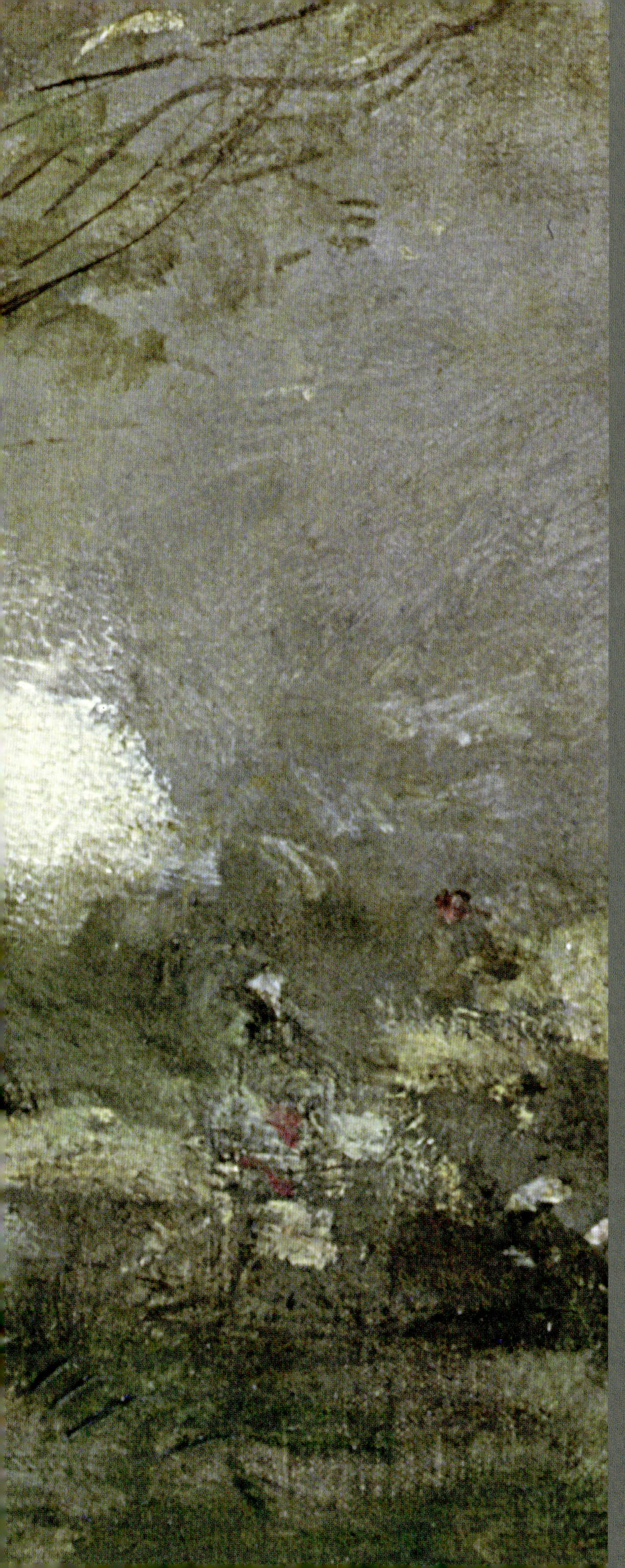

A **soothing** color

19TH–21ST CENTURIES

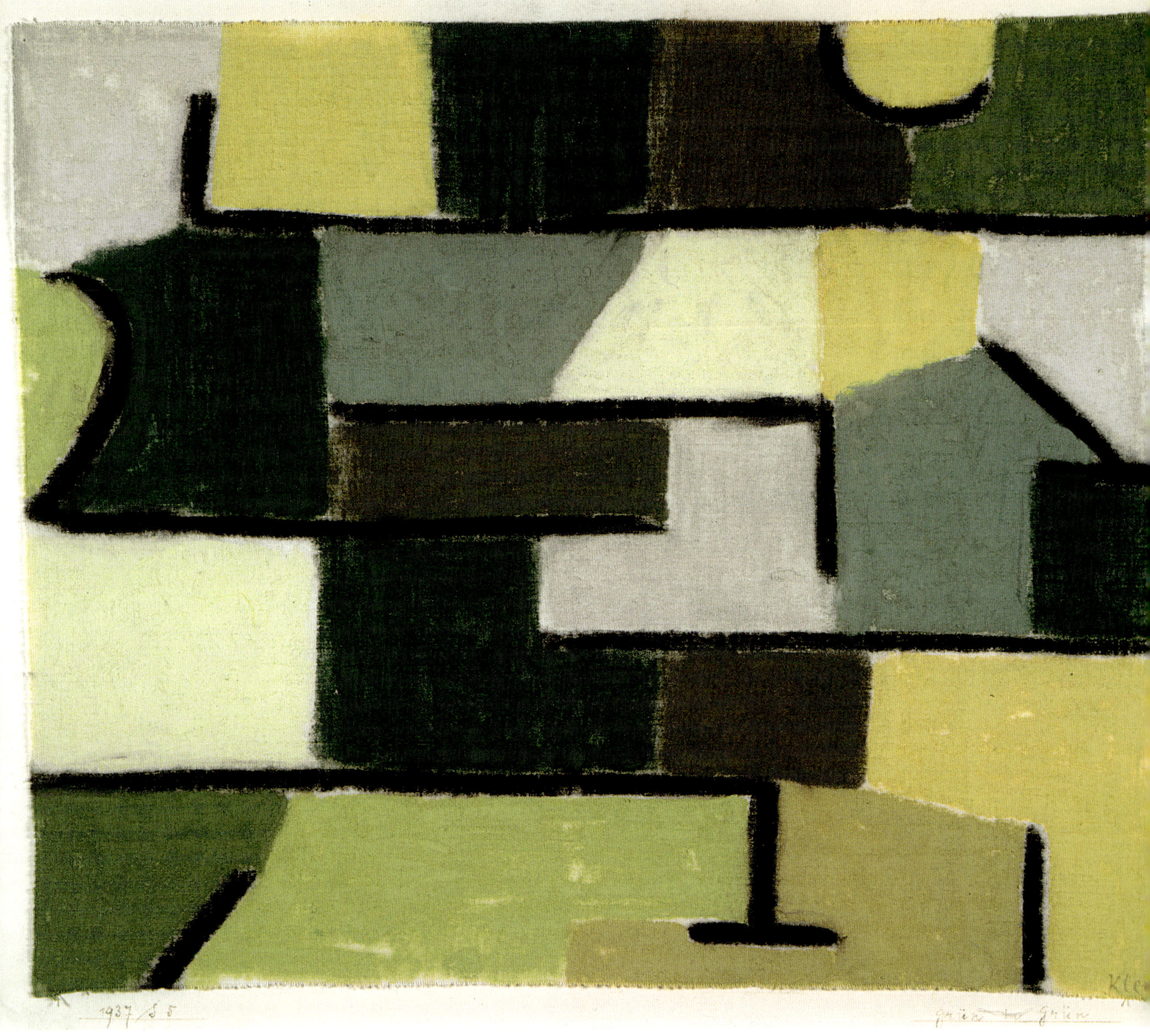

The history of green in the contemporary period is one of highs and lows. Sometimes in fashion, sometimes less conspicuous, sometimes admired, often scorned, green had to wait for the most recent times to truly come into its own. Long discredited by scholars who saw it only as a "complementary" or second-rank color, neglected by painters who complained about its instability and the poor quality of the pigments required for obtaining it, rejected by fashionable women who blamed it for not being flattering enough, suspected by the common run of people who continued to believe it brought bad luck, outstripped in all areas by blue, red, black, and even white or yellow, green occupied a modest place in daily life and artistic creation.

That situation showed tentative signs of change in the second half of the nineteenth century. Green slowly regained value when urban dwellers felt a renewed attraction to the country, nature, and vegetation. But it was the following century especially that discovered or rediscovered its virtues. Over the course of the decades, green was attributed with more and more benefits, its ties to health and hygiene were reestablished, it was sought after as a source of revitalization, restoration, and renewal, and it was widely introduced into urban centers and suburbs to break up the overwhelming domination of grays, browns, and blacks. Sports, vacations, and outdoor activities took over from there, gradually transforming the life of Europeans into a frantic quest for green and greenery: green spaces, green classes, green vacations, green foods, green energy, green revolution. Green was no longer only the color of nature, hope, and freedom, it was also the color of health, hygiene, leisure-time activities, attractiveness, and even civic responsibility.

More recently, the virtues attributed to green have reached new heights and taken on an ethical dimension. Now everything must be green, the color that soothes and saves. In many countries the adjective has become a noun used to designate a political movement or party that makes defending the environment one of the platforms in its campaigns. The link between "green" and political ecology has become so strong that it is impossible today to pronounce the word without its immediately taking on political connotations. Green is no longer so much a color as an ideology. Is that grounds for celebration or for worry?

A fashionable color

Unappreciated for most of the eighteenth century, green experienced its first revival among the "fashionable" colors in the 1780s to 1800s, first in Germany and then gradually throughout the rest of Europe. This new taste went hand in glove with the movements for freedom and new ideas. Moreover, as Goethe underscored in his *Treatise on Color*, it affected the bourgeoisie and the business world more than the nobility. In France it was under the Directory (1795–1799) that the color green returned to the forefront, both in clothing and in furnishings. The phenomenon lasted under the Consulate and the Empire, and even well into the Restoration of the Bourbons. In Italy the new rage for green followed almost the same chronology as in France, but it was longer lived, enduring well into the nineteenth century. Elsewhere, in Spain and Scandinavia, the style was less pronounced and more circumstantial, depending upon the strength or weakness of the influence exerted by Paris and France. Only England resisted the general trend, although not entirely: in 1806, when the British Parliament was entirely renovated, red was chosen for the high chamber, the House of Lords; green was chosen for the low chamber, the House of Commons. Even in the United Kingdom, green appeared to be a bourgeois and "progressive" color.[1]

PAGE 180: **THE MUSIC OF GREENS**

All of Klee's works possess an undeniable musical dimension. But when they fall within the range of greens, they seem to resonate with a particular intensity, that of youth, freshness, and freedom.

Paul Klee, *Vert dans verts*, gouache on paper, 1921. Berne, Kleezentrum.

THE GREEN EMPIRE

In France, during the First Empire, green was in fashion as much for clothing as for furniture and decoration. The Sèvres porcelain factory, which had achieved great feats in the range of blues under Louis XV, had to extend its palette and offer new green shades, henceforth combined with brilliant golds.

Sèvres vase in the style of François Gérard, c. 1810. Compiègne, Musée national du Château.

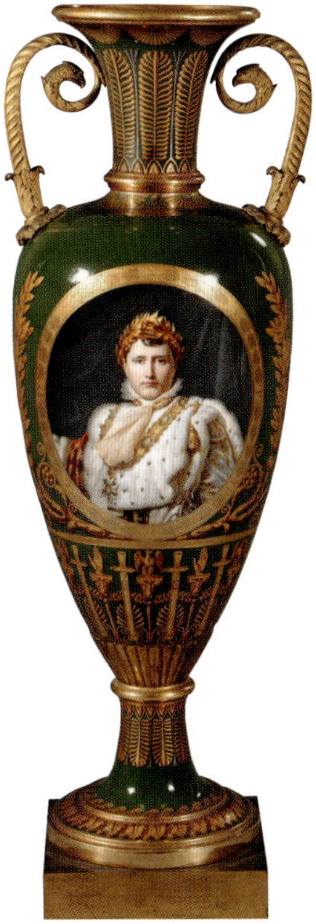

That said, for the styles of the period from 1790 to 1830, there was green and then there was green. At first the color was decidedly dark and more or less bluish, its shades owing to the abundant use of Prussian blue and its derivatives; subsequently it became lighter and created a delicate romantic palette with white and pink on dresses and hangings. Sometimes for a holiday or a show more vivid colors would be added, red or yellow, for example, to create an exotic or "troubadour" atmosphere. But that was true especially in the period from 1820 to 1850. Earlier in France, in the era of the First Empire, greens were still relatively dark and combined with "Pompeian" reds or crimsons and bright gold tones. Military uniforms granted them a place they had never before known, and for the first time they influenced the uniforms of allied and neighboring countries. A persistent myth holds that Napoleon was at the origin of this "Empire green" style, green being his favorite color. Although it is true that he showed a preference for green throughout his life, he was not in the least responsible for the popularity of green throughout Europe at the turn of the eighteenth–nineteenth centuries. Green was in fashion before he ascended to the imperial throne—and even before his appearance on the military and political scene—and remained so long after his demise in 1815.

As an aside, this color did not bring good luck to the Emperor and may have caused his death at Sainte-Hélène in 1821. In his Longwood residence many rooms were in fact decorated in green, a particularly toxic green obtained from copper shavings dissolved in arsenic. This was "Schweinfurt green," developed in that German town in 1814 and rapidly distributed throughout Europe to make paints, dyes, colorants, and painted papers. Now, exposed to humidity, arsenic evaporates and in strong doses becomes dangerous. That is undoubtedly what happened at Sainte-Hélène and explains why arsenic was found in Napoleon's hair and under his fingernails. If he really was poisoned, it was not by his English guards or by any of his enemies or companions, but probably by the arsenic vapors released by tapestries, fabric, leather, and paintings. Schweinfurt green and Saint-Hélène's humid climate were solely responsible.

The toxicity of this product was not recognized until quite late, about mid-century. That explains in part green's declining use in furnishings beginning in the 1860s. With fatal accidents occurring more often (notably in children's rooms) and the danger of arsenic vapors and derivatives having been affirmed by chemists and health professionals, green gradually stopped being used on walls and furniture, even though for a long time some manufacturers still claimed, not entirely in good faith, that Schweinfurt green was not dangerous.[2] Here, for example, is what the head of the Zuber & Cie factory in Mulhouse wrote to Friedrich Goppelsröder, a chemistry professor at the University of Basel, in 1870, after Goppelsröder had drawn the attention of the public authorities to the harmfulness of arsenic-based greens in furniture and decor:

> In France as in other countries, no law forbids the use of Schweinfurt green. . . . The color of this green is so beautiful and so brilliant that it has not yet been entirely replaced because of these effects, and so it continues to be used not only in France but even in Germany, a country where it is strictly prohibited by law.
>
> In Italy, this beautiful green is so prized that we are often asked for papers entirely covered in this green, even though it is known that they can sometimes be harmful. But we have not heard of any accidents there because the climate is dry and the apartments spacious and airy. In central and northern European countries, we now only apply Schweinfurt green in small quantities on papers to give the greens their final brilliance. I maintain that in this case, its use is entirely inoffensive. . . . To want to prohibit all trace of arsenic in papers is to go too far and to hurt business unjustly and needlessly. We are ready to answer for all our products.[3]

The usual defense but a waste of time. The public refused to believe such claims and throughout Europe gradually rejected green papers and dyes, especially as accidents and anecdotes seemed to confirm green's age-old reputation as a color that brought bad luck. Some people came to loathe it. That was the case with Queen Victoria who, when she was widowed, developed a phobia for green and banished it from all the royal palaces, notably Buckingham Palace where, if we are to believe the gossip columns, it has still not made a comeback.

In the nineteenth century, however, there was a fear of green even more famous than Victoria's: Schubert's, which became mythic in Austria and Germany. For reasons escaping us, the great musician claimed that he was "ready to go to all ends to avoid that cursed color."[4] The short life of Schubert, dead at the age of thirty-one in 1828, was such a series of sorrows, failures, and suffering that we may well wonder whether his fear of green, an impossible color to totally avoid, was not justified.

In the second half of the nineteenth century, green may have gradually disappeared from furnishings and daily life, but that was not the case with clothing. Some fashionable women remained faithful to it and continued to consider it a soothing or romantic color. That was true of Empress Eugenie, one of the most beautiful women of her time, admired throughout Europe, where she set fashion trends for European society. Unlike Queen Victoria, she loved green and wore it in the evening for balls, theater, and the opera. It is true that in the 1860s dye manufacturing was making progress, and lighting no longer consisted of candles and oil lanterns as during the Ancien Régime, but now involved gas lamps. The light from gas was different and produced new effects. Moreover, Lyon dyers, together

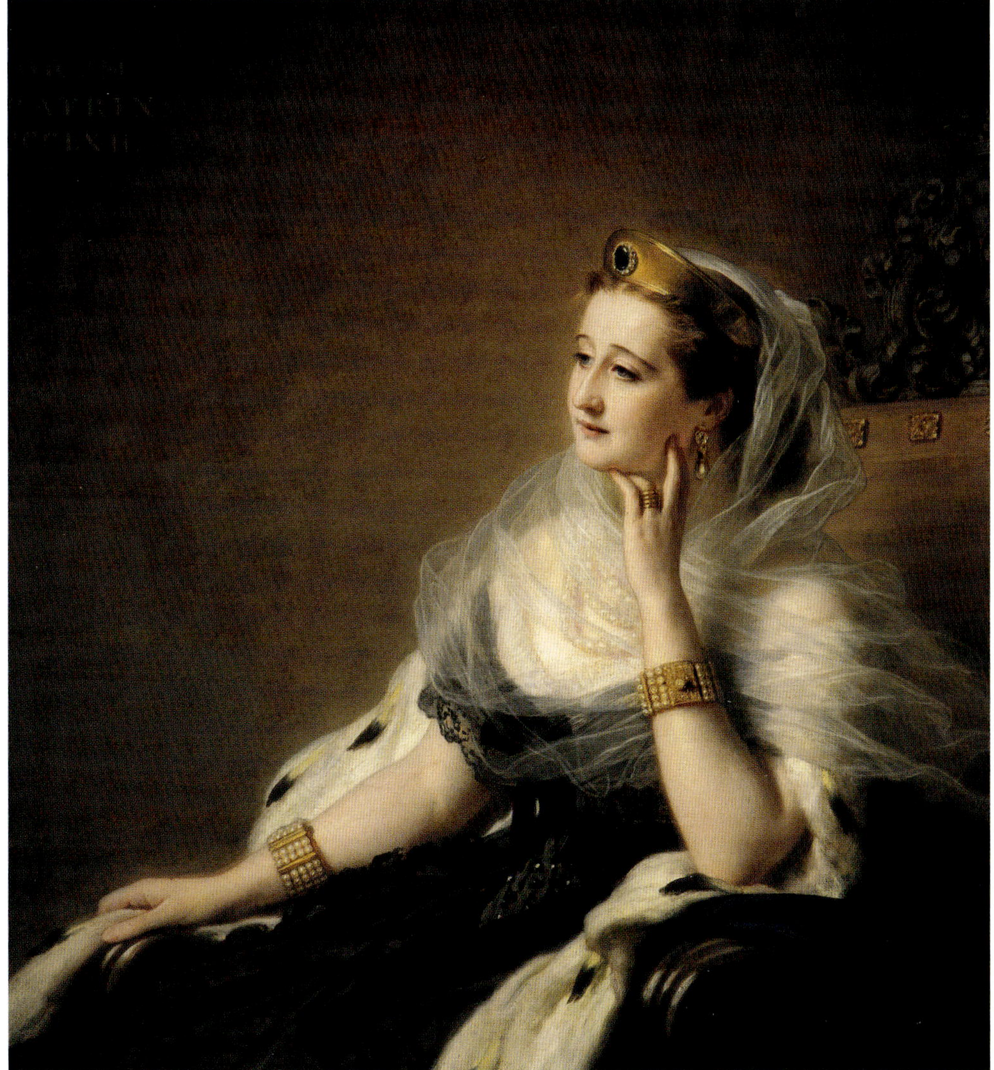

EMPRESS EUGÉNIE

Empress Eugénie loved green. She wore it for evenings at the ball, the theater, and the opera, taking advantage of the progress made in dyeing in this color range (notably on silk) and the new gas lighting. The green of her gowns was even more remarkable because of the way it contrasted with her splendid hair sprayed with gold dust.

Franz Xavier Winterhalter, *Empress Eugénie*, detail, 1862. Private collection.

with German chemists, perfected a new green dye, dense and luminous, that shimmered magnificently on silk: aldehyde (a type of dehydrogenated alcohol) green. Empress Eugenie was the first to wear this new shade of green, and the surprising play of light on it was all the more sensational because of her habit of misting her brown hair with gold dust. Green and gold: perfect harmony. Eugenie was imitated immediately in the courts as in the towns. Dyestuffs inspired by aldehyde green made their appearance in the industry for dying fabrics in bright shades: iodine green, methyl green, almond green. All these products were cheaper than the dye used for the empress's gowns, but they were more or less toxic, which limited their widespread use.[5]

Return to the palette

SEA GREEN

The sea has long been described and represented with colors. Medieval illuminators and Renaissance painters attributed to it a very broad palette. It was not until the modern period that artists reduced it to three dominant colors: green, gray, and blue. By choosing a dark, saturated green here, the young Monet creates a violent image of the sea, very unlike the one his Impressionist friends would later offer.

Claude Monet, *The Green Wave*, 1866–1867. New York, Metropolitan Museum of Art.

Dye production was not the only area in which progress was made throughout the nineteenth century; pigments progressed too, but more tentatively. In the range of greens, the invention of Prussian blue had allowed the preceding century to diversify the range of dark tones. Painters continued to use it extensively, especially since this pigment cost much less than natural ultramarine, imported from far away and comparable to a precious mineral.[6] Mixed with chrome yellow, Prussian blue produced beautiful green shades that were vivid, translucent, and nontoxic. But it was a volatile pigment with a strong tendency to fade. Many nineteenth-century painters fell victim to it: Constable, Delacroix, Monet and most of the Impressionists, Van Gogh, Gauguin, and Picasso even later still. Chrome yellows were hardly more stable moreover; they deteriorated and turned ocher, or even brown, so that a green pigment obtained by combining Prussian blue and chrome yellow was hardly resistant to the effects of light or time. Painters like Sisley and Seurat had painful experiences with it; for Sisley, most of his greens turned yellow, and on Seurat's major work, *Sunday Afternoon on the Island of La Grande Jatte* (1884–1886), the green lawn is now dotted with brown spots because of the darkening of the chrome yellow. Conversely, in nineteenth-century painting, many blue, yellow, or white pigments—zinc white, for example—became greenish over time, and in some paintings, green became dominant with age as it was not originally.

Over the course of the centuries, European painting had little luck with green pigments: plant greens did not hold up, earth greens did not cover well, malachite greens were expensive, those with a natural ultramarine base even more so, copper greens were corrosive, toxic, and turned black or brown over time, and greens with a Prussian blue base faded and turned grayish or

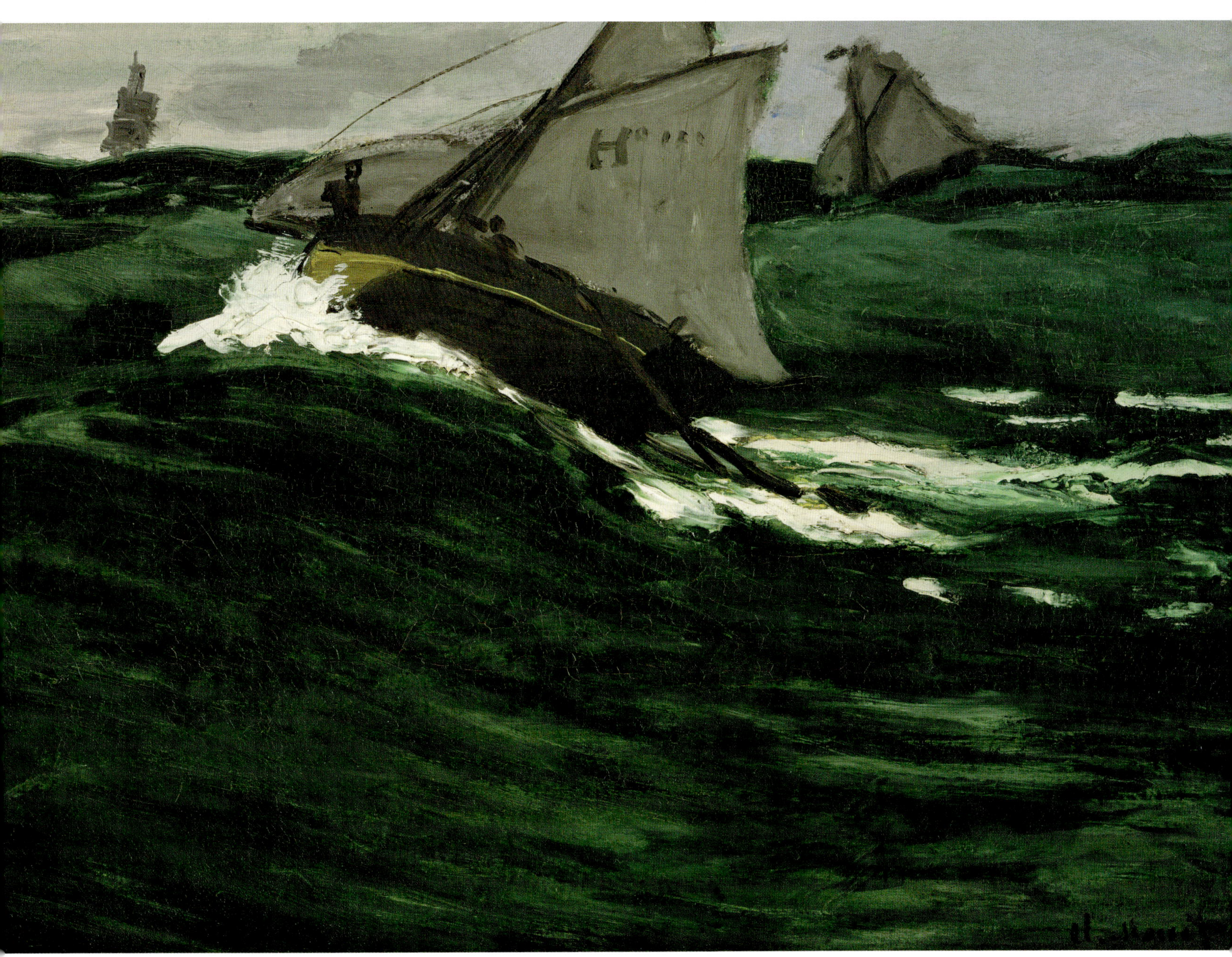

GREEN IN DIVISIONIST PAINTING

Seurat followed some of Chevreul's principles very closely, notably "optical mixing": two colors juxtaposed tend to merge optically and to be perceived by the eye as forming only a single color. Most of the greens in *La Grande Jatte* are produced in that way by the juxtaposition of yellow and blue points. But Seurat's chrome yellow–based pigments failed him; they darkened, and in certain places the green turned brown.

Georges Seurat, *A Sunday Afternoon on the Island of La Grande Jatte*, 1884–1886. Chicago, Art Institute.

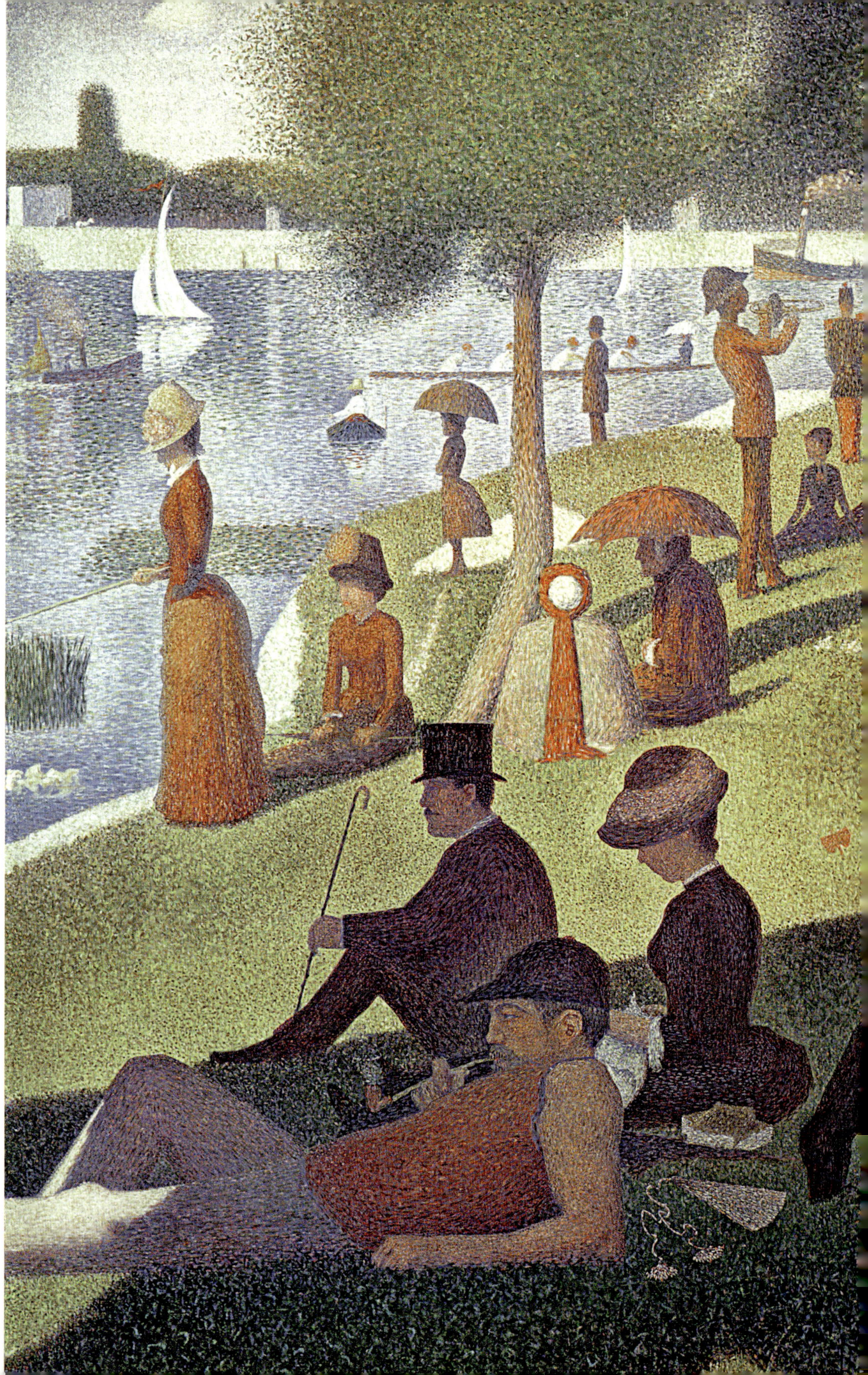

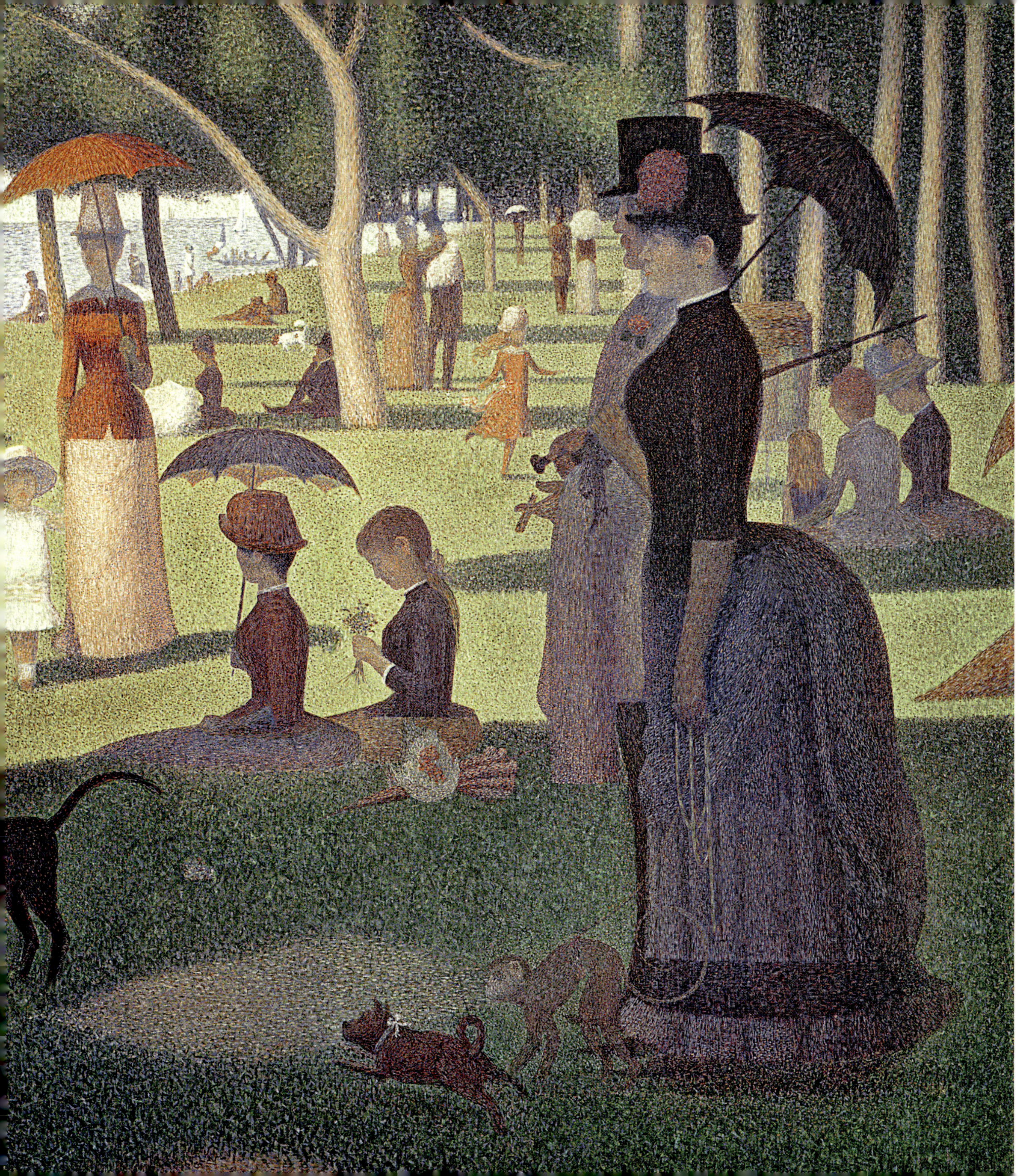

yellowish. From the sixteenth to the nineteenth centuries, all the great painters complained of the greens that were available and, like Veronese, dreamed of "green pigments as good in quality as the reds."

Important progress was finally made in 1825–1830 when French (Guimet) and German (Gmelin, Köttig) chemists perfected artificial ultramarine blues and greens, with bases of kaolin, silica, soda, and sulfur. But even though these new green pigments were more stable than greens with a Prussian-blue base, and even though they cost infinitely less than those with a natural ultramarine or cobalt base (cobalt green, perfected at the end of the eighteenth century and sometimes called "emerald green," cost a fortune), painters did not trust them. Ingres and Turner tried them but did not find them satisfactory; neither did Monet originally. It was not until the 1880s that artificial ultramarine greens finally found their rightful place on the palettes of the great painters. Renoir and Cézanne were among the first to put faith in them and to derive from them subtle mixes.[7]

In the meantime, another invention had changed the work of painters and landscape painting: the soft metal tube, hermetically sealed and easily transportable, which allowed artists to work outside. This was the invention of John Goffe Rand who, after much trial and error, perfected his definitive formula in 1841. The soft paint tube was not marketed in Europe until 1859–1860. After that, young artists left the studios and went out into the country to try to capture on canvas the beauty of nature, the diversity of plant life, the play of shadow and light, reflections on water, and changes in weather. Landscape painting found itself transformed and, with it, the role reserved for the color green in pictorial creation.

Since the late Middle Ages the place of greens in European painting had been in continual decline. "Great painting" had used it modestly, as mythology, history, allegory, biblical episodes, and religious themes did not lend themselves very well to abundant use of this color. Only landscape painting granted it a proper place for representing the plant world, but landscape painting remained poorly regarded and, as we have just said, green pigments were hardly satisfactory. Still today, we often have the impression that painters during the Ancien Régime neglected the spring and vivid colors when they represented the countryside, meadows, woods, hills, or forests, giving preference to autumn and dark tones. That is a distorted view, created by the way greens have turned brown and blues have evaporated, a view that the most skillful restorations have not managed to correct.

That was no longer the case in the second half of the nineteenth century; everything changed, or nearly. Not only did green pigments evolve and become more stable, blues less costly, and yellows more reliable, but young painters now worked outside, freeing themselves from all academicism and returning landscape painting to its rightful place. Colors grew lighter, tones became livelier and purer, and new attention was given to the range of greens. In France the painters of the Barbizon school, Camille Corot

ROMANTIC GREENS AND GRAYS

The critics have sometimes been harsh with Corot when he tried to translate daydream or memory onto canvas by overusing iridescent mists and grayish fogs. *Mortefontaine*, however, escapes all criticism and is even considered one of the high points of Romantic painting.

Jean-Baptiste Corot, *Memory of Mortefontaine*, 1864. Paris, Musée du Louvre.

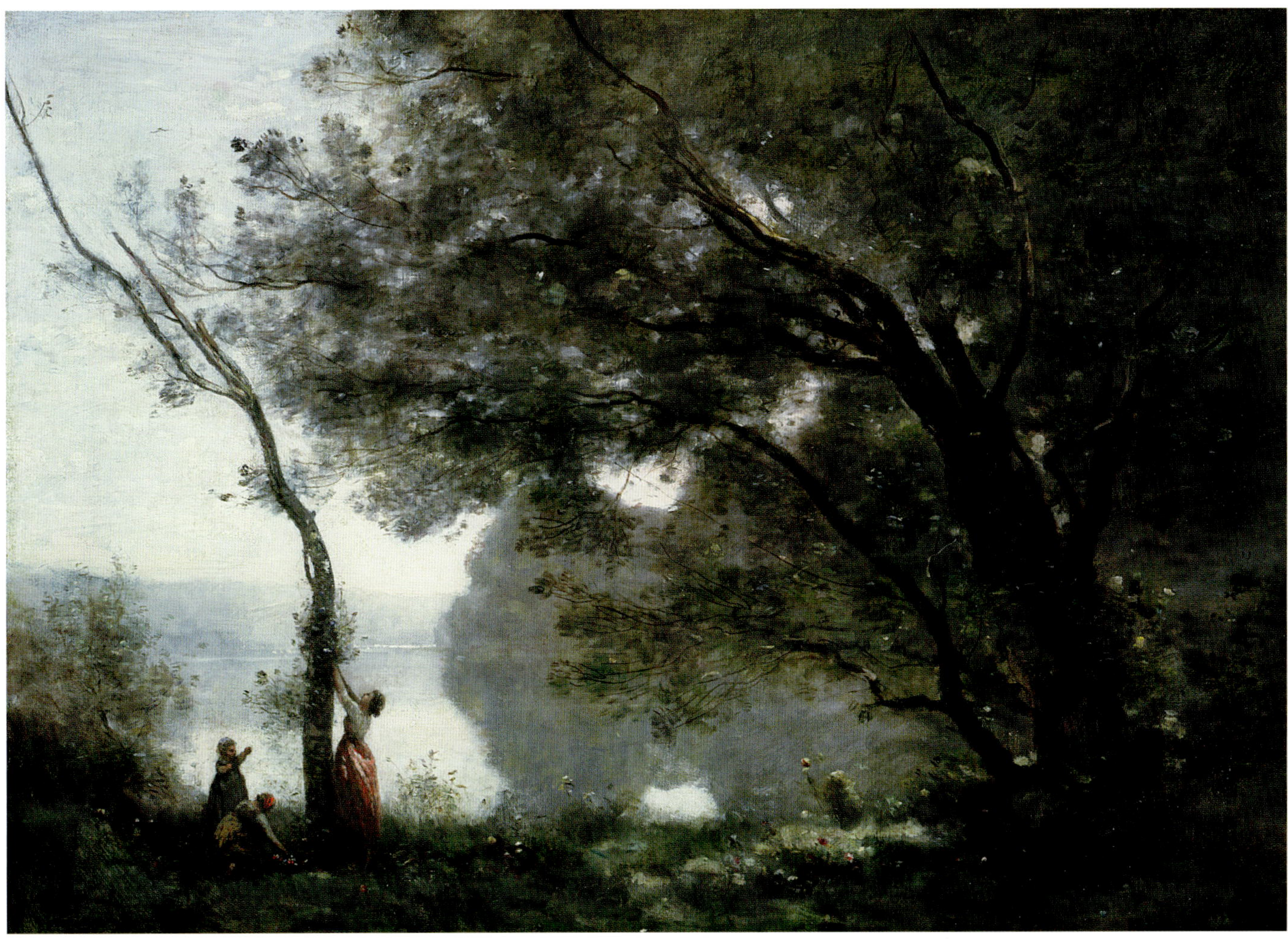

and Eugène Boudin, proved to be forerunners in these areas in which a few Italian veduta painters and English landscape painters preceded them. But it was the Impressionists who took the decisive step, even if their beginnings were difficult. Originally criticized, mocked, and even ridiculed, they eventually won a share of public support for the innovations they proposed. Color was at the heart of their concerns. They did not attempt to reproduce forms realistically or precisely, but to suggest them through color and light. The paint strokes are fragmented, shades broken down, and contrasts multiplied to produce vibratory effects like those of the sun and clouds in trees or on the surface of water. Hence the new palettes, within which green occupied a notable place for the first time in a long time.

Evidence of this new attention to the range of greens is provided by the manuals meant for young artists. Beginning in the 1850s, the recipes for producing greens became more numerous, advice and

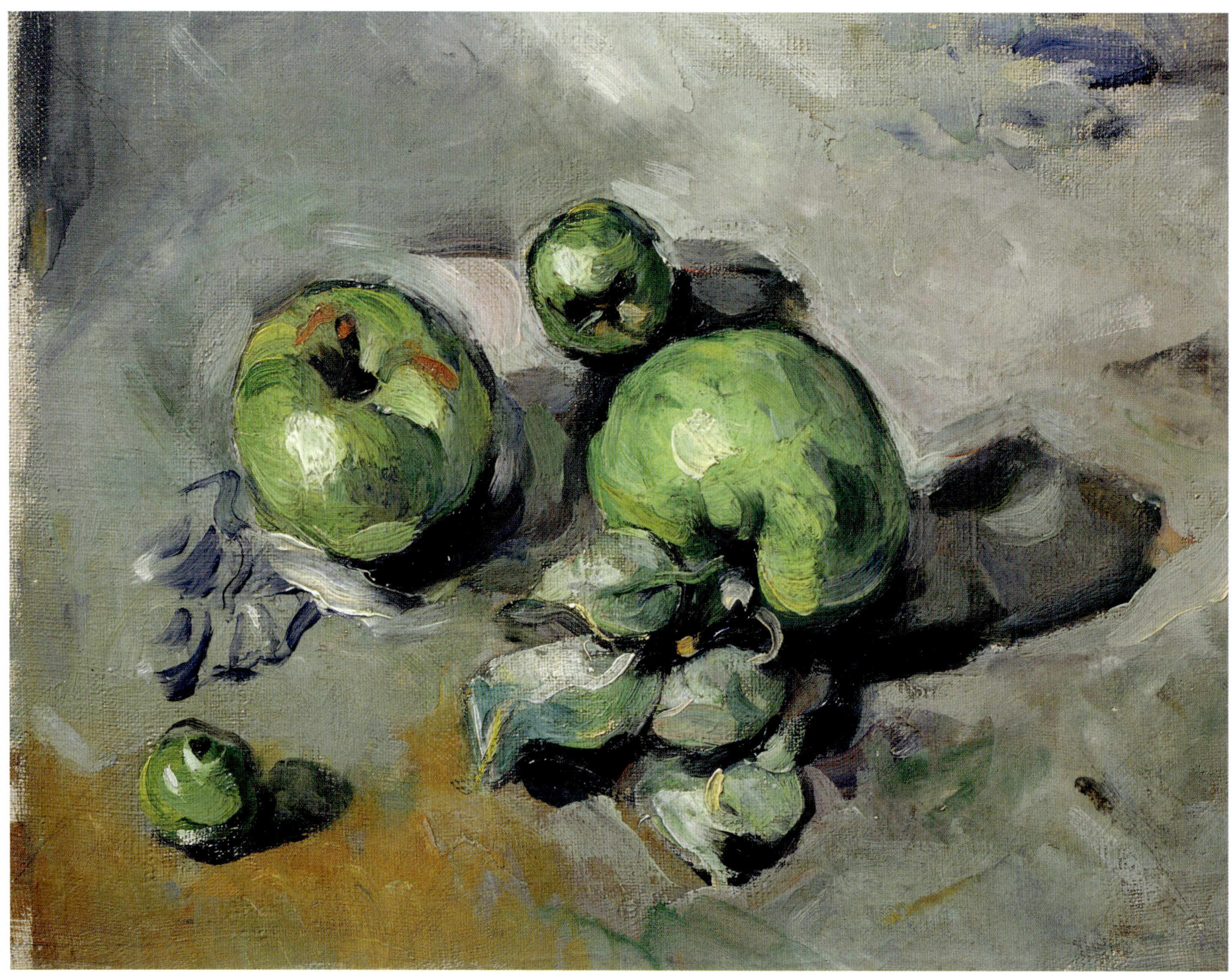

commentary more precise and concrete, and a previously unknown rubric made its appearance: "landscape greens." For example, we learn that to obtain a delicate green meant for "spring leaves," it was sufficient to mix Prussian blue and chrome yellow, add a little zinc white and "a touch of very vivid Venetian pink."[8] Pink in green: that is most certainly an innovation!

POLYCHROMATIC GREEN

Cézanne was the painter of apples par excellence. In his work they can assume any color and can even be totally polychromatic. In these undeniably green apples, we can thus note the presence of white, blue, yellow, brown, gray, red, black, and even a bit of purple.

Paul Cézanne, *Green Apples*, c. 1873. Paris, Musée d'Orsay.

Chevreul and the scientists did not like green

This improvement remained limited and short-lived however. In the second half of the nineteenth century, scientific theories deeply influenced artistic creation, and the hierarchy of colors on the palette suffered the consequences. Since green was not a "primary," or first-rank, color for scientists, it was no longer one for artists, not even for those who practiced landscape painting and worked outdoors. For many, green was simply "complementary," a second-rank color whose main function was to contrast with red and show it to good advantage. Here, for example, is what Vincent Van Gogh wrote to his brother Théo in September 1888 regarding his painting *The Night Café*, now part of the Yale University collection. The work shows a large room in the middle of which sits a billiard table, with other tables and chairs lining the walls:

> I tried to express with the red and the green the terrible human passions. The room is blood red and dull yellow, a green billiard table in the middle, four lemon yellow lamps radiating orange and green. There is conflict everywhere, an antithesis of the most different greens and reds. . . . The blood red of the walls and the yellow-green of the billiard table, for example, contrast with the little soft Louis XV green of the counter, where there is a pink bouquet.[9]

For painters as for scientists, green had become red's opposite, which lowered it a notch in the genealogy of colors. Hierarchically, it was placed on the same level as orange and purple, "complementaries" of yellow and blue respectively. Of course, that was not a new status for it—already in the seventeenth century painters had denied green the standing of a "primitive" color—but in the nineteenth century, it was a status that took on greater and greater scope and that contributed to the

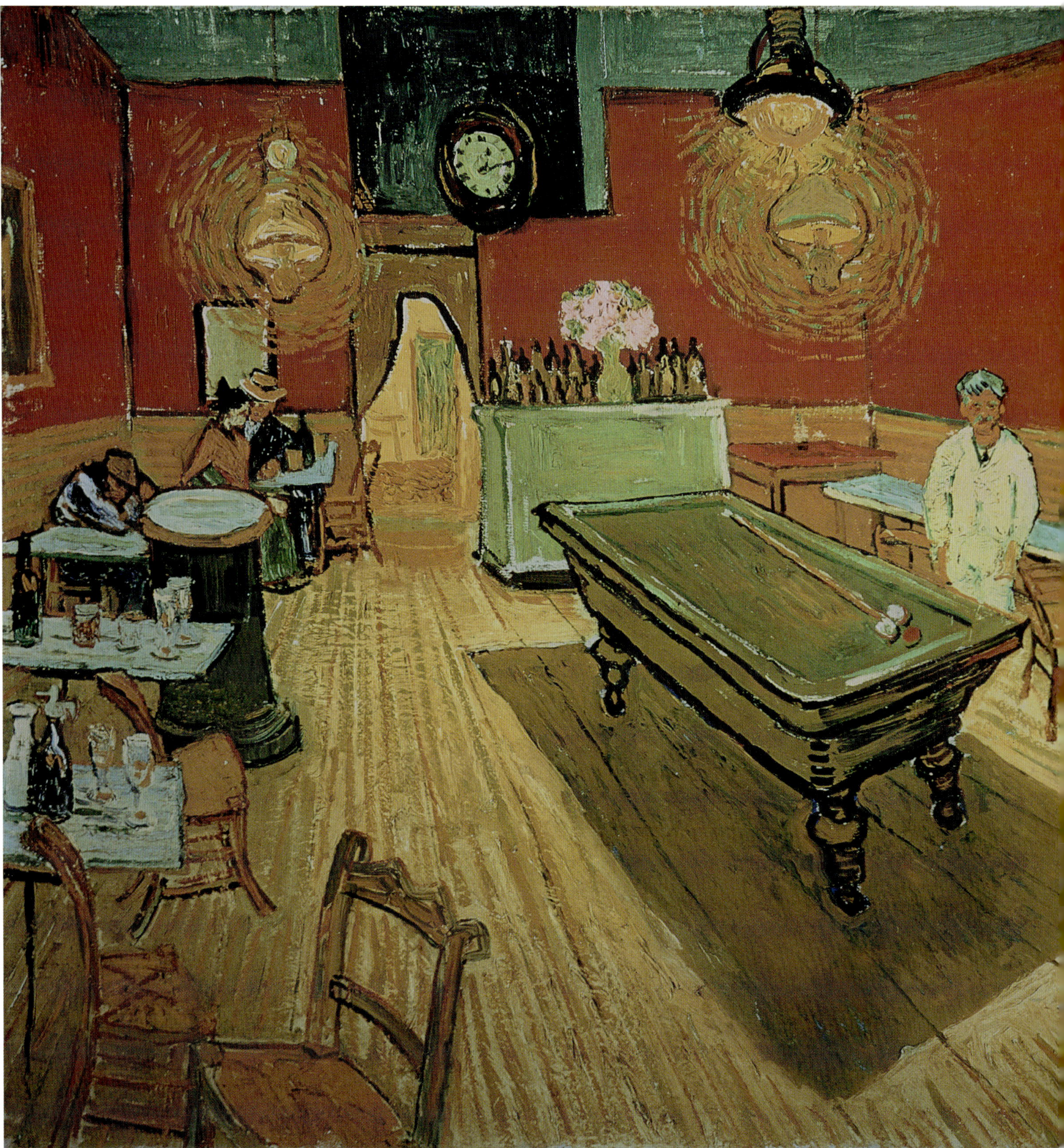

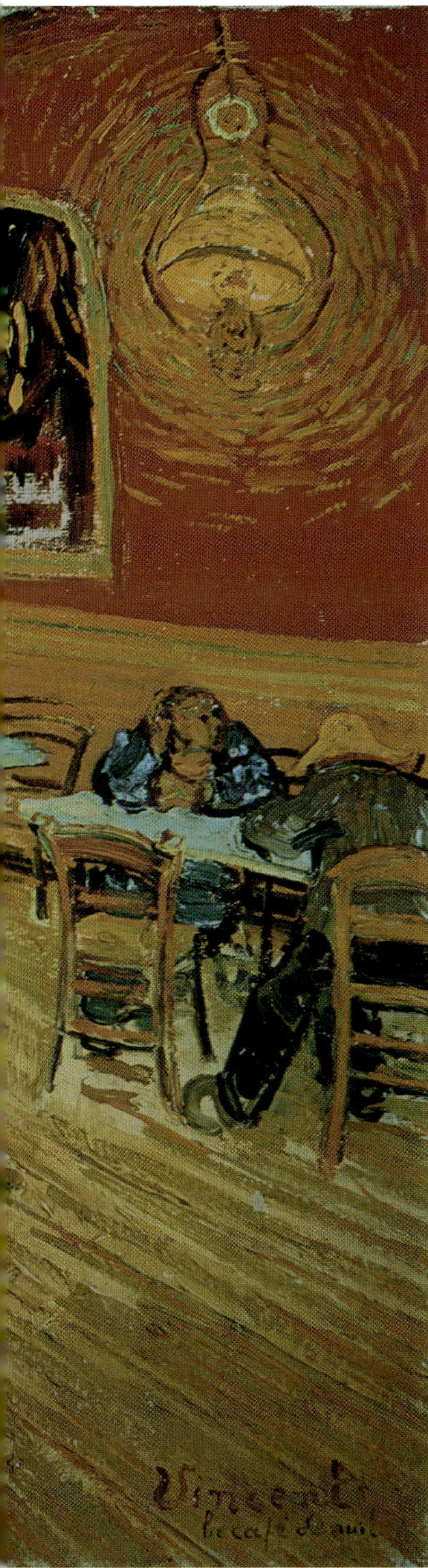

decline of green, not only in the world of the sciences and arts but also in material culture and everyday life.

For the moment let us remain with the painters. The issue of contrasts had become for them one of the central questions, and henceforth any painting was organized around various plays of oppositions: contrasts in value, shade, intensity, warmth, quantity, but above all, contrasts between the primary colors and their complementary colors. Everyone sought the so-called "harmony of complementaries." This quest seemed to them increasingly justified over the course of time as chemistry and physics established scientifically the old empirical distinction that painters made on their palettes between the simple colors and the mixed colors. Henceforth, for science as for art, there were the "primary" colors (blue, red, yellow) and the "complementary" colors (green, purple, orange). The relations that the first group had with the second were defined by increasingly scientific rules to which many artists adhered—and would continue to adhere for many decades.

In this area one work played an essential role, that of Michel-Eugène Chevreul, *De la loi du contraste simultané des couleurs*, published in 1839 and immediately translated into several languages. Director of the Gobelins tapestry works in Paris, Chevreul sought to understand why certain dyes did not produce the color effects that one would expect of them. He knew very well that many dyestuffs were chemically unstable—"which any artist ought to know"—but he also had the intuition that optical problems, tied to the proximity of the colors, specifically added to chemical problems. He discovered that the perception of colors was conditioned by their neighbors, and he drew from this a certain number of laws. Among the most important, one concerns "optical mixing" (two colors juxtaposed

GREEN AS THE OPPOSITE OF RED
Through the violent contrast of green and red, Van Gogh claimed that he wanted to express "the terrible human passions" in this famous painting. That is obvious, but he also followed Chevreul and consciously or unconsciously featured the opposition of a primary color and its complementary color.

Vincent Van Gogh, *The Night Café*, 1888. New Haven, Yale University Art Gallery.

have a tendency to fuse optically and to be perceived by the eye as forming only one); another, the play of primary and complementary colors (a primary color and its complementary color mutually brighten and enhance one another, whereas a primary color and its non-complementary color darken or muddy one another). But this thick scholarly volume contained many other rules, laws, and principles, as well. Despite its complexity, it quickly exerted a great influence in painting circles, and one of the tasks of the critic today is learning who read and who did not read Chevreul.[10]

For our purposes Chevreul's observations and principles mark a new decline for the color green. Not only did optics confirm what chemistry had long made clear, that green was not a primary color, but painters themselves no longer needed to use green pigments or even to mix blue and green on their palettes or their canvases; the optic blend, that is, the juxtaposition of a touch of blue and a touch of yellow, sufficed. It was no longer the material that produced green, nor the painter or the brush, it was the eyebrain combination. Green no longer existed materially; it became a kind of illusion, the union of blue and yellow taking place in the eye of the beholder.

FANTASY GREEN

"Le Douanier" Rousseau may not have been a great painter, but he was a true colorist, especially in the range of greens. To present supposedly exotic vegetation, he used artificial ultramarine green, a recently invented pigment, less expensive than cobalt green and less unstable or dangerous than the old copper greens. This luxurious vegetation, copied in magazines, harbors wild animals that Rousseau himself said terrified him.

Henri Rousseau, *Jungle with Tiger and Hunters*, 1907. Private collection.

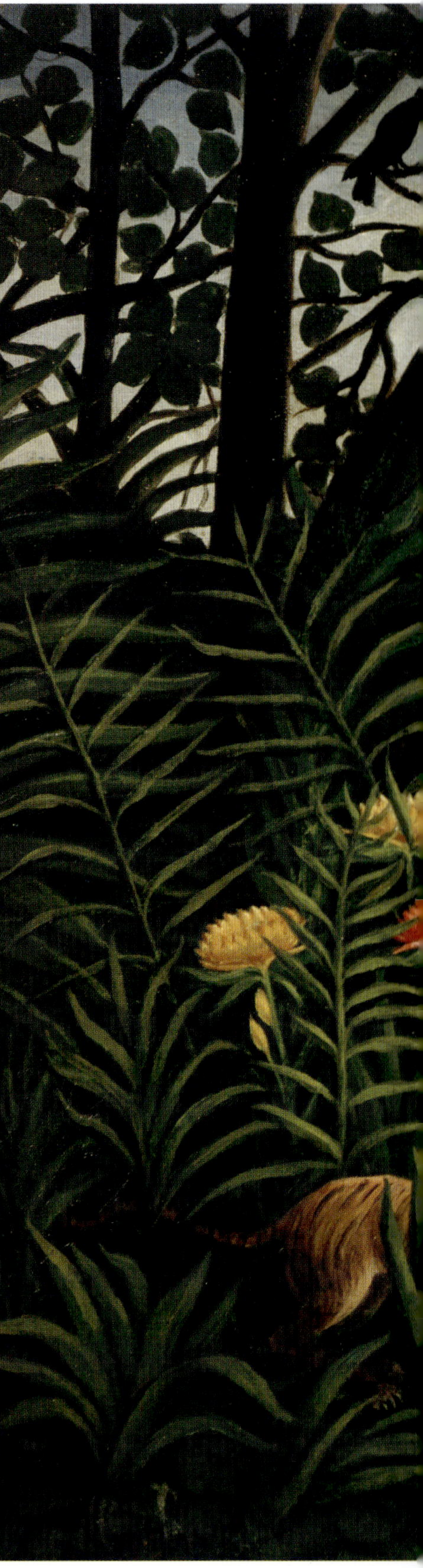

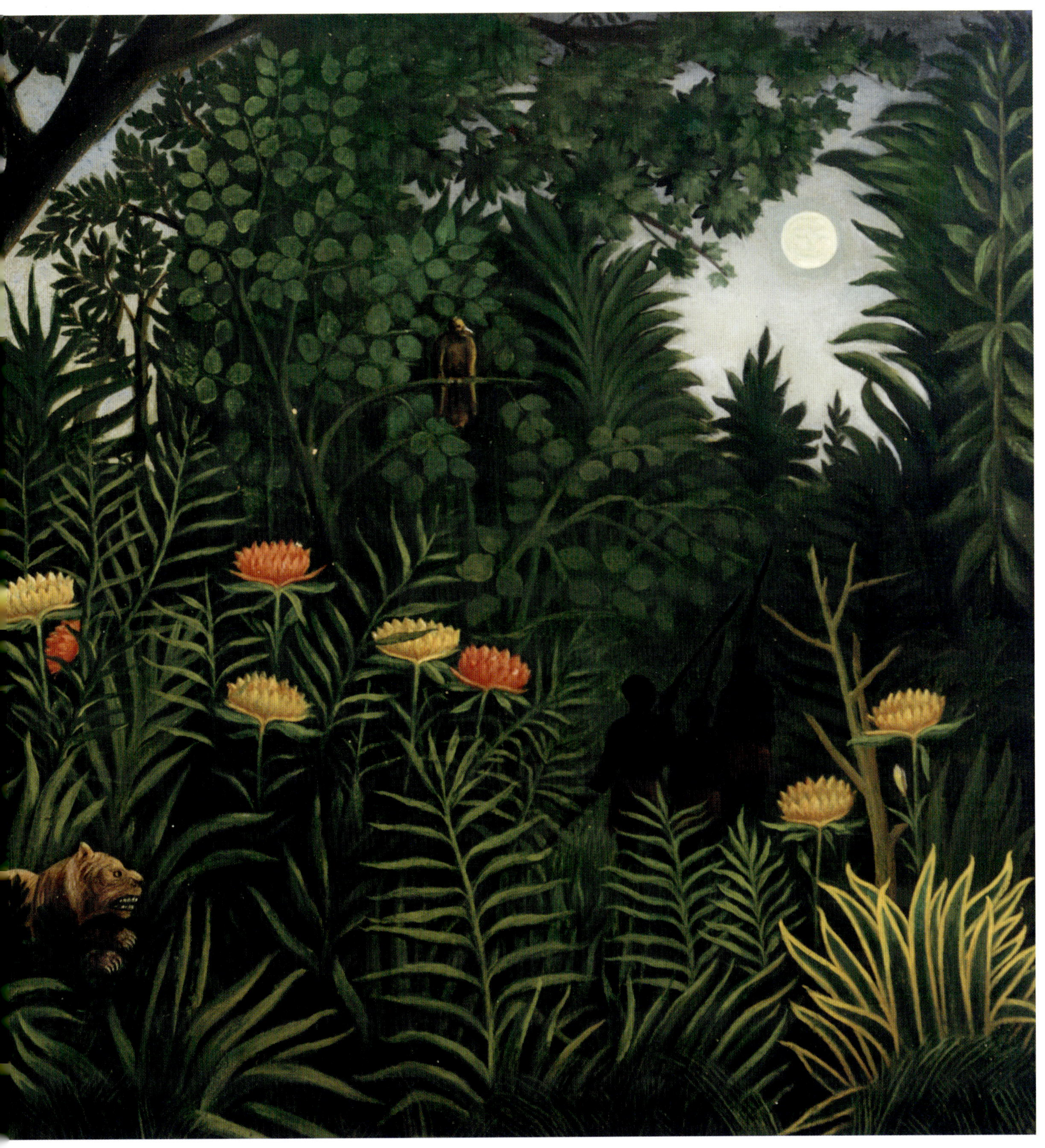

Some artists—Impressionists, Post-Impressionists, Pointillists—followed Chevreul's theories to the letter and abandoned green pigments, as four-color photomechanical reproduction processes (silk-screening, printing) would later do. Others, in greater numbers, remained faithful to this color and used it in the traditional manner, but they seemed obsessed by the opposition of primary and complementary colors that Chevreul had established into law. So it was that, beginning in the 1880s, Pissarro chose for the frame or the stretcher the complement of the principal color in the painting: for a predominantly reddish sunset, a green frame; for a spring scene full of delicate greens, a reddish-pink frame.[11] He had read Chevreul. Not all painters in the second half of the nineteenth century had done so, but they all had probably read the summaries of his theories that the art critic and popularizer Charles Blanc (1813–1882) had offered in his various works, notably his *Grammaire des arts du dessin*, a best seller first published in 1867 and reissued many times. Blanc was easier to understand than Chevreul and for that reason exerted a greater and more direct influence on painters. Here, for example, is what he writes regarding the juxtaposition of green and red:

> If one combines two primary colors, yellow and blue, for example, to make a binary color, green, this last color will attain its maximum intensity when side by side with its complementary color: red. . . . Reciprocally, red placed beside green will appear more red.[12]

Henceforth, art submitted to science and accepted as incontestable truth this distinction between primary and complementary colors. Even the painters who claimed to free themselves of all theory and rely solely on the eye or instinct accepted it without the least objection. That is even more astonishing given that, if we think about it a little, this distinction was pure convention, simply one of many ways to classify colors, unknown for centuries in which, nevertheless, artistic creation thrived and masterpieces were produced. Moreover, for science itself, and for the techniques it generated, the distinction was ambiguous since, depending upon whether it was a matter of an additive or subtractive synthesis, the three primary colors and the three complementary colors were not the same. And finally, from the social perspective—the most important one for the historian—this hierarchical distinction between two color groups had no foundation, no reason to be. Similarly, excluding black and white from the color order had no cultural basis. For Western society, its codes, practices, emblems, and symbols, there really were six basic colors: white, red, black, green, blue, and yellow; and that was true for the thirteenth century or the seventeenth century or the nineteenth century. Following far behind were the five second-ranking colors: gray, brown, pink, purple, and orange. And then . . . then there was nothing more, at least no more colors, only shades and shades of shades.

A FAUVIST WHO LOVED GREEN

Like all the Fauvists, the young Van Dongen was a remarkable colorist, often bold in his harmonies, sometimes violent, always harmonious. Shaded with blues and blacks, unusual for the Fauvists, his greens are magnificent.

Kees van Dongen, *Woman in a Black Hat*, 1908. Saint Petersburg, State Hermitage Museum.

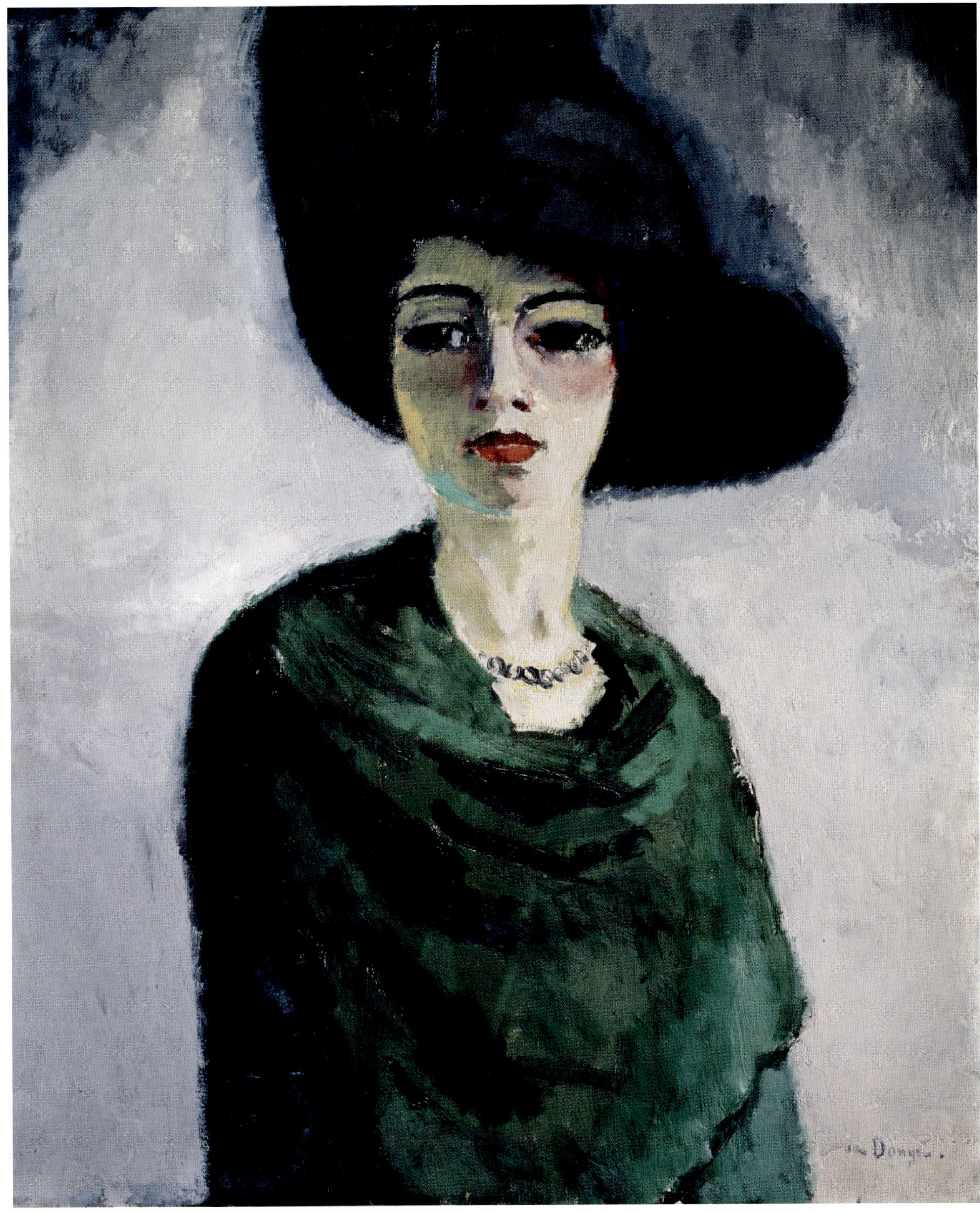

Neither did Kandinsky or the Bauhaus

GREEN: AN IMMOBILE COLOR?

Kandinsky's theories on color are quite outdated, especially when they claim to be universal. But even in their time, some of his assertions were already unusual or provocative. That is the case when he declares that green is a static, passive color "comparable to a fat cow . . . capable only of ruminating and contemplating the world through its stupid, inexpressive eyes."

Vassily Kandinsky, *Green Emptiness*, 1930. Nantes, Musée des Beaux-Arts.

In the late nineteenth and early twentieth centuries, it was hard to find any artists or creators who still accepted those simple ideas. For classifying colors, the hierarchies proposed by physics and chemistry seemed preferable to them, more modern, more ambitious, and more "true." Scientism and positivism had laid waste to most of color's domains, and green was perhaps the principal victim. Not being a primary color, not belonging to the special world of black and white, it was degraded, scorned, forgotten. Bauhaus teachings are a good example: priority was given to the sacrosanct blue-yellow-red triad, combined with black and white. The De Stijl movement followed the same course, and a painter like Mondrian entirely excluded green from his canvases in his abstract period. For him as for many others, "green is a useless color."[13] In fact, if statistics were meaningful in this area (which I doubt) and if frequency ratings could be established, color by color, for all of twentieth-century European painting, the rarity of greens would be glaringly apparent. Even abstract painting (let us think of Dubuffet here), which sometimes makes color a theme in and of itself, abandoned green, perhaps even more so than representational painting. It was not a primary color! Only modest amateur painters who still practiced the art of landscape painting allowed a little green on their canvases.

On top of this reductive, sometime misdirected scientism, on top of all the innovations brought about by the physical sciences (splitting the atom, for example, which dazzled or obsessed certain painters) were added other theories, just as disastrous for the color green. That was the case with theories of psychology, physiology, and symbolism. They invaded the arts of the twentieth century and were often, unfortunately, rubbish, claiming universality whereas these areas are

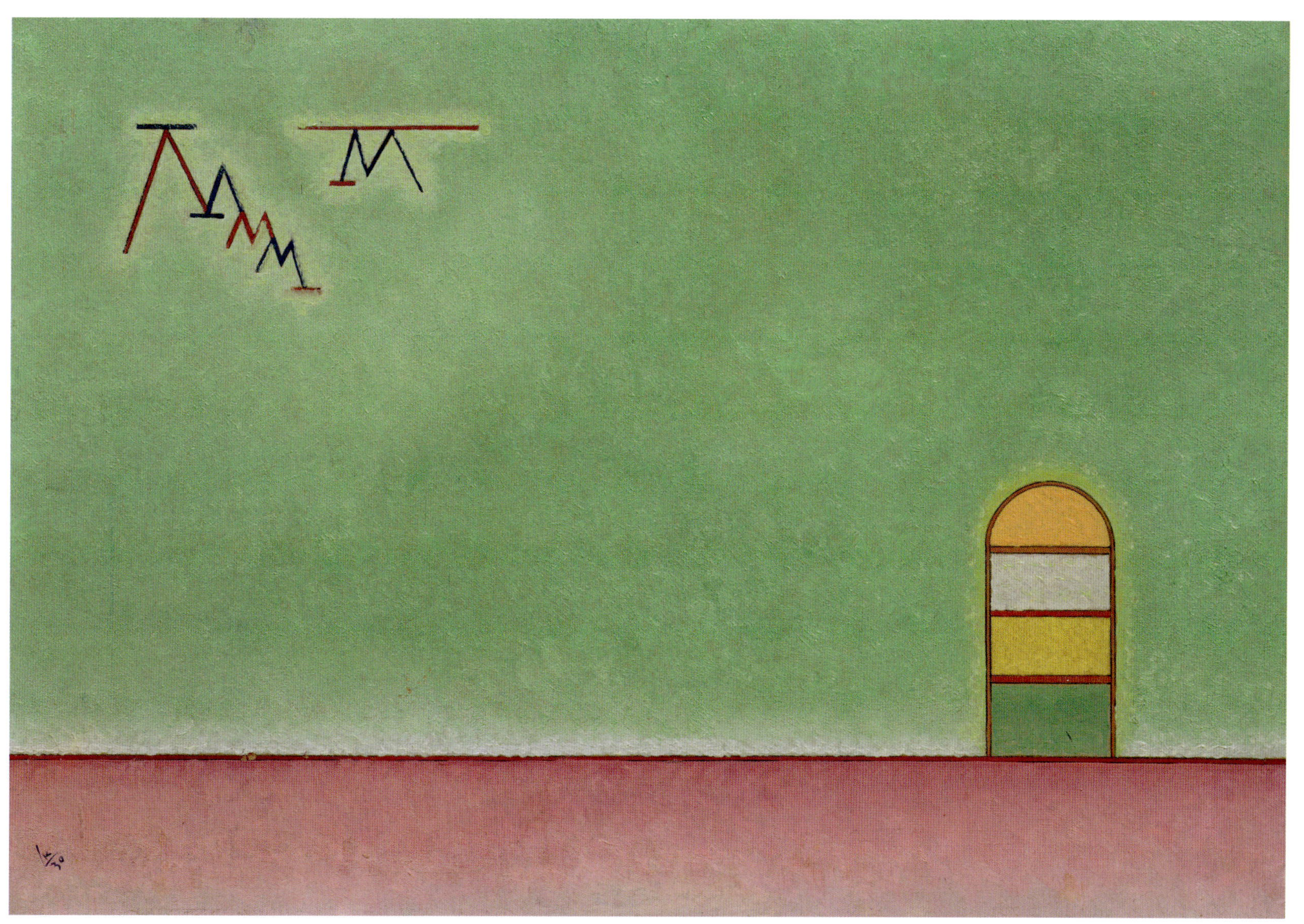

all culturally—strictly culturally—based. Even the greatest of painters succumbed to them, in the image of Vassily Kandinsky. No matter how much we may admire his painting, we must recognize that his writings on color—especially in his best-known book, *Concerning the Spiritual in Art* (1911)—have aged badly. Everything involving the emotive power of colors, their inner resonance for the viewer and their supposedly cosmic meaning is entirely without universal significance. It all depends upon who is doing the viewing, in what context, what time period, and with what sensory and cultural baggage. What Kandinsky tells us about the relationships that colors have with the human soul applies only to Kandinsky himself and cannot be set up as a general rule. And what he tells us about each color is seriously dated and cannot be transposed as is to other centuries and other societies. Here are a few examples of the "truths" that he sets forth: white is a profound and creative silence; black is a nothingness without possibility; gray represents hopeless immobility; red is hot, agitated, and possesses immense power; purple is a cooled red; brown is a hard color; orange irradiates everything that surrounds it; blue obeys a movement of retreat, so much so that an all-blue surface seems to withdraw from us. Europeans in the first half of the twentieth century could partially accept such claims, no doubt, but they cannot in the least be projected onto the past or extended to the entire planet.

But it is perhaps with regard to green that Kandinsky developed his most singular and debatable ideas. Not only does he make green an amorphous color lacking character and personality—whereas for centuries in the West green was a dynamic color, the color of change, disorder, youth, love, freedom, and transgression!—but he freely proclaims his total disdain for this color:

> Absolute green is the most anesthetizing color possible. It moves in no direction at all and has not the least consonance of joy, sadness or passion; it demands nothing, attracts nothing. This permanent absence of movement is certainly a beneficial property for tired men and souls, but becomes very tiresome after a certain amount of rest. . . . Passivity is the characteristic property of pure green, a property that gives it a kind of unctuous air of self-satisfaction, however. That is why, in the area of colors, green corresponds to what represents, in human society, the bourgeoisie; it is an immobile element, self-satisfied, limited in all directions. This green is similar to a fat cow, full of good health, lying down, rooted, capable only of ruminating and contemplating the world through its stupid, inexpressive eyes.

To compare green to a fat cow is taking quite a risk! Kandinsky does just that, and in this astonishing text he seems to be one of the greatest enemies that the color green has yet to encounter over the course of its long history.

At Bauhaus Kandinsky was the colleague of two other color theorists who similarly seemed to hold green in low esteem and to assign it a minor role in artistic creation: Johannes Itten (1888–1967) and Josef Albers (1888–1976). In his famous chromatic circle Itten once again and as always gave priority to the three primary colors—red, yellow, and blue—and claimed repeatedly that "the effects of contrast must be the basis of all aesthetic research on the colors." Albers took up some of the laws of simultaneous contrast set forth by Chevreul but further insisted on the relativism of perceptive effects and rejected any preestablished system of harmony. The works that these two published at the ends of their lives, *Art of Color* by Itten (1961) and *Interaction of Color* by Albers (1963), had (and continue to have) a considerable influence on the teaching of color in art schools in Europe and the United States. At best we can say that they are hardly favorable toward green, a secondary, negligible, and useless color.[14]

Design, heir to Bauhaus and the teachings of Johannes Itten and his followers, provides an obvious example. What place did it grant to green? None, or just about none. Only the present ecological movement lets it play a certain role in industrial production, but for decades designers and creators neglected or scorned green. Why? Because it was not a primary color! What will someday set science, art, and industry free from this pernicious classification of colors? Scientific and artistic Europe existed for millennia without knowing the distinction between primary and complementary colors and was no worse off for it.

Staying with the history of design, let us recognize that it was hardly inventive in the domain of color and was often content with easily accepting scientific theories and rudimentary symbolism. Seeking to make color appropriate to the function of objects, it believed in a general chromatic truth, as if there truly were pure colors and mixed colors, warm colors and cool colors, close colors and distant colors, dynamic colors and static colors. Forgetting the strictly cultural nature of the physiology and symbolism of colors, design claimed to create "universal codes." Not only do such ambitions make us smile today, but more importantly they often drove away consumers, thus running counter to the desired ends: to harmonize practical and aesthetic satisfaction.

Johannes Itten's famous remark, meant for Bauhaus students in 1922 but adopted by design as its watchword for decades, is for the historian undoubtedly one of the most debatable claims ever made regarding colors: "The laws of color are eternal, absolute, timeless, as valid in the past as at the present moment."[15] Such a statement, all by itself, does away with cultural relativism in one fell swoop and, with it, all of the human sciences.

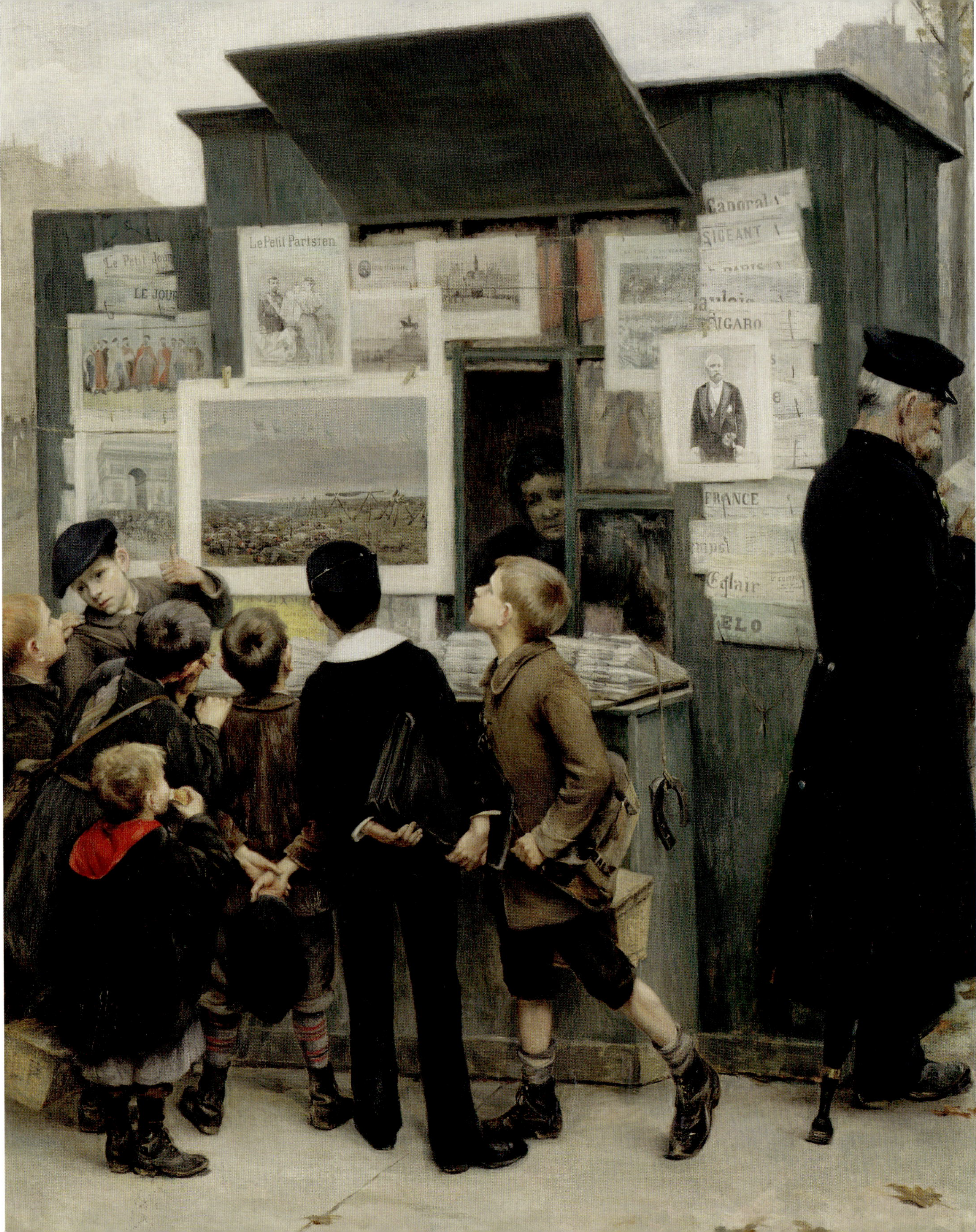

Le Petit Parisien
FRANCE
Eclair

Green in everyday life

THE GREEN OF EVERYDAY LIFE

In big cities at the end of the nineteenth century, a new shade of green made its appearance on the street scene and in the world of public gardens: dark green. This shade echoed another that, in the same period, became pervasive in offices, schools, post offices, train stations, and government buildings: administrative green.

Paul Legrand, *Before Detaille's The Dream*, 1897. Nantes, Musée des Beaux-Arts.

At the end of the nineteenth and beginning of the twentieth centuries, the minor place of green in daily life was partly due to those reductive theories, whether they came from science, industry, or art. But it was also the product of long-held beliefs: green was uncertain, it faded in the light, it disappeared, darkened, yellowed; or on the other hand, green was dangerous, corrosive, toxic, caused diseases, sometimes deadly ones; or once again and most importantly, green brought bad luck, it was the color of witches, the devil, and all the forces of evil. These beliefs, widespread throughout Europe, mixed together recognized facts regarding painting and dyeing with age-old superstitions. Trying to eradicate them was an impossible task. All the same, there was another reason for the minor place green occupied in material culture and everyday life, a reason that was neither chemical nor symbolic, but ethical: green was not a dignified, sober, moral color. It was a frivolous color that it was better to avoid. Here once again we come upon the legacy of the Protestant Reformation and its classification of colors into two groups: "honest" and "dishonest." Green remained in the bad group.

That distinction, which appeared in the sixteenth century, was still very much alive in the second half of the nineteenth century, when European and American industries began to mass produce consumer goods on a large scale. Most of those goods fell into a color range in which white, black, gray, and brown dominated and bright colors were excluded. Only blue, considered good or neutral, remained in the game. Red, yellow, and green were rejected. This industrial palette was not in the least imposed by the chemistry of colorants but very much by the Protestant ethic, which, as the sociologist Max Weber (1864–1920) demonstrated, exerted a decisive influence on economic activity and the birth of capitalism.[16] In the second half of the nineteenth century and still well into the twentieth, large-scale industrial and financial capitalism on both sides of the Atlantic was essentially in the hands of Protestant families who imposed their values, standards, and principles.

Thus, for many decades in England, Germany, and the United States, standard production of objects for use in everyday life was accompanied by moral and social considerations largely related to this Protestant ethic. To it we owe the colorless palette of the first mass-produced consumer goods; articles and tools for everyday life, household appliances, office equipment, telephones, cameras, bicycles, and cars (to say nothing of fabrics and clothing) usually fell within a spectrum that went from white to black by way of the grays and browns. It was as if the palette of vivid colors, perfectly authorized by the chemical industry, was forbidden by the civic moral code.[17] Green was one of the victims. It was considered unstable and superficial, capricious and seductive, too cheerful, lively, and garish: better to use it sparingly for the masses and give precedence to blue, gray, or black.[18]

In fact, until the 1950s green was rarely used for everyday objects or for décor and furnishings. Only rooms meant for rest were sometimes painted or hung with green, but in general these were pale, timid, grayish greens, the deep, heavy greens of nineteenth-century bourgeois houses surviving only among a few provincial notables. They were less toxic than before, but beginning in the 1920s, modern décor, or what passed for it, hardly ever made use of green. Even in bathrooms and swimming pools, green, which had long been the color of water in Europe, had to give way to white or blue. Green was certainly not totally absent from the realm of everyday life, but its place was a modest one.

BABAR'S GREEN SUIT

From the beginning Jean de Brunhoff's hero has worn his eternal suit of a lovely, fresh green, so that eventually that shade has taken on his name: "Babar green."

Jean de Brunhoff, *King Babar*, Hachette Books, 1939.

It may have been in the world of toys, books, and pictures for children that green found its niche between the two World Wars. Here codes were more relaxed, practices less restrained, and colors more joyous. A good example is provided by a remarkable hero: Babar, the kindly elephant created by Jean de Brunhoff in 1931, whose picture books enjoyed great success before and after World War II. Very different from the creatures invented by Walt Disney, who are always agitated and sometimes vulgar, Babar is not at all like other heroes; he is large, gray, calm, honest, a bit talkative, and most importantly, dressed in an unusual green suit with a white shirt and a red bow tie. Only for official ceremonies do we see him dressed differently. His suit is not an ordinary green but a soft, sensible green, a kind of "spring green," perfectly solid and neither tending toward yellow or blue. It distinguishes the king of the elephants from all the other characters—only Babar wears green—and livens up his adventures. It is a green for dreaming, a "gay green" as late medieval French might have said, a "Babar green" as French commonly says today.[19]

In contrast, modernity added to the palette of greens some unsightly, sometimes repulsively ugly tones, but meant to be that way—greens that did not fade, did not get dirty, were based in the landscape, and allowed one to hide. Hence their use in clothing for professions

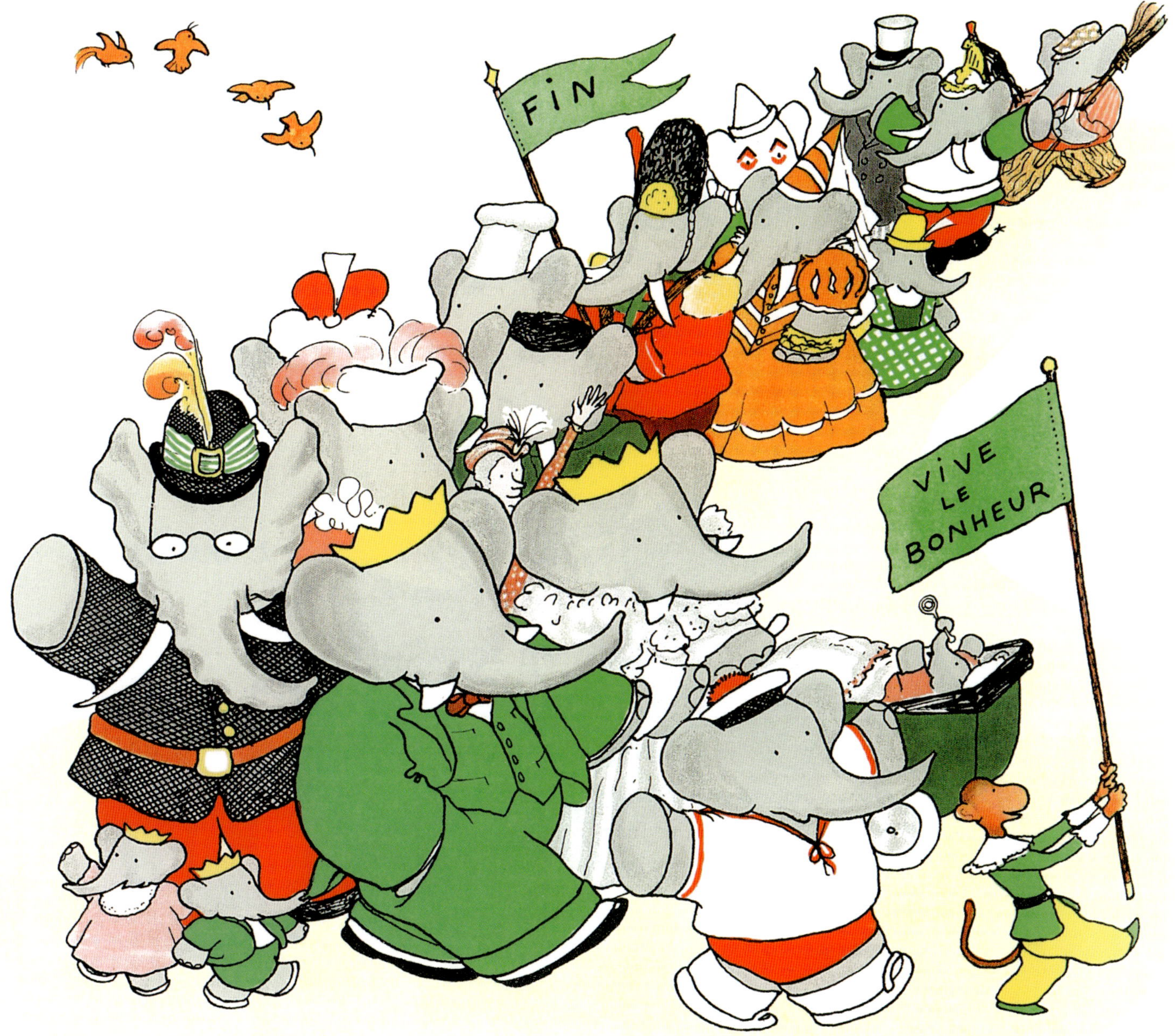

having to do with dirt or garbage and especially for military uniforms. They are all part of a "mustard" or greenish-yellow range. The best known example is "khaki," a shade of the wider palette, somewhere between brown, yellow, gray, and green. The word itself does not come from the French name for the exotic persimmon fruit (*kaki*) but from a Hindustani term meaning "earth color" or "dust color." It was in fact the British soldiers of the Indian armies that first adopted uniforms of this indefinable, indiscernible shade in the

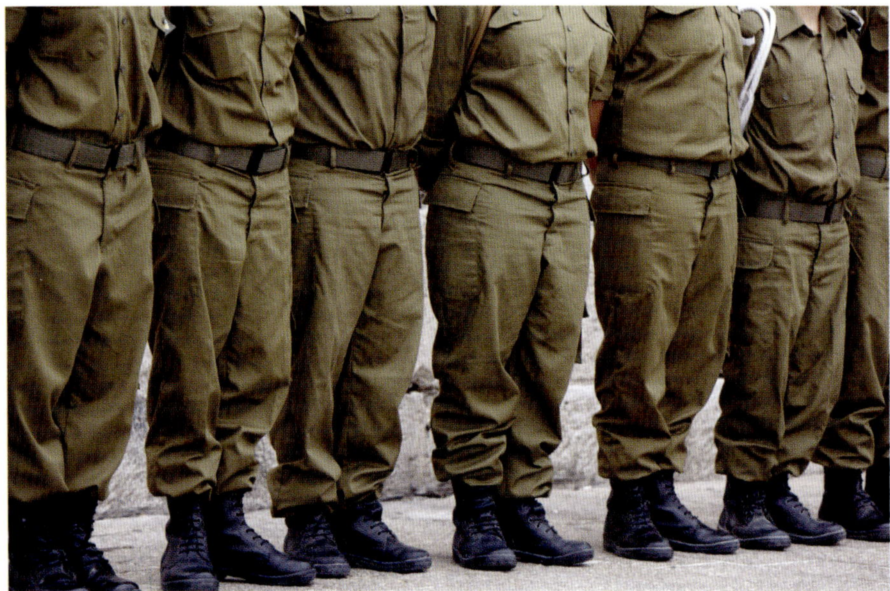

BROWNISH GREEN: KHAKI
Somewhere between green, gray, yellow, and brown, the khaki of military uniforms can take on infinite shades. They all seem dirty, deathly, and sad, and they are often unpleasant to look at.

second half of the nineteenth century. This marked a sharp rupture with the vivid colors of traditional uniforms (since the Middle Ages, soldiers were supposed to be visible from a distance and to be proud of wearing the emblematic colors of their princes or regiments) and, by the same token, a new way of waging war. The British example was soon imitated. One after another, Western armies adopted khaki or khaki-like uniforms, making it easier for soldiers to be camouflaged in landscapes dominated by browns and greens. More recently, these shades originating with the military found a place in some civilian clothing, notably for young rebels ready to change the world and society, self-proclaimed antimilitarists but paradoxically dressed in military surplus. Certain fashion designers and couturiers followed suit in the 1970s and made fashionable brownish-green shades that most people, one or two generations earlier, would have worn only under duress. These styles were short-lived and not significant in the long history of the color green.

The greenish gray (*feldgrau*) of the German uniforms in World Wars I and II met with less success among fashion designers. It is true that it had not left good memories and that this particular shade recalled an everyday green totally lacking in appeal: "administrative green." This color made its appearance in the 1900s both on walls and furnishings in offices. Public administration in France, Italy, Germany, and elsewhere made wide use of it, especially in government buildings, train stations, and post offices. But it was also found in private businesses and in any place the public was received by employees or secretaries and most of the work done there involved files, papers, stamps, and forms. Drab, sad, dark, or grayish, this green was supposed to be neutral, "standard," and functional, in the image of the places it permeated. Its popularity lasted until the 1970s, and in certain places where modernity was slow to penetrate, it never entirely disappeared. It is the emblematic color of bureaucracy.

Nature in the heart of the cities

Let us go back again several decades to the end of the nineteenth and beginning of the twentieth centuries, to the period when green had not yet undertaken its great ecological revolution and its role in daily life was still limited. Artists, writers, scientists, manufacturers, designers, fashion designers, executives, and officials were not particularly interested in the color green except in two areas: leisure and health. Urban Europe was increasingly industrialized and polluted and suffered from a cruel lack of greenery. Thus, beginning in the 1860s, new policies aimed at conserving or introducing green spaces in the centers and at the peripheries of cities.

Victorian England set the example by protecting the few remaining woods and parks and creating a number of public squares and gardens. That was an innovation because parks and gardens in earlier centuries mostly belonged to royalty or nobility, and the public was only granted access to them on certain days and under certain conditions. Henceforth, municipalities or associations managed the new green spaces in urban areas and established very open policies. At the same time, in average-sized towns measures were taken to encourage the creation of private gardens and gardening practices. Specialized journals and magazines appeared, while others enjoyed considerable new success, such as the famous *Gardener's Chronicle* that was first published in 1841. Gardening was becoming a pastime, even a passion.

The English example was soon imitated throughout Europe: protecting existing green spaces; safeguarding and renovating historical gardens; creating many small public gardens and squares; the appearance of "green belts" separating big cities from their suburbs and "green links" connecting the town to the surrounding countryside; the birth of the "garden city" that sought

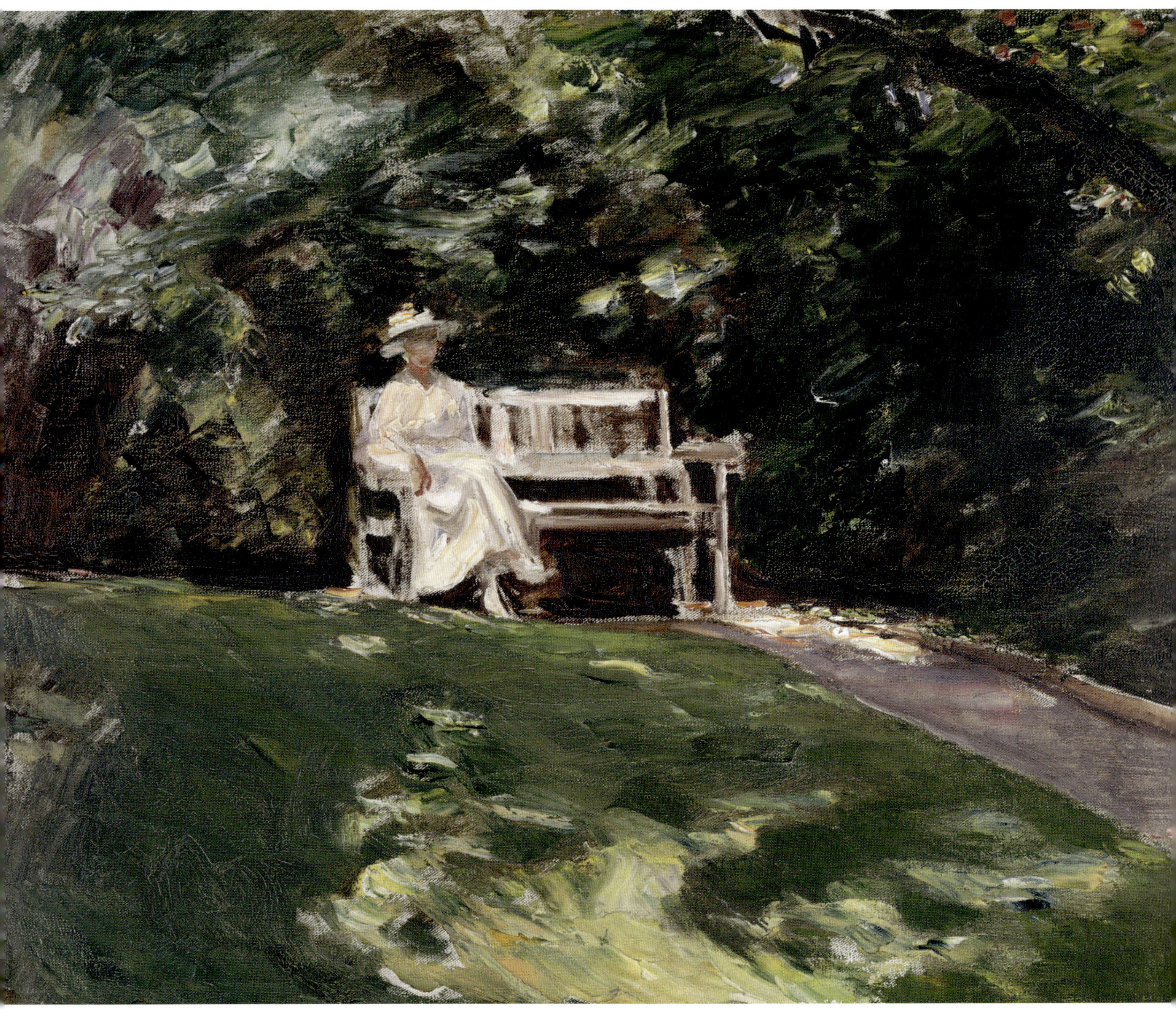

GREEN IN THE HEART OF THE CITY

In the second half of the nineteenth century, the creation of many squares, parks, and gardens introduced nature into the heart of the big cities. Everything was green in them, not just the trees and bushes, hedges and lawns, but also the gates, palisades, fences, and even the attendants' uniforms. Only benches and chairs were sometimes a different color.

Max Liebermann, *The Garden Bench*, 1917. Berlin, Neue Nationalgalerie.

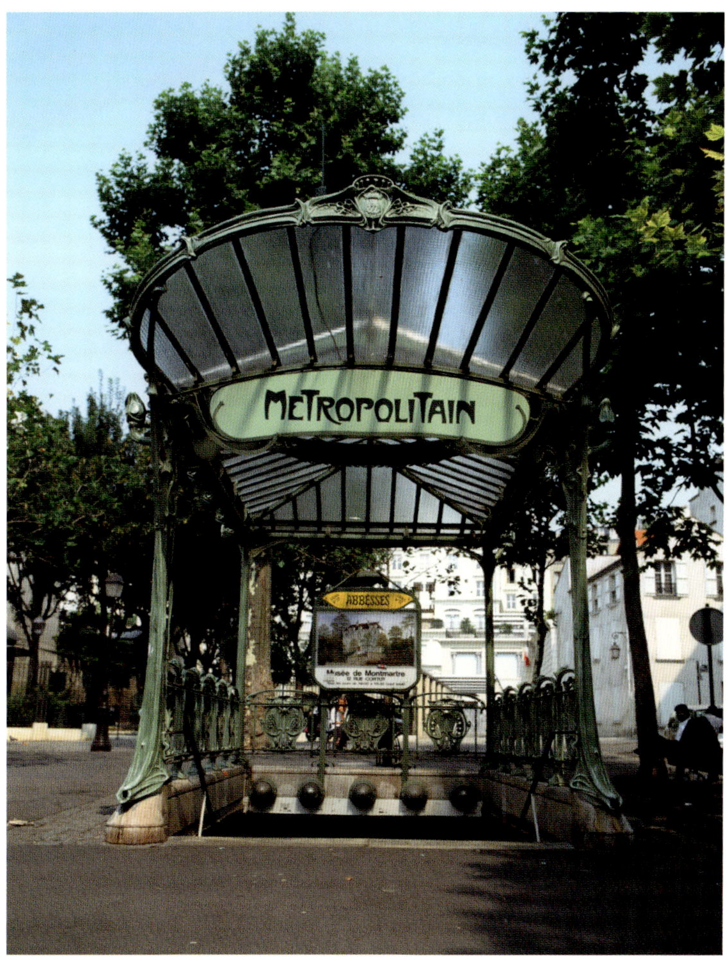

ENTRANCE TO THE ABBESSES METRO STATION IN PARIS

Designed by Hector Guimard, 1900.

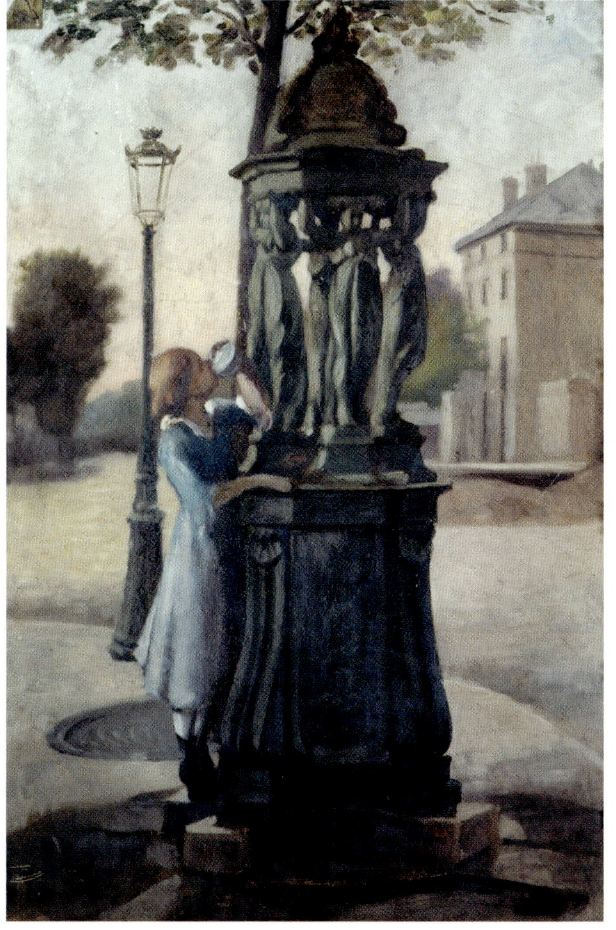

FOUNTAINE WALLACE

André Gill, *Fontaine Wallace à Montmartre*, watercolor, c. 1880. Paris, Musée Carnavalet.

to integrate green landscapes into residential, commercial, and industrial zones; the appearance of places reserved for children, walking, and sports activities. Town planners, architects, and landscapers competed in their inventiveness in creating green spaces, giving them structure and a new look, introducing exotic trees and plants into them, using modern materials, assigning the décor to well-known artists, and staying as close as possible to the styles of the times. Until the 1930s green spaces were places of intense creativity.

The promoters of gardens and public squares were all the more motivated as doctors and health professionals proclaimed their many benefits. Of course, the idea that contact with nature was beneficial for one's health was a very old one—it was already present in ancient Rome, touted by Virgil and Horace—but in the last half of the nineteenth and the early twentieth centuries, at the time of the second industrial revolution, when the pollution and diseases that ensued affected all the large European cities, this idea returned to the forefront with a vengeance. Subsequently, studies and publications multiplied, insisting upon the undeniable virtues of parks and gardens and the need to establish them in the heart of cities. In our time this quest for green space has taken on considerable scope, not only on the level of health but on the civic plane as well; every city has a duty to expand its green spaces. If we are to believe the doctors and psychologists, the simple

THE GREEN OF PARKS AND GARDENS

Vallotton, a painter who should be better known, was an admirable colorist, playing with large, dark, flat surfaces broken by a few touches of very vivid color. Here, pervasive dark greens, large patches of shadow, three faintly sketched silhouettes, the white of clothing, and a tiny red ball are enough to create a mysterious, almost threatening atmosphere. The danger seems to be there behind the green of the trees and in the red of the ball.

Félix Vallotton, *The Ball*, 1899. Paris, Musée d'Orsay.

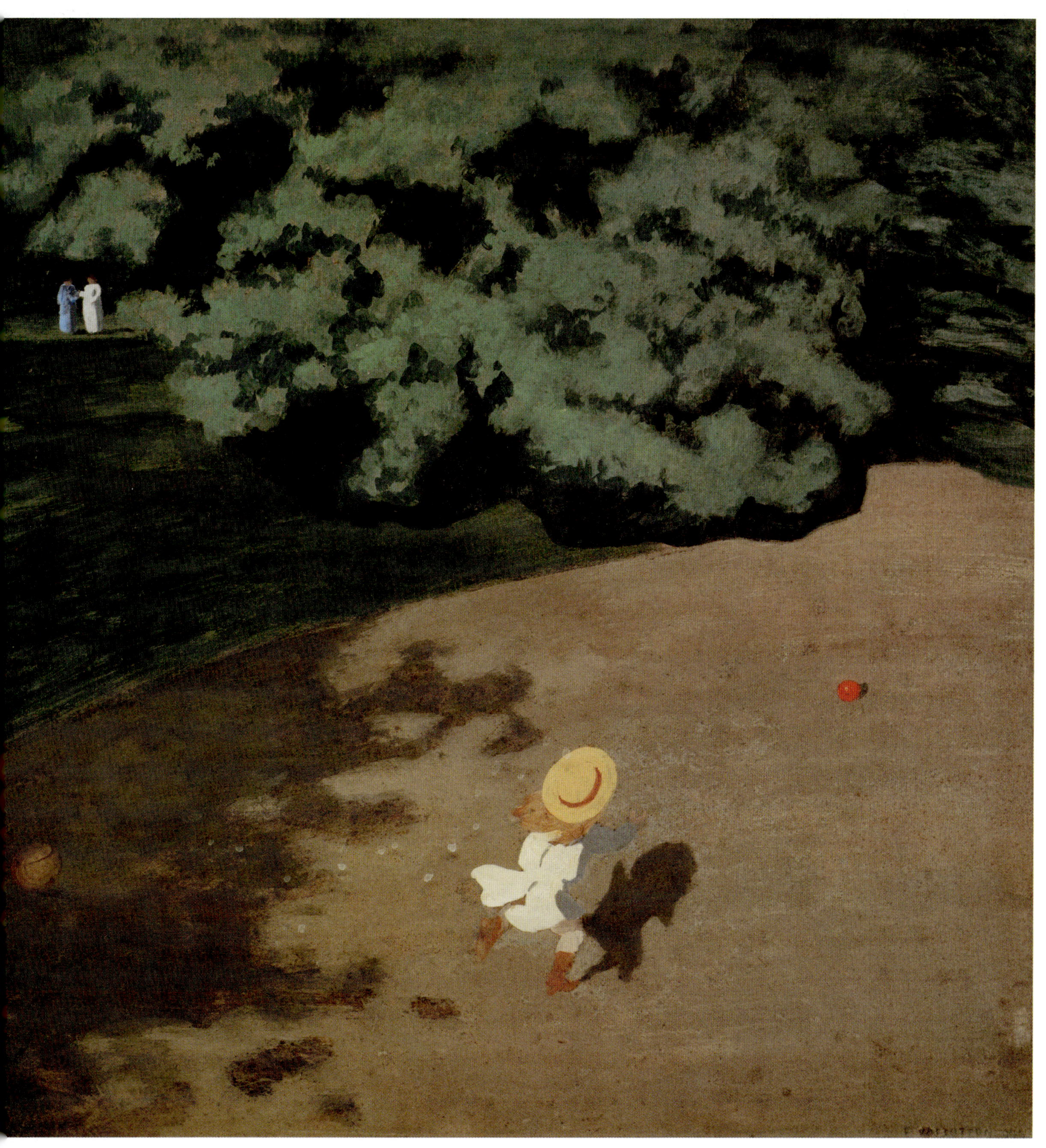

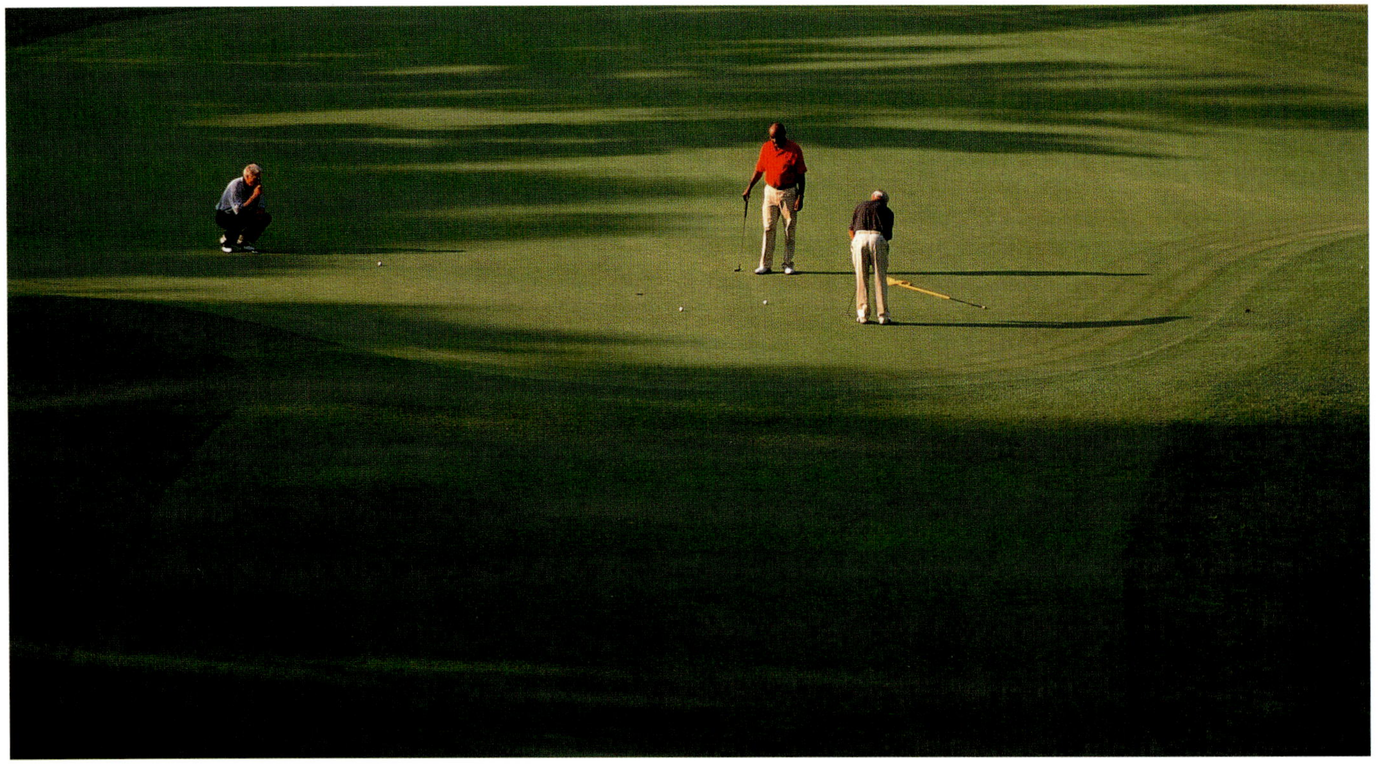

A BIG GREEN SPACE: THE GOLF COURSE
On sports fields, colors are ubiquitous and an essential part of the ritual, whether it is a matter of a Roman hippodrome, a feudal tournament, a soccer match, or a golf course.

sight of a few trees and a little vegetation is supposed to be relaxing and stress-relieving; it lowers blood pressure, creates psychological well-being, promotes positive emotions, and increases optimism. Here again, green appears to be the color of hope.

In the public garden everything was green, not only the trees, bushes, hedges, lawns, and plantings, but also the chairs and furniture, gates and fences, sheds, kiosks, signs, palisades, arches, garbage cans, and even the uniforms of the park attendants. Delicate or fresh green for the plants, dark or grayish green for the objects; in the public square the palette of greens was extremely vast. The holy of holies was the "theater of greenery," a protected place where the public could come sit in a sea of plants of all scents and shades and sometimes watch shows. Whichever way one looked, whatever object one gazed upon, the color green was present.

In the 1900s, in the center of towns, the green of plants and hygiene merged with the green of health that originated at the end of the Middle Ages and quietly infiltrated the whole modern era. Medicine and pharmacology had long had green for their emblematic color, probably because for centuries most remedies had a plant base. In many European universities green was the color of the gown distinguishing doctors and pharmacists in academic ceremonies, and on battlefields it was the color of the insignias or short capes they wore in the various army corps. Subsequently, the crosses indicating pharmacies also became green and greatly contributed to making this the color of the health professions.

That is still largely the case today, notably in hospital settings: the green of the surgeons' scrubs and operating rooms, the green of the corridors and patients' rooms, the green of packaging for medical materials. French has coined an expression for the specific shade of green used in hospitals: *vert clinique*—clinical green. The choice of the term owes less to visual reasons, as is sometimes claimed (green light supposedly being the most neutral, the least glaring in operating rooms), as to historical, emblematic, or symbolic reasons.[20] Green is the color of medicine and the pharmacy. There are exceptions, of course (in Italy, for example, pharmacy crosses are red), and recent practices are trying to diversify the hospital palette (blue and white are assuming increasing roles there), but green is still—and has long been—a soothing, sanitary, medical color. Proof is provided daily by the best-selling medicine in Europe: aspirin. In most European pharmacies aspirin is sold in a green or predominantly green box. This is the traditional sedative green of the pharmacopoeia.

More proof is provided by all the places where hygiene and freshness are necessary or required (dental offices, physical training rooms, fresh produce shops, protected areas, and so on): green is the dominant color there. Contemporary urban codes have made it not only the color of health and hygiene but also the color of cleanliness, healthiness, purification. In many towns and regions garbage cans themselves have become green and, with them, garbage trucks, garbage bags, sewer pipes, and any material ensuring public health. Henceforth, green cleans, green refreshes, green purifies, in the image of mint and all menthol products.

There is another area belonging to contemporary society that similarly combines hygiene, health, outdoor activities, and the plant world: sports. Sports also cultivates on a large scale the virtues of the color green, beginning with the protective benefits of the lawn on which many exercises and competitions take place. That green has a dual function, both pragmatic and symbolic: first, to cushion the falls and soften the blows; second, to remind us that on any green surface is decided the fate of one party. Here we again find one of the oldest symbolic aspects of green, the color of destiny. Whether it is a matter of the green meadow where medieval tournaments and ordeals took place, the green baize for games or cards that appeared in the sixteenth and seventeenth centuries, the modern sports field, or even the green carpet of the corporate board room, the meaning is the same: on green surfaces, decisions are made, fate is decided, luck chooses its side. That is particularly true on the sports field; the green there is not so much that of soft and soothing grass as of fate in the process of being played out. Table tennis is the most obvious proof of this; even though it is played indoors and involves neither impact or violence, it takes place on a green surface. Similarly, billiards is played on green felt, just as a great number of indoor sports are played on green linoleum or wood floors. Green is the color of games and gaming. That is why it is ubiquitous in the world of sports.

On the ground, at least. On the jerseys of the players, it was relatively rare until just recently. When modern sports began in Scotland and England in the second half of the nineteenth century, competitors first wore white or black uniforms. Then red and blue quickly came to be added. On the other hand green, yellow, and purple are more recent, and pink and orange newer still. In France, for example, it was not until the 1950s and 1960s that two first-division soccer clubs played in green (Saint-Étienne) and yellow (Nantes). But obviously there are exceptions. Hence, Ireland's national green, present on all sports fields—rugby fields in particular—even before the country definitively gained independence in 1920. Or again the famous "green jacket" worn for one year, since 1949, by the winning golfer of the Masters Tournament, one of the four great annual competitions. This green was originally the color of the organizing club in Georgia, the Augusta National Golf Club.

Another somewhat different example is the green that represents Oceania in the series of Olympic rings. There it is a matter of an athletic color that was not chosen but imposed. The rings had been established on paper in 1912–1913, but events made it so that they could not be flown on the Olympic flag until the Olympic Games in Anvers in 1920. Each ring represents one continent and possesses its color: red for America, yellow for Asia, black for Africa, blue for Europe, and green for Oceania. The first three colors seem to have been chosen according to ethnic considerations (and also perhaps slightly racist ones): red for the continent of the redskins, yellow for that of the yellow peoples, and black for that of the blacks. The other two, though, are trickier to interpret. Blue, associated with Europe, appears to be an old cultural legacy; blue has been Europe's favorite color since the eighteenth century, and it is also the color other societies around the globe use to symbolize it. But where does the green for Oceania come from? Why this choice? Oceania has no special relationship, either natural or cultural, to this color. In fact, it was a matter of elimination. Five of the six basic colors were already taken—four for the first four rings and white for the background of the flag—only green remained for the fifth ring. Oceania became green and seems gradually to be forming an attachment to this color, chosen for it by solemn European gentlemen who had never set foot on its soil and who probably had no intention of ever doing so. First imposed from without, green was nevertheless accepted by Oceania, and is now embraced and proudly displayed on the playing fields.

Green today

Everything just said about green in relationship to the city, gardens, sports, hygiene, health, and cleanliness is still completely applicable today.

In certain areas this has taken on a growing, even invasive dimension. That is true on the civic and political planes. Long neglected by political parties and trade unions, since the 1970s green has become the color claimed by various movements and trends in public opinion that center on environmental protection and eco-responsible attitudes in their programs and their demands, not only in Europe but on other continents as well. Their positions include questioning consumer culture, giving up polluting and nonrenewable energy sources, defending health and well-being, supporting fair trade and a whole assortment of demands for peace, democracy, and social justice. Although they differ on many issues (socialism, regionalism, communitarianism, feminism, thirdworldism),

GREEN SIGNS AND SIGNALS

A forest of signals, emblems, and symbols of all colors surrounds us today in the urban world. Here we have the European organic food—"*agriculture biologique*"—logo (still called "*Eurofeuille*"—"Euro leaf") and a pharmacy cross.

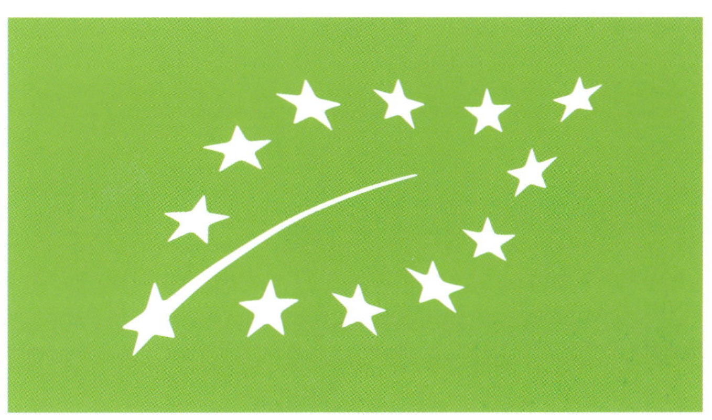

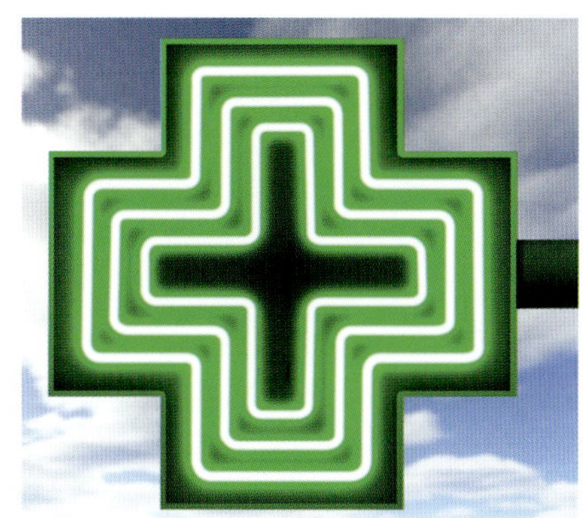

these movements all recognize one another and unite as a federation around the color green, in the image of a nongovernmental organization whose name itself is a program: Greenpeace. Throughout the world this organization and others like it fight against threats to the environment and seek to promote a "green attitude."

Thus, in a few decades green has become what it has hardly ever been since Roman or Byzantine antiquity: an ideological and political color. In many countries political parties have formed that have chosen the name of the color itself for the name of the party: *Les Verts* in France, *Die Grünen* in Germany, *I Verdi* in Italy, and so on. The European example has spread rapidly to the entire world. In 2001 in Canberra, Australia, representatives of eighty green parties signed a common charter, the "Global Greens Charter." In Europe itself, beginning in 1990, many green parties have become government parties. Others have remained in the opposition, but they all joined forces in 2004 to become the European Federation of Green Parties, which a bit later became the European Green Party. Today this organization includes thirty-two national environmental parties.

One area of ecology in particular deeply involves the color green: organic agriculture. Organic agriculture aims at promoting biodiversity, respecting the natural world and its cycles, returning to natural products, and prohibiting chemical fertilizers and pesticides as well as genetically modified organisms. The resulting products—which must obey strict guidelines—are recognized in Europe and the United States by different logos, marks, or labels that are all green in color and accompany the words "*bio*" or "organic." Green is the color of organic agriculture just as it is the color of environmental politics.

This phenomenon has taken on such scope that it has become difficult today in the burgeoning world of marks and signs to display the color green without its immediately assuming an ecological dimension of one kind or another. Similarly, it is nearly impossible to admit that one's favorite color is green without immediately being labeled as a defender of the environment, natural energy, and organic farming, or even as a radical eco-activist. A single current of thought seems to have laid siege to the use and symbolism of green, which is no longer so much a color as an ideology. A few decades ago it was red that was similarly held captive by a too-powerful symbolism. To say that one liked red was to be categorized immediately as a "communist." Today green is the victim of the same hasty and reductive identifications.

Moreover, political parties and currents are not solely responsible for these chromatic deviations. Organizations, institutions, firms, and businesses set the example. Afraid of not being in the know, of not appearing politically or ethically correct, they use green at any occasion. Contemporary emblems and coats of arms are the first examples. Although green (*sinople*) has always appeared relatively infrequently in European heraldry, there are countless communities and organizations today that have granted themselves coats of arms in which green in the dominant color. Some have even renounced their traditional coats of arms, sometimes many centuries old, to adopt a new blazon in which green is featured. Others have changed red or black to green. Still others have added a green component (bend, saltire, or chevron) to their age-old shields. The same phenomenon occurs with business firms and companies; logos that are green or contain green are the current rage. They supposedly validate the image of the moral character they represent, attract consumers, and silence detractors. Sometimes abandoning a previous logo devoid of green for a new one featuring green is so crass that it undermines its desired end. A famous American company specializing in fast food thus recently changed the color upon which it displayed its emblem: a huge yellow M. This M was shown on a red background; today in many countries it appears on a green background, supposedly highlighting the "natural" and "eco-friendly" quality of the food you can buy there.

The current popularity of green in logos and advertising is not entirely the result of such simplistic strategies or ideological offshoots. It also corresponds to the public's obvious attraction for it, even to long-term preferences. For more than a century in Western Europe, all the opinion polls very consistently show that green comes in second after blue when people are asked to name their favorite color.[21] The results are identical in all countries, from Italy to Norway, from Finland to Portugal. They are the same, or nearly, for the two sexes, for the various socio-professional categories, and for all age groups.[22] Above all—and this is undoubtedly the most important thing for the historian—they have hardly varied, if at all, for as long as such polls have existed, that is, since the end of the nineteenth century. Despite the appearance of new technologies, new lighting, new mediums for the color, despite all the changes in society and sensibility that have accompanied them, the results remain unchanged from one generation to the next. Whether it is 1890, 1930, 1970 or 2010, blue always comes first, between 40 and 50 percent of the responses; then green, about 15 to 20 percent; red comes in third, a bit lower at 12 to 15 percent; white, black, and yellow are well behind, between 3 and 6 percent. As to the other "second-rank" colors (pink, orange, gray, purple, and brown), they only get to share the crumbs.[23]

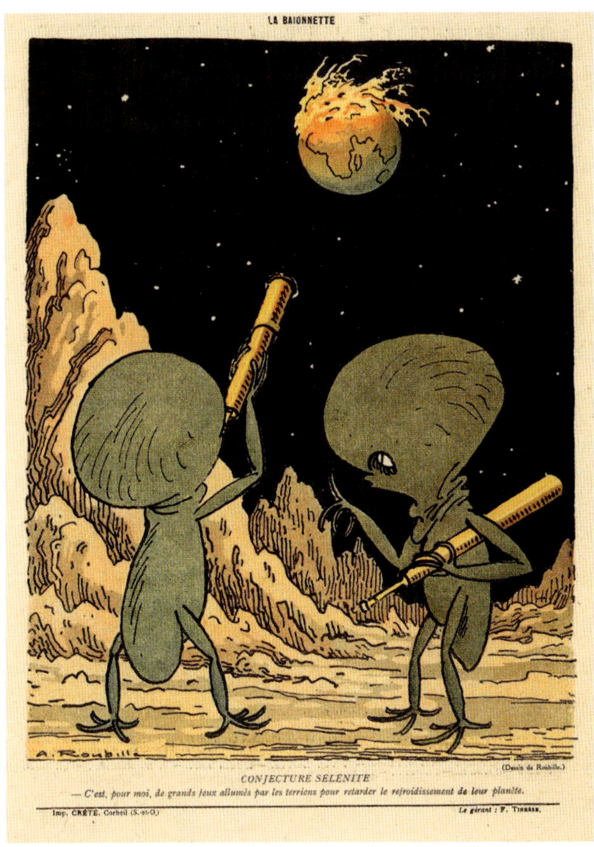

THE LITTLE GREEN MEN
More greenish than green, our contemporary Martians are the heirs of the sprites, trolls, elves, goblins, and imps of the Middle Ages.

Auguste Roubille, "The War Seen from Other Planets," 1918. Drawing published in the satiric weekly *La Baïonnette.*

Now as in the past, green is the favorite color of one out of five or six people in Europe. That is not very much compared to blue (nearly one person out of two), but it is better than all the other colors. Especially because, conversely, less than 10 percent of people asked were found to hate green, while that percentage is higher for yellow, black, and even red.[24] Among those enemies of green, most of them admitted to being afraid of it; green was supposedly pernicious, harmful,

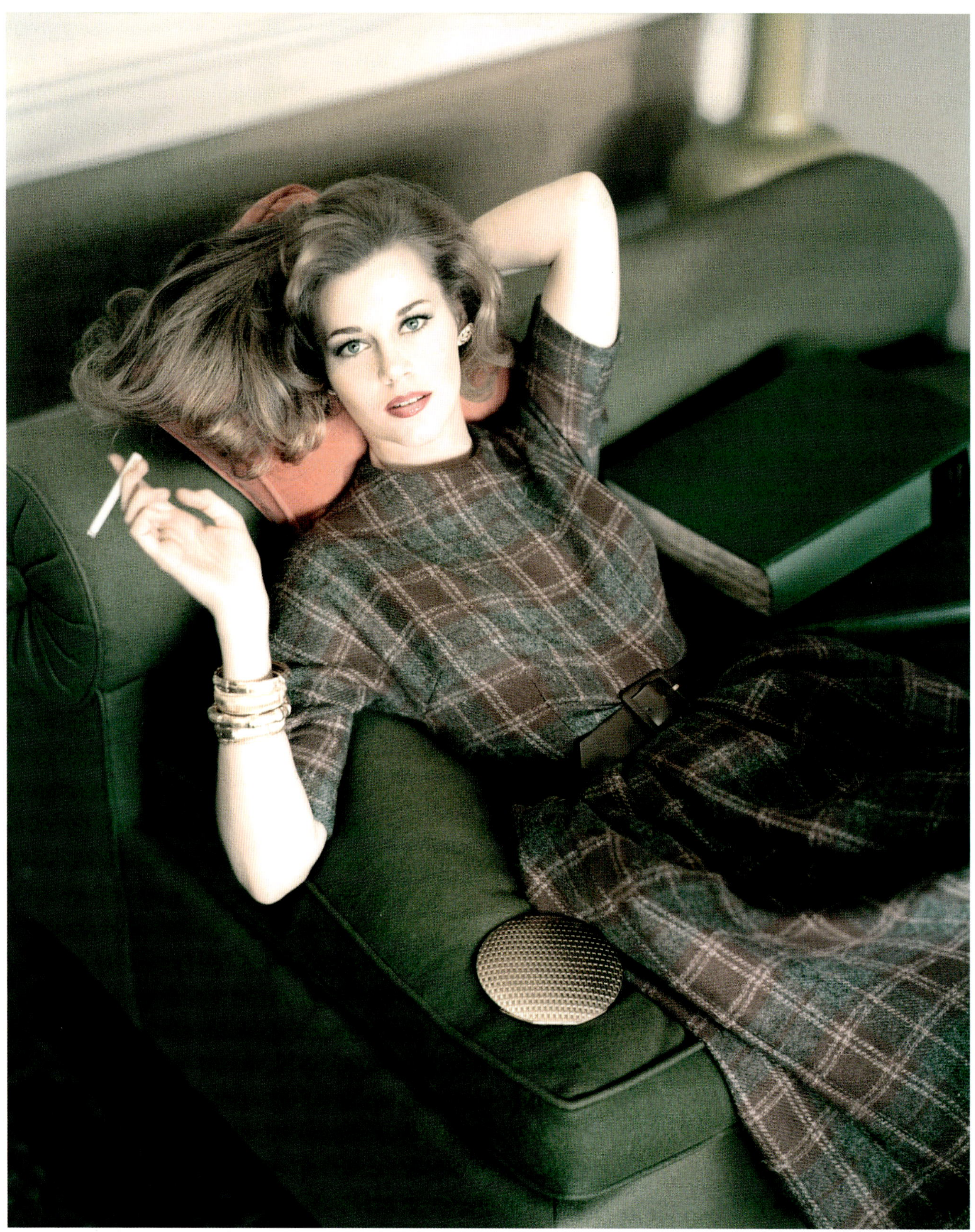

JANE FONDA

For courtly symbolism of the thirteenth century, green was the color of youth, love, and beauty. And, for women, green eyes were considered the most seductive. Seven centuries later, nothing seems to have changed very much.

Jane Fonda photographed by P. Horst, c. 1959.

unlucky. The old medieval superstitions are still at work and do not seem on the verge of disappearing.

Just as instructive as the color preference polls are the ones that ask individuals to associate a color with a concept. There have been many such studies in Europe and the United States over the last decades. Even if we must be cautious in considering their results, they quite faithfully reflect the contours of contemporary color symbolism in the West. Many notions are spontaneously associated with green. Some are negative: poison, evil spells, envy, avarice, jealousy.[25] Others, more numerous, are positive: calm, freshness, youth, harmony, sympathy, nature, friendship, confidence. An agitated, unstable, often transgressive color in the past, green seems to have settled down quite a bit. Its role in signal-system codes (permission, authorization, right-of-way) and in the return to nature (green spaces, environmental protection, ecology in all its forms) has no doubt contributed to this.

Nevertheless, in these associations between a color and a concept, a triad clearly emerges and represents the true symbolic power of the color green in contemporary Western societies: health, freedom, hope. That is not new but has taken on considerable dimension today, influencing numerous areas of material culture, everyday life, artistic creation, and the imagination. Green is healthy, invigorating, robust. It is free and natural, ready to fight against all artifice, any obstacle, all authoritarianism. Above all, it is rich in myriad hopes, as much for the individual as for society. Formerly neglected, rejected, unloved, green has become the messianic color. It is going to save the world.

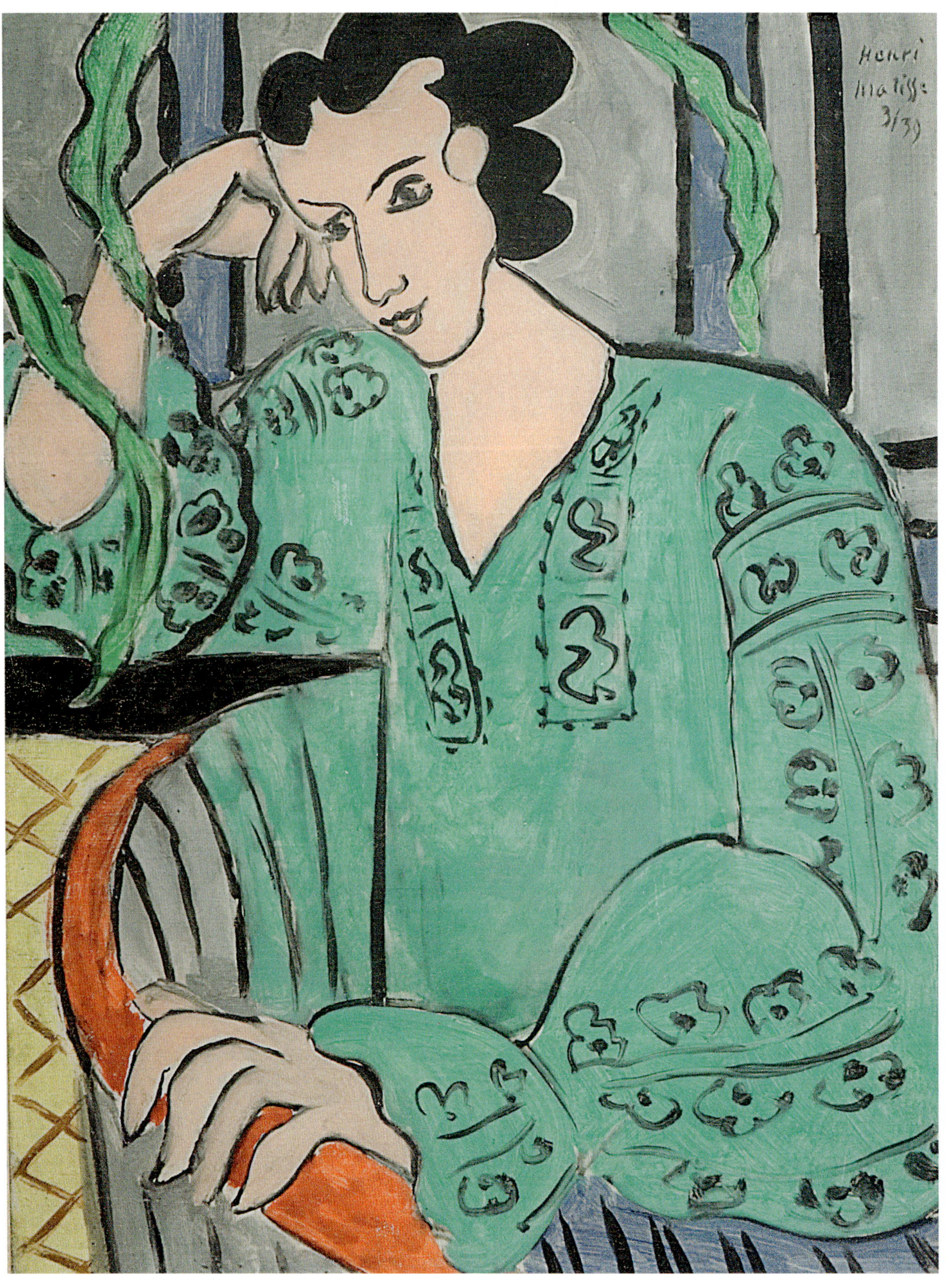
Henri
Matisse
3/39

Acknowledgments

Before taking the form of a book, this social and cultural history of the color green in Europe was the subject of my seminars for many years at both the École Pratique des Hautes Études and the École des Hautes Études en Sciences Sociales. I thank all my students and auditors for the fruitful exchanges we had then.

I would also like to thank all those close to me—friends, relatives, colleagues, students—whose advice, comments, and suggestions I have profited from, in particular: Brigitte Buettner, Pierre Bureau, Yvonne Cazal, Marie Clauteaux, Claude Coupry, Jean-Pierre Criqui, Adeline Grand-Clément, François Jacquesson, Philippe Junod, Claire Lesage, Christian de Mérindol, Anne Pastoureau, Laure Pastoureau, Anne Ritz-Guilbert, Olga Vassilieva-Codognet.

Thanks as well to Éditions du Seuil, to Claude Hénard and the whole Beaux Livres team, especially Nathalie Beaux, Caroline Fuchs, Karine Benzaquin, Marie-Anne Méhay, Bernard Pierre, Renaud Bezombes, and Silvain Chupin. Everyone has worked to make the present volume a very beautiful one.

Finally, I offer an affectionate thanks to Claudia Rabel, who once again has made me the beneficiary of her constructive criticism and efficacious rereadings.

MATISSE'S GREENS

From his Fauvist period until the end of his life, Matisse retained a pronounced taste for vivid colors and contrasting tones. He excelled in the play of saturation and desaturation, especially in the ranges of blues and greens.

Henri Matisse, *The Romanian Green Blouse*, 1939. Private collection.

Notes

An **uncertain** color

1. I have borrowed this expression from L. Gernet, "Dénomination et perception des couleurs chez les Grecs," in *Problèmes de la couleur*, ed. I. Meyerson (Paris, 1957), 313–26.

2. P. G. Maxwell-Stuart, *Studies in Greek Color Terminology*, 2 vols. (Leiden, 1981).

3. Among abundant bibliographical sources, see E. Irwin, *Color Terms in Greek Poetry* (Toronto, 1974); A. Grand-Clément, *La Fabrique des couleur: Histoire du paysage sensible des Grecs anciens* (Paris, 2011), 72–130.

4. Ibid., 118–21 and 415–18.

5. W. E. Gladstone, *Studies on Homer and the Homeric Age*, vol. 3 (Oxford, 1858), 458–99; H. Magnus, *Histoire de l'évolution du sens des couleurs*, trans. J. Soury (Paris, 1878), 47–48; O. Weise, "Die Farbenbezeichnungen bei den Greichen and Römern" in *Philologus* 46 (1888): 593–605. For the opposing view, see K. E. Goetz, "Waren die Römer blaublind" in *Archiv für lateinische Lexicographie und Grammatik* 14 (1906): 75–88, and 15 (1908): 527–47.

6. For example, L. Geiger, *Zur Entwicklungsgeschichte der Menschheit* (Stuttgart, 1871).

7. See especially *Die geschichtliche Entwicklung des Farbensinnes* (Leipzig, 1877), translated into many languages.

8. For example: *caerulus*, *caesius*, *glaucus*, *cyaneus*, *lividus*, *venetus*, *aerius*, *ferreus*. Magnus's hypotheses are taken up again by K. E. Goetz in the article cited in note 5. On the difficulties of saying "blue" in ancient Greek, see M. Pastoureau, *Bleu: Histoire d'une couleur* (Paris, 2000), 23–30.

9. The etymology that connects *caeruleus* to *caelum* (the sky) hardly stands up to either phonetic or philological analysis. Nevertheless, see the hypotheses of A. Ernout and A. Meillet, *Dictionnaire étymologique de la langue latine*, 4th ed. (Paris, 1979), 84. It proposes an ancient (unattested) form, *caeluleus*. For the authors of the Middle Ages, who practiced etymology based on a different body of knowledge than that of twentieth-century scholars, the link between *ceruleus* and *cereus* is a given.

10. Among the strongest opponents of Magnus's hypotheses and evolutionist theories, see F. Marty, *Die Frage nach der geschichtlichen Entwicklung des Farbensinnes* (Vienna, 1879), and G. Allen, *The Colour Sense: Its Origin and Development* (London, 1879).

11. For example, W. Schultz, *Das Farbenempfindungssystem der Hellenen* (Leipzig, 1904).

12. See A. De Keersmaecker, *Le Sens des couleurs chez Homère* (Brussels, 1883).

13. F. Nietzsche, *Morgenröthe* (*Aurore*) (Berlin, 1881), aphorism 426.

14. See the summary by A. Grand-Clément, "Couleur et esthétique classique au XIXe siècle: L'art grec antique pouvait-il être polychrome?" *Ithaca: Quaderns Catalans de cultura clàssica* 21: 139–60.

15. J. Geoffery, "La connaissance et la dénomination des couleurs," *Bulletin de la Société d'anthropologie de Paris* 2 (1879): 322–30.

16. B. Berlin and P. Kay, *Basic Color Terms: Their Universality and Evolution* (Berkeley, 1969).

17. See especially H. C. Conklin, "Color Categorization," *American Anthropologist* 24, no. 4 (1973): 931–42. Another debatable idea that is difficult to eradicate: many sociologists and psychologists accept the assumption that women, "whatever their occupations," are better at distinguishing and naming colors than men are (many examples appear in women's magazines and popular works on psychology, fashion, cooking, and so on).

18. Many recent studies have shown that, upon reaching adulthood, those born blind possess the same knowledge of colors and the same chromatic training as those with sight.

19. A. Grand-Clément, "Les marbres antiques retrouvent des couleurs: Apport des recherches récentes et débats en cours," *Anabases* 10: 243–50. Also see by the same author *La Fabrique des couleurs*, cited in note 3.

20. A. Ernout and A. Meillet, *Dictionnaire étymologique de la langue latine*, 4th ed. (Paris, 1979), "virere."

21. F. Lavenex Vergès, *Bleus égyptiens: De la pâte auto-émaillée au pigment bleu synthétique* (Louvain, 1992).

22. J. Baines, "Color Terminology and Color Classification in Ancient Egyptian Color Terminology and Polychromy," *American Anthropologist* 87 (1985): 282–97.

23. L. Luzzatto and R. Pompas, *Il significato dei colori nelle civiltà antiche* (Milan, 1988), 130–51; J. André, *Étude sur les termes de couleur dans la langue latine* (Paris, 1949), 179–80. In the second century BCE Terence had already described the German thus in his play *Hecyra*: "*magnus, rubicundus, crispus, crassus, caesius/cadaverosa facie*" (3.4.440–41). Treatises on physiognomy from the late Empire fully confirm this disregard for curly red hair, a pale complexion, and blue or green eyes.

24. A. Grand-Clément, "Couleur et esthétique classique au XIXe siècle: L'art grec antique pouvait-il être polychrome?" article cited in note 14.

25. As well as A. Grand-Clément's thesis cited above in note 3, see the catalogs of two recent and particularly instructive exhibitions: *Die Farben der Götter* (Munich: Glyptothek, June–September 2008); *Roma: La pittura di un impero* (Rome: Quirinal, September–January 2010).

26. *Natural History*, bk. 35, chap. 12 and passim; bk. 36, chap. 45. See J. Gage, *Couleur et culture: Usages et significations de la couleur de l'Antiquité à l'abstraction* (Paris, 2008), 14–33.

27. Seneca, *Letters*, 86, 114, and 115.

28. M. Pastoureau, *L'Étoffe du diable: Une histoire des rayures et des tissus rayés* (Paris, 1991), 27 and passim.

29. Pliny, *Natural History*, bk. 31, chap. 62.

30. See the fine study by J. Trinquier, "*Confusis oculis prosunt virentia* (Sénèque, *De ira*, 3, 9, 2): Les vertus magiques et hygiéniques du vert dans l'Antiquité" in *Couleurs et visions dans l'Antiquité classique* (Rouen, 2002), 97–128.

31. They sometimes used colorless, finely cut beryl as a magnifying glass (from which is derived the German word for glasses: *Brillen*).

32. André, *Étude sur les terms de couleur*, 181–82.

33. J. André, *Alimentation et cuisine à Rome*, 4th ed. (Paris, 1981); and J. André, *Être médicin à Rome* (Paris, 1984).

34. Petronius, *Satiricon*, ed. A. Ernout (Paris, 1922), chap. 70, sec. 10.

35. C. Landes, ed. *Le Cirque et les courses de chars, Rome-Byzance* (Lattes: Musée archéologique Henri Prades, 1990) (Paris, 1990).

36. A. Cameron, *Circus Factions: Blues and Greens at Rome and Byzantium* (Oxford, 1976).

37. André, *Étude sur les terms de couleur*, 181–82.

38. Juvenal, *Satires*, bk. 9, lines 183–208 (trans. M. Pastoureau).

39. G. Dragon, *L'Hippodrome de Constantinople: Jeux, peuple et politique* (Paris, 2012).

40. I am drawing here on the work of François Jacquesson, "Les mots de couleur dans les textes bibliques," *Histoire et géographie de la couleur*, ed. P. Dollfus, F. Jacquesson, and M. Pastoureau (Paris, 2012), 69–132. See also A. Brenner, *Colour Terms in the Old Testament* (Sheffield, 1982).

41. The same is true for the lexicon regarding animals and plants, changing from one version to another and from one translation to another, the number of species continuing to grow over the centuries.

42. F. Jacquesson, article cited in note 40.

43. Long obvious, this absence of blue has been debated by some scholars who have associated all the occurrences of purple with blue. This association seems out of place to me. See Pastoureau, *Bleu: Histoire d'une couleur*, 37–41; F. Jacquession, article cited in note 40.

44. C. Meier and R. Suntrup, *Lexicon der Farbenbedeutungen im Mittelalter*, 2 vols. (Cologne and Vienna, 2012). See especially the dictionary of meanings for the colors discussed, with many citations, in vol. 2.

45. An immense publishing endeavor, the *Patrologia latina* by Jacques-Paul Migne includes 217 volumes published between 1844 and 1855 (plus four index volumes, 1862–1865). All the Christian authors appear in it, from Tertullian to Pope Innocent III.

46. F. Jacquesson, *La Chasse aux couleurs à travers la* Patrologie latine (Paris, 2008) (online at the LACITO-CNRS research site).

47. See *Dictionnaire d'archéologie chrétienne et de liturgie*, vol. 3, fasc. 2, col. 2999–3002, which takes up the work of German authors F. Bock, *Geschichte der liturgischen Gewänder im Mittelalter*, 3 vols. (Berlin, 1859–1869), and J. Braun, *Die liturgische Gewandung in Occident und Orient* (Fribourg-en-Brisgau, 1907).

48. Allow me to refer to my own work here, notably "L'Église et la couleur des origines à la Réforme," *Bibliothèque de l'École des chartes* (1989), 147 : 203–30.

49. Patrologia latina, vol. 217, cols. 774–916 (colors in cols. 799–802).

50. Strangely, the holidays of the Virgin are missing from Lothar's treatise. But in this period she was already associated with white almost everywhere.

51. *Quia viridis color medius est inter albedinem et nigritiam et ruborem* (Patrologia latina, vol. 217, col. 799).

52. At the end of his chapter on liturgical colors, Lothar specifies that in certain cases purple can replace black (but not for Good Friday) and in exceptional cases yellow can replace green (as dyeing in true green was a difficult endeavor).

53. This tendency toward unity and the essential role played by green are confirmed by the famous *Rationale divinorum officiorum*, an immense encyclopedia on all the objects, signs, rituals, and symbols linked to the celebration of divine worship, compiled by Guillaume Durand, future Bishop of Mende, in 1285–1286. Colors are discussed in chapter 18 of book 3. See the edition by Fathers Davril and Thibodeau in the collection *Corpus Christianorum*, vol. 140, bks. 1–4 (Paris, 1995).

54. See *De Anima* and *De sensu et sensato*.

55. *Galbinus* must be compared to the modern German *gelb*, yellow, despite the doubts of some philologists. In classical Latin this term is rare and reserved for fabrics and clothing. Martial seems to have been the first to use it. Later, in low Latin, it occurs more frequently and eventually gives rise to most of the words designating the color yellow in the Romance languages. See note 23, André, *Étude sur les termes de couleur*, 148–50; note 9, Ernout and Meillet, *Dictionnaire étymologique*.

56. See the excellent forthcoming thesis by Marie Clauteaux, *Les Couleurs du corps . . . dans les manuscrits enluminés des Xe–XIIe s.*, defended in Paris (EPHE) in December 2012.

57. Let us cite as an example *Annales Xanthenes* (the Annals of Xanten and of Lorsch), ed. G. Waitz (Leipzig, 1839), 56–57 and passim.

58. Even if this was a period of climate warming, it seems unlikely that the western coast of Greenland was particularly verdant, any more than Iceland or Norway. The reasons for choosing this name must be sought elsewhere. It may have been a matter of propaganda, meant to attract colonists (the Icelandic colony in Greenland numbered four thousand inhabitants at its height and only came to an end in the fifteenth century); it may have been as matter, as I think, of a prophylactic name.

59. P. Miquel, *L'Islam dans sa première grandeur* (Paris, 1967).

60. There are few works on colors in the Quran. I rely here on the study by Djamel Koulouchi (forthcoming) in the *Cahiers du Léopard d'or* 13 (2013) (*Histoire et géographie de la couleur*).

61. There are rare exceptions to the presence of green on flags, and they involve countries where the secularism of the state is or was affirmed by the constitution (Turkey, Tunisia). Will this "secular" rejection of green resist the pressures of recent Islamic revolutions? Nothing could be less certain.

A **courtly** color

1. M. Pastoureau, *Bleu: Histoire d'une couleur* (Paris, 2000), 49–83.

2. As clearly shown by the sumptuary laws and clothing decrees that appeared in the second half of the thirteenth century and proliferated in the following one. They will be addressed in the next chapter.

3. M. Pastoureau, "Voir les couleurs au XIIIe siècle," *Micrologus: Natura, scienze e società medievali* 6, no. 2 (1998): 147–65.

4. On the essential distinction between bright and brilliant as expressed by Saint Bernard, permit me to cite myself: M. Pastoureau, "Les cisterciens et la couleur au XIIe siècle" in *L'Ordre cistercien et le Berry* (colloque, Bourges, 1998), *Cahiers d'archéologie et d'histoire du Berry* 136 (1998): 21–30.

5. Green did not become cool until later, between the fourteenth and seventeenth centuries.

6. J. Trinquier, "*Confusis oculis prosunt virentia* (Sénèque, *De ira*, 3, 9, 2). Les vertues magiques et hygiéniques du vert dans

l'Antiquité," *Couleurs et visions dans L'Antiquité classique*, ed. L. Villard (Rouen, 2002), 97–128.

7. See J. Gage, "Colour in History" in *Art History* (1978), 1: 108.

8. Gage, *Couleur et culture*, 61.

9. Bonaventure, *Opera omnia* (Rome, 1882–1889), 2:321, 4:1025, 5:27.

10. This is the oldest conserved stained glass. The problem is knowing what proportion of the glass in place is original.

11. Beginning in the fourteenth century, blue began to replace white as the color of air. But it would not become air's definitive color until the sixteenth century.

12. Among abundant bibliographic sources, let us cite especially E. Gilson, "Le Moyen Âge et la nature," in *L'Esprit de la philosophie médiévale* (Paris, 1944), 345–64.

13. The restricted meaning of "orchard" as a space planted with fruit trees applies especially in vernacular languages. In Latin the word *pomarium* designates such a place.

14. See the collective work *Vergers et jardins dans l'univers médiéval*, in the collection *Senefiance*, vol. 28 (Aix-en-Provence, 1990). See also J. Harvey, *Medieval Gardens* (London, 1981); *Jardins et vergers en Europe occidental (VIIIe–XVIIIe s.)* (Auch, 1989) (Flaran, vol. 9); V. Huchard and P. Bourgain, *Le Jardin médiéval, un musée imaginaire* (Paris, 2002).

15. Gen. 2:4–25.

16. As in the famous image of the garden of the Saint-Gall abbey, known through a detailed map dating from the ninth century.

17. Guillaume de Lorris, *Le Roman de la Rose*, ed. A. Strubel (Paris, 1992), lines 1350–1403.

18. Gen. 1:9–13.

19. John 20:14–18.

20. M. Pastoureau, "Introduction à la symbolique médiévale du bois," *Cahiers du Léopard d'or* 2 (1993): 25–40.

21. These are abstract theoretical associations, linked to "correspondences" between the colors and various natural elements that the late Middle Ages enjoyed establishing. In images, especially miniatures, these associations are rarely found.

22. *Roman de la Rose*, ed. F. Lecoy, line 706.

23. The French *printemps* comes from the Latin phrase *primum tempus*. Not until the fourteenth century did it eliminate its competing *primevere* (from the Latin *primum ver*), standard in the Middle Ages. The word only survives in modern French as the name for the primrose flower, a plant often associated with spring.

24. P. Mane, *Le Travail à la campagne au Moyen Âge: Étude iconographique* (Paris, 2006), 305–19.

25. P. Mane, *La Vie des campagnes au Moyen Âge à travers les calendriers* (Paris, 2004).

26. From which we get the middle English "to flirt," which becomes the nineteenth-century French *flirter*. See A. Rey, ed., *Dictionnaire historique de la langue française*, new edition, vol. 2 (Paris, 1998), 1142.

27. Most dictionaries of old and middle French omit this particular meaning of the verb *s'esmayer*. Of course it often means "to be afraid" or "to worry," especially in the fifteenth century, but the meaning "to wear the May" is well attested in chronicles and bookkeeping documents.

28. Chantilly, Bibliothèque du musée Condé, ms. 65, folio 5.

29. Ballad 68. The fifteenth-century spelling was modernized.

30. Jean Renart, *Guillaume de Dole*, ed. J. Lecoy (Paris, 1962), line 1164 and following. Translation by J. Dufournet revised by M. Pastoureau.

31. The Floral Games of Toulouse, established in 1323, are the distant heirs of the Roman games. From the first, the prize presented to the winning poet was a violet. Later, specific prizes were created for the author of the best sonnet (a hawthorn flower) and the most beautiful ballad (a marigold).

32. Maia is one of the very ancient Roman divinities. Some authors make her the wife of Vulcan. Others make her a mortal beloved of Jupiter and mother of Mercury.

33. Similarly, the Rogation Days, the three days preceding the Thursday of Ascension, are a Christianized version of ancient pagan rituals linked to fertility. In the course of processions through the fields, the priests bless the new plant growth and the faithful ask God to favor the harvest. Established definitively in the Carolingian period, this Christian holiday, like Palm Sunday, gives plants, green, and greenery the place of honor.

34. At the end of the Middle Ages, purple became a negative color, sometimes the sign of affliction, more often the sign of treason.

35. M. Pastoureau, "Ceci est mon sang: Le christianisme médiéval et la couleur rouge" in *Le Pressoir mystique: Actes du colloque de Recloses*, ed. D. Alexandre-Bidon (Paris, 1990), 43–56.

36. A. Schultz, *Das höfische Leben zur Zeit der Minnesinger*, 2nd ed., vol. 2 (Leipzig, 1889); J. Bumke, *Höfische Kultur: Literatur und Gesellschaft im hohen Mittelalter*, vol. 1 (Munich, 1986).

37. In medieval Latin *adulescentia* usually did not designate the third age of life (from twelve to about twenty years old) but the fourth (from twenty to thirty years old or even older).

38. M. Pastoureau, "Gli emblemi della gioventù: La rappresentazione dei giovanni nel Medioevo," in *Storia dei Giovani*, vol. 1, eds. G. Levi and J.-C. Schmitt (Rome and Bari, 1994), 279–302.

39. E. Heller, *Psychologie de la couleur: Effets et symbolique* (Paris), 92–93.

40. In Middle High German, *Minne* is synonymous with *Liebe*.

41. On the medieval symbolism of linden, allow me to cite my own study, "La musique du tilleul: Des abeilles et des arbres," in *L'Homme, le végétal et la musique*, ed. J. Coget (Parthenay, 1996), 98–103.

42. For a good example of a scene of amorous jest under the linden, see the famous *Codex Manesse* (Zurich, c. 1300–1310), folio 308 v°.

43. See the study by J. Trinquier cited in note 30 of the first chapter of this book.

44. I thank Christian de Mérindol for this precious bit of information.

45. Not only the shield but also the knight's coat of arms, his banner, and his horse's quarter sheet are monochromatic and can thus be seen from a great distance. That is why the texts speak of the *vermilion knight*, the *white knight*, the *black knight*, and so on.

46. The choice of the word describing the color red sometimes conveys additional information: thus a *vermilion* knight is of high birth (even while remaining a worrisome character); an *affocatus* knight is quick-tempered; a *bloody* knight is cruel and the bringer of death; a *russet* knight is treacherous and hypocritical.

47. Two blacks exist in the symbolism and sensibility of the feudal period: a negative black related to mourning, death, sin, or hell; and a highly esteemed black, which is a sign of humility, dignity, or temperance. This second black is monastic black.

48. See the complete inventory of monochromatic Arthurian knights in G. J. Brault, *Early Blazon: Heraldic Terminology in the XIIth and XIIIth Centuries, with Special Reference to Arthurian Literature* (Oxford, 1972), 31–35. See also the examples cited by M. de Combarieu, "Les couleurs dans le cycle du *Lancelot-Graal*" in *Senefiance* 24 (1988): 451–588.

49. M. Pastoureau, *Traité d'héraldique*, 2nd ed. (Paris, 1993), 116–21.

50. Ibid., 51–52.

51. M. Pastoureau, "La forêt médiévale: un univers symbolique," in *Le Château, la forêt, la chasse: Actes des IIe Rencontres internationales d'archéologie et d'histoire de Commarque (23–25 sept. 1988)* (Bordeaux, 1990), 83–98.

52. Do we need to be reminded that the French word *sauvage* comes from the Latin *silva* (the forest)? That the one who inhabits or frequents the forest is *sauvage* (*silvaticus*)? This etymological relationship exists in the Germanic languages as well. In German, for example, there is an obvious link between the noun *Wald* (forest) and the adjective *wild* (wild).

A **dangerous** color

1. In Old and Middle French, the word *sandragon* (*sandrac, sandaraque, sang du dragon*, and so on) usually designates a red pigment obtained from the reddish resin of the cypress tree. A few authors sometimes confuse *sandragon* with *réalgar*, another red pigment made from a natural sulfide of mercury.

2. On the linden and its rich, always positive symbolism (music, medicine, love), see P. Leplongeon, *Le Tilleul: Histoire culturelle d'un arbre européen* (Paris, 2013).

3. M. Pastoureau, *Bestiaire du Moyen Âge* (Paris, 2011), 191–92.

4. More indulgent, Thomas de Cantimpré maintains that if frogs mated at night, it was out of modesty! *De natura rerum*, ed. H. Böse (Paris, 1973), 307–8.

5. J.-C. Schmitt, *Les Revenants, les vivants et les morts dans la société médiévale* (Paris, 1994), passim.

6. See the next chapter.

7. On Martians, amid the abundant and often disappointing, even dismaying literature, see K. S. Robinson, *Les Martiens*, 2nd ed. (Paris, 2007).

8. Amid a very plentiful bibliography, see especially for the beginning of the modern period: J. B. Russel, *The Devil in the Modern World* (Cornell, 1986); M. Carmona, *Les Diables de Loudun* (Paris, 1988); B. P. Levack, *La Grande Chasse aux sorcières en Europe au début des temps moderne* (Seysell, 1991); R. Muchembled, *Magie et sorcellerie en Europe du Moyen Âge à nos jours* (Paris, 1994); P. Stanford, *The Devil, a Biography* (London, 1996).

9. On the demonology of Jean Bodin, see S. Houdard, *Les Sciences du Diable: Quatre discours sur la sorcellerie (XVe–XVIIe siècle)* (Paris, 1992); S. Clark, *Thinking with Demons: The Idea of Witchcraft in Early Modern Europe* (Oxford, 1997).

10. Accounts and descriptions of sabbats appear in E. Delcambre, *Le Concept de sorcellerie dans le duché de Lorraine au XVIe et au XVIIe siècle*, 3 vols. (Nancy, 1949–1952); P. Villette, *La Sorcellerie dans le nord de la France du XVe au XVIIe siècle* (Lille, 1956); L. Caro Baroja, *Les Sorcières et leur monde* (Paris, 1978); C. Ginzburg, *Le Sabbat des sorcières* (Paris, 1992); N. Jacques-Chaquin and M. Préaud, ed., *Le Sabbat des sorciers en Europe (XVe–XVIIIe s.)* (Grenoble, 1993).

11. M. Blümmer, *Die Farbenbezeichnungen bei den römischen Dichtern* (Berlin, 1892), 154–59.

12. J. Ziegler, "Médecine et physiognomie du XIVe au début du XVIe siècle," *Médiévales* 46 (2004): 89–108.

13. The first formulation of this famous saying we may owe to Henry Boguet (1550–1619), a well-known demonologist and prolific writer in his time. See L. Röhrich, *Lexikon der sprichwörtlichen Redensarten*, new ed. (Fribourg-en-Brisgua, 1994), 1:112–17.

14. A. Ott, *Étude sur les couleurs en vieux français* (Paris, 1899), 49–51.

15. C. de Mérindol, *Les Fêtes de chavalerie à la cour du roi René: Emblématique, art et histoire* (Paris, 1993).

16. On the composition of poisons, see F. Collard, *Le Crime de poison au Moyen Âge* (Paris, 2003), 59–72. The term *verdastre* appeared in Middle French about the mid-fourteenth century to describe the color of a poison. It was the first color adjective constructed using a suffix (*-astre*, now *-âtre*). *Rougeastre* and *blanchastre* (reddish and whitish) are more recent (late fourteenth century), *noirastre* and *jaunastre* (blackish and yellowish) more recent still.

17. J. Berlioz, "Le crapaud: un animal maudit au Moyen Âge?" in J. Berlioz and M.-A. Polo de Beaulieu, ed., *L'Animal exemplaire au Moyen Âge (Ve–XVe s.)* (Renne, 1999), 267–88; Pastoureau, *Bestiares du Moyen Âge*, 191–92, 211–13.

18. F. Collard, ed., *Le Poison et ses usages au Moyen Âge* (Orléans, 2009).

19. M. Pastoureau, *Noir: Histoire d'une couleur* (Paris, 2008), 95–105.

20. M. Pastoureau, "Un enchanteur désenchanté: Merlin" in *Mélancolies du savoir: Essais sur l'œuvre de Michel Rio*, ed. M. Arent Safir (Paris, 1995), 95–106.

21. G. J. Brault, *Early Blazon. Heraldic Terminology in the XIIth and XIIIth Centuries* (Oxford, 1972), 29–35.

22. See the works listed by D. Brewer and J. Gibson, *A Companion to the Gawain-Poet* (Woodbridge, 1997). See also A. R. Gilbert, *Medieval Sign Theory and Gawain and the Green Knight* (Toronto, 1987).

23. Christine de Pizan, *Le Livre de la mutacion de Fortune*, vol. 1, ed. S. Solente (Paris, 1959), 71. My thanks to Olga Vassilieva-Codognet for having drawn my attention to this important text for the study of the symbolism of green in the early fifteenth century.

24. B. Hell, *Le Sang noir: Chasse et mythe du sauvage en Europe* (Paris, 1994), passim.

25. Allow me to cite my own book here, *Jésus chez le teinturier: Couleurs et teintures dans l'Occident médiéval* (Paris, 1997). See also F. Brunello, *L'arte della tintura nella storia dell'umanita* (Vicenza, 1968), which is more concerned with the chemical and technical history of dyes than with the social and cultural history of dyers; Brunello, *Arti e mestieri a Venezia nel medievo e nel Rinascimento* (Vicenza, 1980); D. Cardon, *Le Monde des teintures naturelles* (Paris, 2003). The work of E. E. Ploss, *Ein Buch von alten Fraben: Technologie der Textilfarben im Mittelalter*, reprinted many times (6th ed., Munich, 1989), follows the recipes and recipe collections more closely than the artisans who used them.

26. Lev. 19:19; Deut. 22:11.

27. M. Pastoureau, *L'Etoffe du diable: Une histoire des rayures et des tissus rayés* (Paris, 1991), 9–15.

28. M. Pastoureau, "La couleur verte au XVIe siècle: traditions et mutations," in *Shakespeare: Le monde vert: rites et renouveau*, ed. M.-T. Jones-Davies (Paris, 1995), 28–38.

29. In practice, it could happen that taboos and professional regulations were transgressed. Perhaps two different coloring materials were not mixed in the same vat, perhaps fabric was not immersed in two successive dye baths of different colors to obtain a third color, but nevertheless exceptions were made for badly dyed wool cloth. When the first dyeing did not come out as hoped (which happened relatively often), dyers were allowed to immerse that same cloth in a darker dye bath, generally gray or black (with a base of alder or walnut bark and roots) to try and correct the faults of the first bath.

30. That is why truly white clothing was rare in medieval societies. The use in dyeing of certain plants (saponins) and washing powders with an ash or ore base (magnesia, chalk, ceruse) gave whites grayish, greenish, or bluish tones and took away from their brightness. As for bleaching with chlorine or chlorides, that process did not exist before the late eighteenth century as this substance was not discovered until 1774. Bleaching with sulfur was possible, but not yet perfected, it ruined wool and silk. Cloth had to be immersed in a diluted bath of sulfurous acid for an entire day. If there was too much water, the bleach was ineffective; if there was too much acid, the fabric was damaged.

31. Henri Estienne, *Apologie pour Hérodote* (Geneva, 1566), ed. P. Ristelhuber (Paris, 1879), 1: 26. It is also possible that for the Calvinist scholar, as for all his fellow Protestants, green was a dishonest color that all good Christians should avoid in their dress. Red and yellow were even worse, of course, but black, gray, blue, and white were preferable to green. All the great Protestant reformers were very much in agreement about this sober and dignified palette, already recommended by the moralist prelates of the late Middle Ages. In many areas man-made green was thus the victim of the Reformation's chromoclasm. On this chromoclasm, see

A. Agnoletto, "La 'cromoclastia' del reforme protestanti," *Rassegna* 23/3 (September 1985): 21–31; M. Pastoureau, "La Réforme et la couleur," *Bulletin de la Société d'histoire du protestantisme français* 138 (July–September 1992): 323–42.

32. Nuremberg, Stadtbibliothek, Ms. Cent. 89, fol. 15–16 (copy from the early fifteenth century). This lawsuit has already been noted by two authors who have recognized its importance: R. Scholz, *Aus der Geschichte des Farbstoffhandels im Mittlealter* (Munich, 1929), 2 and passim; F. Wielandt, *Das Konstanzer Leinengewerbe: Geschichte und Organisation* (Constance, 1950), 122–29. I want to thank my dear departed colleague O. Neubecker here, who helped me as a young researcher to read late fourteenth-century German documents, difficult to decipher paleographically.

33. This was the famous *Plictho* by Giovanni Ventura Rosetti, the first edition dating to 1540. See S. M. Evans, H. C. Borghetty, *The "Plictho" of Giovan Ventura Rosetti* (Cambridge, MA, and London, 1969). An allusion to this same process can be discovered already in a Venetian manual from 1480–1500, in the collection of the Como municipal library (G. Rebora, *Un manuale di tintoria del Quattrocento* (Milan, 1970), but the actual steps of the process are not described. Generally, in the first printed dyeing manuals from the sixteenth and seventeenth centuries, most of the formulas or chapters are devoted to red or blue; green plays a very minimal role. On the collections of recipes for dyers from the Middle Ages and the sixteenth century, see the work cited in note 25 by E. E. Ploss, *Ein Buch von alten Farben*. A project for a data bank assembling all the medieval recipes for color (dyeing and painting) has long been under study: F. Tolaini, "Una banca dati per lo studio dei ricettari medievali de colori," *Centro de Richerche Informatiche per i Beni Culturale (Pisa). Bollettino d'informazioni* 5 (1995): fasc. 1:7–25.

34. Other documents will no doubt some day tell us that we must go back further, perhaps even much further, to encounter the oldest evidence of such knowledge and practices. The problem, as always, will be to clearly distinguish theoretical knowledge from actual practice, isolated experiments from widespread use. For now, let us be content with this date and this observation: in the second half of the fourteenth century in western Europe, those specialists in color, the painters and dyers, already knew that by mixing blue and yellow they could obtain green. Of course, they did not do this often because various physical, regulatory, or conceptual obstacles prevented it, but they sometimes did so.

35. The deceitful nature of the color green was still very much emphasized by nineteenth-century language events, proverbs, sayings, and adages. See, for example, the note on the word *vert* in the *Trésor de la langue française* (online).

36. M. Pastoureau, "L'homme roux: Iconographie médiévale de Judas," in *Une histoire symbolique du Moyen Âge occidental* (Paris, 2004), 197–212.

37. R. Mellinkoff, "Judas's Red Hair and the Jews," *Journal of Jewish Art* 9 (1982): 31–46; M. Pastoureau, "Formes et couleurs du désordre: le jaune avec le vert," *Médiévales* 4 (1983): 62–73.

38. E. Heller, *Wie die Farben wirken*, 2nd ed. (Hamburg, 1999), 132–34.

39. Ibid., 133.

40. Bk. 12, fable 7.

41. M. Pastoureau, *Traité d'héraldique*, 2nd ed. (Paris, 1993), 100–121. C. Boudreau, *L'Heritage symbolique des hérauts d'armes. Dictionnaire symbolique de l'enseignment du blason ancien* (Paris, 2006), 2: 1042–46.

42. Many modern translators of chansons de geste and tales of chivalry for the twelfth and thirteenth centuries go astray by translating the frequent expressions *vert heaume*, *ver hiaume*, *verz elmes*, and *verdz eumes* as *heaume(s) vert(s)*—green helmet(s). This is a matter of steel helmets with brilliant, changing reflections, not green ones (Latin *varius*, not *viridis*). Some have even thought that a *cheval ver* was a green horse (!) whereas it is simply a spotted or dappled one (*Equus varius*). See Ott, *Étude sur les couleurs en vieux français* (note 14), 49–51, 138–39. For a different opinion, see M. Plouzeau, "*Vert heaume*: Approches d'un syntagme," *Senefiance* 24 (*Les Couleurs au Moyen Âge*) (1988): 591–650.

43. Pliny mentions these pits several times in his *Natural History* with regard to what he calls the *minium sinopium*: pigments, dyes, cosmetics, health and beauty aids. Pliny the Elder, *Natural History*, bk. 35, chaps. 6, 31.

44. On this subject, let me cite my own study, "Une couleur en mutation: le vert à la fin du Moyen Âge" in Académie des inscriptions et belles-lettres, *Comptes rendus des séances* (April–June 2007): 705–31.

45. Sicile, *Le Blason des couleurs en armes, livrées et devises*, ed. H. Cocheris (Paris, 1860), 61–65.

46. F. Rabelais, *Gargantua* (Paris, 1535), chap. 1.

47. Sicile, *Le Blason des couleurs*, 77–126.

48. F. P. Morato, *Del significato dei colori* (Venice, 1535).

49. L. Dolce, *Dialogo nel quale si ragiona della qualità, diversità e proprietà dei colori* (Venice, 1565).

50. J. Gage, *Couleur et Culture* (Paris, 2008), 119–20.

51. On Jean Robertet and his work, see P. Champion *Histoire poétique du XVe siècle* (Paris, 1923), 2: 288–307; ed. M. Zsuppan, *Jean Robertet: Oeuvres* (Paris, 1970).

52. On gray as symbolic of hope in the late Middle Ages, see the fine article by A. Planche, "Le gris de l'espoir," *Romania* 94 (1973): 289–302.

53. Published by Alice Planche in the article cited in the preceding note.

54. For this analysis of Jean Robertet's poem and the quotations accompanying it, I relied on a manuscript from the first half of the sixteenth century housed in the Bibliothèque de l'Arsenal in Paris: ms. 5066, folios 108–12. Many painted female figures accompany the text. They personify each of the ten colors presented, and each wears a dress of the color in question. Thanks to my friend Claire Lesage for bringing this manuscript to my attention and facilitating my work at the Bibliothèque de l'Arsenal.

A **secondary** color

1. The "chromoclasm" of the Reformation still awaits its historians. On its iconoclasm, on the other hand, there are some excellent recent works: J. Philips, *The Reformation of Images: Destruction of Art in England (1553–1660)* (Berkeley, 1973); M. Warnke, *Bildersturm: Die Zerstörung des Kunstwerks* (Munich, 1973); M. Stirm, *Die Bilderfrage in der Reformation* (Forschungen zur Reformationgeschicte, 45) (Gütersloh, 1977); C. Christensen, *Art and the Reformation in Germany* (Athens, GA, 1979); S. Deyon and P. Lottin, *Les Casseurs de l'été 1566: L'iconoclasme dan le Nord* (Paris, 1981); G. Scavizzi, *Arte e architettura sacra: Cronache e documenti sulla controversia tra riformati e cattolici (1500–1550)* (Rome, 1981); H. D. Altendorf and P. Jezler, eds., *Bilderstreit: Kulturwandel in Zwinglis Reformation* (Zurich, 1984); D. Freedburg, *Iconoclasts and Their Motives* (Maarsen, Holland, 1985); C. M. Eire, *War against the Idols: The Reformation of Worship from Erasmus to Calvin* (Cambridge, MA, 1986); D. Crouzet, *Les Guerriers de Dieu: La violence au temps des guerres de Religion*, 2 vols. (Paris, 1990); O. Christin, *Une révolution symbolique: L'Iconoclasme huguenot et la reconstruction catholique* (Paris, 1991). To these individual or collective works must be added the scholarly and voluminous catalogue of the *Iconoclasme* exposition (Berne and Strasbourg, 2001).

2. Jer. 22:13–14; Ezek. 8:10.

3. J. Wirth, "Le dogme en image: Luther et l'iconographie," *Revue de l'art* 52 (1981): 9–21.

4. The violent sermon, *Oratio contra affectationem novitatis in vestitu* (1527), in which he recommends all honest Christians wear sober and somber colors and not "*distinctus a variis coloribus velut pavo.*" *Corpus reforatorum*, 11: 139–49. See also 2: 331–38.

5. *Institution de la religion chrétienne* (1560 text), 3.10:2.

6. See, for example, Jean-Baptiste Oudry's reproaches to his colleagues at the Académie de Saint-Luc in his *Discours sur la practique de la peinture*, written in 1752 and published by E. Piot in *Le Cabinet de l'amateur* (Paris, 1861), 107–17.

7. S. Bergeon and E. Martin, "La technique de la peinture française au XVIIe siècle," *Techné: La science au service de l'histoire de l'art et des civilisations* 1 (1994): 65–78, especially 71–73.

8. M. Pastoureau, "La couleur verte au XVIe siècle: traditions et mutations," in *Shakespeare: Le monde vert: rites et renouveau*, ed. M.-T. Jones-Davies (Paris, 1995), 28–38.

9. We lack the space here to discuss in detail Newton's discoveries and the profound consequences they had on scientific and philosophical discourse regarding color. We must be content with referring to the immense bibliography devoted to them. In French one can conveniently read the works of M. Blay, *La Conceptualisation newtonienne des phénomènes de la couleur* (Paris, 1983) and *Les Figures de l'arc-en-ciel* (Paris, 1995), 36–77. One can also read or reread *Opticks* by Isaac Newton, published only in London in 1702 or, for an easier approach, the summaries and explanations of it offered by Voltaire in his work, *Éléments de la philosophie de Newton mis à la portée de tout le monde* (Paris, 1738).

10. Aristotle did not devote any one work to color. But it is present here and there in many of his works, notably in *De anima*, in *Libri meteologicorum* (with regard to the rainbow), in works on zoology and especially in *De sensu et sensato*. It is perhaps in this treatise that his ideas on the nature and perception of color are presented most clearly. In the Middle Ages a treatise circulated that was specifically devoted to the nature and vision of colors, *De coloribus*. It was attributed to Aristotle and thus often cited, glossed, copied, or interpolated. This treatise was not the work of Aristotle or Theophrastus but probably of a later peripatetic school. Nevertheless, it exerted great influence over the encyclopedic knowledge of the thirteenth century and notably over the nineteenth book, *De proprietatibus rerum* by Bartholomaeus Anglicus, half of which was devoted to colors. There is a good edition by W. S. Hett of this treatise in Greek in vol. 14 of the *Loeb Classical Library*: Aristotle, *Minor Works* (Cambridge, MA, 1980), 3–45. As for the Latin text, it has often been published with the *Parva naturalia* by the Greek philosopher. On Bartholomaeus Anglicus and color, see M. Salvat, "Le traité des couleurs de Barthélemy l'Anglais" in *Senefiance* 24 (*Les Couleurs au Moyen Âge*) (1988): 359–85. On the subject of colors in Aristotle and thirteenth-century Latin authors who were

influenced by him, also see P. Kurcharski, "Sur la théorie des couleurs et des saveurs dans *De sensu* aristotélicien," *Revue des études grecques* 67 (1954): 355–90; B. S. Eastwood, "Robert Grosseteste's Theory on the Rainbow," *Archives internationales d'histoire des sciences* 19 (1966): 313–32; M. Hudeczek, "*De lumine et coloribus* (selon Albert le Grand)," *Angelicum* 21 (1944): 112–38.

11. Similarly, given a classification system like this, one would hardly think of mixing red and blue to get purple. In fact, until the sixteenth century purple was almost always presented as a mix of blue and black and not red and blue. Moreover, its most common Latin name (*subniger*) and its use in the liturgy and the vestimental customs for mourning show clearly that purple was a sort of subblack or semi-black, and not a color close to red or crimson. This idea had to wait for Newton and his focus on the spectrum.

12. A. E. Shapiro, "Artists' Colors and Newton's Colors," *Isis* 85 (1994): 600–630.

13. All the more so because, even with regard to the scientific world, Newton kept his discovery secret for almost a quarter century. On the consequences of Newton's discoveries in painters' circles, see J. Gage, *Color and Culture* (London, 1986), 153–76, 227–36.

14. It is surprising that glass artists, who had perfected the "silver yellow" technique at the beginning of the fourteenth century, used it so rarely to produce the color green before the sixteenth century. This cementation technique, with a base of metallic salts, colors the surface of glass but not its mass; it revolutionized painting on glass because it allowed the artist to color the glass partially without resorting to cuts or insertions in the lead cames. On glass already tinted blue the surface application of this silver yellow could produce green shades through superimposition; glass artists in the fourteenth and fifteenth centuries knew this but hardly ever did it.

15. For panel painting it is likely that the use of a new binder—linseed oil—beginning in the late fourteenth or early fifteenth century led to experiments of all kinds for using and combining pigments differently. The combination of blue and yellow to make green may have arisen from these experiments.

16. See the catalogue from the exhibition *I Tempi de Giorgone* (Florence, 1978), 3: 141–52. See also D. Rosand, *Peindre à Venise au XVIe siècle* (Paris, 1993), and M. Hochmann, *Venise et Rome, 1500–1600: Deux écoles de peinture et leurs échanges* (Geneva, 2004).

17. B. de Patoul and R. Van Schoute, *Les Primitifs flamands et leur temps* (Tournai, 2000), 114–16, 630–31.

18. Long restricted to panel paintings, these analyses have multiplied in recent years with regard to miniatures. They are no longer so much chemical as physical. To identify a pigment, it is no longer necessary to take a sample or microsample from the pictorial coat. It is only necessary, for example, to cast one or several specific rays of light on that coat and to observe how the light behaves in contact with the material. Or through microspectronomy it is possible to analyze the molecular structure of one or another part of the pictorial surface. Or, again, to use neutronic activation to highlight individually the various components of the pigment. In short, the new procedures now in use are less cumbersome than earlier ones, no longer harm the pictorial coat and allow more precise identifications. By the same token, analyses have become more numerous and extend to all the artistic practices involving color. See R. M. Christie, *Color Chemistry* (Cambridge, UK, 2001).

19. Paris, BnF, ms. latin 6741. On this manuscript, A. Giry, "Notice sur un traité du Moyen Âge intitulé *De coloribu et artibus Romanorum*," *Mélanges publiés par l'École pratique des hautes études* 35 (1878): 207–27.

20. I. Villela-Petit, *La Peinture médiévale vers 1400: Autour d'un manuscrit de Jean le Bègue*, thèse de l'École nationale des chartres (Paris, 1995), recipe n° 295, 207–09. This thesis is forthcoming. Until it is published, one can consult the summary of it in *Positions des thèses soutenues par les élèves de la promotion* published by the École Nationale des chartes (Paris, 1995): 211–19.

21. B. Guineau, *Glossaire des matériaux de la couleur et des termes techniques employés dans les recettes anciennes* (Turnhout, 2005), passim.

22. *Liber magistri Petri de Sancto Audemaro de coloribus faciendis*, ed. M. P. Merrifield, *Original Treatises Dating from the XIIth to the XVIIIth Centuries on the Art of Painting*. . . (London, 1849), 129.

23. It is true that the treatise is unfinished and essentially constitutes reading notes that Leonardo da Vinci undoubtedly did not have the time to shape (even though some scholars consider his thinking to be already fully apparent in the work). On this treatise, the manuscript of which is kept in the Vatican Library, see A. Chastel and R. Klein, *Léonard de Vinci: Traité de la peinture* (Paris, 1960); 2nd ed. (1987).

24. On the pigments used by Vermeer and their costs, J. M. Montias, *Artists and Artisans in Delft* (Princeton, NJ, 1982), 186–210.

25. A detailed commentary on this diagram can be found in M. Pastoureau, *Noir: Histoire d'une couleur* (Paris, 2008), 140–43.

26. L. Savot, *Nova, seu verius nova-antiqua de causis colorum sententia* (Paris, 1609).

27. A. De Boodt, *Genmarum et lapidum historia* (Hanau, 1609).

28. F. d'Aguilon, *Opticorum libri sex* (Anvers, 1613).

29. Pliny, *Natural History*, bk. 33, sec. 158: 56. See J. Gage, *Couleur et culture* (Paris, 2008), 35.

30. On this invention, see the beautiful and scholarly catalogue of the exhibition, *Anatomie de la couleur* (Paris, BnF, 1995) ed. F. Rodari and M. Préaud. See also the treatise by J. C. Le Blon, *Colorito, or the Harmony of Colouring in Painting reduced to Mechanical Practice* (London, 1725), which acknowledges its debt to Newton and affirms the primacy of three basic colors: red, blue, and yellow. On the history of color engraving considered from a long-term perspective, see the study by J. M. Friedman, *Color Printing in England, 1486–1870* (New Haven, CT, 1978).

31. R. Boyle, *Experiments and Considerations Touching Colours* (London, 1664), 219–20.

32. See A. Mollard-Desfour, *Le Vert: Dictionnaire de la couleur* (Paris, 2012), 153–54.

33. Cited without reference by J. Amandeau, *Louis XIII et le cardinal de Richelieu . . .* (Paris, 1913), 85.

34. A. Somaize, *Grand Dictionnaire des précieuses* (Paris, 1661), passim.

35. See, for example, *Le Satirique de la cour*, an anonymous play published in 1624.

36. Thanks to my friend Frank Lestringant, great specialist on Alfred de Musset, for providing me this information.

37. J. Kott, *The Bottom Translation: Marlowe and Shakespeare and the Carnival Tradition* (Evanston, IL, 1987).

38. M. Pastoureau, "L'homme roux: Iconographie médiévale de Judas," in *Une histoire symbolique du Moyen Âge occidental* (Paris, 2004), 197–211.

39. From the Romantic period to the present, green's bad reputation among theater people is well attested. It is for earlier periods that research still needs to be done.

40. Still today in Brittany a sailor will not paint the hull of his boat green or board a boat with a green hull. This taboo seems limited, now at least, to this one region of France and Europe. See M. Pastoureau, *Les Couleurs de nos souvenirs* (Paris, 2010), 161–62.

41. G. Lacour-Gayet, *Les Idées maritimes de Colbert*, 2nd ed. (Paris, 1911), 15.

42. Pastoureau, *Les Couleurs*, 157–58.

43. On the beliefs and superstitions surrounding green, H. Bächtold-Stäubli, *Handwörterbuch des deutschen Aberglaubens*, vol. 3 (Berlin, 1931), col. 1180–86.

44. Pastoureau, *Les Couleurs*, 158–59.

45. Sura 18, verses 65–82.

46. For psychoanalysis, losing a "glass" shoe at the ball is obviously losing one's virginity. See note 49 below for the famous study by Bruno Bettelheim.

47. In the version by the Grimm brothers, the slippers are silk, embroidered with gold and silver.

48. The *Trésor de la langue française* offers a long entry on "*vair*" that is well worth reading.

49. B. Bettleheim, *The Uses of Enchantment* (Chicago, 1976) (French translation: *La Psychanalyse des contes de fées*, 2nd ed. (Paris, 1999).

50. A few critics have noted that glass must not be so fragile after all since Cinderella's evil stepsisters try to force the slipper on and go so far as to mutilate their feet and make them bleed. In vain!

51. On the symbolism of *sinople*, see M. Pastoureau, "Une couleur en mutation: le vert à la fin du Moyen Âge," in Académie des inscriptions et belles-lettres, *Comptes rendus des séances* (April–June 2007): 705–31.

52. See Gage, *Color and Culture* (note 13), 153–76, 227–36.

53. M. Pastoureau, *Bleu: Histoire d'une couleur* (Paris, 2000), 123–34.

54. Hence "Macquer blue" and "Köderer green" in about the 1750s; they were magnificent, certainly, but were not easy to fix on cloth and held up badly to light and washing. See M. Pinault, "Savants et teinturiers" in *Sublime indigo*, exhibition catalogue (Marseilles and Fribourg, 1987), 135–41.

55. This blue flower is featured by Novalis in his unfinished novel *Heinrich von Ofterdingen*, published posthumously in 1802 by Ludwig Tieck, his closest friend. The novel recounts the legend of a trouvère in the Middle Ages on a quest for a small blue flower seen in a dream. On the novel and its reception, see Gerhard Schulz, ed., *Novalis Werke commentiert*, 2nd ed. (Munich, 1981), 210–25 and passim.

56. The first Parisian traffic light was located at the intersection of Sébastopol and Saint-Denis Boulevards. It was entirely red; green did not make its appearance until the early 1930s.

57. Another tradition reports that Desmoulins asked the crowd to choose between blue and green as the rallying color. The crowd chose green. Desmoulins then supposedly attached a green ribbon to his hat. Unable to do the same, the patriots assembled around him supposedly collected linden leaves—a great number of those trees were planted in the Palais-Royal gardens, property of the Duke of Orléans.

58. From 1792 until 1815, green was one of the colors of the royalist companies sowing unrest in various regions of France. They often wore green scarves or ribbons—hence the nickname of *verdets* that they were sometimes given.

59. On the history of the Italian flag, see E. Ghisi, *Il tricolore italiano* (Milan, 1931); G. Mattern, *Die Flaggenwesen Italiens zur Zeit der französischen Revolution und der napoleonischen Aera* (Fribourg, 1970).

A **soothing** color

1. E. Heller, *Psychologie de la couleur: Effets et symbolique* (Paris, 2009), 98.

2. P. Ball, *Histoire vivante des couleurs: 5000 ans de peinture racontée par les pigments* (Paris, 2005), 227–29.

3. Quoted by B. Jacqué, *Les Couleurs du papier peint* (Rixheim, 2006), 20–21.

4. M. Pastoureau, *Les Couleurs de nos souvenirs* (Paris, 2012), 158.

5. Heller, *Psychologie de la couleur*, 100–101.

6. Prussian blue was also less expensive than cobalt blue, discovered or rediscovered in 1802.

7. On all this, see Ball, *Histoire vivant des couleurs*, 350–58.

8. M. E. Cavé, *La Couleur: Ouvrage approuvé par M. Eugène Delacroix pour apprendre le peinture à l'huile et l'aquarelle*, 3rd ed. (Paris, 1863), 114.

9. Quoted by G. Roque, *Art et science de la couleur: Chevreul et les peintres, de Delacroix à l'abstraction*, new ed. (Paris, 2009), 331–32.

10. On Chevreul's influence on painting in the nineteenth and early twentieth centuries, see the fine book by Georges Roque cited in note 9.

11. Ibid., 300–301.

12. C. Blanc, *Grammaire des arts du dessin*, 5th ed. (Paris, 1880), 562.

13. Quoted by Heller, *Psychologie de la couleur*, 102.

14. See M. Pastoureau, "Couleur, design et consummation de masse. Histoire d'une rencontre difficile (1880–1960)" in *Design, miroir du siècle*, exhibition catalogue (Paris, Grand Palais, May 19–July 25, 1993) (Paris, 1993), 337–42.

15. J. Itten, *Werke und Schriften* (Zurich, 1972), 24.

16. M. Weber, *Die protestantische Ethik und der Geist des Kapitalismus*, 8th ed. (Tübingen, 1986). This work first appeared in the form of two articles in 1905 and 1906.

17. Isador Thorner, "Ascetic Protestantism and the Development of Science and Technology," *The American Journal of Sociology* 58 (1952–1953): 25–38; Joachim Bodamer, *Der Weg zu Askese als Überwindung der technischen Welt* (Hamburg, 1957).

18. On this Protestant chromoclasm, see M. Pastoureau, "La Réforme et la couleur," *Bulletin de la Société d'histoire du protestantisme français* 138 (July–September 1992): 323–42.

19. In the picture books featuring Babar's adventures, green plays a more important role than in all other children's publications. It is a recurring motif from one story to another. All the elephants are gray, but each wears different-colored clothing: a red dress for Queen Celeste; black jacket and red pants for old General Cornelius; red and white sailor suit for unruly Arthur; light blue and pink for young Pom, Flore, and Alexander, and of course the green suit, white shirt, and yellow crown for Babar. To the clothing palette of the elephants, we must add the eternally yellow shirt of Zephyr the monkey and the black dress of the Old Lady.

20. It is also sometimes claimed that on green hospital clothing and in surgery and operating rooms, blood seems less red, more brown, and thus less frightening.

21. These polls appeared in Germany in the 1880s and 1890s, in the United States about 1900, and then spread throughout the West after World War I. Although still in their infancy, marketing and advertising were already sponsoring them. The method used to conduct such polls has hardly changed over the decades: stop passersby in the street and simply ask them, "What is your favorite color?" In order to be valid and included in the count, the answer must be clear and spontaneous; one true color name, not two or three, no adjectives describing the shade, absolutely no quibbling or hairsplitting about whether the question involves clothing, furnishing, paint, and so on. It is a simple, direct question and must be answered in a simple, direct manner. What is at stake is not some practical experience of the color or its material aspect, but how it exists in the imagination.

22. For small children, however, red and yellow are cited as favorite colors nearly as often as blue is.

23. Heller, *Psychologie de la couleur*, 4–9; M. Pastoureau, *Dictionnaire des couleurs de notre temps: Symbolique et société contemporaines* (Paris, 2003), 16–174 and passim.

24. Heller, *Psychologie de la couleur*, 4, 89 and pl. 1.

25. For these three vices, however, green is slightly outstripped by yellow. Ibid., pl. 6.

Bibliography

1. General works

Berlin, Brent, and Paul Kay. *Basic Color Terms: Their Universality and Evolution*. Berkeley, CA, 1969.

Birren, Faber. *Color: A Survey in Words and Pictures*. New York, 1961.

Bomford, David, and Ashok Roy. *Colour*. London, 2000.

Brusatin, Manlio. *Storia dei colori*. 2nd ed. Turin, 1983. Translated as *Histoire des couleurs*, Paris, 1986.

Conklin, Harold C. "Color Categorization." *American Anthropologist* 75, no. 4 (1973): 931–42.

Eco, Renate, ed. "Colore: Divietti, decreti, discute." Special number of *Rassegna* (Milan) 23 (September 1985).

Gage, John. *Colour and Culture: Practice and Meaning from Antiquity to Abstraction*. London, 1993.

Heller, Eva. *Wie Farben wirken*: *Farbpsychologie, Farbsymbolik, Kreative Farbgestaltung*. Hamburg, 1989.

Indergand, Michel, and Philippe Fagot. *Bibliographie de la couleur*. 2 vols. Paris, 1984–1988.

Meyerson, Ignace, ed. *Problèmes de la couleur*. Paris, 1957.

Pastoureau, Michel. *Bleu: Histoire d'une couleur*. Paris, 2000.

———. *Couleurs, images, symboles: Études d'histoire et d'anthropologie*. Paris, 1989.

———. *Dictionnaire des couleurs de notre temps: Symbolique et société*. 4th ed. Paris, 2007.

———. "Une histoire des couleurs, est-elle possible?" *Ethnologie française* 20, no. 4 (October-December 1990): 368–77.

———. *Noir: Histoire d'une couleur*. Paris, 2008.

Portmann, Adolf, and Rudolf Ritsema, eds. *The Realms of Colour. Die Welt der Farben*. Leiden, 1974.

Pouchelle, Marie-Christine, ed. "Paradoxes de la couleur." Special number of *Ethnologie française* (Paris) 20, no. 4 (October-December, 1990).

Rzepinska, Maria. *Historia coloru u dziejach malatstwa europejskiego*, 3rd ed. Warsaw, 1989.

Tornay, Serge, ed. *Voir et nommer les couleurs*. Nanterre, 1978.

Vogt, Hans Heinrich. *Farben und ihre Geschichte*. Stuttgart, 1973.

Zahan, Dominique. "L'homme et la couleur." In *Histoire des mœurs*, ed. Jean Poirier, vol. 1, *Les Coordonnées de l'homme et la culture matérielle*, 115–80. Paris, 1990.

Zollinger, Heinrich. *Color: A Multidisciplinary Approach*. Zurich, 1999.

Zuppiroli, Libero, ed. *Traité des couleurs*. Lausanne, 2001.

2. Antiquity and the middle ages

Beta, Simone, and Maria Michela Sassi, eds. *I colori nel mondo antiquo: Esperienze linguistiche e quadri simbolici.* Siena, 2003.

Bradley, Mark. *Colour and Meaning in Ancient Rome*. Cambridge, 2009.

Brinkmann, Vinzenz, and Raimund Wünsche, eds. *Bunte Götter: Die Farbigkeit antiker Skulptur*. Munich, 2003.

Brüggen, Elke. *Kleidung und Mode in der höfischen Epik*. Heidelberg, 1989.

Carastro, Marcello, ed. *L'Antiquité en couleurs: Catégories, pratiques, représentations*, 187–205. Grenoble, 2008.

Cechetti, Bartolomeo. *La vita dei Veneziani nel 1300: Le veste*. Venice, 1886.

Centre Universitaire d'Études et de Recherches Médiévales d'Aix-en-Provence. *Les Couleurs au Moyen Âge. Senefiance*, vol. 24. Aix-en-Provence, France, 1988.

Ceppari Ridolfi, Maria A., and Patrizia Turrini. *Il mulino delle vanità: Lusso e cerimonie nella Siena medievale*. Siena, 1996.

Descamps-Lequime, Sophie, ed. *Couleur et peinture dans le monde grec antique*. Paris, 2004.

Dumézil, Georges. "*Albati, russati, virides*." In *Rituels indoeuropéens à Rome*, 45–61. Paris, 1954.

Frodl-Kraft, Eva. "Die Farbsprache der gotischen Malerei: Ein Entwurf." *Wiener Jahrbuch für Kunstgeschichte* 30–31 (1977–1978): 89–178.

Grand-Clément, Adeline. *La Fabrique des couleurs: Histoire du paysage sensible des Grecs anciens*. Paris, 2011.

Haupt, Gottfried. *Die Farbensymbolik in der sakralen Kunst des abendländischen Mittelalters*. Leipzig, 1941.

Istituto Sorico Lucchese. *Il colore nel Medioevo: Arte, simbolo, tecnica: Atti delle Giornate di studi.* 2 vols. Lucca, 1996–1998.

Luzzatto, Lia, and Renata Pompas. *Il significato dei colori nelle civiltà antiche*. Milan, 1988.

Pastoureau, Michel. "L'Église et la couleur des origines à la Réforme." *Bibliothèque de l'École des chartes* 147 (1989): 203–30.

———. *Figures et couleurs: Études sur la symbolique et la sensibilité médiévales*. Paris, 1986.

———. "Voir les couleurs au XIIIe siècle." In *View and Vision in the Middle Ages*, 2: 147–65. *Micrologus: Nature, Science and Medieval Societies*, vol. 6. Florence, 1998.

Rouveret, Agnès. *Histoire et imaginaire de la peinture ancienne*. Paris, 1989.

Rouveret, Agnès, Sandrine Dubel, and Valérie Naas, eds. *Couleurs et matières dans l'Antiquité: Textes, techniques et pratiques*. Paris, 2006.

Sicile, héraut d'armes du XVe siècle. *Le Blason des couleurs en armes, livrées et devises*. Ed. H. Cocheris. Paris, 1857.

Tiverios, Michales A., and Despoina Tsiafakis, eds. *The Role of Color in Ancient Greek Art and Architecture (700–31 B.C.)*. Thessaloniki, 2002.

Villard, Laurence, ed. *Couleur et vision dans l'Antiquité classique*. Rouen, 2002.

3. Modern and contemporary times

Batchelor, David. *La Peur de la couleur*. Paris, 2001.

Birren, Faber. *Selling Color to People*. New York, 1956.

Brino, Giovanni, and Franco Rosso. *Colore e città: Il piano del colore di Torino, 1800–1850*. Milan, 1980.

Laufer, Otto. *Farbensymbolik im deutschen Volsbrauch*. Hamburg, 1948.

Lenclos, Jean-Philippe, and Dominique Lenclos. *Les Couleurs de l'Europe: Géographie de la couleur*. Paris, 1995.

———. *Les Couleurs de la France: Maisons et paysage*. Paris, 1982.

Noël, Benoît. *L'Histoire du cinéma couleur*. Croissy-sur-Seine, 1995.

Pastoureau, Michel. "La couleur en noir et blanc (XVe–XVIIIe siècle)." In *Le Livre et l'Historien: Études offertes en l'honneur du Professeur Henri-Jean Martin*, 197–213. Geneva, 1997.

———. *Les Couleurs de nos souvenirs*. Paris, 2010.

———. "La Réforme et la couleur." *Bulletin de la Société d'histoire du Protestantisme français* 138 (July–September 1992): 323–42.

4. Problems of philology and terminology

André, Jacques. *Étude sur les termes de couleurs dans la langue latine*. Paris, 1949.

Brault, Gerard J. *Early Blazon. Heraldic Terminology in the XIIth and XIIIth Centuries, with Special Reference to Arthurian Literature*. Oxford, 1972.

Crosland, Maurice P. *Historical Studies in the Language of Chemistry*. London, 1962.

Giacolone Ramat, Anna. "Colori germanici nel mondo romanzo." *Atti e memorie dell'Academia toscana di scienze e lettere La Colombaria* (Florence) 32 (1967): 105–211.

Gloth, Walther. *Das Spiel von den sieben Farben*. Königsberg, 1902.

Grossmann, Maria. *Colori e lessico: Studi sulla struttura semantica degli aggetivi di colore in catalano, castigliano, italiano, romano, latino ed ungherese*. Tübingen, 1988.

Irwin, Eleanor. *Colour Terms in Greek Poetry*. Toronto, 1974.

Jacobson-Widding, Anita. *Red-White-Black, as a Mode of Thought*. Stockholm, 1979.

Kristol, Andres M. *Color: Les Langues romanes devant le phénomène de la couleur*. Berne, 1978.

Maxwell-Stuart, P. G. *Studies in Greek Colour Terminology*, vol. 2: ΧΑΡΟΠΟΣ. Leiden, 1998.

Meunier, Annie. "Quelques remarques sur les adjectifs de couleur." *Annales de l'Université de Toulouse* 11, no. 5 (1975): 37–62.

Mollard-Desfour, Annie. *Le Dictionnaire des mots et expressions de couleur: Le noir*. Paris, 2005.

Ott, André. *Études sur les couleurs en vieux français*. Paris, 1899.

Schäfer, Barbara. *Die Semantik der Farbadjektive im Altfranzösischen*. Tübingen, 1987.

Sève, Robert, Michel Indergand, and Philippe Lanthony. *Dictionnaire des termes de la couleur*. Paris, 2007.

Wackernagel, Wilhelm. "Die Farben- und Blumensprache des Mittelalter." In *Abhandlungen zur deutschen Altertumskunde und Kunstgeschichte*, 143–240. Leipzig, 1872.

Wierzbicka, Anna. "The Meaning of Color Terms: Cromatology and Culture." *Cognitive Linguistics* 1, no. 1 (1990): 99–150.

5. The history of dyes and dyers

Brunello, Franco. *L'arte della tintura nella storia dell'umanita*. Vicenza, 1968.

———. *Arti e mestieri a Venezia nel medioevo e nel Rinascimento*. Vicenza, 1980.

Cardon, Dominique, and Gaëtan Du Châtenet. *Guide des teintures naturelles*. Paris, 1990.

Chevreul, Michel Eugène. *Leçons de chimie appliquées à la teinture*. Paris, 1829.

Edelstein, Sidney M., and Hector C. Borghetty. *The "Plictho" of Giovan Ventura Rosetti*. London, 1969.

Gerschel, Lucien. "Couleurs et teintures chez divers peuples indo-européens." *Annales ESC* 21 (1966): 608–63.

Hellot, Jean. *L'Art de la teinture des laines et des étoffes de laine en grand et petit teint*. Paris, 1750.

Jaoul, Martine, ed. *Des teintes et des couleurs*. Exhibition catalogue. Paris, 1988.

Lauterbach, Fritz. *Geschichte der in Deutschland bei der Färberei angewandten Farbstoffe, mit besonderer Berücksichtigung des mittelalterlichen Waidblaues*. Leipzig, 1905.

Legget, William F. *Ancient and Medieval Dyes*. New York, 1944.

Lespinasse, René de. *Histoire générale de Paris: Les métiers et corporations de la ville de Paris*. Vol. 3, *Tissus, étoffes . . .* Paris, 1897.

Pastoureau, Michel. *Jésus chez le teinturier: Couleurs et teintures dans l'Occident médiéval*. Paris, 1998.

Ploss, Emil Ernst. *Ein Buch von alten Farben: Technologie der Textilfarben im Mittelalter*, 6th ed. Munich, 1989.

Rebora, Giovanni. *Un manuale di tintoria del Quattrocento*. Milan, 1970.

Varichon, Anne. *Couleurs: Pigments et teintures dans les mains des peuples*. Paris, 2000.

6. The history of pigments

Ball, Philip. *Histoire vivante des couleurs: 5000 ans de peinture racontée par les pigments*. Paris, 2005.

Bomford, David, et al. *Art in the Making: Impressionism*. London, 1990.

———. *Art in the Making: Italian Painting before 1400*. London, 1989.

Brunello, Franco. *"De arte illuminandi" e altri trattati sulla tecnica della miniatura medievale*. 2nd ed. Vicenza, 1992.

Feller, Robert L., and Ashok Roy. *Artists' Pigments: A Handbook of Their History and Characteristics*. 2 vols. Washington, D.C., 1985–1986.

Guineau, Bernard, ed. *Pigments et colorants de l'Antiquité et du Moyen Âge*. Paris, 1990.

Harley, Rosamond D. *Artists' Pigments (c. 1600–1835)*. 2nd ed. London, 1982.

Hills, Paul. *Venetian Colour*. New Haven, CT, 1999.

Kittel, Hans, ed. *Pigmente*. Stuttgart, 1960.

Laurie, Arthur P. *The Pigments and Mediums of Old Masters*. London, 1914.

Loumyer, Georges. *Les Traditions techniques de la peinture médiévale*. Brussels, 1920.

Merrifield, Mary P. *Original Treatises dating from the XIIth to the XVIIIth Centuries on the Art of Painting*. 2 vols. London, 1849.

Montagna, Giovanni. *I pigmenti: Prontuario per l'arte e il restauro*. Florence, 1993.

Reclams Handbuch der künstlerischen Techniken. Vol. 1, *Farbmittel, Buchmalerei, Tafel- und Leinwandmalerei*. Stuttgart, 1988.

Roosen-Runge, Heinz. *Farbgebung und Technik frühmittelalterlicher Buchmalerei*. 2 vols. Munich, 1967.

Smith, Cyril S., and John G. Hawthorne. *Mappae clavicula: A Little Key to the World of Medieval Techniques*. Philadelphia, 1974.

Technè: La science au service de l'art et des civilisations. Vol. 4, *La couleur et ses pigments*. 1996.

Thompson, Daniel V. *The Material of Medieval Painting*. London, 1936.

7. The history of clothing

Baldwin, Frances E. *Sumptuary Legislation and Personal Relation in England*. Baltimore, 1926.

Baur, Veronika. *Kleiderordnungen in Bayern von 14. bis 19. Jahrhundert*. Munich, 1975.

Boehn, Max von. *Die Mode: Menschen und Moden vom Untergang der alten Welt bis zum Beginn des zwanzigsten Jahrhunderts*. 8 vols. Munich, 1907–1925.

Boucher, François. *Histoire du costume en Occident de l'Antiquité à nos jours*. Paris, 1965.

Bridbury, Anthony R. *Medieval English Clothmaking: An Economic Survey*. London, 1982.

Eisenbart, Liselotte C. *Kleiderordnungen der deutschen Städte zwischen 1350–1700*. Göttingen, 1962.

Harte, N. B., and Kenneth G. Ponting, eds. *Cloth and Clothing in Medieval Europe: Essays in Memory of E. M. Carus-Wilson*. London, 1982.

Harvey, John. *Men in Black*. London, 1995. Translated as *Des hommes en noir. Du costume masculin à travers les âges*. Abbeville, 1998.

Hunt, Alan. *Governance of the Consuming Passions: A History of Sumptuary Law*. London, 1996.

Lurie, Alison. *The Language of Clothes*. London, 1982.

Madou, Mireille. *Le Costume civil: Typologie des sources du Moyen Âge occidental*, vol. 47. Turnhout, 1986.

Mayo, Janet. *A History of Ecclesiastical Dress*. London, 1984.

Nixdorff, Heide, and Heidi Müller, eds. *Weisse Vesten, roten Roben: Von den Farbordnungen des Mittelalters zum individuellen Farbgeschmak*. Exhibition catalogue. Berlin, 1983.

Page, Agnès. *Vêtir le prince: Tissus et couleurs à la cour de Savoie (1427–1447)*. Lausanne, 1993.

Pellegrin, Nicole. *Les Vêtements de la liberté: Abécédaires des pratiques vestimentaires françaises de 1780 à 1800*. Paris, 1989.

Piponnier, Françoise. *Costume et vie sociale. La cour d'Anjou, XIVe–XVe siècles*. Paris, 1970.

Piponnier, Françoise, and Perrine Mane. *Se vêtir au Moyen Âge*. Paris, 1995.

Quicherat, Jules. *Histoire du costume en France depuis les temps les plus reculés jusqu'à la fin du XVIIIe siècle*. Paris, 1875.

Roche, Daniel. *La Culture des apparences: Une histoire du vêtement (XVIIe–XVIIIe siècles)*. Paris, 1989.

Roche-Bernard, Geneviève, and Alain Ferdière. *Costumes et textiles en Gaule romaine*. Paris, 1993.

Vincent, John M. *Costume and Conduct in the Laws of Basel, Bern, and Zurich*. Baltimore, 1935.

8. The philosophy and history of science

Albert, Jean-Pierre et al., eds. *Coloris Corpus*. Paris, 2008.

Blay, Michel. *La Conceptualisation newtonienne des phénomènes de la couleur*. Paris, 1983.

———. *Les Figures de l'arc-en-ciel*. Paris, 1995.

Boyer, Carl B. *The Rainbow from Myth to Mathematics*. New York, 1959.

Goethe, Johann Wolfgang von. *Materialen zur Geschichte der Farbenlehre*. 2 vols. Munich, 1971.

———. *Zur Farbenlehre*. 2 vols. Tübingen, 1810.

Halbertsma, Klaas Tjalling Agnus. *A History of the Theory of Colour*. Amsterdam, 1949.

Hardin, Clyde L. *Color for Philosophers: Unweaving the Rainbow*. Cambridge, MA, 1988.

Lindberg, David C. *Theories of Vision from Al-Kindi to Kepler*. Chicago, 1976.

Magnus, Hugo. *Histoire de l'évolution du sens des couleurs*. Paris, 1878.

Newton, Isaac. *Opticks or a Treatise of the Reflexions, Refractions, Inflexions and Colours of Light*. London, 1704.

Pastore, Nicholas. *Selective History of Theories of Visual Perception, 1650–1950*. Oxford, 1971.

Sepper, Dennis L. *Goethe contra Newton: Polemics and the Project of a New Science of Color*. Cambridge, 1988.

Sherman, Paul D. *Colour Vision in the Nineteenth Century: The Young-Helmholtz-Maxwell Theory*. Cambridge, 1981.

Westphal, John. *Colour: A Philosophical Introduction*. 2nd ed. London, 1991.

Wittgenstein, Ludwig. *Bemerkungen über die Farben*. Frankfurt am Main, 1979.

9. The history and theories of art

Aumont, Jacques. *Introduction à la couleur: Des discours aux images*. Paris, 1994.

Ballas, Guila. *La Couleur dans la peinture moderne: Théorie et pratique*. Paris, 1997.

Barasch, Moshe. *Light and Color in the Italian Renaissance Theory of Art*. New York, 1978.

Dittmann, Lorenz. *Farbgestaltung und Farbtheorie in der abendländischen Malerei*. Stuttgart, 1987.

Gavel, Jonas. *Colour: A Study of Its Position in the Art Theory of the Quattro- and Cinquecento.* Stockholm, 1979.

Hall, Marcia B. *Color and Meaning: Practice and Theory in Renaissance Painting*. Cambridge, MA, 1992.

Imdahl, Max. *Farbe: Kunsttheoretische Reflexionen in Frankreich*. Munich, 1987.

Kandinsky, Vassily. *Über das Geistige in der Kunst*. Munich, 1912.

Le Rider, Jacques. *Les Couleurs et les mots*. Paris, 1997.

Lichtenstein, Jacqueline. *La Couleur éloquent: Rhétorique et peinture à l'âge classique*. Paris, 1989.

Roque, Georges. *Art et science de la couleur: Chevreul et les peintres de Delacroix à l'abstraction*. Nîmes, 1997.

Shapiro, Alan E. "Artists' Colors and Newton's Colors." *Isis* 85 (1994): 600–630.

Teyssèdre, Bernard. *Roger de Piles et les débats sur le coloris au siècle de Louis XIV*. Paris, 1957.

10. The history of the color green

Heinermann, Theodor. "Die grünen Augen." In *Romanische Forschungen* 58–59 (1949): 18–40.

Kinney, Muriel. "Vair and Related Words: A Study in Semantics." In *Romanic Review* 10 (1919): 322–63.

Laurien, Jean-Michel. "*Über die grüne Grenze* ou la longue marche des lexies colorées." *Contrastes* 7 (1983): 79–95.

Mollard-Desfour, Annie. *Le Vert: Dictionnaire de la couleur: Mots et expressions d'aujourd'hui (XXe-XXIe siècles)*. Paris, 2012.

Pastoureau, Michel. "Une couleur en mutation: Le vert à la fin du Moyen Âge." In Académie des inscriptions et belles-lettres, *Compte rendus des séances* (April–June 2007): 705–31.

———. "La couleur verte au XVIe siècle: Traditions et mutations." In *Shakespeare: Le monde vert: Rites et renouveau*, ed. Marie-Thérèse Jones-Davies, 28–38. Paris, 1995.

———. "Formes et couleurs du désordre: Le jaune avec le vert." *Médiévales* 4 (May 1983): 62–73.

Trinquier, Jean. "*Confusis oculis prosunt virentia* (Sénèque, *De Ira*, 3, 9, 2): Les vertus magique et hygiéniques du vert dans l'Antiquité." In *Couleurs et visions dans l'Antiquité classique*, ed. Laurence Villard, 97–128. Rouen, 2002.

Vignes, Laurence. "Histoire de vert." In *Les Enjeux sociaux du langage: Hommage à Bernard Gardin* (*Synergies France* 5), 124–35. Paris, 2006.

Photography credits

©ADAGP, Paris 2013: 199 (Kees Van Dongen), 201 (Vassily Kandinsky).

Agence Bio: 217 bottom left.

Agence martienne: 219.

AKG, Paris: Nimatallah: 12, 16; Glasshouse Images: 15; akg-Images: 17, 74, 82, 157, 163; Roger Lichtenberg: 23; Erich Lessing: 56, 187, 213; De Agostini Pict. Lib.: 79; Rabatti-Domingie: 120, 187; Roland and Sabrina Michaud: 164; André Held: 194.

BnF, Paris: 47, 59, 60, 63, 67, 68, 85, 92, 97, 100–101, 106, 108–109, 110, 112, 113, 127, 131, 143, 153, 175.

Bodleian Libraries: 96.

Bridgeman Giraudon: Private collection: 20; Private collection/photo Heini Schneebeli: 29; National Gallery, London, Great Britain : 50–51 (detail), 77; Victoria and Albert Museum, London, Great Britain: 68; Musée Condé, Chantilly, France: 104; Hambuger Kunsthalle, Hamburg, Germany: 139; Museumslandschaft Hessen, Kassel, Germany/Ute Bunzel: 140; National Gallery of Scotland, Edinburgh, Scotland: 149; Comédie française, Paris, France/Archives Charmet: 156; Birmingham Museum and Art Gallery, Birmingham, Great Britain: 162; Private collection/Bonhams, London, Great Britain: 168 left; Rafael Valls Gallery, London, Great Britain: 168 right; Private collection/Christie's Images: 169; Goethe National Museum, Weimar, Germany: 173; Louvre, Paris, France: 178–179 (detail), 191; The Art Institute of Chicago, Illinois, United States: 188–189; Professor Hans R. Hahnloser Collection, Bern, Switzerland: 194–195.

British Library: The British Library Board: 75, 95.

Corbis: Horst P. Horst/Condé Nast Archive: 220.

Fotolia: Pete Laz'e: 217 bottom right.

Courtesy of Hachette Jeunesse Licenses: © Librairie Hachette 1939: 207.

© Succession Henri Matisse, photo André Held/AKG: 222.

HPHE: Millet Library/Christian and Byzantine Collection: 41.

Collection: Interfoto 10–11 (detail), 43; Jean-Paul Dumontier: 88, 91, 99, 122–123; Artothek: 134–135 (detail), 145, 146, 197; Artothek/Christie's: 160–161.

Leemage: Luisa Ricciarini: 21, 27; Aisa: 22, 32–33, 185; Electa: 26, 115; DeAgostini: 34, 37; Photo Josse: 102; Selva: 107; Bayes/Lebrecht: 144; North Wind Pictures: 176; FineArtImages: 199; Godong: 208; Heritage Images: 211 right; Imagestate: 214.

Picture-desk/The Art Archive: Museo del Prado Madrid/Gianni Dagli Orti: 86–87 (detail), 132.

Roger-Violet: Carnavalet Museum: 211 left.

RMN-GP: Louvre, Paris: Peter Willi: 44; Gérard Blot: 119; Michèle Bellot: 170; BPK Berlin: Gudrun Stenzel: 48, Jörg P. Anders: 136 (detail), 147, 210; The Metropolitan Museum of Art/Image of the MMA/Gift of J. Pierpont Morgan, 1917: 52; The Metropolitan Museum of Art/Image of the MMA/Rogers Fund and the Cloisters Collection, by exchange, 1950: 73; RMN/DR: 183; Musée d'Orsay: Hervé Lewandowski: 192; RMN-GP: Gérard Blot: 201, 204.

Scala Florence: Courtesy of the Ministry of Cultural Heritage and Att: 55; Austrian Archives: 150.

Zentrum Paul Klee, Image Archive, Bern, Switzerland: 180.

Image research by Caroline Fuchs, Marie-Anne Méhay and Karine Benzaquin-Laidain

The extract on p. 202 is from *Du Spirituel dans l'art et dans la peinture en particulier de Vassily Kandinsky*, translated from the German by Pierre Volbout © Éditions Denoël, Paris, 1969.

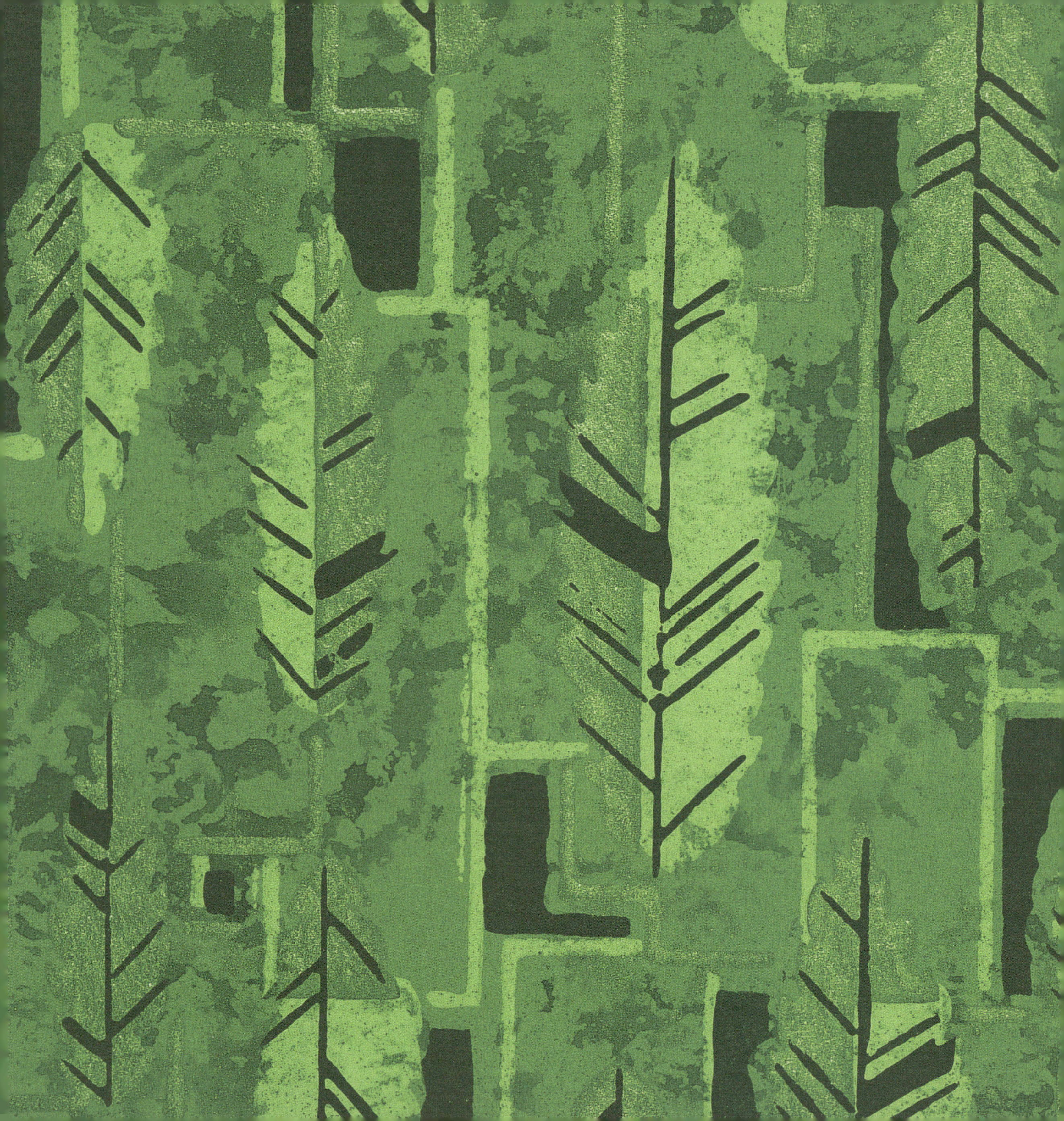